101 WWE Matches To See Before You Die

By Samuel 'Plan

For my close friend, Ash, without whom this wrestling lark wouldn't be half as much fun

DPC Publishing, Incorporated
North Carolina

Samuel 'Plan
101 WWE Matches To See Before You Die

ISBN-10: 0692548823

Editor: Matthew McIntyre
Cover Image: Charles McCarthy
Cover Design: Trey Cox

Contact

Samuel 'Plan is very active on social media.

To contact him:

Twitter: @LOPPlan

Facebook: Samuel Plan

Columns by Samuel 'Plan can be found on:

www.wrestlingheadlines.com / www.lordsofpain.net

To listen to "The Right Side of the Pond" weekly podcast, please visit www.blogtalkradio.com/lordsofpain

Table of Contents

Introduction

What would you say if I told you professional wrestling was not "real"?

Perhaps you would snort in derision. Perhaps you would sigh in exasperation. Perhaps you would simply wave a hand in dismissal. Whatever it is you would do, one thing is a certainty; you would say that you *know* it is not "real."

Professional wrestling was created in an age when it was easy to ensure people did not get hold of information you did not want them to get hold of. Kayfabe – an old carny term meaning "protect the secrets of the business" in pro wrestling vernacular - was an impenetrable layer of fiction that shielded the audience, in order to create a wrestling fandom to which the world's greatest work was still "real." Now, though, professional wrestling finds itself in an age where it is practically impossible to stop people from getting hold of information you do not want them getting hold of. The internet is an unstoppable permeation of instant communication that means a global audience can learn of breaking news within seconds. The result is the industry having no choice but to admit openly its preconceived nature, where fans, promoters, talent and anyone remotely involved with the business freely confess that professional wrestling consists of choreographed matches with predetermined outcomes.

So of course you would tell me that you know wrestling is not "real," because everybody knows that it is not. But I wonder, though: if you can tell me with confidence what it is not, could you tell me also what professional wrestling *is*? Many terms have been bandied around, including the likes of "sports entertainment," "male soap opera" and "simulated sport." The problem is these terms stem from outmoded philosophies, fashioned at a time when it was much easier to convince the world of professional wrestling's sporting element precisely because there was less willingness to discuss its scripted side. It seems strange that, at a time when wrestlers actively and freely acknowledge the difference between their real selves and their on-screen characters in interviews and on social media, the industry continues to cling onto receiving pro wrestling as simulated sport. The result is an industry with one foot planted firmly in its past while the other tries to drag itself into the 21st Century; in other words, an identity crisis.

It is the belief of this writer that none of the terms used to describe professional wrestling today do the profession any justice and instead only limit professional wrestling to the sneering sphere of reception it has now endured for decades. Sports entertainment as a term, for example, carries as much stigma as the term professional wrestling does because of its use as an obvious euphemism, and the overall impression that the ardent use of these terms creates is of an apologetic business unwilling to take itself seriously. Instead, it denigrates its most brilliant achievements by labelling them with simplistic terms, populist in their design so as to achieve nothing other than the easing of mass public reaction to what remains ostensibly a vibrant, garish melodrama.

These problems can be remedied, though, because of the unusual turning point in history the industry now stands at. Never since the advent of WWE's holy trinity - Hulkamania, Rock'n'Wrestling and WrestleMania - has professional wrestling faced such potential for radical change. The world's new digital age is presenting unfamiliar challenges which in turn present a unique opportunity to begin turning the general perception and reception of professional wrestling among both uninformed, mainstream audiences and elitist, internal audiences to something far more positive and proud.

Such is the bold intention of this book, *101 WWE Matches To See Before You Die*. Among the pages that follow, you will read a series of explorations musing on the factors that make up the very DNA of WWE as a promotion, highlighting in turn the most pressing questions and issues facing all of professional wrestling. By the time you have finished, hopefully you will have come to agree with me that the increasing transparency and confessional nature of the business is not an obstacle in need of overcoming or avoiding but a challenge offering a chance for a radical evolution. Understanding wrestling's past will better prepare us for postulating philosophies intended to help it survive whatever it is the future holds. Now is the time to reassess professional wrestling's identity.

It is important to note that the opinions and analyses presented in these pages come solely from my understanding and disposition as a life-long professional wrestling fan, drawn from my personal philosophy as regards to how professional wrestling is best received. Nevertheless, it is my hope that this book can be read and enjoyed thoroughly by ordinary, everyday fans in need of a ticket – like me – but also by those fans so enamoured they made the decision to become an active contributor to the business; hopefully, any professional wrestler, promoter or similar industry insider will enjoy reading my opinions just as much as the ticket holding fan-boy.

Essentially, I am here to share my outlook on professional wrestling and attempt to convince you, dear reader, of its benefits. As I seek to shift the contexts in which we converse about professional wrestling, the focus will primarily be on the creative aspects of professional wrestling in WWE; its use of character, its approach to storytelling and so on. These ideas are far more malleable and open to debate, and this approach stems from the grand idea I intend to argue: that professional wrestling is a performance art capable of telling stories in as artistic and complex a manner as any other form of high art, and it is in such a vein that any future prosperity, or so-called "wrestling boom," may lie.

The methodology is quite simple. First, you must understand that this is not a list of the best matches in WWE history, or a list of my individual favourites as the author. This is a selection of 101 matches from WWE's past, regardless of their quality, that best allow us to explore pertinent issues regarding the many facets of the promotion and the wider business, so that we may better understand both. Matches will be reviewed with an interpretive brand of analysis and the issues underpinning them will be inspected and scrutinised to help broaden our thoughts and understanding of what professional wrestling is and, more importantly, what it could be.

On a more specific level, the list will be separated into six sections. The first section, running from #101 to #96, will focus on the core proposition of a new frame of context in which to receive professional wrestling - as performance art. It will cite examples proving how much more worth there is in this approach compared to the traditional sport or sports entertainment philosophies. The second section, running from #95 to #68, will build on section one by examining professional wrestling in terms of genre on both literal and conceptual levels, exampling both this new approach's unmitigated potential and the current limitations we ourselves impose on the industry courtesy of our currently dated outlooks.

In section three, running from #67 to #43, the book will strive to better understand the industry's general character, its most prevalent challenges and its powerful appeal in light of this fresh philosophy, while the fourth and fifth sections, running from #42 to #30 and #29 to #11 respectively, will work in conjunction by beginning the creation of an independent grassroots fan history of the world's most influential and powerful professional wrestling promotion; part four will look at the most anomalous and affecting individuals in the company's history and part five at the promotion's most notable historical turns of events.

Finally, the sixth section will provide the all important Top Ten; with a new way to receive professional wrestling conceptualised, a present day reappraisal of identity conducted and the process of a fan built history having been started, the list will round out with a miscellany of philosophical propositions climaxing with a look at WWE's own answer to the ultimate question: "Who is the best WWE wrestler of all-time?"

Once you have reached the far side of these pages, you will have read a series of explorations that challenge all of your preconceptions about WWE; it's past, present and future, biggest stars and most profound moments, its challenges, its promise and its identity will all be scrutinised. Hopefully, you will have been convinced to take professional wrestling that little bit more seriously as a legitimate art form, one capable of achieving as much as history's greatest pieces of literature, film, music or theatre. This great industry may never face as a big a challenge like the one posed by the Digital Revolution, but the time has come to embrace that challenge as a positive rather than a negative. Now is the time to seize an opportunity afforded to us, the wrestling fans, to ask the question, "What is professional wrestling?" When you have watched these 101 matches and read these 101 musings, you may just have a different answer to that question than the one you do now.

So I ask now only that you approach this book with an open mind. Some of the ideas suggested are far more radical than others, but if you, dear reader, are willing to accept at least the possibility of change then maybe, just maybe, so will someone else too.

Chapter 1

Professional Wrestling as Performance Art

#101
William Regal vs. Chris Benoit
No Mercy
October 8th, 2006

As you begin this journey, it is imperative to clarify that, for the sake of historical accuracy, the ensuing explorations must take account of and discuss Chris Benoit the professional wrestling performer, albeit with the caveat that praise written in his favour is done so exclusively from the perspective of his ring work and *only* his ring work. Chris Benoit's actions immediately prior to his death were inexcusable and monstrous, but his work inside the ring endeared him as one of the greatest wrestlers to lace up a pair of boots.

Any dispassionate appraisal of Chris Benoit's work should lead you to the inescapable conclusion that part of what made him so appealing to watch was his dedication to realism. He was a wrestler unafraid to work stiff and, once he had acquired the decades of experience he enjoyed at the tail end of his career, few could match him. William Regal was one of those few. Though not lauded as much as he deserves in more vociferous critical circles, Regal is a man like Benoit who seems to relish any opportunity to ramp up the physicality.

Though enjoyment of both men's most intense work carries inherent sadism, its appeal is undeniable. Theirs was a visceral quality that possessed a perverse physical beauty. Whenever the two got together, particularly at as late a stage in their careers as 2006, the result was an exhibition that supposes the very assertion this book will now make: that performance art is professional wrestling's transcended state.

What is meant by performance art? There is a famous phrase that "professional wrestling is not ballet;" I would contend that it is much closer to ballet than people concede. Like any performance art, professional wrestling is the presentation of a physical medium wherein a performer utilises their body, voice and objects to convey artistic expression. Professional wrestlers do this through a specific physical discipline learned over a period of years and mastered over a period of many more. In the end, each wrestling match is its own composition, with the best of their kind telling stories in one form or another, some being as moralistic as fables and others as brainlessly entertaining as a summer Hollywood blockbuster.

To select this match as the perfect proponent of my performance art theory carries with it a certain irony; while watching, you get a strong impression that Chris Benoit and William Regal both respect the art form so much that they may still quite possibly view it as closer to sport than anyone else would dare. As such, their work in #101 is somewhat reductive. It is in the small, almost unnoticeable moments - blocking chops with forearms, landing chops onto an open head wound and deploying hard head butts to escape an arm trap – that Benoit and Regal create a match eschewing consciously stunning visuals in favour of a more down-to-earth grit that is no less entertaining and twice as relatable.

This match, on a philosophical level, is perhaps as far removed from the predominantly theatrical approach of WWE as you can get as a result, and it is perhaps such refreshing uniqueness that allows any viewer to fall so easily in love with the composition. The passion is infectious, bleeding through the performances and translating into a brilliant eleven minute bout. Its unapologetic zeal and tone is a pertinent lesson for those claiming to be proud of their chosen profession. Its dense action and well-judged, methodical pace result in a collaboration exuding confidence which, in every sense, watches as an unmitigated triumph.

One question remains, though: does it tell a story? WWE are big on promoting the idea that their performers are more than just athletes and that they are much more like storytellers. While the tight focus on athleticism and durability in this match may feel refreshingly different, it still endures the same subconscious stylistic expectations from its audience. In other words, it had to still feel like a WWE match.

The answer to the posed question all depends on what we mean by story, of course. On the one hand, this match fails to allegorise anything specific, as other matches will succeed in doing later in the list. It has nothing to say in terms of social commentary or even about the history of the business of which it is so clearly reverential. At first glance, it is essentially all surface level; just two men assaulting one another physically in the hope of achieving a victory. It really is, rather simply, just a professional wrestling match.

That is the point.

Though its story does not stem from a desire to comment, it does stem from its desire for the wonderfully fun nature of professional wrestling and its essential tenant – beat the other guy up until you can keep his shoulders on a canvas for three seconds or make him submit – to speak for itself. So goes the narrative purity at the core of this piece.

Essentially, #101 is a succinct composite of the soul of professional wrestling – its emotion, fluidity, grit, and physicality. Therein is the irony; in its lack of desire to do anything other than just *be* professional wrestling, it is a match that perfectly exhibits professional wrestling's ability to be more than what it is. It combines sublime choreography with a restrained pace and enthused realism, which all together allow it to go beyond melodrama or simulated sport into the realms of performance art.

By viewing #101 as performance art, despite its apparent desire to be nothing more than an old fashioned pro wrestling match, this soulful bout becomes a powerful representation of professional wrestling's future. Over the course of its existence, professional wrestling has been met with contempt because of the perceived notion that it chooses to convey itself as, at least to some degree, a sport. Even the term "sports entertainment" refuses to let go of this outdated identity. As soon as knowledge of professional wrestling's predetermined nature came to light, the wrestling fan knew too much. However, this is not, as many would claim it to be, a bad thing. It simply demands change. What is the best sort of change? It is to embrace the very elements of professional wrestling people have tried to shy away from. If WWE wishes to present itself as a form of storytelling, I say embrace it. Do not limit reception to old fashioned ideas that prevent a wrestling match from being anything other than an exercise in pretend; such ideas are reductive and at odds with the modern wrestling world. Rather, be proud of the fact that professional wrestling is a unique entity because of its strange heritage. Like no other art form, professional wrestling can tell stories of any kind, from abstract human emotion like jealousy, friendship and loyalty, to aspects of life such as success, fame and competition, to personal histories or metaphoric pitches regarding changes within the pro wrestling industry itself.

There are whispers in #101 of other issues we will come to explore later, but the reason this bout has been deemed must-see is because of its silent proposition that professional wrestling carries an inherent state of transcendence that I hope you will come to be onside with. Of course, viewing professional wrestling as performance art presents its own questions and a need for certain redefinitions, the most prescient of which is the very nature of how we think about what we see unfold. Every action and reaction becomes a part of a grand fiction and, rather than being about athletes pretending to fight, it becomes about the nature of the characters involved and the reason for their dispute; not a match, but, crucially, *a story*.

#100
Randy Orton vs. Shane McMahon
No Holds Barred Match
No Way Out
February 15th, 2009

To perform a character convincingly requires an ability to commit to the fiction and ensure your audience loses sight of the fact that what they are seeing is a fabrication. In professional wrestling, it seems like a rarity to come across such strong character-driven work.

It is important to understand the definitions being used here and the difference between character and gimmick. The former is established over a number of months or perhaps years and conditions the fans into expecting certain mannerisms, actions and reactions, predisposing them to know how a particular character would react in any given situation. For example, the fans would expect the sociopathic Viper character portrayed by Randy Orton to react differently in any given situation to how the confidence-exuding Best in the World character portrayed by CM Punk would. Conversely, the term "gimmick" gives a more one-dimensional impression. It is not about progression or growth or semantics, or anything really. It is a purely surface level portrayal that constantly threatens to devolve into parody. Repo Man, Skinner and Mantaur were gimmicks. Randy Orton, Chris Jericho, Steve Austin, Bret Hart, Ultimate Warrior and others are quite the opposite: fully realised, three dimensional characters that could be built upon, fashioned, formed and then deployed with greater creative liberalism.

These might seem like obvious distinctions to anyone who has watched professional wrestling for some time, but it has become all too easy to forget that what we see on screen is in every possible way a fiction. This is made even trickier an obstacle by the fact that some characters are not quite as clearly fleshed out as your Vipers, Best in the Worlds or Rattlesnakes. Instead, some wrestlers, such as John Cena, simply portray amplified versions of themselves. Those are still fictional characters, though, and an example of a performer performing, and taking professional wrestling as a performance art makes these ideas easier to remember; even, to encourage. This second choice is one of the long forgotten master-classes in character performance from WWE history that exemplifies these assertions.

It is quite a shame that nobody seems to think about this encounter very much, given it came in the midst of Randy Orton's most enthused work to date. When you watch the match back now, you may be reminded just how good the man is. Orton pretty much achieves complete performance perfection. His offense looks realistic, his reactions are believable, he plays the crowd with incredible ease and his expressions and movements show him to be completely and utterly devoted to the character of the Viper. If you watch closely enough, you will come to understand that Orton is lost entirely to the fiction of the match's story, with innumerable tiny touches in the content that lead to his own complete suspension of reality - from selling every punch in a convincingly dazed manner to such infinitesimal details as holding onto Shane just to keep himself upright, as anybody would in a real world fight.

The usage of weaponry is well judged. The tease of its initial introduction is exactly the right way to begin setting up the more awkward props like tables and trash cans; we see them, but they're not used until much later. Such subtle insertion of the more fantastical elements of the story becomes a trademark. The spots themselves are timed wonderfully, as action unfolds in a borderline suicidal manner with Shane giving off the impression that he is willing to use his body in whatever way necessary. Even after a cringe-worthy landing off a Coast-to-Coast, for instance, he still scrambles back to his feet to dive his way through an announce desk. The way both men play off these spots feels improvisational; Orton's reaction to getting hit with the monitor is difficult to define as either legitimate or a grand sell, and the climactic superplex through the table – which sees both men bear the brunt of the impact – results in Orton logically hesitating before trying a cover, in turn meaning Shane's few added moments of recovery time are what allow him to kick out.

Given this is an arrogant, sociopathic multiple-time World Champion going against an average Joe fighting simply to defend his family honour and avenge his father, you can believe Orton would initially go it alone, excusing the early absence of his henchman Cody Rhodes and Ted DiBiase. When things don't quite go to plan, and Orton is lying prone for Shane's killing stroke through the announce desk, only then do his cronies show up to save their boss. When they do, it is the most classic display of villainy counteracted by viable underdog heroism. McMahon's comeback does not strain the realms of believability, yet maintains enough agency to win you over to his cause. The way this emotionally accessible underdog story unfolds is intelligently plotted, with effectively placed spots meaning the composition's discourse unfolds fluidly and with rapidity. Coupled with the submission to character we see from Orton, where every minor action is dictated by the self-imposed rules of his creation - from the way he tells DiBiase to get Rhodes to the back to the way he writhes and slithers on the canvas when he is battered relentlessly by Shane and his steel chair - the atmosphere feels utterly irresistible. It is a breathtaking piece of character wrestling, committing to the theatre while never becoming cartoonish.

Orton suffered criticism at the time for the slow pace at which he would wrestle. The result of his conscious stylistic choices was a wave of reception that labelled his act boring and him as an inadequate performer. Such judgments change once you alter the frame of context in which you receive his work. When thinking of this match as a piece of performance art, what once seemed like a languid simulation of athletic contest becomes the aforementioned complete commitment to character, allowing even this most unnoticeable of matches to become something much more than what it may at first seem to be. There is an argument that says when many wrestlers try to act, they fail miserably. The Randy Orton in this match *is* The Viper, the performer consumed completely by his portrayal of the character's wanton desire for evisceration. This is not a heel wrestling; it is a maniac playing with his victim. Such total subjugation to character is incredibly impressive.

Furthermore, take this definition of character in wrestling and apply it to other matches you think you know well and you may find they have much more to them than you originally believed. I have already been using such grandiose language in this book as "transcended state," but such a state can be easily achieved in professional wrestling, not just as the industry moves forward but also for matches that have already happened. In truth, there is little grandiose in the theory at all. It is actually quite simple. Do not just take what you see happen in a given wrestling match as two performers pretending to compete with one another while loosely adhering to a sort of awkward melodrama they are not well enough equipped to pull off. Think deeper than that; view it in terms of art, fiction, character and achievement.

Now, of course, it is not being supposed that all the achievements I have lauded this match with, and the one that preceded it, were purposefully designed, but that impression – if you have been given it - highlights yet another clarification we need to make as we continue to develop this particular approach toward professional wrestling: the ability and freedom to interpret. Like any great art form, performance or otherwise, professional wrestling can be subjected to a degree of interpretive analysis, where matches and feuds are seen to achieve things not necessarily consciously intended. As a result, the observations made in these first two reviews, and the observations that will be made in the ninety-nine others still to come, are representative of only a single interpretation of the match being analysed; they are not claiming each bout's achievements were accomplished purposefully, but that they were accomplished regardless of intent.

When following such a route of creative interpretation, it is amazing the kind of allegory you can witness any given professional wrestling match create.

Chapter 2

Allegory, Comment and Metaphor

#99
Bret "Hitman" Hart vs. Mr Perfect
Semi-Final Match
King of the Ring
June 13th, 1993

As a story told in the ring, #99 provides the viewer with a relatable human element residing in each one of us, and so too does it represent a conceptual idea challenging the starkly defined lines of good and evil: competitiveness.

Even though the predetermined element of professional wrestling dictates that matches can even at their best only ever *feel* competitive, that does not mean that, by extension, there is no competitive element to the endeavour. These ideas are not limited to this one industry either. Competitive spirit burns within us all, though its ferocity differs greatly among individuals. What you have in this particular match is both warning against and active encouragement of the spirit of competition, displaying both its moral dangers and the success it can catalyse all in one half hour block. In real terms, it feels like an impassioned effort from the two individuals involved to outdo their critically acclaimed outing at Summerslam 1991, while in creative terms its deliberate muddying of the babyface / heel definition discusses the benefits and pratfalls of being more than just a wrestler; of being a competitor. You witness a positive crusade to be the best through the Hitman's exhaustive efforts and incredible endurance, but so too do you see the corrupting nature of the desire to win take hold of Mr Perfect.

On both these literal and creative levels, the message is clear: never surrender in the face of past achievements, always seek to prove yourself to be the best at what you choose to do and beware the will to win. #99 takes the ideas #101 is fuelled by and greatly exacerbates them, transforming a piece of sports entertainment into artistic expression that acts as an allegory on what competitiveness can help you achieve.

Part of this match's complex nature comes from what is effectively the elephant in the room: their more famous Summerslam 1991 Intercontinental Championship match, which many people would rate above this King of the Ring rematch in qualitative terms. Truly it was an instant classic, but crucially so is this later encounter. The difference between the two is that #99 was more than just a show-stealer; it was a third of Bret Hart's famous effort capable of contending for the best one night performance in WWE history. Perfect was in superior physical condition himself due to the absence of the back injury that had plagued him at Summerslam '91 and, together, both men prove able to use the psychology created by their previous tussle to create a more nuanced sequel.

Like most Hart matches, this is one that finds benefit in its careful plotting. The pace begins methodically, with long smooth exchanges of wrestling holds creating a steady foundation upon which the two then deploy sudden explosive spurts of momentum. Each of these spurts lasts only a short while before the pace settles back down again and, with such an approach stretched across the duration of their encounter, the whole outing feels, as the best wrestling matches always do, like an exhilarating roller-coaster ride, the action more engaging because of the resultant emotional peaks and troughs. Couple this approach with the way they are able to effectively generate an atmosphere of tension through their characters' respective tentativeness, born logically from their previous clash, and what you end up with is an enthralling powerhouse of a piece. Granted, given the talent of both men involved it is difficult to justify expecting anything less than complete self-assurance, but even the way the pair interact with one another flows so well that it borders on a form of physical poetry.

Hyperbolic rhetoric being damned, the craftsmanship on every level is stunning.

Once Perfect's thirst for victory excuses itself use of more questionable tactics, the match then morphs into a typical Hart beat down, albeit one where the ongoing resilience and irrepressible drive of the Hitman translates into prestige for the King of the Ring moniker. While many of his illustrations in the ring would carry the same sense of growth and recession #99 possesses, that he would often employ such a methodology so effectively does not render this particular encounter's brilliance moot whatsoever. In a lot of ways, it's Hart's ever faithful and proven methodology toward the physical action that creates such a strong and stable foundation for Perfect to build his nuanced, teetering psychological framework upon in the first place, with the two coupling together in a symphonic marriage of style and purpose where eerything either man does feeds into the performance of his partner, creating a testament to their generous professionalism, their unbridled talent and their love of the art form.

It is all too easy to gush about this beautiful entry for pages and pages. The realism created by the cumulative effect of the many factors explored is propelled by the generosity of both individual performances, which together preach what good chemistry can help create in the squared circle. Hart and Perfect were famously big fans of one another, meaning their performances are vigorous in both the physical and psychological arenas. While often we have witnessed wrestlers getting a little too enthusiastic in the ring, creating melodrama rather than art, it is the match's surface-level simplicity that helps prevent such a phenomenon from occurring. Though the psychology becomes increasingly complex as events progress, it is ultimately an uncomplicated story fully aware of its immediate role; the middle part of Hart's trilogy that night, it was sandwiched by encounters with two very famous villains, meaning that Perfect's gradual dissension into moral ambiguity, and the resulting muse on the dangers of competitive spirit, is fitting in tone and tempered in purpose, believably allowing Hart to appear as the hero fighting from the knees up.

It is a jigsaw of a wrestling match, with all pieces playing an equally important role in making up the final, stunning picture. All those pieces are slotted into place at all the right times and the result is another master class, and its lessons are many. It teaches us that Hart and Perfect were one of the all-time great in-ring pairings, their matches rightfully deserving of the reputation of necessary viewing for anyone wanting an introduction to WWE and its history. It is proof of what a little originality and greater effort can help any professional wrestler achieve, exhibiting a self-assured approach that actively embraces the role it has been given and does the best with it that it possibly can, leading to a multi-layered psychological density that even the greatest performers of today may struggle to match.

Most importantly of all, though, it is a supreme exhibit further proving the worth of pro wrestling when received as performance art. It possesses an allegory that reads as an exploration of the varying facets of competitive spirit, be they positive or negative. It is a muse on the nature of professional wrestling in both kayfabe and real world terms; it is a pioneering attempt to bring a degree of doubt to the concrete and unwavering black and white realms of wrestling morality; it is a simultaneously simple and complex performance; and it is an example-setting show of two performers and their refusal to accept mediocrity, delivering a superior and more intelligent sequel to their original outing. It is competition, with oneself, with one's peers and with history.

When you boil that idea down to its rawest, simplest and most exposed form, it is a match that leaves you with the one inspirational question you should ask yourself in any of your life's endeavours: what's stopping me?

#98
CM Punk vs. Brock Lesnar
No Disqualification Match
Summerslam
August 18th, 2013

This next entry allows us to continue building the performance art frame of context by bringing together the ideas we have thus far established – matches are stories driven by entirely fictional characters that, in their best examples, provide allegory, comment or metaphor, like any art form. The preceding match on this list had statements to make regarding competitive drive and the moral confrontations it can lead us to, which is an issue with literal applications to how we think about professional wrestling as an industry or business. #98 is more expansive an example of the performance art philosophy, instead relating a universal human experience: friendship, and the bitter results of when it fails.

#98 has poisonous intention pulsating through every moment, the pure unfiltered hate that swells inside of the grimy twenty-five minutes putrid and believably raw. It is visceral and affecting with an aesthetic as unflinchingly brutal as its psychology. The performances of both wrestlers allow the viewing fan to feel consumed by their nightmarish tale. The story leading into this match was of the ruination of a trusted friendship, a betrayal of faith and the corruption of love. It is a simple, irrepressible, unrelenting emotional experience. It exhibits the same methodology as #100 did before it - CM Punk, Brock Lesnar and the man they both have in common, Paul Heyman, are wholly displaced, courtesy of their commitment in both character and event, by the match's fiction.

The wheels for this titanic clash started turning months beforehand, when Paul Heyman sank his corrupting claws into the then likeable CM Punk. Once his poison began to take root, Punk's already large ego was inflated to uncontrollable proportions, so much so that his confidence-breeding Best in the World ideal turned from being an athletic quest of self-confirmation to a self-perpetuated nightmare of insecurity and covetous envy. The WWE Championship did not escape this perversion intact either; it stopped being an affirming accomplishment for Punk and transformed violently and disturbingly into a source of possessive obsession. Then, two consecutive losses to the self-proclaimed champion of the very people Punk had become paranoid about – The Rock – resulting in the loss of his coveted championship started a shocking descent for the Best in the World culminating with his humbling, world-shattering defeat at the hands of The Undertaker's vaunted Streak in New Jersey. CM Punk thus left the company, retreating to the isolation of his home to reflect on his failures, but more importantly freeing himself of Heyman's incessant corruption in doing so. Upon his return, Punk possessed renewed clarity of purpose, keeping Heyman at arm's length to ensure such torturous experiences were never again repeated.

Spurning the devil turned out to be an unwise venture, though, inviting a fresh hell. Seeing that his iron grasp over a man that might genuinely be the Best in the World was broken, Heyman opted to kill him off instead; if Punk would not be his, he simply would not be. Heyman's spurned love for CM Punk, perverse as it was for having been born from Punk's ability to afford obscene success, caused him to begin a new quest: the evisceration of his prodigy, in which he would play upon Punk's blind faith in their friendship to paint his own self the victim. The key component needed to ensure this strategy's finality was Brock Lesnar.

This was a story, and ultimately a match, that made Lesnar's character clear as day. He is Heyman's nuclear arsenal. He is a monster whose detestation of the rest of humanity stems from the fact that Heyman is his only link to the inferior species; Heyman's character, after all, is not a good example of a human being. As a result, the Beast Incarnate, fuelled solely by his misanthropic outlook on the planet he inhabits, is perhaps the most dangerous entity in WWE's fictional universe. His contempt for the human condition is bred by his transcendence of it, where Eat, Sleep, Conquer, Repeat is not just a mantra but the very essence of his existence. He is a simple, primal force of nature targeting whatever it is Heyman chooses to target; in this case CM Punk.

As you should be able to tell, the story was undeniably one of the most epic WWE had built in years when viewed through the performance art lens. When all of these factors collided, what occurred was an explosively violent, frighteningly destructive, fantastical parable where the best in this world had his path toward retribution blocked by an entity beyond anything this world could ever offer. The word "masterpiece," or an equivalent of it, applies to all the matches analysed thus far; this high fantasy of betrayed friendships and the suicidal quest of one man clashing against the physical manifestation of the devil's evil is no exception. It is an almost biblical setting that translated into an incredible work of art in the form of #98.

The bout's visceral, animalistic nature is largely constructed out of the aesthetic Punk's performance breeds; he is able to show, in this match, a dedication in his bumping that only a talent like Lesnar could exclusively afford him. Truly, this remains one of Punk's finest showings; his unflinching enthusiasm in such a legitimately dangerous composition, one of his greatest attributes. He treats his body as nothing more than a weapon, diving around in full kamikaze mode with a reckless intention that implies both his character's narrow mission statement and the emotional intensity fuelling the feud: he just wants to get his hands on Heyman. This is a Punk that does not care about winning or losing matches, or about his own future. It is a Punk willing to martyr himself to his own cause, and that his performance exhibits this in real terms, despite the obvious repercussions, is a testament to the commitment that prompted this bout's selection. Further, whereas the idea of this being one of Punk's finer performances perhaps stems from its physical aspect, for Lesnar it is instead the sense of a more overt theatricality. He talks smack here more frequently than usual, with enjoyment more than once evident on his expression. It seems as Punk resigns himself to the ugly necessity of his mission, Lesnar apparently enjoys the ugly necessity of Heyman's.

It is dissecting the positives of both individual performances that hints at their greatest achievement that night: they use the fiction of the story and motivation of their characters to marry up their creative outlook with an effective execution pitched perfectly. The naturalistic way they play off their size differential without ever making it the bout's primary focus allows the match's creative to breathe without being stifled by the requisite athletic ergonomics. The swinging sense of momentum is catalysed not by fabricated plot twists but rather strategic mistakes made by each, allowing the pace to alter enough to keep interest piqued but not so much that the action feels unfocussed. And the ferocity of their respective showings continues to unfold at an impressively sustained rate.

Most impressive of all is the maturity of the ending; a dark and quite disturbing curtain call and a reminder of the stark reality that when friendships fail, more often than not, everybody loses. Whether that is Punk's lack of revenge denying him necessary closure, Heyman's slavery to his own worst nature denying him his one redeeming friendship or Lesnar's inability to dominate thoroughly reminding him of his fallibility, this parable's bleak conclusion was, in varying degrees, one detrimental to the lives of all the characters involved.

This was a story without a happy ending, relating through its physical medium experiences many of us feel we have endured. With #98, what you have is a magnificent piece of physical art that only pro wrestling could compile so affectingly. This encounter should only ever be about its emotional significance, something that will remain obvious regardless of the passage of time, where the viewer is elevated to the level of participant by the nature of the infectious delivery of perennially relevant issues. It is the dramatic representation of an enhanced element of real life; it is wrestling as metaphor, a state unachievable in any circumstance other than when we consider it to be performance art. It is, like #99 before it, wrestling's transcended state that, when reached, proves a professional wrestling match can put itself to some very revealing uses.

#97
CM Punk vs. The Rock
WWE Championship
Royal Rumble
January 27th, 2013

As performance art, matches can act as metaphor; metaphors that can teach us about the wider industry in a manner we may not otherwise be tempted to think about it. I am referencing, specifically, historical concepts such as periodisation, teleology, post-modernism and more. Both #97 and #96 were chosen together to example how we, as an audience, can learn from the metaphor found in wrestling matches when approaching them as performance art to better our understanding of the business's evolution; in this specific instance, a promotion's changing identity through shifts in memory.

WWE identifies its history through specific periods. Populist opinion regularly identifies the Golden Age of the 1980s to early 1990s, the New Generation Era of the mid 1990s and the Attitude Era of the late 1990s to early 2000s. Following the conclusion of the Attitude Era – with the most popular theory marking WrestleMania X-Seven as the end date – the company moved then into what many refer to as a Ruthless Aggression Era in the early to mid 2000s and the PG Era of the late 2000s; I prefer to see them collectively as one and the same: the Brand Extension. Then, of course, came the Reality Era of the early 2010s.

Each of these periods have issues unique to themselves to be explored at varying points later in the book but, for now, understand that WWE treats its own history in the context of these periods. Such treatment gives us an insight into the perceptions that WWE and its fans have of the company's changing identity through the years and, of these perceptions, perhaps the most obvious is in the reverence in which the Attitude Era is held. Fans remember it with the misty eyes of nostalgic favouritism and the company has, in recent years at least, bought into such glorification. Such historical misrepresentation is unhealthy. Not only does it tempt a gross misunderstanding of the past and how WWE has gotten to where it is today, it also threatens to leave forgotten the greatest elements of the company's other eras. Ultimately, it limits our understanding of WWE's history and evolution.

Thankfully, there are indications this favouritism is beginning to change. As the last vestiges of Attitude began disappearing - Shawn Michaels, The Undertaker, Triple H, Mick Foley, Big Show, Kane, The Rock and "Stone Cold" Steve Austin all, in their own ways, fading from prominence to some degree - younger stars made names for themselves in the latter days of the Brand Extension. CM Punk forced his way into WWE's highest echelon, the fans forced Daniel Bryan's way to the same spot, while The Shield tore roster positioning wide open. As the power of the company's future grew at an increasingly exponential rate, the unbending reverence of the most nostalgically beloved period in company history faded away. This shift, though still ongoing at the time of writing, became strongest specifically during what many call the Reality Era; WWE's most recent period.

The revolution of CM Punk, rise of Daniel Bryan and consistent quality of The Shield were all part of this shift that not only naturally championed fresh, enduringly popular stars to replace the largely maligned, corporately sponsored favoured few of the Brand Extension but, more presciently, may have set the Reality Era on a course to, in years to come, displace even the untouchable reputation of the Attitude Era itself. #97 is, accidental or otherwise, a striking metaphor of this changing view of WWE's past, one that takes the man some would argue to be a harbinger and icon of the Reality Era, CM Punk, and pits him against a similar harbinger and icon of the Attitude Era, The Rock. The resulting composition hints at the future of the company's perception, where longing for a return of Attitude's hyperactivity is displaced by an appreciation of Reality's cerebral maturity.

Perhaps due to the general apathy to WrestleMania and The Road that led to it that year, it is tempting to recall a hostile response to this match and ignore what it teaches. Watching it back now may shock, as you will rediscover the level of passion bleeding through the piece. The Rock cuts an opening promo that frames this match as a crusade for the people, playing up to his moniker as The People's Champion more literally than perhaps ever before. The situation escalates from a title match between a part-time legend and the longest reigning champion in a quarter century to a tale of overcoming adversity, emotively framed by Rock's intense recollection of his mother's battle with cancer. Punk's reign is, thus, afforded new status: an unstoppable tyranny subjugating the people Rock fights for. A revolutionary tone results.

The match features old school wrestling psychology before an explosive intensity brings a chaotic climax, but what makes #97, together with its Elimination Chamber sequel, so special is its post-modern embrace of structural conceits most associated with the frenetic environment of Attitude from which The Rock spawned. Throughout both matches, The Rock has moments where he looks set to devolve their psychological chess game into the balls-to-the-wall brawling style that he'd carved his success on, while CM Punk parodies the tropes that so memorably watermarked Attitude. In #97, their first of two encounters, The Rock goes to strip the table early on for a Rock Bottom, while CM Punk not only outright mocks doing the same later but, in the immediate, actively puts the table back together with a smug grin and a wag of his finger, condescendingly denying The Rock use of the cliché. Similarly, the ending to the match – The Shield interfering leading to a restart - pays tribute to the over-booked style of the same preceding era; it is this tribute that ultimately enables The Rock's victory, as it did so many times in his heyday.

Taken to the next level in their climactic confrontation at Elimination Chamber, the subtle winks are reborn as utilised conceits, though notably being employed by CM Punk. The sub-textual metaphor changes as a result. Where before Punk's attempts to prevent The Rock from creating a familiar environment to win failed to earn himself the victory, in the sequel he alters the strategy to fight fire with fire. The methods he had mocked The Rock for trying to use in #97, he instead actively embraces - CM Punk strips the table, encourages his manager to provide numerous distractions, causes the infamous ref bump and tries to use the championship belt to earn an illicit third WWE title win. This embrace of Attitude proves to be just as responsible for his second failure as his denial of it was for his first, though. The ref bump means his ten-plus count on The Rock following a GTS goes undetected, and his use of the title as a weapon leads to a moment of capitalisation where The Rock is able to nail the deciding Rock Bottom.

By the time The Rock has scored his second win – more as a result of Punk's failures rather than his own successes – you get a sense that Punk was simply a strategist confronted by an unfamiliar that he was unable to adapt to; playing The Rock at his own game was as ill-advised as trying to prevent him from playing it at all.

This post-modern embrace translates ultimately into a metaphorical proposition of how memory of the Attitude Era is changing, where nostalgic praise is being replaced with warranted objective criticism. Though The Rock notably wins both matches with Punk, the reception to those wins is what speaks volumes, providing the validation that this composition's metaphorical content was very much an accurate reflection of fan sentiment. The condescending anxieties felt toward the Attitude Era, portrayed metaphorically by Punk's character's actions here and in the sequel, are clearly shared in real terms by a fan base vociferously rejecting the thought of a legendary Attitude Era talent of yesteryear triumphing over a Reality Era cornerstone of the here and now.

One question remains unanswered, though. If pervading opinion and memory is changing, what exactly is it changing into?

#96
The Shield vs. Kane and The New Age Outlaws
WrestleMania XXX
April 6th, 2014

This particular choice of match may seem highly unusual. Amounting to little more than a two and a half minute tag team squash, this is not so much about the content as it is the execution, result, and how these answer the questions posed by #97.

As a group, The Shield's story was one dominated by the theme of renaissance: in traditional tag team wrestling thanks to the Rollins / Reigns title run; in the six man tag format that, in WWE at least, had hardly ever been given a semblance of utility thanks to their mastery of controlled chaos; of the product as a whole, thanks to their unapologetic desire to reach the top no matter what. There is a reason The Shield cemented a reputation as arguably the greatest group in WWE history and, in years to come, when historical reappraisals look back on the Reality Era, the Hounds of Justice will be stood right alongside the likes of Punk and Bryan as leviathan players, if not above them.

#96 is indicative of all these ideas. It exhibits their strengths as a team and as individual talents, of WWE's faith in them as the future and of their fervent drive as performers to be the highlight of any show. They had less than three minutes of ring time to work with and managed, in that time, to create something metaphorical and entirely must-see. What they achieved with this squash was sublime.

Being a squash match, it is naturally a one-sided affair. The Shield blow the roof off, tear the opposing team apart and leave almost without breaking a sweat with a strikingly blistering pace. Admirably, that does not create a sense of bluster, as it may threaten to do with less focussed performers utilising less established acts. The entire duration is clear and lean. The execution is without distraction resulting in an intense snarl of an encounter. It is a tour of the best of The Shield, the match acting solely as a platform for them.

The match's greatest achievement perhaps comes before the bell even rings, though. The way each combatant's entrance plays is tremendous. The Shield, in an indication of their generally hostile regard of the past, interrupt Road Dogg before his trademark act on the microphone is complete, only for the Hounds to, in turn, get interrupted by the deafening explosive pyro of Kane. If viewed literally, as sports entertainment would facilitate, this would no doubt betray a sense of expediency that the evening's script demanded. When viewed as interpretive performance art, it plays out as aggressive posturing between both units. The Shield are not prepared to listen to the tired act of a decades old tag team, while Kane is not going to allow the young upstarts to get away with puffing out their chests without doing likewise himself. It all creates added psychological depth to what otherwise would perhaps feel like a standard, if slightly more entertaining than usual, squash match.

At this stage, it is imperative to keep in mind certain assertions. First, that the performance art interpretation of this match creates a sense of posturing psychology and confrontational intonation that may otherwise be crushed under the weight of its squash match vices. Second, The Shield as a group of stars is as recognisable with the Reality Era as the likes of Punk or Bryan, perhaps increasingly so as time goes on. Third, their act was predicated upon a sense of competitive ferocity in both character and performer; the characters are there to tear apart the competition and the performers are prepared to bring the fight to the highest locker room echelon because of their burning desire to reach that very same level. Finally, recall the issue explored in the preceding selection: immoderate praise of a flawed time in the company's past finally being offset with appropriate cynicism, allowing WWE and its fans to move on from an obstructive obsession with the past.

If you combine all of these factors, the metaphor underlying this short piece of work should become obvious. This is the Reality Era, seen here in the guise of The Shield, squashing not just the Attitude Era, in the guise of Kane and The New Age Outlaws, but more conceptually a damaging preoccupation with the past. Further still, in keeping with this view, #96 exhibits how this change in identity extends even to the very nature of WWE's product. It sees a new form of professional wrestling cast aside its outdated forbear, as you witness wrestling's long-standing, predominant approach of pure fabrication utterly displaced in favour of a revitalised philosophy predicated on fictionalised realities, where storylines and characters are inspired increasingly by real world circumstance.

Again, remember that The Shield's characters are as competitive onscreen constructs as the real world performers appear to be in the locker room, at least going on the impressions they give during media interviews, through social media and so forth. The Hounds are able to translate that real world desire to be the best into their fictional characters, who seek the justice that comes with their own ongoing success. Conversely, as the younger brother of the fantastical Undertaker character, Kane is as far from a factually rooted product as can be, and his partners the Outlaws, though less fantastical, still come from the same period famed for zany, off-the-wall antics and implausible storylines. Then consider that the former squashes the latter.

In the Attitude Era, even through the Brand Extension days, WWE have continued to pursue the tried and tested fictionalised universe of wrestling, where characters like Kane are able to thrive despite their whimsical nature because of the required suspension of disbelief. Such ideas worked just fine before the explosion in accessible information. But the 21st Century began a plague that has nagged at WWE, perhaps at all promotions, for the better part of fifteen years now: the internet. The increase in the number of people who could readily access the World Wide Web, escalated further with the advent of broadband, has led to a business far more exposed than it has ever been. Suddenly, the Internet Wrestling Community (IWC) was born as an entire subculture of wrestling fandom that has been seen as more a bad thing than a good one. WWE for the longest time did not seem to know how to adapt, and soldiered on with a style of wrestling product that, until this point, had always worked. Pure fiction had always been fine and they would stick to it.

As fans rightly or wrongly believed they were more informed about the business, their opinions became more vocal. Critical praise became more infrequent as common show goers became self-styled “armchair bookers.” Not only did this lead to the advent of revised ideas of the past explored in the preceding entry, but more generally WWE found it harder and harder to maintain a creatively forward-thinking approach because news of storylines and show results would leak before they could even execute any given idea.

However, as fans have dragged the real world into WWE’s fictional reality more and more, the company has slowly mastered the art of balancing their storytelling intention with utilisation of what fans believe they know but think they shouldn’t. The result is a new style of an old method: fictionalising fact, where WWE take a piece of information that has become widespread knowledge via the internet, cover it in a thin layer of fiction, offer it back and proceed after judging the reaction. Such a methodology is where the term “Reality Era” perhaps originates – fans can no longer be as sure about what is real and what is not, at least in part refashioning an ambiguity we once called kayfabe.

While it may be extreme to say WWE has managed to rebuild kayfabe through this new found method of harnessing internet leaks as a weapon against the so-called smart fan, there can be no denying that they have gone some way to re-establishing a degree of ignorance among wrestling crowds - most notably the IWC - that the entire industry once functioned upon. The story of the Reality Era, historically, may yet be about WWE becoming the first wrestling promotion in the world to realise how to operate at peak efficiency in an age where many said it was no longer possible.

This match selection is, thus, all about change. The Shield (major stars of the Reality Era) squashing Kane and the Outlaws (major stars of the Attitude Era and, more importantly, the past) not only proves WWE are reacting positively on the back of the critical shifts evident in popular reception to #97, it also speaks for their wider alteration of identity by metaphorically representing the replacement of one generation with another, and of yesteryear's pure fiction with the fictionalised realities of today.

These enlightening ideas further prove the might of professional wrestling as a performance art. In this case, metaphorical creative expression betters our understanding of WWE's growth over the years, and its changing perception of self today.

Chapter 3

Developing Genre in Professional Wrestling as Performance Art

#95
Mark Henry vs. The Big Show
World Heavyweight Championship
Survivor Series
November 20th, 2011

Arguing that performance art is a transcended state for professional wrestling presupposes that the currently pervasive sports entertainment philosophy is a limiting one; let us now turn to examining that presupposition. It is in putting the performance art method into practice once again that facilitates this examination through a very important, rather revealing concept: genre. Firstly, this chapter will explore how we are able to identify genre in pro wrestling as performance art, before then going on to evidence how this new idea of genre opens new creative ground by enabling us to cast aside sports entertainment's needless, self-evident constrictions.

Changing our philosophy to pro wrestling naturally changes our conversation regarding it. Use of vaguely defined terms different to us all, such as "prestige" or "momentum," become, thankfully, redundant as we shed the need to construct the framework necessary for a simulated sport. Championships no longer need to function as the affirmation of achievement, but instead become simple MacGuffins needed only to set stories in motion; it doesn't matter if they "mean anything" to fans because they "mean something" to the characters. Indeed, talent are characters before they are competitive athletes too, as seen in #100's McMahon / Orton Street Fight.

Central to it all, however, is the change in how we receive matches.

As sports entertainment, matches are simulated athletic contests mitigated by theatrical demands for drama and emotion. They are constructed, with preordained results, so as to achieve specific effects. Over time, the ways certain kinds of matches are constructed give birth to habit which, in turn, through persistent usage, becomes unspoken semantic rules. These rules eventually come to shape popular and critical reception to matches of all kinds. If the rules are evolved, reception may be more positive. If the rules are too radically strayed from or ignored, reception may be overly negative. If the rules are strictly followed, reception will be prototypical.

Put simply, over the years fans have come to expect sports entertainment matches of all kinds to watch a certain way, carry a certain tone and play out in a certain manner depending on how they can be categorised – through stipulation; through show; through weight class etc.

Then apply the change to performance art and think of matches not as mere simulated contests but, rather, more as fictional constructs. Sports entertainment's silent rule sets affecting reception transform into performance art's genre definitions that categorise matches according to their defining characteristics – stipulation; show; weight class etc. This enables us to begin categorising matches into such genres according to their defining characteristics. In some instances, such as stipulation matches, this is rather quite easy. In others, such as weight class, it demands more nuance. Altogether, it reshapes our reception to pro wrestling from the literal world of sports entertainment to the liberal world of performance art.

#95 is a strong example of this method of identifying and re-categorising pro wrestling matches as performance art genres. The presence, and often prominence, of super heavyweights has long been a recurring conversation among WWE circles. The company has developed a strongly negative reputation for favouring larger men, and fans continue to contend that there is more to the game than simple size. Though perhaps frequently over-exaggerated amongst the fiercer critical element, there has always been an undeniable presence of these "big men" on the roster, and many of them, despite their limitations, have held the company's most prominent accolade. From Ultimate Warrior all the way to The Great Khali, there have been plenty of World Champions favoured for their look rather than their acumen, much to vehemence of many. This fierce contention of the issue stems from sports entertainment's semantic expectations of these larger talents.

#95 confidently subverts those expectations in the most unbelievable manner, building upon the startling over-achievement of Henry and Show's preceding match the month before at Vengeance. This more serialised approach to the narrative of their feud creates a sense of tension that rests in the air and sees the viewer waiting to watch the ring implode a second time as it had done in their prior encounter. Indeed, everything unfolds like a ticking time bomb, and the two performers manipulate the tension in a manner as equally effective as any match wrestled between two smaller stars.

This encounter does have flaws. They perhaps play on the tension a little too long with the more sluggish action, and their overuse of finishing moves seems unoriginal. Truthfully, their first encounter is the superior match, telling a more substantive and comprehensive story. It is worth checking out in itself; it, too, is a startling over-achievement. Henry and Show appeared to have made a conscious decision at that stage to push one another and prove that super heavyweights can wrestle as varied an affair as any 230 to 250 pound individual could. And while #95 remains an overachievement, at least by popular definitions, why choose the inferior second part over the superior first? It boils down to a simple fact: it is, by virtue of its highest point, far more must-see.

Big Show performs an elbow drop off the top rope.

When he does so, the crowd goes ballistic. A superplex that implodes the ring followed the next month by a 440 pound top rope elbow drop is all the proof you need of these men's superior intentions. It's unfathomable, and Henry kicks out to boot. The apparent lack of room for dramatic growth generated by an early over-abundance of ineffective finishing moves is instantaneously disproved, shattering conventions again when it feels as if there were no more left to shatter. I challenge anyone to find anything more must-see than a 440 pound, 7" tall giant climbing to the top rope of a wrestling ring, standing up straight and delivering, on point, a diving elbow drop.

In a match that deliberately seeks to turn the stereotype on its head by following the same path they had so successfully followed once already and for Show to commit himself so unexpectedly to such a spot – the kind of immortal moment that is often saved for a much bigger show like WrestleMania – shows their desire to really put an exclamation mark on the end of their contradictory work. For "contradictory" is the word that most definitely should read as the tagline for their entire feud. Their bout at Vengeance shocked a great many people; so gloriously gross was its overachievement. They then followed that up with the lighter iteration that is #95. All of their critical acclaim across both efforts stemmed from the unspoken rules of the "big man" sports entertainment match that has stood in WWE for many years being turned on its head. It is thanks to the conventions challenged with this two-part argument for more open minds, preached by two of the better super heavyweight talents in company history, that we can thus identify the new, performance art pro wrestling "super heavyweight genre."

When people think of super heavyweights in WWE, the temptation is to immediately think of the limitations of many of the more infamous members of the weight class. There have almost been too many to count. Even the more popular, successful, talented "big men" have been attacked for their apparent lack of acumen inside the squared circle, rightly or not. When people think of matches involving these larger performers, and particularly in the case of matches consisting exclusively of them, slow pacing, methodical action and a rather boring discourse all come to mind. The lack of high spots – a modern and dangerous addiction for many WWE fans – generates disinterest, and people fatigue quickly because of the unfortunate stigma WWE has developed for favouring this often less than enticing set-up. Big Show and Mark Henry have both been involved in such diatribes. Yet, after the opening statement they made at Vengeance, when this particular match happened, that elbow drop from the top rope was as definitive a statement as could be imagined: ideas about super heavyweights were wrong.

This is a match that speaks very clearly about the nature of the super heavyweight genre in professional wrestling, and most certainly about the negativity felt toward it within WWE fan circles, precisely because of its intention to prove said nature as being inaccurate. Henry and Show, two victims of preconception, instead showed the world that super heavyweights can be as accomplished at storytelling and as impressive athletically than any man half their size. It is a match that clarifies the conventions of the super heavyweight genre by shattering them. Alone, it silences zealous critics, complimented by a one of a kind, must-see moment. Alongside its predecessor at Vengeance, it is the exclamation mark on a remarkable accomplishment.

It is the bar-setter for the genre of super heavyweight pro wrestling in the world's greatest performance art.

#94
Dean Malenko vs. Scotty 2 Hotty
Light Heavyweight Championship
Backlash
April 20th, 2000

Understanding pro wrestling matches as performance art genre, then, clarifies to a great extent the semantic rules imposed by sports entertainment from which said genres draw their definitions. Through viewing #95 as genre, we can see the semantic rules imposed upon "big men" in WWE, but such bondage is not a phenomenon exclusive to one weight class. It is as relevant to the "little man" as it is to talent like Henry and Show.

These "little men" too have suffered from the imposition of perceived convention and, just as super heavyweight bouts carry semantic expectations that help us identify the performance art genre, so too does cruiserweight work. Similarly, just as we are able to identify the super heavyweight genre through the subversion of those relevant preconceptions courtesy of Henry and Show in #95, so too are we able to identify the cruiserweight genre through the subversions of its sports entertainment-bred preconceptions courtesy of the light heavyweight wrestling exampled by Dean Malenko and Scotty 2 Hotty in this next match.

Consider the key change made to the division of smaller talent and the conceptual conflict that it breeds: light heavyweight vs. cruiserweight. Though, on the surface, it may seem like homogeneity, this distinction is an important one.

The Light Heavyweight Championship was officially recognised on WWE television as early as 1997, but light heavyweight wrestling was never allowed to take on a prominent role in the promotion. The Cruiserweight Championship was adopted following the Invasion Angle of 2001 and, from 2002 onwards, cruiserweight wrestling took the "little man" to heights of popularity and relevance in the company that light heavyweight wrestling never managed. With that popularity, however, came a sports entertainment demand to stick to a tighter rule set; after Mysterio's ascension to prominence, the strict stereotypical expectation fans now carry whenever seeing "little men" compete developed in earnest. Thanks to this Mysterio Effect, we fans are as guilty of pigeon-holing the cruiserweights as we are the super heavyweights.

This is contrary to the unfortunately obscure light heavyweight wrestling powerfully exampled in the case of #94. Such matches feel like a different take on the same concept, seemingly more open-minded and less prone to type-casting as its successor proved to be. Familiar tropes can still be found amidst light heavyweight title matches – a brisker pace and greater proportion of aerial offense, for example – but these did not confine to cliché as much as its successor seemed to. Expressed succinctly, the difference is such: cruiserweight matches often functioned in a manner only cruiserweight matches could, but light heavyweight matches operated often in a manner many different kinds of matches could.

#94 is prototypical of the long-dead light heavyweight genre and, by extension, subversive of the later, perennially popular cruiserweight genre; it does things that the cruiserweight genre seemed to actively shy away from doing. It is one of a plethora of strong Light Heavyweight Championship matches that were more varied and open-minded in their approach than later, stylistically stricter cruiserweight encounters would prove to be, and it is in that comparison – and the knowledge that light heavyweight wrestling in WWE is a long-dead genre – that we unravel another sports entertainment rule set fuelled by limitations.

WWE opted to follow the lineage of the Cruiserweight Championship post-invasion, and as the years progressed and the title faded into obscurity off the back of Mysterio's ascension through the ranks, compositions became increasingly confined to sports entertainment expectations of flash and style. By the time the Cruiserweight Championship was retired, with Hornswoggle as champion, you were either a cruiserweight talent or you weren't; in other words, any hope of upward mobility was gone. The more fluidly enabling light heavyweight matches crafted by the likes of Malenko, as in this particular example, had become a rare, if not extinct, breed.

#94 disregards the cruiserweight genre's assumption that machine gun athleticism is necessary as a matter of course, with a central focus largely on Dean Malenko working over Scotty 2 Hotty's leg, It's a psychology-heavy method proving to be an approach as appropriate for those under 220 pounds as anybody else, essentially transforming into an argument for substance over style.

That argument dominates the main span of the action, which stays safely in the realms of a steady heel beat-down, kicking into a higher gear only when Scotty starts his comebacks in the latter stages. It's those final few minutes that really stand out and help propel the piece above the realms of solid, thanks to their patiently constructed sense of escalation. They bust out more moves in their final act than we often see in the entirety of some twenty minute matches – though, importantly, fewer than in any ten minute span of a more familiar cruiser match - and, as a result, the sequences become more engaging. The finish, in particular, seems brutal, with Malenko countering a superplex into a vicious DDT from the top rope.

Substance is *never* sacrificed. Granted, it's fun to see a match finish with fifteen flips turning into a pinning combination, but it's just as fun, and twice as effective I venture, to see it end with a counter DDT from the top rope. There's certainly more grit to it, but substance, grit, believability; these are all just really synonyms for everything our stereotyped sports entertainment view of what smaller wrestlers can and should achieve in the ring denies.

Historically, it is the memory of WWE's cruiserweight genre that has become the predominant tale of the small man in Stamford. It is a story with a less than impressive end, its majority represented by downward trends of interest, prominence and importance courtesy of Mysterio's centricity to the division, and later ascendancy beyond it. When viewing professional wrestling and WWE as performance art, the cruiserweight genre becomes another clear case of sports entertainment dictating, much like in the case of super heavyweight wrestling, everything cruiserweights could *not* do; that cruiserweights could never wrestle anything less than the kind of match a WWE fan would expect to see south of the border. The cruiserweight genre is, thus, forced to carry the weight of style, flash and the adrenaline rush.

The varied substance of light heavyweight work feels like a precognitive subversion because of the cruiserweight genre's resultant pervading legacy. #94's sense of variety and enabling mobility was substituted and displaced by the language, style and, in many cases, the talent of a promotion Vince McMahon had inherited. Taking such a limited, copy-cat approach from the onset may just have doomed the division from the start, meaning Mysterio's transformation from niche performer to outright superstar became the tenth toll of a funeral bell, rather than the first of many examples of upward mobility it could have been.

#94 is a match that helps us identify the boundaries of the cruiserweight genre of performance art in WWE because it exhibits the difference between what the promotion and fans once *allowed for*, compared to what eventually the promotion and fans came *to expect*. Those expectations, though not exclusive, became predominant and ensured the division, when robbed of its crown jewel, came to nothing. The reality of light heavyweight matches such as #94, however, is the feel of WWE, not the feel of imitation. A genre that followed the example of matches like this one may have come to offer more variety, which would offer more upward mobility, which would offer more substance for the larger company, in turn meaning that Mysterio's success could have been a positive example of career progression rather than the exception to a rule of limitation it was.

This composition shows not only what light heavyweight wrestling was capable of before its extinction, but hints also at what more it could have achieved relative to the rest of the company, and the possibilities available for those who could make a name for themselves within its confines. Unlike the preceding entry on this list, it did not actively seek to break conventions because it came before those conventions were ever imposed; conventions that have come to define the WWE fan base's perception of the "little man," limiting most performers of a certain size to enacting a specific role and following variations of a specific formula. To return to my earlier distinction: few matches could end the same way many post-Invasion cruiserweight matches ended, but any of them could have ended with a counter DDT from the top rope.

Thus, it is through this match's surprisingly subdued content we can come to understand the limitations of the current sports entertainment mentality held towards the "little man" and his cruiserweight genre of wrestling.

#93
Edge vs. Randy Orton
Monday Night Raw
April 30th, 2007

There is a reason as to why the two matches evidencing my method - of identifying performance art genre through understanding sports entertainment semantics - were selected for their subversive tendencies: they show how limiting sports entertainment, as a philosophy, has become, obsessing, as it does, with what matches cannot and should not do.

Our next match, however, brings us to the second part of this chapter: framing pro wrestling in terms of performance art genre opens up limitless, expansive new creative potential for the industry, comfortably and confidently casting aside sports entertainment's needless dos and don'ts and obsessing not on what matches cannot and should not do, but rather on what they can – and in some cases should – become.

#93 is a powerful example of this taboo-shattering capability. It places the spotlight on one rather perplexing sports entertainment anathema: heel vs. heel. By reframing this maligned concept in the context of performance art genre, it becomes a clear example of sports entertainment holding professional wrestling back from achieving the true extent of its creative potential by virtue of its increasingly irrelevant ideas.

Why is heel vs. heel conducted, at most, only ever rarely? Fear is the most likely answer; fear of audience disinterest, split reactions, inconvenient responses, lack of drawing power or the provision of an entirely wrong impression. Or it is simply not done - shirking as it does the rules that have stood for decades upon which the entire industry was built – because there is not a "good guy" and a "bad guy." Even with the growth of the babyface vs. babyface dynamic, heel vs. heel remains borderline heretical. Essentially, the problem can be boiled down to a simple question: who would be interested in any fight where the only possibility is to back a villain?

It is my belief that the answer is many. At least, it would be if we could shake off the constraining chains of accepted professional wrestling theory. Place the idea of heel vs. heel in the wider context of artistic expression and storytelling and the view of what a heel vs. heel match may achieve shifts.

Popular audiences often more readily adopt into their sentiment the antagonists of a story than their more heroic counterparts. People like to read about, watch, think about, explore and even strive to understand the "bad guy" in fiction. Considering professional wrestling to be just another form of storytelling or fiction, what then is to stop a heel vs. heel match from working? It's not about professional wrestling heels clashing in an event that threatens to confuse fans emotionally, but rather it's about the presentation of two morally complex characters that popular audiences find appealing and fascinating in their own degree. The prospect of two infamous villains renowned for their capacity for evil clashing in mutually assured destruction carries an undeniable sense of attraction, and no form of storytelling other than professional wrestling possesses the same ability to set popular villains against each other in a shared fictional universe, except perhaps for the comic book (and look how profitable an enterprise that has become).

In WWE, however, this opportunity is being squandered because of an apparent reticence to break the bondage of orthodoxy.

#93 is the match to prove that heel vs. heel is an untapped genre in the world of professional wrestling, carrying the potential for genuinely unique achievement. After all, there is no other set-up in professional wrestling capable of presenting a situation in which we can fully indulge our darkest vices and ugliest desires, meaning there is no other set-up capable of presenting something so affecting (at least if it is judged properly).

It is important we accept that this is a concept that could only work if given the due diligence required. There is no denying heel vs. heel is a risk; I will not shy away from the fact that it so often taunts audience apathy in the face, and can fail easily. These are the reasons why, though, if we are to commit to the idea posited here, understanding this specific match becomes even more important, because *this* is how to do it properly; the genre's benchmark, or instruction manual if you will.

What both Orton and Edge did exemplarily, not just in this match, but throughout the duration of their feud, was remain consistent in character. WWE, particularly, often comes under fire for its lax approach to continuity, but throughout the duration of Rated RKO's dissolution you had a conflict of natures. Edge proved himself at every turn the master manipulator with the gift of a silver tongue; he was the sociopath. Orton, growing out of his Legend Killer gimmick and moving steadily closer towards the eventual Viper character he inhabits today, proved to be ruled by his hot-head and paranoid, impatient outrage; he was the psychopath. By the time they get to finally unload on one another between the ropes, this difference in psychosis is allowed to come to the fore, and as early as the opening exchange. Edge slapping Orton before leading him on a merry chase around the ring to be able to pick his spot is proof of that unconscionable, opportunistic cowardice. Orton's response – brazenly thumbing Edge in the eye, choking him on the ropes – is one fuelled by simple-minded, remorseless anger.

This kind of interaction provides the main narrative drive, dictating how events unfold. It may be a strange story, with the dynamic swinging often back and forth, but even when tempted to view either combatant in a more positive light those character traits remain consistent still. Edge is either the opportunistic coward or the desperate underdog, always playing a cerebral game of chess. Orton is either remorselessly raging or indignantly angry, always finding his energy by feeding off directionless emotion. This poses a question: if character remains consistent, does the crowd simply pick sides in a war of villainy rather than react in ostensibly the "wrong way" to a heel vs. heel situation?

Sports entertainment might dictate that, in this situation, fans de facto try and turn a heel babyface, and that this is a bad idea that can have negative impact on the wider product; an understandable concern. Performance art, however, dictates that fans are simply allowing their own darker side to decide which man they intend to back in this intriguing clash of evils, ensuring that, once all is said and done, both characters will still remain villains regardless; in such a view, the fears founded by sports entertainment suddenly seem unnecessary.

The piece proudly exhibits a myriad of achievement – a furious pace, intense high points, a simmering tone of vitriol and the subtext of a tag team split, all balanced perfectly with the heel vs. heel method. Such accomplishment proves just how missed an opportunity it was to not book this same match for WrestleMania 23. Had the orthodox professional wrestling mindset not existed and the company instead realised the incredible potential of any heel vs. heel encounter when approached as performance art rather than sports entertainment, #93 might just have helped propel WrestleMania 23 to greater critical acclaim. It may have even gone down as one of many WrestleMania classics, instead of sitting unnoticed in the annals of Raw.

More importantly, one wonders, had this been a bout that miraculously found its way onto the WrestleMania card that year in the same guise we eventually got it, just how much louder the debate would be over whether or not heel vs. heel compositions work. There can be no denying this was one occasion where the risk paid off, proving there can be value in the idea if it is done properly - when the concept of villain against villain isn't hesitantly shied away from but actively embraced. In their own way, such encounters present a whole different version of the dream match conversation so many fans enjoy engaging in.

Rated RKO crafted a stunning piece of professional wrestling history in their slow dissolution, culminating with this equally stunning altercation, and their simply masterful stroke of genius was to not ask the crowd to sympathise with them but for them to instead, thanks to the character consistency bravely on show, "embrace the hate." All of a sudden, a pro wrestling audience is presented with an opportunity to do what they seem to enjoy doing so often: cheer the better bad guy. What fun it proves as well. The result is an instantly classic clash between two endlessly intriguing fictional characters, belonging to performers who expect a level of maturity and intelligence from their audience and who show no desire to talk down to them. It is proof that, with the proper execution and the right approach to pro wrestling – performance art, not sports entertainment - heel vs. heel matches cannot only work, but could become a genre all their own; just imagine the possibilities that creates.

It is but one example of innumerable others showing how the limiting, suffocating impositions of sports entertainment are, in this 21st Century, utterly unnecessary. It shows that, if we change our view of the industry to the performance art philosophy being championed among these pages, I believe we can blow the industry's creative potential wide open to a previously unseen, unknowable degree; and there is no reason as to why we cannot implement that change today.

There is only one possible problem: WWE's reputation. WWE are infamous among fan circles – especially the most cynical – for being creatively unbending; dogmatically inept, in their worst moments. WWE also happens to be the very originator of sports entertainment in the first place. Combining these together presents a tough question: how responsible is WWE for creating sports entertainment's limitations in the first place? Is there any point in suggesting a change of our pro wrestling conversations if WWE's mind-set is an unyielding one?

Before going further then, we must pause our development of genre in pro wrestling as performance art to briefly inspect the truths of WWE's creative character: are they rigidly doctrinal, as is tempting to believe, or are they actually willful progressives, open to new possibilities?

Chapter 4

WWE as Apostate

#92
The Brotherhood vs. Seth Rollins and Roman Reigns
No Disqualification Tag Team Match
WWE Tag Team Championships
Monday Night Raw
October 14th, 2013

Truthfully, there is an inherent irony in play as this book now turns to uncovering whether WWE is a promotion responsible for limitation and as obsessive over their dogma as fans often claim. It was in WWE, of course, that sports entertainment was founded and first implemented; at the time, a new philosophy that liberated the industry and took it to soaring, new heights. Yet, as the years go by, WWE's reputation becomes, it seems, increasingly negative.

There are many reasons for that, some of which may even be justified, but the idea that WWE is severely adverse to change in either the grand historical sense or the individual, more intimate sense is inaccurate. Tackling this head-on presents the issue Chapter 4 wishes to argue: WWE is a pragmatic creative liberal before it is anything else which, far from being a dulled, unimaginative regressive, more times than not will show inventive willingness, creative environment and rebellious tendencies. This chapter will now take a very quick look at some pertinent examples.

If IWC folklore is to be believed, and dirt sheet reports taken as the gospel they are most certainly not, the bipolar state of tag wrestling in WWE may be because of a flippant attitude to the genre. It has become a fan-held myth that WWE sees no worth in the format and that such an outlook remains one of their many ongoing sins. For the sake of this list, it is this myth that presents a strong, clear example of a WWE status quo that may simply not exist and rather has been imposed upon the company due to the collectively perceived reality of a sometimes overly impassioned fan base.

All through the years, there are incidents proving WWE see more than enough value in the tag team format to act as an attraction match, as exemplified by this selection. #92 is the culmination of an issue that had been brooding between The Authority and the Rhodes family for some time. The feud began out of singles competition – first Cody, then a returning Goldust – but its climactic bouts were both tag team matches. More specifically, they were tag team matches utilised as attraction; first at Battleground, in what became the evening's greatest achievement, then in the case of #92, as the championship main event of Monday Night Raw. #92, in particular, even came complete with main event style ring introductions.

Incredibly fluid interaction between Rollins and Cody and a prototypical hot streak that sees Goldust get the best of both of his opponents each play in the match's favour, but its greatest strength eventually grows to be the see-sawing momentum. While the No DQ stipulation plays its part, it does not suffocate the apparent desire to compile a classical composition adhering to prototype, making this a prime cut of WWE's personal definition of tag team wrestling.

Thematically, the composition, like the feud from which it stemmed, is strong in undertones of fraternity; while Goldust and Cody were close half-brothers, The Shield were brothers in all but blood too. Moments of peril, therefore, take on fresh and emotive weight. While The Shield are too good a trio of villains for one to really feel sympathy in even their most pained moments, the Rhodes' do nothing but evoke emotion en masse. Every anguished expression feels that much more immersive because of their real world bond known widely among fan bases. That same manipulation of fan knowledge is a great expression of the Reality Era in action, as well as the fierce effectiveness of the storyline now culminating. Every time either Goldust or Cody maintains momentum over their enemies by themselves, it feels all the more valiant.

Reigns would go on to become a controversial figure, as we know, but his impressive interactions with Cody halfway through the piece - when the action kicks up a gear - remind of how he reached his (perceived) favoured position today. Reigns' reaction to Cody's offensive is appropriately intoned as one of outrage at the prospect of a man arrogant enough to think they can get the better of him, while Cody himself is the cog responsible for increasing the speed of the chaos. It is in this transition to the final third that sees the No DQ stipulation play into the bout's advantage the most, as Shield's numerical superiority is brought to the forefront.

By the time Goldust cuts off the famous Shield Triple Powerbomb with a steel chair, the narrative has the complete immersion of the live crowd in hand. The use of the chair is suitably restrained though, as once again the focus proves to be on storytelling over visuals and aesthetic. Such restrained simplicity allows drama to breathe rather than drown in multiplicity of carnage. Such multiplicity does find itself growing the closer the combatants reach their finish; however, albeit for good reason - it excusably affords the reappearance of Big Show in a moment tying the raging tag skirmish into wider storylines, allowing the Rhodes' victory to feel all the more triumphant.

The forethought and careful crafting behind this match and the feud it culminated all so clearly on show simply cannot be denied, and most certainly support the dismissing of the fan myth of WWE's disinterest in the tag team format.

When the storyline calls for it, WWE is more than prepared to deploy tag team wrestling as a major attraction. Even the briefest glance through their history supports that to a great extent, peppered as it is with tag team wrestling of all kinds in major placements. Whether it be the reformation of famous factions such as D-Generation X at Summerslam 2009 or the in-ring return of a living legend such as "Never Before, Never Again" at Survivor Series 2011; whether headlining major pay-per-views such as Team Nexus vs. Team WWE at Summerslam 2010 or headlining throughout the ages, from Austin and Undertaker vs. Kane and Mankind in the Attitude Era to Batista and Undertaker vs. John Cena and Shawn Michaels during the Brand Extension; WWE is far from shy in embracing tag team wrestling as an effective, important and vibrant aspect of their product today and in the farthest reaches of their past. Lest we forget, the very first WrestleMania was headlined by a tag team match.

#92 provides a strong and recent example of a story-driven tag team match utilised as a major attraction in a high profile position on the card, culminating a tag team-heavy feud. It proves that sometimes there is little truth in our predominating perceptions of WWE; that they are not always guilty of the crimes levied at them. Sometimes there is only a fan crafted cynicism unable to stand up to the scrutiny of a careful and level-headed examination of WWE's past, both recent and distant. In turn, this serves to reinforce further the underlying idea being posited within this chapter: WWE is not as artistically castrating as we fans often claim it to be. Rather, it is more open-minded than it may at first seem, capable of both purposefully pursuing the deconstruction of its own established creative trends and generating a freeform atmosphere for the individual performer too.

#91
30 Man Royal Rumble Match
Royal Rumble
January 24th, 1999

Let us now turn to supporting those latter two statements then, beginning with the proposition that WWE is capable of purposefully pursuing the deconstruction of its own established creative trends. What better example to offer than one of the quietest yet most radical subversions of genre in their long history, found amidst one of their most sacred creative quarters: Royal Rumble.

#91 sits right in the middle of the infamous Attitude Era, when the overriding creative philosophies of the time were as unapologetic as ever, resulting in quite incredible television which never feared to experiment. A heel walked out of WrestleMania the victorious champion; the authority figure became a power couple; tag team Ladder matches and Hell in a Cell matches came to be; the Montreal Screwjob changed the world; even the briefest overview of the Attitude Era evidences historical precedent that WWE is more than capable and willing to ignore convention and, at times, seek actively to destroy it. #91 is indicative of that phenomenon.

Have you ever heard of a two-man Royal Rumble?

The Royal Rumble is an hour-long festival of professional wrestling fun because of its unique design. It is a simple concept, different enough to forever feel fresh and flexible enough to always surprise. Reducing such a sacrosanct idea down to a glorified singles match sounds like creative suicide; such is the temptation to characterise this oddity of iteration. Despite the typical thirty-strong field, the story revolved so much around one rivalry – Stone Cold Steve Austin vs. Vince McMahon – it is hard to think of any other example in Rumble history where the other twenty-eight participants were as incidental as they were here.

It would be pointless to explain just how hot an angle Austin vs. McMahon was when at its zenith. Few words could do it justice. Whether the vicarious fantasy it provided of the every-man freely beating his boss to a withered and bloody pulp, or the eternal appeal of an underdog overcoming insurmountable odds, or simply the feud's visceral character, even tiny moments led to palpable responses from the fans, both raucous and tense. It is such tension that earmarks the opening minutes on this occasion, creating an atmosphere that excites still today.

In the midst of all this match's unlikely successes, you are constantly reminded of why Austin is considered to be of such a high calibre as a performer. He uses the vocal crowd to intensify his work as the story progresses, playing up to their obvious investment at every turn. The way he enthuses the live audience in the first couple of minutes by teasing the expected elimination of The Chairman, only to go right back and open a new proverbial can of whoop-ass on him is masterful. What helps is the unintentional humour derived from McMahon's melodramatic physical parlance too. He plays the cowardly heel perfectly.

When the match opens up to others, performers get a chance at seizing the spotlight with Road Dogg and Kane both having notably entertaining appearances. A constant whisper in the back of your head is telling you, however, the Austin / McMahon aspect is not over, and that whisper grows louder and stronger when McMahon himself returns to the commentary booth to adopt a role he had long since left behind. By the time Austin returns, there's a sense of everything you've sat through, in the meantime, being ultimately irrelevant. It's a strangely cyclical situation. When Austin and McMahon are around, all eyes are on them; if neither is there, you find yourself waiting for their return. By removing those characters from the action for an extended period of time, the match somehow becomes even more about them. It is, therefore, easy to become dismissive toward everything else going on.

Retrospect helps make that less of an issue now, although only through mild bemusement. It is hard to escape the sense of endless filler, though, and there's no single character you feel justified in rooting for in Austin's absence. The little interest shown in allowing other performers to play upon their unique assets evidences a production strategy attentive only to that centric Austin / McMahon dynamic.

Despite the bleak picture this paints, though, these sins are easy to forgive. When Austin finally reappears in characteristically whimsical fashion, it's an adrenaline shot in the arm of a match suffering cardiac arrest. The excitement returns, and with it the crowd. The fact that he largely leaves Vince to the commentary team until everyone else is eliminated maintains credence to the central narrative drive and returns the sense of building tension; it's a time-bomb they let tick away for as long as they can before blowing it up. Indeed, it is Austin's performance that really ties this entire affair together. His respect as a performer for the little touches helps add to the entertaining whole, such as taking a break from the ring for the express purpose of tossing ice water in McMahon's face. The excitement builds slowly in tandem with the tension and, by the time of the final eliminations, there's a giddy rabidity that begins taking over, erupting when Austin is finally alone to step outside the ropes and begin what you hoped was going to be the longest ass kicking of all-time. The beat-down is still thoroughly enjoyable today.

Everything about this Rumble match is audacious. The certified winner did not win. A $100, 000 bounty sub-plot was introduced and discarded early, ultimately with no lasting effect on proceedings. Twenty-eight of the bout's participants were inconsequential. The fact that it contained the first-ever female Rumble entrant became an after-thought. While there are some other Rumble entries that centred largely on one, maybe two individuals – with 2000 being prominently all about The Rock and Big Show for example – none were ever quite so dismissive to its Also Rans. No other Rumble match took its timeless concept, the popularity of which is predicated upon its potential for variety, chaos and surprise, and tore the rulebook up so entirely that it then watched like a glorified singles match.

1999's Rumble was a platform solely for the ongoing Austin / McMahon saga. The way that story is portrayed throughout the bout's duration has no bearing on any character other than those two, yet instead of being dull and uninspiring it comes off a roaring success. The excitement when Austin and McMahon are present truly is palpable. When neither of them is there or when only one is on screen, the same excitement simmers away like a bubbling volcano before building to a spectacular emotional eruption. Even passing interactions become memorable moments. Perhaps glorified singles match is misleading; perhaps it is simply a glorified beat-down, hijacking a fan-favourite event.

Whatever tag line we choose to give it, though, one thing remains: it was company driven subversion. WWE took one of their golden concepts and, if only for this one year, melted it down and reformed it unapologetically into something designed to take advantage of the incidental present. Your inner-critic may tell you there is plenty in the 1999 version of the Royal Rumble to dislike, resent, deconstruct and, in its worst moments, perhaps even hate. Hopefully though, what you should find, rather like me, is that you cannot help but admire it. Austin's performance, McMahon's melodrama, the inclusion of an ultimately pointless bounty subplot and The Rock's walk-on cameo turn a self-indulgent and audacious affair into the vital proof that, when WWE commits to usurping its own ideas, it can come up with something as remarkably successful as it is remarkably original; the most fitting thing of all, of course, being that if a Royal Rumble ever showed unbridled attitude it was 1999's.

#91 was not just subversive, but successfully so. The historical precedent is there, then. This book's suggestion of a paradigm shift is not necessarily a vein one. If WWE can commit to disrespecting one of its most beloved concepts as brazenly and as gloriously as they did in the instance provided by #91 – indeed, #91's entire Era - why can they not do so on a grander scale also?

#90
Kurt Angle vs. Chris Benoit
WWE Championship
Royal Rumble
January 19th, 2003

As #91 hints, and as the very invention of sports entertainment goes to prove, WWE's behemoth of success is founded upon the very desire to rock the boat; hostile territory talent raids and the invention of WrestleMania are two obvious examples from its early modern history. It is not immune from elements of conservatism and dogma – perhaps the decade of the Brand Extension is this personality trait at its grossest – but WWE will often allow, if not encourage, the radically different.

Perhaps a contributing factor to the perpetuating cynical beliefs of especially older fans today is that these efforts are not always aggrandised. WWE has a bad habit of placing too much emphasis on specific moments in time and, with the reach of their propaganda machine, those mistakes often firmly embed themselves as historical fact. Nine times out of ten, while these moments are integral elements of WWE's history, they are not quite as pivotal as they are made out to be. "Redefined"; "legendary"; "of all-time"; these are terms that WWE obsesses over in their own skewed presentation of the past and, in such an environment of verbosity, smaller, more intimate latitudinarianism is lost in the shuffle. In conjunction with the obvious mitigation of Chris Benoit's presence, such is the case with #90 on this list; by no means is it a match that changed the world, but it remains a dramatic departure from stylistic norms, proving the artistic avant-garde to as often be a relative normality in WWE as it is a paradigmatic shift.

In a lot of ways, #90 is WWE enjoying a moment of traditional simplicity; and it pays dividends for them. The creative approach is not necessarily to shake up the WWE mantra, but rather to strip it away. Much like their reputations in the ring, Benoit and Angle go for a no-

nonsense approach that almost flies in the face of the Savage / Steamboat foundation built in Pontiac. With #90, what we have is not a World Wrestling *Entertainment* match but a World *Wrestling* Entertainment match. The desire to emphasise that second word could not be more evident from the moment the story begins either, with Team Angle ejected before the bell tolls, literally doing away with a cliché plot device.

The lack of wasted movement – so often a tag line for a WWE classic – is utilised for the sake of realistic grit rather than intense pacing, flirting with the Japanese strong-style's sense of hyper-realism where the action organically dictates their ring positioning. So too is there little wasted time. The pace is constant from the opening. They opt for more haste and less speed, moving briskly, but without rushing, and suckering the viewer in with the resultant frenetic violence. They do what so few others have been able to: successfully translate a show of intensity as a portrayal of unfiltered desire; like with #101's Benoit / Regal showpiece, the feel of unashamed masochistic enjoyment turns this match into a confessional.

Benoit and Angle prove themselves masters of their chosen craft as they transition seamlessly from submission to submission, even adding in a couple of other moves in between just to show off their skill. It is only when things seem as if they can't be improved upon further, that Benoit and Angle break out their superlatives. After having gone to great effort to swerve us away from WWE tropes early on, they show, in the last act, that they've stripped away the foundation in order to simply rebuild it.

They keep the finish itself restrained and calm, contrasting all the excess of the final act with a whisper of almost dismissive realism: Angle wraps up the leg of his opponent in a grapevine. On the surface, it watches as an attempt to prevent Benoit crawling to the ropes once again. When thought about, it instead watches as a certified effort from Angle to not only trap Benoit away from the ropes, but to neutralise Benoit's evidenced capability of reversing Angle's advantage into disadvantage. Angle disables Benoit in more than one way and the result is both a literal and metaphorical submission from the challenger – with nowhere to crawl and no way to counter, Benoit finally backs down and Angle takes the round. It's an almost, "Ok, ya got me!" moment, with Benoit tipping over the proverbial king piece in the face of his checkmate.

It's easy to imagine matches that attempt to shift paradigms to the left of the spectrum to be so widely lauded in their execution that they get promoted until we're fit to vomit – see the WrestleMania X Ladder match. Some, however, go unnoticed. #90 had no lasting effect on the in-ring product. Yet, for twenty minutes, two of the best to ever lace a pair of boots went out and whispered in our ear that wrestling is more than just the same thing we see every week. This is a wink at the audience, a gentle nudge in the arm that, in actuality, wrestling is a variable beast that can be tweaked and modified and be all the more effective for it. This match represents a stripping down of modernisation, a pure hearted soul largely void of the grandeur that modern Western pro wrestling has normalized. The result is an overwhelmingly effective opus for both involved. Just watch how the fans react: with a standing ovation.

I doubt there was as deep a level of planning that went into it as I have managed to draw out of it, but that's beside the point. As standard with the performance art philosophy, whether it was *designed* to happen is irrelevant. What is relevant is the fact that it *did* happen and it happened in WWE. This match shows freeform experimentation in the

'E, and these conscious formulaic imbalances pop up with what might be, to some, quite surprising frequency; just because such knowing whispers get drowned out by the tsunami of rhetoric that more dramatic moments in time are bombarded with does not disprove their existence. Such existence is an imperative fact, considering I am attempting to alter the way you, dear reader, may approach professional wrestling and WWE. This is a company more creatively liberal than it is given credit for, less suffocating than it is believed to be; the proof is in the in-ring product. What is sweeter than matches akin to the unheralded classic that is #90?

Hopefully by now, any negative ideas you may have had regarding WWE's tendency to subscribe invention in a stifling top-down approach may be in question. WWE is a company that allows room for subversion and invention, on occasion pursuing it actively as a promotion in the most unexpected places; and successfully so may it be said. Coupled with both the dispelling of the kind of fan myths that are made fact solely through their pervasive application, and a recognition of less grandiose but no less original matches that reject WWE's norm, we can begin to refashion entirely our understanding of WWE's character: it is an environment that cultivates rather than curtails.

This conclusion is inescapable when viewing WWE compositions through this book's new performance art analytical prism, transforming, as it does, WWE matches into invaluable source materials from which to draw fresh understanding of how genres have developed, grown, evolved and should function in the industry we know today. So to culminate this inspection of WWE's creative character, let us do a case study of a specific sub-genre to examine in greater detail. By examining the evolution of

Money in the Bank as a match, we can see in action all of the traits touched upon in these last three reviews.

Chapter 5

A Case Study: The Money in the Bank Sub-Genre

#89
Chris Jericho vs. Chris Benoit vs. Christian vs. Edge vs. Kane vs. Shelton Benjamin
Money in the Bank Ladder Match
WrestleMania 21
April 3rd, 2005

The Money in the Bank Ladder Match sub-genre provides a case study that highlights, in play throughout a single historical narrative of birth, growth and recession, the three elements of WWE's creative approach explored in Chapter 4: talent afforded the space to innovate in #89's original version; formula created by the fans (albeit in this case indirectly), leading to #88's WrestleMania XXVI version; and the company's willingness to subvert formula resulting in #87's 2010 Smackdown-exclusive version. This, in turn, both continues to certify that the performance art paradigm shift proposed by this book is by no means a lost cause and, more importantly, points to the best uses of WWE's brand of subversion and reinvention, proving them not just a creative liberal but a pragmatic one at that.

It would be remiss not to begin any examination of Money in the Bank without first touching on the Ladder Match as the mother genre. It will be dealt with in more detail later, but it is worth stating here that it is a genre that has become integral to WWE's machinery; perhaps the most popular in WWE today, courtesy of the iterations within it being naturally verbose. That popularity translates across the pro wrestling world too. Money in the Bank was perhaps, at the time of its first inception, the peaking of this popularity and a maturation of the new fangled multi-man Ladder Match concept, born from the tag efforts at the turn of the century. It is an ultimate coming-of-age that brought together the disparate ideas that permeated both key ages in the ladder's history: pre and post-Tables, Ladders and Chairs (TLC).

It is also worth noting, at this stage, that WWE is a creature of habit at a basic level. If something goes down well with fans, WWE will rinse and repeat in the face of demand for more. Alas, they can sometimes too often forget that familiarity breeds contempt and the more matches of one kind you have, the more diluted they become, even if their popularity remains constant. Over the course of its lifespan, Money in the Bank as a sub-genre has inevitably changed, but whether that change is a progressive or recessive one is up for debate. Not only has the basic format altered radically given its relatively short existence, but the philosophy has altered too. Money in the Bank began in the realms of relative decency before, just like its TLC forebear, devolving into violent voyeurism. Psychology was increasingly substituted for stunt work and the spots escalated to a needlessly dangerous level. All the while, fans demanded a sub-genre adhering to the rule of "more is more." It is because of these reasons that it is the very first Money in the Bank that remains the best of its kind.

My reasoning is multi-faceted. First and foremost, though, is the roster of talent. The number of competitors, in this case a mere six, while still too many for my liking proved a great deal more manageable than the later variants of seven, eight and, in some cases, ten. More importantly than numerical value, the participants here indicate a contemplation of design later efforts would eschew for the convenience of occupying directionless talents. There's a great variance in styles, with each competitor bringing their own instantly recognisable methodology and being as equally capable of putting together a breath-taking composition as their multiple opponents. This equality of athletic skill is matched by a similar equality in prominence; there is no single mega-star that stands out above all others, making the pre-determined result that much more difficult to predict by the viewer.

This difference of styles becomes the major theme; in large part thanks to the creative space they are afforded. Kane's size determines the opening lines, while Benjamin's athleticism provides the most memorable crescendos. Edge and Christian's use of weaponry evidences their experience in similar environments, Jericho is as reliable a chorus as ever and Benoit's grit becomes the defining, affecting refrain. Such an approach makes the action watch as seamless, with transitions in story so natural the entire discourse plays out in what feels like much less time than actually passes. Unfortunately, this does not prevent the usual haphazard tone that is inevitably born in this specific offshoot of the parent genre. There are moments of bizarre and inexplicable psychology that, for fans who like their substance, threaten to shatter the atmosphere. Endearingly, though, any such nonsensical incidents are graciously fleeting.

The pace is steadier without being less exciting; fewer men in the same time allows for more breathing room, where fans are allowed to soak in the spectacle before the next big moment occurs. Fans are allowed to pop loud for big moves because such moves aren't cut short in favour of the next suicidal spot. It's not necessarily an obvious factor, but this basic structure was lacking by the time the 'Mania iterations were retired, as the spots accumulated to the extent that, were you to blink, you would miss a possibly pivotal moment in your pausing for breath. In this case, the match is able to retain its intensity without denigrating itself with farce. It remains real.

Each of the six pulls their weight equally, as well. Benoit is certainly the standout and, despite the ensemble cast, seems to take the lead as the primary protagonist when the story unfolds. It's interesting seeing Benoit come into the match injured, the perfect vehicle for him to exhibit the fortitude with which he always tried to gain the win. Kane's performance shows the kind of self-assurance and in-character enthusiasm we've come to expect from him and is, in large part, a driving force behind the sympathy evoked for Benoit – he targets the arm in the first third and attempts to take Benoit out completely at the culmination. While Edge is the victorious villain, it's really Kane that provides the antagonistic drive. Benjamin gives us the human highlight reel we would come to expect in later years, though which here benefits from novelty. Edge gives us an early iteration of his Ultimate Opportunist character, notably in his winning moment, though most of his other activity during the match, if quietly competent, remains relatively unimpressive – rather like two of his fellow Canadians.

The finish is another pristinely judged example of how to get the right reaction from the fans, though. After all the excitement and exhilaration, the end comes with a standard, simple-as-you-like chair shot to an injured arm, contrasting the dangerous complexity of the respective quests to victory with an infuriating moment of obvious simplicity; so stark is the contrast, it is an entirely legal moment that feels like it should be wholly disallowed. Not only does that give you a precursor to Edge's eventual character, and intriguingly his cash-in as well, but it complements the match itself, which stands as a thrill ride ending on an irascibly simplistic note in order to garner resentment for the man you're meant to hate.

Generally speaking, there is a clearly defined purpose to #89. On a literal level, that purpose was to get Edge "over," but I think each individual had an achievement in mind regardless of whether it was to steal the show, to innovate a sub-genre or to create what would eventually become the predominant means of pushing new main event talent. It is a piece that knew where it was going, didn't become tangential and remembered what it was there to do. I feel there's a lesson to be learned in that.

Contempt is not the only negative bred by familiarity; so is sloth. Like WWE, most franchises will simply revisit what worked the first time, especially if popular reception never wanes in its positivity. In doing that, however, the creative force loses its focus. Stories get lost, messages drift away and, before you know it, the creative has dwindled into nothing more than an old, reliable but stagnated cash machine. This is exactly what happened to the Money in the Bank sub-genre; it lost its way because the more it added, the crazier fans went.

More, more, more is not always well-advised and, while Money in the Bank has in recent years made progress in creating lasting success, its record of hits and misses still leans too heavily in favour of the latter. It still, as a sub-genre, entertains the majority of fans, but how often is its use justified? The record speaks for itself. To varying degrees, the victories of Damien Sandow, Dolph Ziggler, Alberto Del Rio, The Miz, Kane, Jack Swagger, CM Punk's first time, Mr Kennedy and Rob Van Dam all failed to generate prolonged, sustained success. In some cases, the failure was outright and immediate. In others, though followed by relative short-term success, it did nothing for main event longevity. Furthermore, how many other unlisted victors got the win because the company had little other choice, indicating the bout's occurrence as more an increasingly problematic obstacle than a naturally occurring benefit? Yet, in this first instance, Edge's win saw him take the next step to becoming a certifiable company centrepiece.

#88
Kofi Kingston vs. Jack Swagger vs. Christian vs. Matt Hardy vs. Kane vs. Drew McIntyre vs. Evan Bourne vs. Dolph Ziggler vs. MVP vs. Shelton Benjamin
Money in the Bank Ladder Match
WrestleMania XXVI

Part of the problem with Money in the Bank as a sub-genre, since its inaugural iteration, has been the decisions made regarding who should win, and then betting the success of that often unsubstantiated performer's presence in the main event entirely on the idea of the cash-in. As the match became a needless annual fixture at WrestleMania without a plan in mind for a specific talent moving forward, it seemed that interest in how to wisely utilise the concept waned. Cash-ins became formulaic and predictable, and winners were chosen often, it felt like, simply to shock or to give a wrestler something to do for a little while. In other words, the outcomes of the later WrestleMania Money in the Bank bouts became an ends in and of themselves, rather than a useful means, as was the case with the original.

Interestingly, the worst example of this phenomenon would occur in the very same edition that would provide also the worst example of the match in action, with both elements together marking a creative low point for an idea in desperate need of rejuvenation. As the sub-genre grew, became cockier and, eventually, perhaps felt impervious to critique – and in some quarters it likely was - it plumbed new creative depths and transformed into a victim of formula adhered to because of a positive consensus among fans. It became a *monstrosity* in the shape of Money in the Bank VI.

It was a match doomed almost from the start, given the number of participants that would weigh down, cripplingly, its creative opportunities. It is difficult to imagine a feasibly worked ten man Ladder Match of any kind on any show, but to then give those ten men twelve minutes at a WrestleMania is ludicrous. What results is a jarring, unrealistic rotation of bodies (by this stage in the bout's growth a certifiable structural conceit), where any given performer spends an unconvincing amount of time away from the action before showing up to be part of a single spot before immediately being swapped out again. With such an approach, it is borderline impossible to suspend disbelief.

The same goes for the distinct lack of psychological sense, with multiple examples of spots that deconstruct the narrative. The most infuriating example would be the use of two halves of a broken ladder as stilts; though this may create a cute visual and a decent image on a future highlight reel, when it occurs in a match surrounded by demonstrably functional ladders in an environment punctuated by urgency, it is an inexcusable moment of illogic; the worst effect being that the moment, like so many others on show, has spawned a series of increasingly outrageous successors elsewhere. Such incongruities could be easily dismissed if they were not quite such superfluous reminders that the piece is a staged performance aiming only to startle the viewer. This, in turn, becomes worse by virtue of botches and mistiming plaguing the duration, with even the climactic moment of Swagger's win going awry; it remains a small mercy this embarrassment was edited to be much shorter on later home video releases.

Though some positives remain – namely the performances of Christian, Matt Hardy, and Kane – the indulgent, perhaps lazy number of participants, the non-existent psychological logic, a number of poor showings and a slew of bad timing all stacks up to make this the ugliest, nastiest train wreck of the entire WrestleMania Money in the Bank collection; perhaps of the entire sub-genre, for that matter. It evidences the sub-genre at its most indulgent, exampling its worst habits and outcomes in one inglorious misfire.

If the first Money in the Bank at WrestleMania represents the concept at its very best, then the final Money in the Bank at WrestleMania represents the concept at its very worst. It strips the bout down and reveals it for what it really is: an ugly logistical nightmare.

Yet, for all the wrong reasons and perhaps because it chose not to strive for something greater than the literal sum of its parts, it fashions a sense of entertainment all its own, passing beyond the point of being bad and touching the level of so bad it is good. Perhaps good is too strong a word; entertaining, though, certainly not. By simply indulging, utilising only spot after spot without any reasoning that could stand up to analytical scrutiny, it hit its stride in the oddest way possible. #88 evidences no tone of pretension, or of upward aspiration. It operates on such a functional level it comes off as no-nonsense, trying to be nothing more than the pro wrestling equivalent of a B-Movie. #88 is, ultimately, mindless entertainment.

Rewatchability can be added to its short list of positives then, but let it be known that any pessimistic enjoyment found from its lack of quality aside, the lessons that #88 teaches could not be more important. While it remains vital for us to not draw any direct links of causation between two sub-genre iterations separated by half a decade, comparisons do indicate the basic evolution that watermarked the first chapter in the concept's lifespan: uncontrolled growth.

The major turning point was the addition of extra participants. For example, WrestleMania 22's immediate sequel was still a passable match. Though it failed to attain the same critical success as its predecessor, it successfully avoided the majority of pitfalls #88 and its ilk fell prey to. By the third instalment, however, things began to become increasingly homogenised. The first time eight men were utilised, expediency became more important and, as a result, room for creative expression narrowed significantly. Rather than playing off the renowned styles of the competitors, the creative enterprise shifted instead to being about how complex the ladder spots could become. The ladder itself became increasingly central to the action, with huge swathes of the matches at WrestleManias 23, XXIV and the 25th Anniversary clearly being built around how to utilise the prop in a manner nobody had before. While not particularly worth condemnation in theory, in practice it became an ineffective, distracting approach, more often than not leading to the same unbelievable spots (i.e. Kingston's stilts).

In short, WWE got carried away. The more Money in the Bank matches they had at WrestleMania, the more ludicrous the set-pieces became and the more diluted the stories' integrity felt; frustratingly for the more restrained viewer, their popularity grew too. The focus in the fictional universe, as a result, felt less and less about winning and more and more about the needless, hard-to-reason effort put into deploying the ladders dangerously. Essentially, the concept lost sight of its original purpose and collapsed under the weight of its own enthusiasm. Worst of all, this focus on increasing danger and decreasing purpose born from the multiplication of bodies that Money in the Bank has brought seems to have spread, with Ladder Matches across promotions now reaching heights of such danger it grows hard to support - and in some cases excuse - the work being done within their confines.

#88 stands as a testament to everything Money in the Bank should not be but, more often than not, had unfortunately become. If the first was the zenith of the multi-man Ladder Match concept, #88 was its lowest point reached by mindlessly pandering to the perceivably incessant demands for more, more, more. Between these two cornerstones in the sub-genre's history, the story was one of increasing enthusiasm and diminishing artistic returns, where the concept was much more a force for bad than good despite the warm regard in which it was held; it became much more of an obligation than an opportunity; and winning it transformed into much more of a threat than a promise.

#87
Smackdown! Money in the Bank Ladder Match
Money in the Bank
July 18th, 2010

In the same year #88 occurred, of course, WWE decided to gift Money in the Bank its own pay-per-view in the summer, essentially allowing it to take up the King of the Ring mantle for a new generation. For some, this was a development equal parts promising and stinging. On the one hand, it broke the chains that had for so long constricted the intrigue and broader sense of development in WrestleMania undercards (even if it would ultimately be an opportunity failing to blossom as late as five years later).

On the other, it created another show where the ladder genre was utterly indispensable. The upward trend Money in the Bank VI so brashly embodied was set to go on unimpeded and, if the danger continued on the up, the concept may have necessitated a rest if for no other reason than decency, safety and good taste.

Luckily, what that first Money in the Bank pay-per-view would offer in the form of #87 was a much needed rewrite. Though that rewrite did not necessarily reduce the danger, it was able to distract performers from further escalation – though perhaps not moderation - with a return to strong storytelling and greater creative merit; it changed the direction of the future.

A major key to success in #87 is talent positioning, with Big Show having an especially fine hour in one of his career's best. His presence becomes a prevalent factor very early and his use throughout is consistently well judged. #87 could almost be labelled a "Big Show match" because he is so central to the action, despite him not winning and even being absent for the entire third act. Without being over-used, he bookends the story with a pair of very notable absences; a clever judgement, creating structural efficiency that avoids, by default, any problems generated by having the World's Largest Athlete in as bespoke an environment as Money in the Bank. Even the ways his absences are explained narratively show a refreshed maturity in approach. They never feel awkwardly shoe-horned in, being instead interwoven with the wider action. The best part is, because of this necessary plot device, the match provides us with interesting, wowing spots, some of which are refreshing for their simplicity; Christian free-falling into Show from on high for example, or a pile of ladders trapping Show under an avalanche of steel before Kane starts launching men into said pile like human missiles. Big Show's deployment is supreme; he dominates as he should whenever present and is removed convincingly whenever needed, and with profound positive effects on the composition's broader sense of achievement.

He is, of course, not the only man involved, though, and every competitor takes to their individualised roles with aplomb in this instance. Christian and Matt Hardy both serve well as anchors – as they had months previously in #88 – while, perhaps because of the advantage lent by youth, Cody Rhodes and Dolph Ziggler both take a lot of the harder hits and perform some of the more exciting ladder climbs; in a strange way, it's almost like a passing of the torch between an aged generation of progenitors to a fresh generation of prospectives. For those progenitors to be part of such a glorious reinvention seems fitting.

Kofi does well as the resident stunt man, throwing himself around in a manner reminiscent of Shelton Benjamin. Kane is handled well too, ensuring his presence is known throughout, but never quite hogging the spotlight. His victory, as a result, is neither as irritatingly sudden as Swagger's had been months earlier, nor as predictable as some later victories would prove to be. It simply feels as though it makes sense, with Kane's nostalgic appeal leading to a notably positive reception upon the result - a testament to the performer's enduring talent if ever there was one.

Moving away from specific performances and turning to the overall action, the key to success is, yet again, variety. Switching from high spots involving Kingston to brawls involving Kane to hardcore action involving Big Show is the kind of kaleidoscopic material that makes the run-time fly by, the match more engaging and the overall tone generally less threatening. The method is prevalent throughout, resulting in a thoroughly enjoyable composition you can watch over and over again and never get bored with. It was a level of achievement unattained since the sub-genre's inaugural and defining outing.

This is a version of Money in the Bank that returns to the original methodology of making the styles of the performers involved the focal point, rather than the tools they need to use to win. There's a renewed sense of purpose in how the discourse unfolds, as the size, capability, characters and star power of the combatants informs positioning, execution and participation, rather than the stunts alone informing the storytelling. In the years that followed, the dangerous and unending rising of bars that had dogged the sub-genre since its first two years slowed, putting pause to the excessively dangerous.

Though the sub-genre has continued to misfire on the follow-ups, the matches themselves have at least become a little more open-minded ever since. As recently as 2014, the format was put to original use once more as the Rollins and Ambrose feud took centre stage in almost the same way the Austin and McMahon feud did in the previously reviewed 1999 Royal Rumble. The years of its life plagued by a concerning formula of fan-pandering hardcore styling seem to have been consigned to the past. #87, then, provides another key cornerstone in the historical narrative of the sub-genre, as important to its growth and change as #89 - the first and best - and #88 - the last at WrestleMania and undoubtedly, at that point in time, the worst. In returning to a philosophy much closer to the original, like all great franchise reboots Money in the Bank rehabilitated itself into something a little more palatable for the little more cynical. Though the preoccupation with escalatory stunts persists to this day, so too does the thankful avoidance of catastrophe that felt so inevitable were the worrying trends of the WrestleMania Years to have continued.

Perhaps most vitally for this list, though, given its desire to alter your perceptions of the industry and reform stipulation into the concepts of genre to which I frequently refer, the watershed subversion of formula that was #87 saw, if only for a passing moment in history, the real potential of the Money in the Bank idea unlocked.

A professional wrestler has to be an intoxicating mixture of many things: an author, an actor, an athlete and, most of all, damn good at what they do. WWE has, among its ranks, some of the best and most talented authors, artists and, perhaps most impressively, *athletes* in the world. The environment created by Money in the Bank is, thus, one able to showcase a unique potion of equal parts artistic endeavour and athletic achievement the likes of which you cannot find anywhere else in the world, including in widely acknowledged performance arts already in existence. It is the kind of advert that WWE should want: a means to showcase hardcore action, high flying athleticism, larger than life giants, young, unformed athletic talent they can nurture in the future and some of the most talented and hardworking athletes they have nurtured in the past. From an external perspective, Money in the Bank gives WWE, and fans in general, a means to dispel cynicism and prove just how great professional wrestling is and can be. From an internal point of view, it can remind believers of just how amazing this great performance art is by highlighting the variety of unique performers that populate it. Such is a sub-genre we can be proud of.

Chapter 6

Judging By Past Example

#86
The Hart Foundation 2.0 vs. Stone Cold Steve Austin, Ken Shamrock, Legion of Doom and Goldust
In Your House: Canadian Stampede
July 6th, 1997

By now, hopefully you will be questioning any previously held assumptions about perceived reticence on WWE's part to progress forwards, innovate, reinvent and, ultimately, change. There are numerous historical examples indicating that WWE are creatively liberal in more than one way. In the specific case of the growth of the Money in the Bank sub-genre, you can see clear indications of how these elements affect WWE's creative directions through time, adding pragmatism to their creatively liberal character.

This latter most idea returns us to the cause we diverted from in Chapter 3: moving our conversation of matches away from sports entertainment towards performance art re-categorises them as genre, which allows us a better understanding of what is expected from certain kinds of matches, what works best for them and how they can break their sports entertainment shackles to reach a transcended state. We saw this in Chapter 5's case study; succinctly put, in moving Money in the Bank away from sports entertainment stipulation towards performance art genre, we discover what works best for the concept and, through that understanding, unlock its true potential as a hype machine for pro wrestlers and their profession.

This, however, is a universal rule we can apply to any such genre or sub-genre in a reframed pro wrestling. One much broader, much older and far more abstract genre to apply the method of learning from past example to would be tag team wrestling.

Tag wrestling has been covered fleetingly already in this book but, for all its enlightening uses, #92's Shield / Rhodes affair remains a limited historical source. Despite providing an example of how some fan myths are unnecessarily damaging, it isn't the best article to exhibit WWE's competency – nay, excellence – with the ensemble casts of the tag team genre; quite possibly the very first special attraction in the industry. #86 goes to prove such excellence, providing an example that #85 would go on to fulfill the promise of.

#86 is, in fact, another incredibly complex beast to dissect. It isn't two-on-two. It's five-on-five, and it's not at Survivor Series. That creates an intimidating set of complexities in structure, particularly given the bout's run-time. It was a hard mountain to climb for the ten men involved; how could such a setup possibly function smoothly and maintain the high standards not only expected but necessitated, courtesy of the rousing success of the pioneering Border Wars angle that had acted as preface? What is more, this challenge came at a time when the company's interest in the tag team format seemed slight and the division was enduring one of its myriad lulls. Amazingly, though, the challenge was not only met, but comfortably overcome thanks to a professional wrestling epic tightly interwoven with focussed action amidst an intensely partisan crowd.

That partisan crowd was inevitable, of course. The emotive Border Wars storyline set Canada against America on a moral battlefield, and the Canadian Hart family, so central to the angle, were here competing in their hometown of

Calgary. Naturally, the reaction for The Hart Foundation is indescribable, the only thing capable of doing it justice really being the match itself. The Canadians keep themselves at the top of the entrance until at full strength, but when they eventually walk towards the ring and stand toe-to-toe with their exclusively American opponents, they do an inimitable job of whipping you into an anticipatory frenzy before anyone even throws a punch.

The fact that Bret "Hitman" Hart, leader of the Hart Foundation, gets an early advantage has the building shaking. When the tide turns, the fans vocalise their disapproval, but the building keeps shaking anyway. The electricity in the voices of the announcers is palpable and it does, admittedly, make you feel a little giddy even now. The Hitman is hugely aggressive, despite being the firmly cemented hero, and you also get a sense that Austin is thoroughly enjoying being able to play the part of the villain again without fears of being cheered by an increasingly countercultural fan base.

It's in the second big brawl of the story that the match clarifies its intention to create something greater than a prototypical tag team affair. It threads its discourse together with a fascinating character arc, starting with Steve Austin injuring Owen Hart's leg. Psychologically, it immediately turns the Foundation into underdogs; they already benefitted from hometown empathy and going down a man incenses that hometown crowd further at a moment it feels impossible. There's a fitting sense of controlled chaos for a couple of minutes after Owen is led to the back and, out of that chaos, Hart vindictively injures Austin's leg in similar fashion. Austin, too, is led to the back and the match turns into a slightly lesser four-on-four affair. The respective return of the wounded not only later creates a much greater sense of narrative thanks to the completion of the arc, but also further exacerbates the eventual finish.

#86 is, ultimately, a catwalk of controlled chaos; the ten men create a match that sees a reaction of equal force for every action taken, without a single moment of the dense, extra-legal activity going unpunished. Tag team wrestling may often be cliché, with its instances of larger scale often denigrated into messy free-for-all, but not here. In the case of #86, ten top talents went out in front of a raucous crowd and decided on something simple but important: be a little different. Instead of a steadily ongoing encounter dictated by genre tropes - heavy on action, low on substance - what you get is a story; an impressive feat in the face of such daunting ergonomic obstacles. That story is one of the oldest in the book - guy gets injured, then ejected and then returns later - but it's done in such a logical way that it becomes something greater than the sum of its parts, rather like the match itself. The reason this stands up as such a defining match in tag team wrestling is due to its refusal to be restricted by the norm. There are no prolonged beat-downs, no faces in peril and no real hot tags. This is not a cliché; this is a composition of tag team wrestling.

Of course, there are other examples of tag team matches that are as structurally efficient, though perhaps few that are quite as resoundingly successful. It is appreciated as well that the difficulties confronting a match consisting of ten men are wildly different to any faced by those involving four. As a result, it may seem that the application of lessons learned here in eschewing the familiar for the original can only go so far. At this stage, I would implore you to remember that it is far easier to do more when less is expected than it ever is to do less when more is expected.

By virtue of the larger than average scale, the lessons learned through this match can be applied to almost any variant of the tag bout; if a rule can be applied to a tag match where there are more, surely it would be easy to distil so it fits a tag match involving fewer. Examples exist wherein that has happened, and the golden rule to follow, evidenced so gloriously in the case of #87's 2010 Money in the Bank redefinition, is simple: allow the story to dictate function, rather than the other way around. In doing so, it is easier to avoid predictable cliché – which #87 does in its own sub-genre rousingly – and in this instance, unlock the creative potential of the tag team genre as an infinitely surprising element of the pro wrestling performance art. The successes would then quickly stack up, regardless of whether there are ten men, four men…or six.

#85
The Shield vs. The Wyatt Family
Elimination Chamber
February 23rd, 2014

To a certain degree, there is a naturally ordained symmetry between #85 and #86. Both proved the culmination of a hugely popular element of WWE's product. In this case, it is two of the hottest stables of their day. As soon as the match's hype graphic appears on the screen, there is a tangible, audible shift in the excitement of the crowd.

In story terms, the set-up was as efficiently simple as you could hope for, with the Wyatts costing The Shield, albeit somewhat inadvertently, a chance to participate inside an Elimination Chamber match for the WWE World Heavyweight Championship. An extra layer of intrigue was also added by the slowly growing seeds of dissension within the ranks of The Shield. Despite the allure of said simplicity, though, impressively there is not a single artist involved who seems content to rest on his laurels. The lesson taught by the preceding review, of putting the artistry before the ergonomics, is eagerly deployed with the promise evident in the Wyatt gimmick since its debut and the show-stealing zeal that had come to watermark The Shield's work.

The method is slightly different to #86's ten man tag, and indeed it had to be. While the build to #85 was simple, efficient and engaging, it was not quite the emotive force of 1997's Border Wars. The reason for the palpable anticipation here was instead because of its dream match quality: of two strongly developed, clearly defined groups of characters, each instantly recognisable, finally clashing following months of speculation. Like #86 before it, #85 recognises its greatest strength and so allows strict adherence to character to inform the discourse. It is the characterisation in this instance, not plot, which proves to be the most invaluable asset; The Shield is driven by their unrelenting and unforgiving sense of justice and appropriation, while The Wyatt Family is framed, as ever when at their most effective, as the Other.

This contrast of fraternal aggression and outsider psychology is the central, powerfully enthralling dynamic informing the omnipresent sense of mutually assured destruction. In the entrances, The Shield comes through the throngs of the crowd all business and the Family enigmatically from the darkness. So as to invoke fear, The Shield communicates their intention clearly without room for misinterpretation, while the Family refuses to communicate anything, maintaining instead their collective opacity. Though the confrontational philosophies of both entities compliment one another resoundingly well, those philosophies are postured in ways that, comparatively, could not be starker. The Shield roars, barks and snarls along with its pulsating anthem while the Family slide through the black with a clapping crowd, methodical and at peace with their spiritual chaos.

Such sense of character cascades down from the units to the individuals. During the opening stand-off, "The Architect" Seth Rollins stands firm in adherence to the apparent game plan while "The Lunatic Fringe" Dean Ambrose paces wildly; a small character moment that goes on to inform the composition's climax, where Ambrose plays the part of the frenzied, despatched maverick responsible for fatally disadvantaging his team. Most impressively of all, however, is the evident psychology of Wyatt's mind games coming to the fore in that exact same moment during the opening. Seeing Ambrose's lunacy so clearly on show becomes The Shield's tell that Wyatt then exploits mercilessly, agitating Ambrose until the Fringe bites; Ambrose's angered response marks the opening to the match, and what follows is an immediate degradation into unrelenting physical warfare. In a way, the Family won this match before the bell even rang, proving that, though The Shield is at home amidst chaos, Bray Wyatt gorges himself upon it.

The action is as masterful in its execution as the character touches exampled above. The opening brawl has the audience frothing at its jaws immediately, and the first pairing of Rollins and Erik Rowan evidences both teams' knowledge of how to play off their differentials with purpose and exactness of vision. Those differentials include the starkly contrasting in-ring approaches of both groups: the Family's smash-mouth physical disregard and The Shield's precisely judged tactics. Even this aspect speaks further to character. Just as the Wyatt view of the world is singular and unforgiving, so is their approach between the ropes. The Shield, in turn, are an entity bred specifically for their crusade, tactically minded, but here confused by a Rubix Cube of an enemy impossible to prepare for. The Wyatt victory seems almost inevitable then, and the right decision for more reasons beyond the literal simplicity of furthering The Shield's dissension as sports entertainment would have it.

The transition into the final third is marked by a sudden, dangerous escalation. Chaos reigns until Rollins is soon stripping tables, Bray and Harper trying to mug him and Ambrose, again proving himself the tell, coming to Rollins' aid without knowing when to stop, brawling with Bray through the crowd to create a crack in the armour; it is the moment the Family requires to capitalise. Once Bray reappears alone, the Family manages to hook a nail into Shield's Ambrose-shaped opening and proceed to tear the pack apart gruesomely, limb from limb. Rollins is mugged on the announce desk and the performers work in some truly ugly visuals and audio as the scene unfolds, leaving Reigns alone to fight a one man war. Though the Big Dog is allowed to show some moments of hope, The Shield has been routed and it's now a pyrrhic last stand. Reigns stays true to The Shield's cause – he shows no hesitation in taking the fight to his superior numbers – but the story has taken a dark turn and, thanks to Harper taking a sacrificial Spear in the name of blind faith for his leader, ultimately the Family gets the win.

#85 is as much an opus within the tag genre as #86 was before it. Their profoundest lesson was putting art before structure, idea before economy. It is important to understand, though, that lessons taught in a specific sub-genre can still be universal in application to the parent genre too, provided they are adapted appropriately. #86 set a benchmark for an entire genre: tag team wrestling. Sometimes, judging by such past example can lead to practical applications in instances of exact replication. These, however, are rare. More often, judging by past example and learning from prior achievements can lead to a *conceptual* understanding that is far more adaptable. #85 showcases such a learning curve. It showcases too the same level of heel vs. heel success seen in the example of #93's Edge vs. Orton piece, proving further the idea of heel vs. heel being a workable genre. This is a match that shouts of the benefits of judging by the past to reform the future; in fact, so well did it do that, it might just have cemented itself as the new past example to be judged by.

#85 is proof of the value of the methodology at the heart of the coming chapters then: in reshaping our understanding of pro wrestling to performance art, we can easier learn from what has come before to refashion and to reach on. In this example, one tag bout featuring fewer performers learned the lessons of its genre's past, written by the standard that is #86; it is pragmatic creative liberalism in action that transforms #86 into a "How to" and #85 a whole new performance art watershed all its own.

This example of developing the tag team genre, and the case study of Money in the Bank before it, have been only two examples of a method we can apply to *all* examples of pro wrestling performance art genre. This is to what we now turn. By looking at, and by learning from, the best past examples of all kinds of matches through the performance art genre-centred analytic, we will discover what works best for those match types, realise the true creative achievements of freshly recognisable opuses and, most importantly of all, create opportunity for future instalments to reach the level of masterpieces like those explored in all chapters thus far.

Chapter 7

Concrete Genre: Understanding Gimmick Matches

#84
Jake "The Snake" Roberts vs. "The Model" Rick Martel
Blindfold Match
WrestleMania VII
March 24th, 1991

In this refashioned performance art view of the industry, "gimmick matches" of sports entertainment form very concrete ideas of genre to which any specific match type will clearly belong. Chapter 7 will focus only on some of the most prescient and / or notable examples of these concrete genre types.

WWE has had a curious preponderance with bizarre, singular experiments over the years, some of which have bordered on ludicrous. The number of these instances can be quite staggering when accumulated. #84 examines a match bred out of this habit utilising a general approach that houses the key to success in such constraining situations for WWE's talent. High concept with slight return, you have two grown men staggering around with black bags over their heads engaging in a degree of slapstick comedy. This is an impossible match to review because, writing plainly, there is no match *to* review.

There are, however, the performances of the two artists, worthy of inspection.

Jake "The Snake" Roberts is widely recognised as one of the best psychologists ever and, oddly enough, if any match concretely proves that assertion it is one with very little actual action: #84. The reason is the necessity of the situation. Without vision, coordination naturally becomes more difficult and, muffled by hoods, so too does communication. If an ability to create content through interaction is limited, then crowd interest is at risk. Formulating a method that still involves that crowd in a manner other than the provision of exciting action then becomes top priority, and is certainly at the forefront of the chosen methodology on show in this oddity of a piece.

What this bout lacked in actual physical combat it makes up for in calling on the crowd to actually take on the role of the third competitor. In #84, you have a thankfully rare instance of professional wrestling as pantomime, almost quite literally so. Roberts does a brilliant job using both his cunning and his support from the fans to win the bout, instead of his physical prowess. Though as much as The Snake's constant involvement of the live crowd helps bring them into the match, Rick Martel does an equally good job at keeping things entertaining by playing up the inept villain. Slapstick comedy doesn't exactly take genius of wit to pull off well, but it takes a rare kind of man in professional wrestling to willingly go to the ring and act the idiot. That degree of humility can sometimes sorely lack in an industry that seductively appeals to uncontrolled growth of fragile ego, and Martel deserves plaudits for his self-deprecating outing that night; it is a highly commendable, if somewhat lunatic episode to his career.

This good humour and the wily involvement of the crowd in dictating how events unfold plugs the gaps in the action with enough animation to keep your attention while, even more impressively, maintaining the cleanliness and crispness of their physical interaction; it transforms a match that, on paper, should have failed miserably into a tremendous accomplishment. The outcome is obvious from the onset: the black hoods look comical, the performers move slowly around the ring exhibiting limited moves amongst limited action, the storyline itself isn't all that engaging and the content that is present is understandably barebones. Yet, for all these pratfalls, they succeed in entertaining.

As unworkable a concept as the stipulation is in principle, and in spite of the ludicrousness, the acclaimed master of psychology, Jake Roberts, partnered with the master character wrestler, Martel, creates a one of a kind professional wrestling match. It is difficult to think of quite any other pairing that a bizarre scenario such as this would have worked quite so well with. Together, Martel and Roberts make something worth noticing out of the insanity; they turned water into wine, as both were so often apt to do.

Hence the inclusion on this list; the Blindfold Match is too remote an incident through the annals of time to warrant being analysed in depth as a genre on its own, but its inclusion here is indicative of the wider problem that has occurred far too often in WWE. Blindfold matches are just one of many bizarre stipulations committed to screen in the world's premier pro wrestling promotion. Good Housekeeping matches; a Kennel from Hell match; Chairs matches; Stairs matches; these are just a handful of madness from the pantheon of weird. Some have not proven to be too bad. Others have proven to be complete misfires. While the lessons found in the midst of #84 cannot necessarily be universally applied in an immediate, practical sense, the underlying attitude just might.

What Roberts and Martel do in their Blindfold Match is recognise their limitations. They do not try to avoid the hard truth that a Blindfold Match affords little in the way of creativity. Instead, they find precisely the right angle by which to attack the myriad obstacles standing between them and success, and the result is a unique bout that provides a genuinely different final product. In the case here, that angle is crowd participation. It almost feels as if the audience is ready to shout, "He's behind you!" in the most traditional British sense of pantomime. They stop only just short of it. Roberts pointing for the crowd to indicate where Martel is brings them into the fold, almost like no other match can; the audience becomes a competitor in an immersive participatory experience. Not only does the general fan get to pretend to be part-hero themselves and feel responsible for allowing their favourite, Jake Roberts, to get his long awaited revenge, but so too do they get to vindictively embarrass the loathed bad guy. While offering Roberts his revenge, they offer Martel a humbling as the Model tries the same method as the Snake only to be undone by an inevitable lack of support.

In more abstract terms, they took the fact that the Blindfold Match was so remarkably different to normality and made it very much the point, embracing it rather than working around it. Obviously it becomes much harder to do this when the nonsense a performer is saddled with is a cage inside a cell surrounded by disinterested dogs, or when victory can only be attained by burying a man alive in concrete, but it is the philosophy that is important, not the practicality.

#84 stands up as the best instance of a strange gimmick being executed with admirable success. The sense of hilarity was embraced – quite overtly in the case of Martel's physical comedy routine – and by embracing the ridiculousness, in not taking the situation too seriously, the match avoided catastrophe. Even the strangest concrete genre types may possess the potential to entertain; all they need do is embrace the farce rather than struggle against it and perhaps then the crowd can disengage their more critical self and go with the flow instead. The results might be camp, but so too might they be fun; and is fun not the beating heart of professional wrestling when all is said and done?

#83
Cactus Jack vs. Randy Orton
Hardcore Match
Intercontinental Championship
Backlash
April 18th, 2004

Consider the hardcore stipulation if you will. Before its advent as a WWE genre in the late 1990s, no disqualification environments had already accrued a number of unconvincing and indistinguishable sports entertainment euphemisms – no holds barred, no disqualification, falls count anywhere, street fights; there were minor differences, but very rarely were those differences adhered to. With the introduction of the Hardcore Championship and the resulting genre, it seemed simply like another additional euphemism for an already exhaustive list had been spawned. Nowhere is there as spent a match type in sports entertainment than "No Disqualification."

I have already discussed in this book the changes seen in the Money in the Bank Ladder Match sub-genre over the years, and how it had been stripped of its original worth and significance. I would say that, due to the nature of the genre's pre-existing alternative titles, the Hardcore Match never really had any unique identity in the first place; and the creation of a rather gimmicky looking title hardly lent it any legitimacy. The division would result in television and pay-per-view matches that far too often descended into realms of comedy to truly present anything close to worthy of bearing the label "hardcore." In an age of attitude, this is one genre that was happy to have none. Instead, it somehow quickly became a parody of itself despite having little to parody in the first place; a parody that perhaps saw it's most unworthy hour in the endless WrestleMania X-8 backstage skits.

Then #83 happened.

This was very much the right match at the right time, with the superior condition of both men contributing to its success. What's intriguing is that this match, along with his later bouts with Edge, really acts as an epilogue to Foley's career-proper. It's a small detail that gets overlooked, but there is an element of a time-warp. We see a great deal of Foley watermarks - backdrops on the ramp, knees into the steps, sliding from the ring to deliver a neck breaker and diving elbows off both ring apron and stage. It makes one ponder what a full-fledged run as Cactus Jack in WWE might have done for his legacy. There's even a wonderfully symbolic moment when Foley appeals to the fans as to whether to use Socko or Barbie…and it's Barbie that wins out, signifying a progression in Foley that we perhaps may not have anticipated at this late stage: goofy fun play time is over; time for violence.

Foley seems to relish taking some sick bumps, ones that play well into the progression of events and do not read as a gratuitous attempt to prove a point that doesn't need proving. Those moments are spread fairly evenly. Foley suffers at the hands of a bed of barbed wire, tearing his arms to bits, while Orton gets launched into thumbtacks. The pain Orton is enduring is clear, not just through his expression, but his hesitation to even roll on his back in the following pin fall attempt. As much kudos as Foley deserves for a performance worth returning for, Orton deserves just as much, if not more, for not just leaving his comfort zone but positively sprinting away from it in the opposite, most horrifying direction.

It's vital Orton gets the right props. The Legend Killer infamously wasn't well liked early in his career. What we get here then is a humbling – not, as you might be thinking, of Orton from Foley, but rather of the audience from Orton himself. The Legend Killer had something to prove. He needed to show that he wasn't just a beneficiary of WWE promotion, but that his hype was deserved. Orton blades, bumps on tacks and undergoes what is very much a humiliating character dissection at the hands of a legend, and he comes out on top. This didn't just validate Orton as a future prospect; it validated him as a performer who was as capable of giving as he was of receiving.

It's an interesting dichotomy, with the two performances proving to be antitheses in their objectives and equal in their achievements. As Orton is validated as the future worth investing in, Foley is validated as a past worth revering.

Indeed, validation is the word of the day: of Orton, of Foley and, most importantly, of the genre itself: hardcore wrestling.

The fact that this bout summons shadows of the famous Cactus Jack / Triple H series should speak volumes for the similar achievements both programmes share, but there's one major difference: the label. Matches with Triple H utilised some of the aforementioned euphemisms. This bout and its spiritual sequel with Edge some years later did not and instead proudly proclaimed themselves to be specifically "hardcore." As #84 embraced its own hilarity, #83 embraced, for the first time in its genre's history, an ability to fashion an identity all its own. What we got as a result was a match that legitimised the entire concept; even, I would say, gave it a reason to exist in the first place.

That identity is key. First, Foley had been given the moniker of "The Hardcore Legend" some time prior to this match, meaning his zeal and enthusiasm in this repulsive beauty has a powerful effect that gave the hardcore genre, until then just another parody of the no disqualification concept, a perverse coming-of-age. Second, pitting Foley against the handsome, talented, promising young Orton presents a real threat of ruination, both visually and creatively. Third, in consciously promoting the match specifically as a Hardcore Match, #83 becomes ultra-violence that very consciously follows through on the aforementioned threat of ruin. Perhaps an argument could even be made that #83 was the real *birth* of the genre.

Thus, this match is the very reason why the hardcore genre deserves to exist. It is a confirmation that the nonsense birthed in its earliest, most unconvincing years was worth it. Sure, the legitimisation written by Foley, Orton and Edge hardly lasted beyond 2006 but, for just a brief couple of years, WWE realised the gravitas such a stipulation could carry, the visual horror it should rightly result in and the important lessons that it should provide: to be pro wrestling's equivalent of grind-house or exploitation cinema. From a practical, real world and compassionate point of view, #83 and its 2006 successor are perhaps best left as two unique outings in the history books. Creatively, though, should WWE ever choose to craft more entries for the hardcore genre's library, these matches provide the perfect past examples to judge from. They prove that, if it wants to be taken seriously as a legitimate genre separate from the myriad euphemistic terms for the identical rule sets of No Disqualification, No Holds Barred, Anything Goes matches or the hundred other non-descript variations thereof, the Hardcore genre requires a greater sense of visual and conceptual horror than its cousins; a conscious embrace of its title and existence as something altogether separate.

Prior to Backlash 2004, "hardcore" didn't really mean a great deal. It carried no impact and struggled to justify its existence under both the weight of the reputation that preceded it and the existence of identical alternatives. Somehow, though, Foley - and, to be fair, Orton too - managed to find a way not to redefine the concept but rather to reaffirm it. Perhaps in that sense (specifically in WWE), Mick Foley isn't the Hardcore Legend as much as he is the Hardcore Progenitor, and #83 isn't a high point of its genre as much as it is a genesis point.

#82
Owen Hart vs. Bret Hart
Steel Cage Match
WWF Championship
Summerslam
August 29th, 1994

Even if you are still not convinced enough to subscribe to this short history of hardcore in WWE, it remains fact that the genre is, historically speaking, among the rather quite young. With these younger genres, it is much easier to analyse historical narrative and find their least imperfect execution to hold up as example, courtesy of their less dense libraries of work. When considering older genres, however, this threatens to become more difficult. Such is the fear when approaching arguably the grandest of them all.

The Steel Cage is one of the oldest, most prestigious and most beloved genres in the entire industry, hosting an endless list of classics. While it perhaps has lost some of its mythical appeal since the advent of its bigger brothers – Hell in a Cell and Elimination Chamber – and despite being diluted by frequency, it is still a genre worth getting excited for. Whenever the cage is deployed, it comes with an atmosphere of Event and carries the promise of an above-average composition. Alas, because of this grandiose state of existence, finding the genre's crown jewel would, therefore, be a daunting mountain of a task. Surprisingly, it was quite the opposite.

There is no point in reticence: #82 is the perfect Steel Cage match in both intention and execution.

The method utilised is exactly what every entry in Steel Cage genre should pursue; the rules for victory are the more limited set where the win can be attained only through escaping the steel construct over the top or through the door. There are no pin falls and no submissions and how that comes to dictate the content is the bout's most glorious accolade.

In typical Hart fashion, the action starts with great fluidity and structural maturity, with Bret returning to the same storytelling construction he used so effectively in the case of #99's confrontation with Mr Perfect. The pace set is a steadily progressing, methodical one, but made to feel more expedient than it is by the escape attempts starting from almost the very beginning. Those escape attempts from both parties are really what the rest of the content is designed to fit around. Given the unique stipulation often put in place in a Steel Cage match and made central here – to win you must escape – there is a constant feeling of progression; from the first escape attempt to the last, even in the face of a relatively methodical discourse, there's a constant feel of moving relentlessly toward the climax because of the centricity placed on reaching the outside of the ring.

The escape attempts themselves come to form many of the tale's peaks. In a modern era where pin and submission is as often a means of winning as escape, it becomes easy to gloss over escape attempts as easily as one would a kick-out from a pin fall. A moment of analysis, though, shows them to be what they are: the piece's strongest dramatic asset. The timing alone is enough to impress. There's no sense of stalling when one of the brothers goes to escape, perhaps speaking volumes for the trust Bret and Owen had in one another and the nature of their easy chemistry. These are two characters that do not walk gradually, or even casually, for the door; they lunge head-long toward it, often literally. And why wouldn't they?

This means the emotional intensity stemming from the story of two siblings embroiled in a war tearing their family apart, while still central to the narrative, never overshadows the prize on offer, nor the other way around; this is still a World title Cage Match, and both men's hasty attempts at escape not only promote the idea that they wish to escape the other brother's raging clutches, but that the World title itself is worth urgent pursuit. Were a World Championship Steel Cage match to ever legitimately take place in a truly competitive environment under the rules of escape imposed here, this is undoubtedly what it would come to look like.

So too do they balance the small, stiller moments of recovery which become gradually longer in logical conjunction with the run-time. The action is not over-stylised as it so often is today, but nor is it too underdeveloped as perhaps it once had been long before. The high spots are neither too dangerous nor too subtle, and it is the aforementioned increasing downtime between them that develops the growing sense of exhaustion so effectively in the later acts. All the way through too, the Steel Cage plays its own part; it never intrudes at the expense of the action, but its imposing, claustrophobic presence is constantly felt.

By the conclusion, you as the viewer are as breathless as the two men battling it out. It is difficult to not be warped back in time to 1994 and imagine yourself sitting on the edge of your seat amidst the sea of fans entranced with the shifting drama. Every move is felt, every swing in momentum dizzying and the lasting impression is left that you were not just lucky enough to witness an incredible thing; that you were also a part of it.

It should be clear, then, as to why I feel this is the benchmark for the Steel Cage genre. As a genre, the Steel Cage is something that can last forever. Even with bigger, badder and more popular versions of it hanging around, it can capture a very unique kind of atmosphere, suck the crowd in like possibly no other genre can and ultimately create a match for the history books; when done affectingly. The problem is it so rarely is. #82 was.

Oftentimes, it feels like the genre can get caught up with bloodshed or with using the walls as a weapon or with executing some kind of memorable "moment" - big men and the wall collapsing or high fliers and extremely dangerous dives from up top. The actual storytelling potential of a Cage match has unfortunately, though only in the majority and by no means exclusively, gotten lost in the shuffle. Such potential is ageless and could work as easily today as it did back in 1994, back in 1984, back in 1974; it does not matter. The urgent, breathless jeopardy that a

Cage match creates for both men inside is enrapturing - a word that describes #82 better than perhaps any other.

The basic approach utilised by the two Hart brothers – that to win in a cage you must escape from a cage – and the believability they employed in portraying their pursuit of the win feels like exactly how to do a Cage match. Forget pin falls, forget submissions, forget interference, forget blood and weapons and gimmicked constructions. The Steel Cage genre is an exacerbated environment in itself where, once again, less is more. You do not need any of the aforementioned mitigation to create drama inside those confines. All you need is a clear focus on the very thing that makes the genre a unique entity; embracing the characteristic of escape creates heart pounding drama like little else in professional wrestling can. It is what #82 does so well; it is what #82 teaches.

#81
30 Man Royal Rumble Match
Royal Rumble
January 22nd, 1994

The Steel Cage is not the only older, more prestigious genre out there, of course. The Royal Rumble remains, to this day, a firm fan favourite almost universally across the entire WWE Universe, and for good reason. It is almost always a match highlight of the year. It remains consistently entertaining and is incredibly difficult to get, for lack of a better term, "wrong." Its unwavering place in the hearts of the WWE faithful across both the world and the years warrants a special look at its most definitive outing and, perhaps in as great a tribute to the invulnerable sense of fun this unique genre possesses, the iteration most representative of its identity is quite far from being known as sitting among the elite.

The 1994 Royal Rumble seems like an incredibly odd choice; one that, even in watching back, threatens to underwhelm. There's a distinct lack of star power – Luger and Hart appearing only late on, when excitement sits on life support - and any variety in the style of entrants is deployed poorly; for a long time in the middle of proceedings, there seems to be a dulling abundance of larger, limited athletes leading to much less enticing action at a critical juncture in the run-time when attention requires reinvigorating.

So why the pick then, given its apparently poor credentials? Well, there are a number of positives, foremost of which are some of the performances. Diesel has an impressively dominant run that glues much of the first half of the bout together, goes down exceedingly well with the live audience and perhaps sets him immediately on the path to stardom later that year. Randy Savage has a fun, albeit brief run of his own with a blazing hot cameo. Shawn Michaels excels as the second longest surviving competitor, being present in the final four, and his raucous showdown with Jannetty gets one of the hottest reactions all night. Bam Bam Bigelow is effortless as the top iron man of the match and the two most important performances of Luger and Hart are, in many ways, textbook. Luger provides explosive energy and Hart cerebral storytelling.

Generally speaking, though, that this Rumble's positives are heavily outweighed by its remarkable mediocrity I do not deny. It is, however, that very mediocrity that sees it placed upon this list. This is a paint-by-numbers Royal Rumble match; so paint-by-numbers it practically writes the manual, "How to Book a Royal Rumble." It is the perfect choice, in that sense, as a genre defining composition, as clearly embracing of its genre's specifically individual identity as #83 and #82 were of theirs.

Whether because of appeal or longevity, Rumble matches often avoid the same kind of criticism other genres can fall prey to. Truthfully, the genre has as many poor entries as it does good ones and many iterations fall into the usual cluster of clichés. None, however, has collected such clichés quite as comprehensively as #81 did. The set-pieces it so heavily relies on to counter the general lack of roster depth might be easy to overlook, even miss, but such set-pieces often help make any Royal Rumble as famous as it can be regardless of its chronological position or relative wealth of star power. What #81 presents undeniably is a blueprint worth showing any non-fan who may be curious as to what a Royal Rumble match watches like.

The commentary, though not quite the zenith of Heenan in 1992, hosts Ted DiBiase doing an admirable job reeling out a list of the kind of tactics the commentary booth will every year refer to: fresh talent targeting weary talent; teaming up on bigger competitors; not wastefully expending energy; even his cries of confusion as the Steiner Brothers refuse to team up highlights the kind of psychology only a Rumble can present quite so efficiently to the tandems of the day. In fact, the abrupt manner in which that Steiner civil war comes to an end is, in itself, a slight example of a different but no less prescient trope. Kwang's green mist is indicative of the extra-legal activity that one might often witness in a Rumble marathon, more prominent examples including the brief use of chainsaws and chairs in 1998 and, more simply but no less memorably, Triple H's post-elimination assault on Mysterio in 2006.

Even specific performances may take cues, with the aforementioned outing of Diesel being the example in this instance. His spree of eliminations and general dominance of the ring is what set him on the path to stardom that would culminate later that very same year, and is a method replicated many times since. Rikishi benefitted heavily from the same approach in 2000, for example, in a performance as much a highlight of that year's addition to the genre as Diesel's was in 1994.

Diesel's performances in more recent years have been highlights for an altogether different reason of course: the cameo. The past is as often a part of a Royal Rumble as the present is, and the genre has become increasingly known for including stars of yesteryear. Though not played for the same sense of circus as it may be today, Bob Backlund's relatively alien presence is at least a figurative example of the philosophy being practiced here. Tenryu and Kabuki are the other alien presences, but it is the role they play in one of the bout's sub-plots that matters most; their obsession with eliminating Luger for their employer is indicative of an early progenitor of the "painted bulls-eye" method that would prove so fitting for the likes of Austin in 1999 and The Rock in 2000.

Elsewhere, Doink provides the kind of comedy that the 2012 Rumble obsessed itself with and the confrontation between Jannetty and Michaels examples the idea of old rivals finding one another amidst the chaos of the battlefield that Cena and Orton so miserably failed to replicate in 2011; Austin and The Rock, however, succeeded inimitably in deploying the same idea in 2001.

The final four at the climax of events is a clear example of the four corner stare-down we get every other year at close of play – one personal favourite example being the variation provided in 2009 where Legacy were treated as a single entity throughout such a closing verse – and this is followed when Luger and Hart have their brief hero vs. hero stare down; a trope replicated in innumerable Rumbles before and after, sometimes at the end of events and sometimes in the middle - Warrior and Hogan in 1990 perhaps being one of the most memorable occurrences of the conceit.

Luger and Hart actually present two other concepts often deployed frequently in the genre. Luger occupies the role of the dominant babyface that sometimes comes to anchor the narrative. His comic book heroism is reminiscent of Hogan before him, of course, but also a precursor to the overpowering shadows cast by The Rock in 2000, Triple H in 2002 and, perhaps to a slightly lesser extent, John Cena in 2013. On the other side of the coin is Hart, who occupies the contrasting role of the underdog babyface to Luger's dominating hero, the plucky athlete we vicariously identify with for overcoming impossible odds lent to him by his injured knee. Benoit in 2004 is an obviously forgotten example of this idea, as is Mysterio in 2006. Rumbles often give us one or the other, with whomever occupying whichever role eventually going on to win; that we get both in a single match might explain the finish, in itself indicative of yet another repeated idea: the joint winner born from an impossible to clarify photo finish.

Ultimately, while by no means is 1994 a universalised list of Royal Rumble set-pieces and cliché, it is an extensive one. It is a remarkable prototype by virtue of its unremarkable intentions. It presented lightning in a bottle; the electric appeal of a Royal Rumble is here distilled into a series of often seen but never less entertaining tropes that together craft a solidly fun hour of action from a depleted and largely directionless roster of talent. #81 *embodies* the genre more holistically and represents the genre's undefined identity more so than any other of its brethren and, in that sense, proves that this particular iteration's habitualness is its most worthy, most necessary, most must-see quality.

#80
Chris Benoit vs. Shawn Michaels vs. Triple H
Triple Threat Match
World Heavyweight Championship
WrestleMania XX
March 14th, 2004

While the Rumble is in a class all its own, it is to the general idea of multi-man matches to which this thesis now turns. There is a precedent of multi-man matches contested under "One Fall to a Finish" rules which we are able to parcel into a single genre because they possess their own sense of collective identity.

Of match types such as the Fatal 4 Way or the Six Pack Challenge, or the multitude of variations thereof, the Triple Threat is the most frequent, arguably the most popular and certainly the most tried and tested; it provides the shadow in which all other spin-offs sit. Admittedly, the Triple Threat has been rather overexposed in recent years, particularly at WrestleMania, and that overexposure has created a debilitating side-effect: coasting. Whenever there is now a Triple Threat match – or indeed any similar multi-man one fall finish match – there is often a sense of sterility, disinterest in originality and a lackadaisical picking and mixing from a preordained bank of set-pieces and psychologies. Unlike in the case of the genre represented by the preceding entry, though, this vault of cliché is not in and of itself sufficiently entertaining. In an environment so potentially singular, it remains a crushingly disappointing recurrence instead.

Recognisable telegraphing of recycled spots within mundane narratives make it increasingly tempting to roll eyes when matches such as the Triple Threat are announced, knowing it can too easily amount to a glorified handicap match, or a prolonged beat-down, or a series of singles bouts with a rotating roster where each combatant has an unconvincing prolonged stint of being floored on the outside. It is from #80 that all this originated, thanks to its overwhelming success at the time.

Like with #81, it is not an all-encompassing list of populist plays by any means but, like with #81, it is an impressively expansive one: the interruption of a submission finisher with a finishing move; a tap out saved by reaching inside the ring and physically grabbing a wrist; a competitor being taken out by a silent, unlikely double-team; a stare-down between the two more storied combatants. It is not being posited here that #80 should be given all the credit for everything seen to unfold in the Triple Threat match genre today, and it certainly isn't a genesis of concept, but it is a progenitor for the modern formula. Every Triple Threat since, as well as even some of its variant cousins too, has included direct replications or transparent riffs on elements played out for the first time – or at least the first notable time – in the running of this WrestleMania XX main event.

Too often these Triple Threat matches become glorified handicap matches and follow a wearyingly simplistic formula you can see unfold before anyone even gets to the ring. However, #80 was a *true* triple threat that could have genuinely flowed in any of three different directions. The trinity of extremely talented performers do a great job of using the stipulation to its fullest effect throughout.

Styles are allowed to mesh to great results. From Benoit authoring entire sequences of the kind of mat-based surgery we knew him for to Michaels peppering the whole affair with his renowned aerial offense of moonsaults and diving baseball slides, all the way to Triple H adding the exclamation marks with his high impact, smash mouth and opportunistic assaults, there are multiple styles showcased to cater to multiple kinds of fan; technique, speed, power, even cerebral opportunism across the board. What this creates is an artistic symphony of professional wrestling. Add in the double suplex spot on Benoit and the nauseating bleeds of Michaels and Triple H and you even have elements to satiate the hardcore taste as well.

As the momentum is never adequately sustained by one of the three men at any stage, it becomes feasible that any one of them can win at any moment. Not only does that mean unpredictability – a trait any Triple Threat match should possess - it prevents any stretch of the discourse hitting a plateau. A constant seesaw of momentum places all three on a single skill shelf, ensuring you pay attention for the duration knowing a Sweet Chin Music can come from nowhere or a Crossface can counter pretty much any move, or even that Triple H could cheat his way to victory through any number of methods. There are multiple moments when one combatant suddenly comes a second away from winning only to get interrupted, and all of those moments are timed with clinical precision.

Content is dense. There's little repetition, despite the clear example of three German suplexes. What moves are repeated fail to become predictable due to the varying degrees of success with which such moves are performed. Our artistic axis play the crowd like a sucker, creating a short-sighted rollercoaster of emotion, blind to the long game and with an outcome that remains muddied to the last. By the time the third act opens, Benoit lies in the wreckage of an announce table, Michaels is dripping with crimson and it's all Triple H's to lose. Michaels and Triple H play up their own rivalry that simmers underneath the immediate and, soon enough, just when you think The Game is on course to gain the victory, he finds himself on the back foot as he too tastes his own blood. The blade jobs aren't necessarily needed but they do transform a thrilling content-laden blitz into a blood drenched, grindingly attrite epic.

Triple H hits Michaels with a Pedigree and it doesn't do it. Benoit puts Triple H in a Sharpshooter and it doesn't do it. Michaels hits Benoit with a Sweet Chin Music and it doesn't do it. There's no recoiling at any stage and no escalation because of the relentlessness, which makes the ultimate finish all the more brilliant and exciting. As if to tie the story all together with a nice ribbon, the finish is granted an epilogue that fashions the single greatest, most real WrestleMania Moment of all-time, as Benoit and Eddie Guerrero hug one another in the promised land of WWE amidst confetti, WWE and World Heavyweight Champion respectively.

This truly is a match which ages well into an ever-better vintage every twelfth month. It is not just *a* triple threat match; it is *the* triple threat match.

In spite of the often employed rhetoric of WWE in its presentation of industry evolution, the real frequency of redefinition is much rarer than the company claims it to be. The word "redefined" is thrown around with far too much levity today. Every now and then, though, a redefinition does occur, be it through a man, men, a company or a match. Hulk Hogan redefined what it meant to be a World Champion. Steve Austin redefined what it meant to be a hero. Edge, Christian and Matt and Jeff Hardy redefined the ladder genre. WWE itself, lest we forget, completely redefined the very nature of professional wrestling. So far, the matches championed in this chapter have not been redefinitions; rather benchmarks or embodiments of identity. The goliath that is #80, however, is all of these things at once, proving a master of its genre to which so many other iterations that have followed have proven slave.

#79
CM Punk vs. Jeff Hardy
Tables, Ladders and Chairs Match
World Heavyweight Championship
Summerslam
August 23rd, 2009

#79 is a master class of a genre not too far removed in its narrative from Money in the Bank, the growth of which was inspected in Chapter 5. In that case study, it was suggested that Money in the Bank as a sub-genre became too ineffectual for the greater good when it became too verbose for its own good. As a similar sub-genre, TLC is analogous; in fact, its birth was very much the amplification in volume of the Triangle Ladder Match witnessed at WrestleMania 2000 and an advent of the philosophy that one day spawned Money in the Bank in turn.

Absence of logic is the greatest sin of a 21st Century Ladder match variant. Even the majority of the better half of modern day Ladder bouts seems overly reliant on the fact that the crowd is going to pop regardless, ridding pro wrestling of its art and reducing it to a reductive anticipatory giddiness of how far Talent A is going to fall. Ultimately, the Ladder match, regardless of which of its many faces it wears, is too often a voyeuristic exercise in cheap thrills at the expense of emotionally intelligent art.

This, to some degree, explains my proclaimed admiration for the minimalist attitude of the inaugural Money in the Bank match in the case of #89 – an admiration felt towards #79 also. Much like the character of their entire feud, Hardy and Punk exceeded expectations, shattered negative preconceptions and put on a hell of a match. It had the same risks as any TLC match, granted, but it dialled those risks down enough to feel more comfortable and safe than shadowed by doom. Perhaps even because of such a comparative restraint, the match made room for uncharacteristic levels of logic that, in turn, ensured actions made sense, and a clearly identifiable story was afforded space to develop. The result was the best singles TLC match ever seen under WWE colours and, yes, a perfect instruction manual for its genre.

A number of early attempts at victory from both parties emphasises the urgency of matters at hand. That urgency is furthered with how little time both competitors waste in introducing the weaponry and, in fairness to them both, those weapons are then used in a way that evades the artificially long and unjustifiable set-ups that can often be found with too great a frequency elsewhere in this sub-genre and its kin. There's less of a sense of fabrication in this instance and more a sense of natural progression. For example, when Punk sets up a table outside the corner of the ring, Hardy cuts him off with offense, allowing Punk to go through said table at a later passage in a manner that feels legitimately surprising. There is also original content too - Hardy being back-dropped on the rim of an unfolded chair; Punk countering a whip into the steps with a leap, only to turn and lunge into a chair shot; a superplex onto a flattened ladder.

Very back and forth, of course a match such as this one is largely reliant upon its sense of unpredictability to maintain the tension and drama. Just as Punk has an advantage, a weapon swings it back to Hardy. Just when Hardy looks set for a killing blow, Punk counters some other way; and this continues throughout. Generally speaking, it's a very good example of collaborative effort. Not only do they share the offense and disadvantage evenly, they both do an incredible job of expressing their character's pent up aggression stemming from the very personal animosity that had, at this point, come to drive their feud. Sometimes, unfortunately in Hardy's case, this characterisation translates into one or two occasions of over-zealous execution which threaten to endanger him or his opponent. Overall, though, it sets a tone that's believable and presents content in a well executed manner. Exemplary is the fact that both men suffer from very few, if any, botches or mistiming, which in an environment such as this one is a danger even the most experienced performers can come to encounter. Also, note the lack of prolonged down time where both men lay sprawled out and battered on the mat; in the midst of all this chaos and brutality, the two of them keep getting up and keep going despite the clear pain they're both in.

Too many times, these TLC matches become too hyperbolic and, ironically, the result becomes something that demands nothing of its audience. It's the pro wrestling equivalent of a cue card; prompts such as, "Cheer," "Boo," or "Gasp" wouldn't be out of place if they appeared on the big screen. It's needlessly dangerous and that it may, one day, end very badly is a bitterly real possibility. Yet with #79, we have a prime example of not just how to make a TLC match as effective as an Iron Man match in its ability to tell a story, but a match that can itself act as a good role model; another blueprint of how to execute well any entry into a specific sub-genre, in this case achieving the same ends with relative safety. The fact of the matter is that good professional wrestling will always get crowds popping; all fans in all crowds are all watching for the same reason. That basic shared interest need not play substitute to the flagrance of props and stunt work.

By dialling it down from eleven, Hardy and Punk created here something unique in the annals of TLC. That it is unique is something of a crime, not just for the sake of safety but for the sake of entertainment too. The stipulation remains perennially popular, and probably always will. People will always cheer the sub-genre and it won't be going away any time soon, or even radically changing. But synthesis is no great demand, and logic by no means a ludicrous expectation. The predominant modern pattern of this particular sub-genre is too much of a demand, ironically because it makes no demands of the fan and too many of the performer. Engaging with a cheap, all too dangerous stunt for a quick fix is no substitute for emotionally intelligent art. #79 presents the best of both worlds; an empiricist's treasure haul; another past example by which to judge future efforts.

Chapter 8

Abstract Genre: Understanding Ideas

#78
Macho Man Randy Savage vs. Jake The Snake Roberts
This Tuesday In Texas
December 3rd, 1991

Thus far, the focus in the development of genre in pro wrestling as performance art has been on the readily identifiable and concrete. The uses of this paradigm shift are far from being quite so limited, however, and can as well be applied to better our understanding of abstract ideas that permeate WWE and the rules we, as fans, impose on those ideas to determine the degree of success by which they are employed. Pro wrestling conversation is rife with the abstract, from umbrella concepts like the undercard and main event scene down to specific ideas about how certain shows (such as WrestleMania) should operate. Even the commonly utilised "events" deployed outside of official ring time to further advance stories are defined by silent rule sets that determine their quality. Developing these concepts into abstract genre types helps us understand them at their best in the same fashion as it helps us understand concrete match types. Chapter 8 now turns to exploring some of the most readily identifiable abstract genres to example this claim, beginning with one of the most common - "the beat-down;" a conceit the potential of which has never been realised in quite as harrowing a fashion as it was in the instance of #78.

The match remains important, providing as it does the emotional charge that eventually comes to contextualise what occurs after its conclusion. The theme that runs through both the match and what comes after is, as it has been often already in examples analysed in this book, simplicity. The participants keep their offensive displays passionate, their respect for the roles they each play unbending and thorough. It is through small touches such as Macho's mistakes stemming from his overwhelming emotional outrage and Roberts taking a break on the outside to stem his opponent's seismic momentum that their encounter becomes a psychological master class.

Their chemistry is a wonderful element to behold. From their promos to their looks to their styles, we have complete opposites and, in a manner that speaks volumes for both individuals, they use that utterly to their advantage. The loud, passionate madness of Macho is pitted against the cool, cold calculations of the Snake. One promo is a convoluted rant, the other a threatening monologue. One wears a blinding myriad of colour, the other muted flame on black. Everything is diametrically opposed, creating an awed, magical atmosphere. Nothing is wasted either. Not only do they refuse to even wait for the bell, they settle into their desired story with economic speed. That story is not the obvious option of Roberts relentlessly beating down Savage in the smothering manner we might see today, but a relentless dissection of Savage peppered with teased comebacks; once again, madness vs. calculation.

Yet, despite its status as a quiet classic, the match itself isn't why it's placed on the list. Of more interest is the beat-down that follows. Certainly, I've come across little as daring for or ahead of its time. Much like how Macho's zealous outrage had lent him a disadvantage in the match, it leads to a horrible turn of events for him afterwards and what follows is shocking even by today's standards.

Like the match preceding it, the beat-down itself is really rather simple. Savage sells the DDTs flailing and rolling around the ring as if in spasms of agony. Roberts mocks Elizabeth before planting Savage with another DDT, positively reveling in Elizabeth's ensuing horror. When you think it can't get worse or more violent, Roberts grabs Elizabeth by the hair and clocks her with a hard right, an action he later relishes during his post-match promo with classic lines like, "It felt so good I should have to pay for that!" and "I could cultivate her into something even I would want!" Such reprehensible behaviour and deeply discomforting phraseology is *pure* villainy.

In the sports entertainment guise of a beat-down, it may watch as familiar. Violence towards female talent was shown on television semi-regularly during the Attitude Era after all and, while something that is heavily shied away from today, is certainly nothing relegated to the far distant past. We should, by rights, be desensitised to it. As performance art, however, what follows #78 is frightfully hard-hitting. There is no humour to be had from it and, beyond that required by the nature of the pro wrestling beast, nor is there any melodrama either. This is an incident not played for laughs or to illicit a cheap reaction from fans. There is very little theatre. It is simple, realistic, frightening; it is a man *enjoying* hitting a woman. That is all. A man grabs a woman by her hair, taunts her then hits her and is shown to have enjoyed doing it.

When viewed as performance art, it is an angle decades ahead of its time.

Roberts and Savage *both* were men ahead of their time, their work proving brave enough to tackle such highly emotive issues as inter-gender violence not just for the sake of entertainment, as perhaps is too easy to claim when taking a traditional view of professional wrestling, but for the sake of hard-hitting, thought-provoking, morally challenging art.

Today, an image-conscious WWE might not have the gall to quite so explicitly tackle an issue like this on their television programming and, if they did, it probably wouldn't be played as straight as it is here, especially while they continue adhering to the outmoded, near-sighted sports entertainment paradigm. One could not blame WWE today for avoiding anything of the nature of #78 because of how pro wrestling is thought of under that current paradigm. The stigmatic reputation of "sports entertainment" has allowed it to shy away from artwork unafraid to challenge its audience. Characteristic melodrama and the bizarre tradition of viewing professional wrestling as a camp, simulated combat sport curtail its ability to challenge, relegating aggressive artistry like that of #78's beat-down to realms of poor taste and bad influence. While a man crashing through a table is dismissed as standard fare, tackling prevalent social issues such as violence towards women is avoided entirely for fear of misunderstanding.

Such misunderstandings that levy blame of violent influence on pro wrestling – found among the uninformed mainstream - is, in fact, the very problem that makes professional wrestling promotions so apparently frightened of image and dismissive of responsibility. Viewing pro wrestling as performance art tackles that fear and dismissal head on, pointing again to the potential we might unlock in an abstract idea as seemingly inconspicuous as the beat-down: another untapped genre.

#78's beat-down is just a man hitting a woman; it was ahead of its time, and so genius because of its reductive realism. It highlighted fearlessly one of the rankest occurrences in our society. What sports entertainment would call a mere beat-down, performance art would call social commentary. The beat-down in professional wrestling as sports entertainment is a regular occurrence, often used to provide only incidental danger or flimsy motivation. With #78, there is a frightful level of perturbing realism, rooted entirely in the safety of a fictional dimension, which not just entertains but challenges its audience - your outlooks on life, your moral beliefs and your ethics as an individual. It brings to the spotlight an emotive social issue and forces you to take a stance on it. It gets you thinking and engaging with the world around you; and it unlocks the powerful, striking, unapologetic and relevant effect any beat-down could have were pro wrestling to shed the bondage of its modern orthodox school of thought.

#77
Kurt Angle vs. John Cena
Smackdown
June 27th, 2002

Establishing new characters memorably is problematic in any form of storytelling, even more so in as constantly variable an animal as professional wrestling. This is why seeking to understand the debut as an abstract genre of its own is a vitally important exercise. Unfortunately, it should be said, WWE have failed on this front more than they have succeeded over the years, considering the ratio of successful talents to unsuccessful, and the real reason for this is rooted amidst one of the promotion's more pervasive creative philosophies from the 1980s.

Often, the squash match and / or undefeated streak is WWE's chosen method to build up empathy for a new fangled star, and prolonged title reigns common among each generation's baby face poster boy. Indeed, it often seems that dominating success is often the first port of call for WWE to create positive impression. However, it is not always effective and is frequently an unstable footing at best. WWE's outdated, insecure portrayals of heroism, in fact, imply an active aversion to vulnerability, where endearing effort is mistaken for uninspiring weakness.

Alas, in this day and age, to be heroic is not enough for a hero to resonate; so too must they be to some degree unbalanced, flawed or, at the very least, embattled. The most beloved heroes of any medium of storytelling have at least one of these characteristics, if not all three. WWE do not appear to share this philosophy, however, much to their discredit. Instead their product subscribes to a far more machoistic sense of hero. This is not, in and of itself, necessarily a problem, but it does mean audiences tire easily, especially in the midst of their own hardship. Audiences would sooner support an underdog not dissimilar to how they feel in life than they would a Superman unafraid of difficulty and consistently outdoing his competition with apparent ease – never more evident than in the very natural and unexpected groundswell of support for unlikely lads such as Daniel Bryan and Dean Ambrose. These issues are embodied by the obvious example of course: John Cena. The reputation that – fairly or unfairly – dogged the majority of his career is the quintessential representation of everything wrong in how WWE so often approaches hero creation – predominantly victorious, rarely showing convincing weakness.

It is, therefore, a great historical irony that Cena's debut is one of the most memorable of all-time. #77 is indicative of what WWE's understanding of heroism is missing, forgetting or actively ignoring. It shows determination in the face of believable adversity. While WWE has often tried to replicate such a situation throughout John Cena's career, it has never worked quite the same way again and the reason is simple: they started letting Cena win. That is to say that the hero having his day only becomes quite as emotive a moment once the villains have had a hundred days all their own. In Cena's personal continuity, that rarely happened outright. Indeed, it was usually the opposite and, as a result, so was the reaction to him. Winning gets wearisome and distant but losing is relatable; that is the lesson of Cena's debut, one that proves both its strength as a method and its qualification for replication.

The opening sets the fast, furious tone that persists in the main and Angle's zeal in selling for Cena, the new kid on the block, is worthy of applause. Deploying his Ankle Lock early portrays a man unwilling to play around with an enemy who is unwilling to play around themselves – an early instance of the pervading story being that Cena is not so much there to win as he is to simply keep up. This entire bout becomes a professional wrestling equivalent to *Rocky*, played out in less than ten minutes.

Cena's performance is, remarkably, one of his most praiseworthy. His show of competency and his level of practical efficiency impress. Psychologically, his multiple pin attempts on Angle do a good job of showing the debutant as a man able to assess his most viable and beneficial tactical options – here, the urgent pursuit of a quick victory over a former World Champion and veteran of the Olympiad.

#77 harks back to Chapter 4: WWE as Apostate, as it represents a WWE prepared to go out on a limb, confident enough in the ability of, and belief in, one of their top stars to not fear making them appear disadvantaged against a new talent. In this short match, the company was able to establish in the minds of the fans, quite firmly, a brand new future prospect, and it just so happens that the individual who became "A Thing" here went on to become and remain "The Thing" for over a decade.

There are many matches throughout WWE history that prove losing can make you more of a star than winning and this is one of them. As an audience, we readily identify with losers and more powerfully so because of their default state as the underdog. Life, it often seems to us all, is filled with crushing defeats. If this match is a less than ten minute pro wrestling version of *Rocky,* it's morality is straight out of *Rocky Balboa*'s most memorable speech. This is a match not about how hard John Cena can hit, but about how hard he can get hit and keep moving forward. The practical application of that moral should be obvious: one can achieve infinitely more in a single, notable, hard-fought, losing effort than ever could be achieved in six months of comfortable victories. Somewhere along the line WWE forgot that when it came to John Cena, and he went from the underdog to the franchise; from the rookie to The Champ; from Rocky Balboa to Apollo Creed. The damage dealt as a result has, at times, felt soul destroying to many a fan.

In this one example, though, the approach has its worth proven beyond a shadow of a doubt. Did Kurt Angle seem any less convincing a top contender after this match? No. And John Cena came out looking like a kid that could become something, not because he didn't lose but rather because we were allowed to wish that he hadn't. His debut was a far stronger, sturdier foundation for that. Just as victory cannot guarantee you success, nor does defeat ever guarantee you failure. Quite the opposite, in fact, and in such a match as this, we as fans may find as invaluable a lesson for life as we do for the performance art we adore so much. It is a prime example of not just WWE's creative liberalism already explored, but also further proof of the potential in professional wrestling that this book's interpretive performance art approach allows us to unlock.

It is these successes that also make it a textbook definition of how to handle the debut match as an abstract genre in professional wrestling. The squash match and the winning streak may have worked in the age of renewed Americana that was the 1980s, where society wanted its insecurities to be reassured with infallible heroes, but structurally it has often proven to be a wavering, unreliable starting point that demands consistent follow-up and punishes even the faintest whiff of the opposite heavily. The result is perhaps as many, if not more, failures than successes. On a social level, both have become emotionally distancing. In the cynical post-9/11 world of today, it is the losing effort that resonates most. Not only did it work in the case of #77, it resulted in arguably the most overwhelmingly successful career in WWE history, perhaps indicating the hard-fought, nail biting loss to be a stronger starting point than any other alternative. Starting at the bottom with a losing but admirable effort is, ironically, win / win; your rank cannot possibly get lower and, precisely because of that, your emotional appeal cannot possibly get stronger.

Simply put, #77 is how to debut a character in a 21st Century performance art.

#76
Bret "Hitman" Hart vs. 1-2-3 Kid
WWF Championship
Monday Night Raw
July 11th, 1994

While #77 is listed for being a brilliant example of how to debut a new character, its qualities as an underdog match are not to be ignored, as it is those very qualities that make it so effective. As another abstract genre, the underdog story is a very useful tool for affording upward mobility that begs questions of its own. The most pressing, of course, is if a well-fought losing effort can be such an elevating experience for any given character as I contend #77's debut of Cena to be, what has anyone to ever worry about? Losing would simply never matter. There is, naturally, a line that must be drawn and the history books provide us with the appropriate instruction manual as to how to draw it in the guise of #76.

Underdog stories are historically proven to be tricky balancing acts, especially if their intention is to push a talent to the next level in anything other than the most fleeting manner. Undeniably, some have built a successful career on the back of the genre, yet many others who were promoted the same way quickly faded back into obscurity thanks to the cocktail of an eventually disinterested WWE and a lack of continuing emotional resonance. As #76 will come to show, in order to work, an underdog story needs to be a perfect storm of the right character, the right structure and the right tone.

Believability is the key term, and despite the lazy, misguided assumption that size differential equates to the most expedient method of generating the emotion required in an underdog tale, it is vital to realise there is a massive difference between being out-sized and being out-matched. It is the latter wherein lies the key to the genre.

Of the myriad factors allowing #76 to be the benchmark it is, that neither man is afraid to play their role is perhaps the primary. The character of 1-2-3 Kid is out of his depth here and Waltman embraces that fact in his performance. He's not afraid to look like he's being outclassed by his World Championship opponent, while at the same time never hesitating when it's his turn to take the offensive. In both his movement around the ring and his execution, he laces his method with vigorous belligerence. In an interesting role reversal found in #99 - Hart vs. Perfect at King of the Ring - Hart is unafraid to show himself as being overly aggressive despite his status as the primary hero in the company. He provides a hasty hostility to counter Kid's fighting spirit, creating a tangible atmosphere of escalation. The more aggressive Hart gets, the more outmatched Kid becomes and the harder he fights as a result, creating a tandem of both desperation and hope on both sides.

That sense of escalation is an important factor to identify. More so than many others, the underdog genre is prone to sloth, opting for jarring segregation in its styling: the underdog starts well, gets beaten down, comes back and wins. The method is just fine in general terms and WWE employ it often, but if you want believability and the vicarious appeal of one man fighting against the odds, then less synthetic rigidity is required. In the case of #76, there are no long spurts of advantage from the champion or challenger, nor any real comebacks from the latter. Instead, in the midst of the champion's aggression, the underdog challenger is forced to take advantage of momentary openings, hesitations or mistakes, building his performance from instantaneous reactions rather than cerebral counteractions, thus generating the aforementioned effect of being outmatched rather than simply out-sized.

This is not to say that Kid isn't afforded his own impressive moments in the sun. Though his opportunities are often gut reactions, Kid does have an answer for Hart's earlier offensives. Similarly, though his own arsenal is kept reductive, it is no less unique, at least in comparison to both the wider roster of the day and his famously deliberate opponent too. Kid's tenacity does not go without mention, and is in fact pointed out on commentary to become an integral part of the story being written. He also has plenty of space to sell heavily every strike of his conservative opposition, meaning that, while never making it the central crux, the size difference is by no means ignored. Even when on the defence then, Kid is given a platform to showcase his talents in real terms as a performer; and Waltman seems to devour the opportunity with glee.

All in all, it's a real fight from the knees up for the challenger, and who can't empathise with that? Though Hart maintains the advantage to a notable degree, the discourse avoids totalities in a manner most other flawed examples of the same genre prove unable to; in other words, it is believable because of its fluidity and more epic for it too. The sense of grand occasion comes from the tempting tease of a lasting memory when Kid saves the match with a rope break just when it looked like the two had re-written the Cinderella story with an ending that shattered the glass slipper. The opportunistic manner in which Kid lands his comebacks prevents him from looking better than, or even on par with, the character ostensibly being portrayed as the best in the world, while never making an underdog victory seem like an impossibility or his fighting spirit neutered.

Of course, Hart's performance is as exemplary too. Hart had an uncanny ability to mesh with whatever style he was wrestling against, which makes this particular effort a worthy memorandum to his adaptability. Outside of the fiction, it should therefore appeal to any Hitman fan if for no other reason than the fact that this match presents Hart with all too rare an opportunity to work with a talent much smaller and more agile than him. His ability to elevate the talent he worked with is never on show better than it is in this instance, and that this gem of an accomplishment is talked about far less than other matches which achieve less is unfortunate.

The bravura performances of both individuals are what work for #76. Like Angle in the preceding entry, Hart is far from embarrassed to make himself appear outplayed by a less experienced character much further down the competitive ranking of the company. Though this is not a debut for Kid, it is most certainly his debut taste of the company's highest peak, the challenge presented by Hart undoubtedly Kid's tallest mountain to climb. The lesson behind it all, the one that makes #76 a pristine embodiment of how to put together an effective underdog story, is that the manner in which you climb matters more than how high you get.

The believability so key to the underdog genre's effectiveness should be fashioned from fluidity in discourse, humility in performer and accessibility of character. #76 has the trinity. The fluidity in discourse comes from the opportunistic offense of both challenger and champion. The humility comes from the ego-free performance from both parties, where Kid is not embarrassed to wrestle as if outmatched and Hart not embarrassed to appear outdone on more than one occasion by a character supposedly much less capable than him. The accessibility comes in the form of the Kid; a man who, for so long having been known primarily as a loser, afforded for himself through blood, sweat and tears an opportunity to succeed in as grand a fashion as possible in his world.

And while he ultimately came up short, there was no shame to be had in the distance that remained.

#75
DDP vs. Christian
European Championship
WrestleMania X8
March 17th, 2002

It is easy to forget the overall quality of wrestling that occurred during the night of WrestleMania X8 all those years ago. The card is filled with sleeper matches: bouts that look like non-events on paper, but in actuality provide some very strong in-ring action. Though the pervading memory is almost exclusively about The Rock vs. Hulk Hogan, the closing bout between Jericho and Triple H is by no means a failure. Austin and Hall have an entertaining showing too, as do Angle and Kane, who exceed all expectations. Other matches are less successful; the Tag title four-way leaves much to be desired, and Edge and Booker T completely overdo it.

Perhaps Edge vs. Booker is the second most interesting match of the night, showing as it does the post-modern approach to "More is More" wrestling on an undercard. I say second most interesting because it is in the case of #75 that we find the most interesting, presenting the opposite attitude. Both matches had barely passable feuds heading into the big night – a shampoo commercial in the case of the former, a motivational speaker in the case of the latter – and both matches consisted of equally talented performers. The comparison, therefore, becomes an interesting one.

Though this is a match unlikely to ever be labeled a WrestleMania classic – a fair critical assessment– it remains nevertheless impressive. The action is clean and crisp, the pace smooth and comfortable. The content is stringed together both fluidly and methodically, though the bout never begins to feel slow. The chemistry truly sings. None of this should be unexpected for any fairly learned fan. When two historically consistent workers are paired together such as these two combatants, who perhaps in some spheres remain unfairly underappreciated, a four to five star effort is nigh inevitable, even when both men are at opposite ends of their careers.

What is it that transforms this strong outing into something great? It is the latter half of the action. The climactic final act utilises a see-sawing momentum to envelop even the most cynical, detached or critical viewer. An entertaining effort then becomes a golden rediscovery for any fan who is unfamiliar with WrestleMania X8, be it because of not having watched it in a long time or, in some cases, never having watched it at all. As if to flaunt how accomplished a pair of performers DDP and Christian both were, the extended climax avoids pratfalls that most false finishing sequences are unable to avoid, as the near falls never become overbearing in their abundance or synthetic in their narrative context.

The bout's run-time is relatively short, unfortunately detracting from any sense of occasion. However, the brevity of the story makes its accomplishments all the more impressive. The approach is simple - traditional even - but by no means evidences an attitude of restriction.

Indeed, such is the entire point. The manner in which this composition is painted upon the ring canvas hits the perfect balance between necessity and ambition. With only six minutes of active ring time, it would be impossible to compile something as complex as the all-time classics, and incredibly difficult to even steal the show; as a result, it concerns itself primarily with helping to *make* the show instead. There is no sense of more is more on this occasion, and the maturity evidenced in not trying to overload their run time with an unseemly degree of content pays dividends. The focus, instead, appears to be on how best to execute the content they do opt to include.

Simply put, this is a match paying more attention to the why rather than being obsessed with the what, turning a six minute arrangement into a verbose accomplishment; verbose, ironically, because of its accepting humility and readiness to play exactly its intended role. Sometimes it can be actively damaging for an undercard match to try and "steal the show." Sometimes it is important, and by no means denigrating let it be said, for an undercard match to be a great undercard match. That's what we have in the example of #75. It is the manner by which it accomplishes this that is the most important point to take away, though. What DDP and Christian do to great effect is something you often hear industry experts constantly preach a need for among talents lower down the company ladder: maximise minutes.

In maximising their minutes, DDP and Christian may not have created an all-time classic, but they did create an unassuming and by no means bashful defence of their qualities as performers in the pro wrestling industry. Whether DDP's near flawless outing or Christian's supreme performance, this is pro wrestling that should encourage any uneducated viewer to extensively research the work of both halves of the equation. Balancing their ambition with imposed necessities, DDP and Christian wrestle a prime showing of their maturity, humility, chemistry and, most importantly of all, individual ability and, in doing so, reveal any under-appreciation of their careers as grossly unfair.

As a rule, "less is more" is almost universal in its success when applied. Success is bred not by an ambition that tries to contemptuously outmatch immediate opportunity because it believes it should have more, but instead by an ambition patient in its understanding of how to get the most out of immediate opportunity so as to afford greater chances at a later date. The idea that any path to the top in WWE is attained by consistently *stealing* the show is historically proven to be inconsistent in its success rate. What #75 proves is that the undercard's primary purpose is instead to help *make* the show; and that there is honour to be had in that. Any match should seek to maximise its minutes. That does not equate to every performer desperately clamouring to make their piece the most dramatic of the night; it instead means to wrestle according to the opportunity afforded and to make the most of what is given. That is exactly what DDP and Christian did.

Sure, it never changed the world, but that's the point; *it was never supposed to.* Therein is the key to the abstract umbrella genre of the undercard match.

#74
Rey Mysterio vs. Kurt Angle
Summerslam
August 25th, 2002

#74 pulls together the preceding three elements discussed in this chapter. It is the debut pay-per-view match of Mysterio in WWE – interesting that it would prove as successful as Cena's against the very same talent – and portrays an underdog story not too dissimilar in design to that seen in #76's Hart / Kid affair. So too does it maximise minutes appropriately, as in the case of the prior entry; a perfect example of achievement in the undercard. It is because of these exemplary achievements that it also presents a premiere example of yet another, far more common abstract genre type: the curtain jerker.

Curtain jerkers are perhaps as important to any show as a main event, especially in the case of pay-per-view. It needs to get the crowd hot, get them excited and amped up and give them a taste of what's to come. It is a hefty, all too unrecognised responsibility, but one Angle and Mysterio appear to relish.

This is the opening match to what many people would name as the greatest Summerslam of all-time. On watching this match alone, you can understand why that is. #74 could actually rank amongst the very top opening matches for any WWE pay-per-view ever. It would be easy to give that moniker to curtain jerkers benefitting from some form of handicap – World title matches, for example, or stimulating stipulation – but #74 has only its intoxicating emotional hook. The underdog method is a little more hyperactive than in the case of Hart vs. Kid, but not too dissimilar. Certainly, it manages to attain that same atmosphere of Mysterio fighting from the knees up. The size differential, while important, does not dominate the story or harm the pace. Of all its supreme accomplishments, though, it is content that leaves the most lasting impression.

#75 was all about a match being fit for its purpose, showing no desire to over-achieve at the expense of the show, the match or the artists involved. #74 is, again, not too dissimilar, but benefits greater from its circumstance. Mysterio is the perfect foil for a technician like Angle to help create a red hot opening gambit for an evening's entertainment. The speed with which both men were able to work and the crisp nature of their execution meant they could ramp up the bout's content in spite of its short run time without damaging quality. It is perhaps because this is only a ten minute match that a conditioned WWE fan might go in with lowered expectations. When the two men hit the viewer with *this*, it astounds. There is no meandering or any long downturns in action that wane interest, or even any booking stunts as was (perhaps) seen in the Hart / Kid composition's false ending. There is, though, still so much going on that it is impossible to take everything in with a first viewing.

The key refrain that makes it all so edge-of-your-seat is Angle's continuing attempts to lock in his signature submission, the Ankle Lock, in the seamless and near invisible way only he could. His arms are like snakes, his hands a pair of snapping jaws as he almost manages to clamp on his devastating finisher from the most impossible situations. It means his performance becomes as swift as Mysterio's own, albeit in a slightly different manner, jolting up the unpredictable tension impossibly high. Importantly, Rey is afforded the opportunity to counter each and every time, answering Angle at every turn to prove him a capable competitor and adding ongoing jeopardy to proceedings. The number of layers to the drama at hand is truly incredible; we get energy, creativity, jeopardy, tension, unpredictability and psychological depth in one fast-paced, swift moving, tight-knit package. "Blink and you'll miss it" has perhaps never been quite so applicable.

The discourse is as praise-worthy as the content. Their impressive pace remains consistent beginning to end, which is exactly what allows the piece to be so utterly loaded with action until it is close to overflowing. The way they move around their environment never hurts proceedings. Like in matches already reviewed, this is an affair that lacks WWE's artificial movement so often needed to reposition the artists for planned spots. There's no dragging one man by the hair down the aisle or to a corner to move the story along. The action is what dictates location, lending a relentless fluidity that ensures no wasted movement (as cliché a phrase as that may be). Take the finish for example: beautifully done and seamless. The end result of allowing positioning to be dictated in such a fashion is that the fan becomes utterly transfixed, lost and forgetful of choreography. It is absolute total assimilation by the fiction; that the match is only ten minutes becomes irrelevant by virtue.

Even when Angle, the villain of the piece, utilises ground and pound offensives to counter Rey's unpredictable innovation – a conceit that often slows Mysterio's bouts to a crawl – the energy never dissipates. The match never once drops down a gear. The conditioning of both performers then becomes another huge plus. While it is fairly easy to see why Mysterio needed top class conditioning because of his arsenal, Angle's vigour never relents in any sphere: the energy begins quite literally before the bell rings and his impact never lessens, every clothesline slapping, every German suplex rattling, every punch carrying its weight. This is not to detract from Rey's outing. Any learned fan should know his approach by now: variety, innovation, uniqueness. This match, however, is a reminder of what Mysterio was before time ravaged his knees and his knees ravaged his capability.

As a match, it also helped cement Mysterio as a brand new highlight of WWE television. The results of this star-making performance speak for themselves; Mysterio would go on to be heavily involved in what some would proclaim the programme of the year as he teamed with Edge to feud with Angle and Benoit over a set of newly minted Tag Team Championships that Autumn. He was rubbing shoulders with the elite from the moment he came to the company and so perhaps, in that sense, his eventual graduation to leagues outside the cruiserweight genre was inevitable.

#74 shows not just the kind of bristling ferocity an effective curtain jerker needs to pursue, but also awareness that there is no substitute for a well-told story. This is a match that had no helping hand. There was no stipulation to help prop it up, no mitigation that made paying attention or vocal reaction in any way a given. What it did have was freshness, clarity of place and purpose, a bulging depth of relentlessly executed content and a sprinting pace that whipped the live crowd into a mania that would come to witness arguably the greatest Summerslam in history. It is arguably the greatest curtain jerker ever. If I am to get really grandiose, it might just be one of the greatest undercard achievements in company history as well. By synthesising the elements involved in a good underdog tale, a strong debut and the maximising of its minutes, #74 finds itself an apparently lost gem in the annals of WWE's past and, most certainly, the "How To" of show opening efforts.

#73
Team Orton vs. Team Kingston
Traditional 5-on-5 Survivor Series Elimination Tag Team Match
Survivor Series
November 22nd, 2009

This ongoing exercise in the development of genre in pro wrestling as performance art is essentially an exercise in identification: do specific kinds of match types, literal or conceptual, consistently exhibit common traits that indicate self-conscious uniqueness, i.e. identity? The matches that best exhibit these common traits to their fullest and most successful potential can then become the standard bearers of their respective genre, be it a concrete or abstract one; they are the historical examples to be learned from and improved upon for future success and growth.

Matches are not the only element of WWE to possess individual identities, though; so, too, do their shows. Of WWE's pay-per-views and television offerings, most beloved in the hearts of fans worldwide are the so-called "Big Four" - seasonal super-shows that have come to represent major waypoints in the calendar year and that to this day, thanks in large part to their longevity over all others, are seen as indispensably special. Indispensable is the key word. The potency of the Big Four ideal is such that, were any one of these shows to ever be scrapped, regardless of its standing among the four, the move would likely be met with outrage. Yet, there is truth to the suggestion that their quality remains inconsistent. Prosperity is what these old timers deserve, I think most fans would agree, and that prosperity can come if we strive to understand the identity of each, revealed among their respective most successful moments.

By applying the same method utilised in this and the preceding chapter to now better our understanding of how WWE approaches these landmark super-shows, we can begin the process of defining their respective identities and just what it is that marks them out, or in some cases *should come* to mark them out, as being different; the Big Four as abstract genres all their own. Defining the identity of the Big Four in this manner would ensure they lose none of their special significance; that they might, or in some cases already have, is such a disappointing prospect that it seems sensible to start with the ugly step-sister of the quartet, and the one that has come perilously close to entering administration in recent years (and perhaps creatively did so a long time ago).

What is it that makes Survivor Series special?

Rather like in the case of Royal Rumble, it is an easy question to answer: the match type. Though the Elimination Tag has been around for quite some time and often occurs outside of Survivor Series, the Series carries a certain awe that can comfortably elevate any entry into the Elimination Tag sub-genre. This is because the Series handles the sub-genre with greater care and respect and treats it more attentively, whether having a multitude of compositions throughout the evening or just one as a show highlight. Thus, if we are to understand what special identity Survivor Series possesses, we must first define the identity of the sub-genre upon which it was built: the Five-on-Five Elimination Tag Team Match. Rather like in the genres presented in the previous chapter of this book, there is one work among the pantheon that could be labelled definitive because of its successes that were born from embracing its idiosyncrasy. That match is #73.

This is a genre all about format. That format is put to textbook use in the case of #73, morphing the bout into a masterful ergonomic portrait from its earliest moments; "Vintage Survivor Series," as Michael Cole would no doubt say.

As the minutes tick on, prototypical tag team conceits come to dominate as the ensemble of performers indulge unashamedly in the uniqueness of the genre. The results give the impression all involved wanted to make full use of the opportunity afforded to them by a Survivor Series 5-on-5; there are quick tags, a strategy of isolation from the bad guys and more stylised offense from the plucky heroes, each of whom is allowed a moment in the sun before, in some cases, being quickly dispatched. One of the more intriguing psychological elements of the sub-genre is allowed plenty of room to come into play through this approach: the numbers game. It is a game that is played beautifully by Team Orton on this occasion, quickly affording the treacherous group a deal of early momentum.

Each participant is used effectively according to their strengths. The workhorses are allowed plenty of time to strut their stuff on stage – Christian; Punk; Kofi. Individually, Ted DiBiase Jr. and Cody Rhodes are both allowed to get their fair share of attention too, allowing them to satisfyingly showcase their abilities in an environment of big names; importantly, they are allowed a number of moments to evidence their capability as a unit as well. Admittedly, each performer sticks to their comfort zone, though there is no hesitation in allowing the various, more unique styles a chance to take centre stage. Perhaps the more idiosyncratic game players actually protrude from the discourse more obviously because of its general conservatism, but that does highlight a number of missed opportunities that disallow the unusual to collide more often, the singular potential of such collisions denied in favour of these generally older or less able competitors being eliminated quickly.

Quick tags continue through to conclusion. The structure, therefore, maintains its motion and avoids dulling thanks to the in-ring pairings being kept fresh. The spacing of eliminations plays also to the strengths of those involved, if denying the aforementioned chances at truly original sequences. They come thick and fast early, but once proceedings are thinned to the most capable performers involved, the pace slows to one more deliberate.

In the discourse's penultimate chapters, the drama heightens considerably. Christian exhilirates with a shock near fall on Orton, a team captain saved by his last remaining lieutenant, Punk. An imposing psychology of intimidation is then deployed by the Viper. He moves to the outside floor, still as stone and staring at Kingston. Again, like with #100's Orton / McMahon fight, Orton is completely engulfed by his character, impressively and silently building to the eventual pay-off without even allowing us to sniff it, while creating an amazingly subtle character touch that embodies the Viper's sociopathic tendencies.

The equally detestable Punk is not without a role to play either, as he does the majority of heavy-lifting at this impasse. His own character is given relevance courtesy of Striker, with the stare-down between the Second City Saint and the Troublemaker from Paradise contextualised as a cautious encounter between former tag champs. The pace is breathless and the atmosphere tense, with Kingston's climactic confrontation of Orton feeling very much at risk courtesy of Punk. So effectively performed is Punk and Kofi's few minutes with one another, in fact, that it feels very much a match within a match. The sense of progression, again lent so brilliantly by the specific format at play, generates an almost gladiatorial feel; that to get to Orton, Kingston must first despatch the gatekeeper, Punk. Also, that Punk is a former World Champion helps create the impression that Kingston is a performer worthy of combating the company's highest echelon, which in turn evidences another benefit of the sub-genre's unique formatting: it is an efficient platform to elevate a star to a new level courtesy of a noteworthy performance on a special kind of night that happens only once a quarter.

The finish proves a sudden, sharp exclamation mark; because the Punk / Kingston chapter was allowed to play out rather exhaustively, the climactic confrontation explodes powerfully in a single second of shocking impression. The exhausting gladiatorial encounter with the gatekeeper leads to a swift killing stroke against the Machiavellian Viper, who so arrogantly stared into the arena from a position of safety. It is a moment of complete tonal contrast and is all the more effective for it, eliciting a feel good win from a genuinely heroic triumph.

Granted, in the end, there's nothing overly awe-inspiring about this match, but its beauty lies in its simple embrace of format; there's no real memorable stand-out moment for the highlight reels and even Kofi's win, big as it was, provided little for him in the long term, tarnishing any sense of legacy the match might have had in different circumstances. However, it does provide an absolutely pristine example of how to utilise the very unique Survivor Series format to its greatest effectiveness. Like all examples listed in the previous chapter and in this one so far, #73 is an unabashed embrace of identity; a "How To" for the traditional 5-on-5 Series.

This is, though, only half the requisite analysis.

#72
Team Austin vs. Team Bischoff
Traditional 5-on-5 Survivor Series Elimination Tag Team Match
Survivor Series
November 16th, 2003

#73 is an exemplar format that highlights Survivor Series' uniqueness by virtue of being the sub-genre's most functional accomplishment. It is not, however, the sub-genre's best example. It is to the best of the sub-genre we must now look to form fully our ideas of how its unique format can be exploited to make Survivor Series into a greater, more special event than many of its fellow pay-per-views.

It is the storyline context that allows #72 to excel the way it does. Austin, a hero famed as an ass-kicker, is reduced to a bound and helpless role that riddles this entire affair with unease. It felt very much like a fresh take on the Career Threatening Match, where the career under threat couldn't even be defended by the man who forged it.

There are a number of noteworthy performances that shape #72 as the greatest of its sub-genre; RVD contributes faster impact chain wrestling in the early going; Jericho and Christian perform with nothing short of the same competence they are rightfully famous for; Orton puts in another of what had become a string of star-making performances across 2003 and 2004 and, while obviously less accomplished than he is today, hangs easily with his far more experienced counterparts; The Dudley Boys operate as strongly as a unit as they always did. Yet, the shadow of Shawn Michaels looms large.

There is growing concern among certain fan circles regarding the reverence WWE afford the Heartbreak Kid that, rightly or wrongly, has heavily influenced the argument of Michaels being the greatest performer in WWE's history. Performances like his in this match are, in their bravura, the undeniable evidence there is at least some worth to the claim. His performance, and the story that then unravels from it, elevate an otherwise forgettable first half to the level of classic that the match now rightfully enjoys.

As the third act opens and Michaels stands alone (his teammates having been eliminated), the antagonists do a wonderful job of keeping a frantic pace going, constantly trying to overwhelm Michaels with numbers. Michaels puts in a convincing effort, teetering on the edge of keeping an advantage but never quite being able to maintain it, before he gets busted open. This watches as an example of the absolutely right time for a blade job and how one can add so much more emotional substance if deployed effectively. Three cocky heels target the bloodied and noble babyface, but it doesn't become a Cena-style beat down where momentum rests comfortably in one corner for extended lengths of time. Instead, Michaels continues to give us tiny glimpses of a miraculous comeback, creating teases of something greater that gives the viewer an emotional anchor but denies them relief from the growing tension. It really is a beautiful piece of narrative structure.

Thanks to the nature of Sweet Chin Music as a finisher, the eliminations come out of nowhere, requiring only a second to come together for our hero. Even the way Michaels reductively *falls* into the pin falls, rather than actively attempting them, lends itself to the bloodied realism. Michaels flops his way into most moves, in fact. The sense of exhaustion is a constant presence that grows to be infectious. It's a man functioning solely on instinct, with that instinct carrying him to the superhuman acts of heroism only professional wrestling can give us, and only when seen as performance art can give us so powerfully.

As Michaels continues flying blindly into the maw of defeat, JR's throat becomes raw with emotion and Bischoff and Austin get increasingly animated at ringside. The crowd begins getting feverish in their anticipation, all on their feet. As the viewer you almost find yourself jumping out of your chair right along with them, even on a fiftieth viewing. Lawler contextualises things well as a matter of believing, a matter of faith. If ever the word miracle can be attributed to a story, this would be it. This immersion all stems from the form Michaels is in, which for most others might be called rare. His timing in the way he moves, being it falling into offense, executing Sweet Chin Music or avoiding attacks, is as fluid as his crimson mask.

Michaels' impossible victory is so close by bout's conclusion it feels tangible, with the idea of the final win almost flashing before your eyes prior to Batista and Orton putting an end to Austin's weekly presence on Raw; a crushing result that silences the crowd in an instant. We never see the ending we want. We never see the hero win out, even though it felt impending as the chaos escalated beyond all control. As Austin's music had for years started with the shattering of glass, his era ended with the shattering of a dream, courtesy of a hard and stark reality; Austin's forced departure was the reality, Shawn's miracle effort to prevent it the dream.

Hence why #72 proved the concept of Survivor Series was an ingenious one. Here, events *really* mattered; every elimination, every move, every decision made by those at ringside all carried desperate consequence. It exhibits the unique identity of Survivor Series as having always been more serialised than episodic, a night of cause, effect, action and consequence that gives fans the rare opportunity to witness and experience repercussions in the immediate, rather than through the familiar delayed gratification akin to pro wrestling. If #73 is the best blueprint for its sub-genre of match courtesy of its functionality, #72 is the best blueprint for the show's conceptual base courtesy of its standing as a pinnacle of achievement. Granted, other iterations have captured the same sense of epic consequence – with Team Cena vs. Team Authority being a more recent example – but none quite so emotively (or indeed, courtesy of this story's bleaker ending, quite so crushingly). It is for that reason that #72 is the greatest 5-on-5 Survivor Series match of all-time.

Unfortunately, for whatever reason, this once unique night, with perhaps the most individualistic identity in WWE, has become a shadow of its former self, the titular concept largely ignored and certainly under-utilised. That's a shame because it is, in truth, the concept of consequence wherein the strength of traditional Survivor Series matches lies; a strength that empowers the very concept of survival in the first place.

Of course, Survivor Series is an intrinsic part of the origin for the modern WWE product. Alongside the Rumble, 'Mania and 'Slam, the Series was another landmark moment, a cornerstone show that continued to develop the framework around which the company is built today. It easy to forget, in fact, its longevity is bested *only* by WrestleMania itself. It should be recognised as the integral element to WWE's own make-up that it is. Presenting its greatest match, both on conceptual and literal terms, pays tribute to these facts and serves as a reminder to any doubters that this is a concept that, when executed effectively, is capable of drawing another unique kind of palpable emotion from fans and, perhaps most importantly of all, is a platform for performers - be they respected vets or questionable young stars – and the stories they tell – be they sweeping epics or incidental classics - to reveal themselves as special in their standing. It is, in that sense, that the Series is not as far removed from its three brothers as is dangerously easy to consider.

#71
30 Man Royal Rumble Match
Royal Rumble
January 25th, 2009

Juxtaposing the unfortunate circumstance that Survivor Series has been subjected to over its lifespan with the unmitigated affection Royal Rumble has grown to be held in is an interesting comparison. Out of the Big Four, it is the Series and the Rumble that can most easily stand apart as unique entities because of their dedication to a specific kind of match: the elimination tag in the case of the former and the titular take on the battle royal in the case of the latter. In that sense, their respective histories are perfect mirror images of one another.

By virtue of this diametrically opposed history compared to that of the Series, an attempt to define Royal Rumble's identity as a show is obviously different too. There is no tale of lost (arguably unattained) glory here like in the previous case. Instead, Royal Rumble enjoys an unwavering, cemented spot in the affections of WWE fans, and rightfully so. As previous reviews have already tried to prove, the titular concept of the show is one of great potential for variety, surprise and entertainment.

Even the most basic approaches to the Rumble match itself – such as in the case of #81's 1994 effort – remain perennially entertaining. Finding the greatest execution of format is not quite as *vital* as in the case of Survivor Series because of this. Even in its more mistaken moments and its earlier, more simplistic days, the Rumble still entertains as a match type and rarely fails to state a case for positioning among Match of the Year contenders. The sub-genre, therefore, has not wanted to quite the extent of the one explored in #73 and #72 because, even if it stumbles, it rarely (if ever) falls down entirely. The exercise of finding the sub-genre's benchmark is by no means any less necessary, though; not for fear of outright failure this time, but rather a desire of ensuring complete success in the future.

#71 is not the austere embodiment of genre #81's 1994 version was, nor as radical a departure as #91's 1999 effort. It treads the line between both to create, simply put, the greatest Royal Rumble match ever. It does not allow classical tropes to limit its creative output, though it does maintain a degree of orthodoxy. Its ultimate achievement is a symphonic mixture of deference and originality, respecting where the sub-genre has come from while fashioning a defining iteration that can hopefully help inspire sequential efforts in the continuing years to come.

This is a Rumble all about mobility. The concept of the Rumble is that any man can win. In practice, the purpose is to establish a popular character as the challenger in the main event of WrestleMania. What 2009 manages so well is the meshing of those two elements together, abundantly clear as early as the entrances of Orton and The Game. The two have a heated exchange that lights up an already hot match, but that comes to an end with the interference of Mysterio and Morrison, who then take centre stage themselves; such a tactic is the lifeblood of the entire affair. Performers from every level of the card interact in tightly timed and creatively constructed incidents that provide the fans with action much more complex than a more prototypical Royal Rumble, where such interactions get lost among a homogenised collage of one-dimensional brawling.

The focus is ever-changing too, with lightning quick transitions between these scenarios, pairings and set-pieces. Whenever the action threatens to still, the next entrant causes a fresh spike, or a new skirmish shifts your focus. The match demands you pay attention and, even after fifty viewings, you are liable to still uncover a hidden gem: the action stopping when Undertaker enters; the showdown between Rhodes brothers; the RKO spree; Legacy triple teams; RVD's shock return; Benjamin's high spots; even Santino's record breaking brevity. Most impressively of all, the composition does not just relate the surface level story of a marathon won, but takes time and care enough to focus in on a whole cast of individual characters from all levels of WWE. From speedsters to legends to giants to shooters, from Triple H, Undertaker, Orton and Jericho to Ziggler, Punk and The Miz, the cast is overwhelmingly prosaic. The resulting fluid variety stemming from such an ensemble approach sees the run-time fly by.

Following the thirtieth entrant, there's a post-modern degree of self-consciousness to how the action unfolds, patiently allowed to play out steadily rather than rushing to a conclusion. Upon the characters left, an unspoken rule is applied: the lower your standing and lesser your experience, the earlier you are eliminated. The breadth of characters is whittled down gradually in accordance to this rule until only the very best remain: Legacy, Triple H, Undertaker and Big Show. It is a final six that plays artistically off of an understanding of character. Legacy are the multi-man unit that work effectively together like a pack of hyenas to take down their chosen victim, together equalling the stature of their remaining combatants, if not outright surpassing it. The Undertaker is the Dead Man, an otherworldly phenomenon with inhuman abilities to absorb punishment and keep coming, the most powerful of these final survivors. Big Show, the real-world giant, stands as the World's Largest Athlete, a towering gargantuan capable of taking down, single-handedly, almost anything that stands in his way, far too heavy to eliminate alone. Then there is Triple H, grizzled ring general famed for his cerebral approach and with enough experience to know how to survive any war into which he is thrust. The most powerful matches up against the most numerically strong while the general tackles the giant. The giant and Phenom then tackle one another until Triple H is left alone with a baying pack of hyenas, whose numbers eventually prove too strong for even his action hero effort.

On an artistic level, this final six - or final four if you choose to view Legacy as a single unit - has never and, to my mind, may never be bettered. The set-up and the story it tells is the strongest expression of performance art in the sub-genre's illustrious history, the crowning achievement of a masterful collaboration that climactically rounds off a Rumble aching to be noticed and very much deserving to be remembered.

This is a Royal Rumble that excels beyond its own unfathomable potential, the opus of its sub-genre and the apex of its format. The action is much more complex, its structure manipulated masterfully and its conclusion aptly suited for a performance art school of reception. It's filled with many wonderful performances; effortless iron man runs have never seen a finer hour and near-eliminations have never been more prominent a part of the excitement and tension (and rarely better executed either).

The Royal Rumble is such a wonderful, beloved concept and, like Survivor Series, an ever-important cornerstone of WWE's year – creatively, financially and in many other terms too. Unlike Survivor Series, its lustre has never waned and grown only stronger across its lifespan. This is because, again, even the worst Rumble matches are still, to varying degrees, somewhat entertaining; the reason this one represents the opus is because the match itself exceeded the already impossibly high expectations people had of it. In every arena one can analyse and critique a match, it is an inarguable success. There have, no doubt, been other greats (1992 and 2001, for instance). None of them are as immersive or as synergetic a piece of art as 2009. In consideration of how to execute the sub-genre's format – of utilising near eliminations for dramatic effect, for example, or spinning together a multitude of alternating narrative threads - this superior piece of work doesn't just race ahead of its brethren, it eclipses them entirely. Star power, structure, storytelling, memorable moments and artistic endeavour, 2009 had it all with each aspect being as intrinsic as the next. It may yet prove to be forever the zenith of the Royal Rumble match, and certainly hasn't been bettered since.

As with Survivor Series, though, seeking a high point of Royal Rumble's unique sub-genre will define only part of its identity as a show. In one of the great ironies of WWE, the key to Royal Rumble as a show is not actually in its crowning match type at all. Though 2009 represents the best of that sub-genre, as a whole show it is far from the cream of the crop. That alone should prove that, in terms of an overall product, Royal Rumble succeeds best when its undercard is as thoroughly enjoyable as its take on the battle royal.

Synergy within a Rumble match is one thing, an element 2009 succeeded undeniably in mastering; synergy between a Rumble match and the matches that precede it (or in some cases follow it) is another thing entirely - the key to creating a great Royal Rumble event rather than just a great Royal Rumble match.

#70
30 Man Royal Rumble Match
Royal Rumble
January 22nd, 1995

A successful undercard can help save a Royal Rumble show while a successful Rumble match is inherent to any great Rumble show; when those two elements are married together successfully, the result is self-reflexive elevation on every front. 1995 is the prime example of such a phenomenon occurring.

It is easy to remember #70 with a bad taste in the back of the mouth. It falls massively short of the average running time and the content is largely forgettable, with only the first successful wire-to-wire effort making it memorable. In isolation, it is both odd and a struggle to sit through. When watched alongside the rest of the show, however, it becomes much more enjoyable, in keeping with the discoverable themes of the evening and proving to be a fun sprint to the event's emotional climax. In striving to account for this transforming view, we uncover just why synergy can make Royal Rumble so special.

When watched alone, it is the severe contravention of the quintessential Rumble tradition that ultimately hurts the piece the most. Reducing the intervals between entrants from ninety seconds to sixty may seem like a small change on paper but, in practice, makes a world of difference. Fictionally, it is given little justification; creatively, it has none. Departures from status quo can sometimes be successful, but often not when they come at such a foundational level; similar abhorrence was felt by many in 2011 when the company expanded the field of participants by ten to a total of 40, despite a struggling and largely impotent roster at the time.

It is because of the sixty second intervals that the action screams by in frenzy. Though the rampancy that ensues is beneficial to a small degree – never before or since has the Rumble felt quite so much like a race toward an attainable goal as it does here – the urgency is rendered inert by the lack of star power. That WWE were struggling with roster depth is painfully clear. The relentless pacing is only half as impressionable as it could have otherwise been because of what sometimes feels like the endless list of irrelevant names and faces.

Michaels and Bulldog – both of whom have performances of equal standing let it be said – help prop up the mercifully short parade of mediocrity. Not only are they, in large part, responsible for gifting the composition its more exciting content, they also lend it what prestige they can. Their names are, by quite a way, the biggest involved, with only Luger's much diminished aura coming close. Their centricity is vital to the match, but also proves historic. There is no denying their efforts are pioneering; previous Rumbles had utilised lengthy iron man runs as a point of attraction, but never had it been made as much of a point as it is with the bookending outings of the Heartbreak Kid and Manchester's Own.

Their presence throughout also feels like a pragmatic effort to combat what might otherwise have been difficult-to-sustain interest; had they turned up only in the final third, for example, the match would have been denigrated to a laborious tedium rather than the quick fire athletic display it is.

Nevertheless, even the talented likes of Heartbreak and Bulldog prove unable to lift this failed experiment from the doldrums of its contemporary demands and, even with its brighter elements and admirable effort to entertain, 1995 sits firmly among the lower ranked entries in Rumble lore.

This observation returns us to the issue of synergy and the role it should always play in Royal Rumble's identity as a show. Though alone #70 watches as a perversely lacklustre Rumble, when watched as the highlight of the wider show it is suddenly lent a new lease of life. The reason: synergy created through theme, established via the interpretive analysis the performance art theory affords.

There is a theme that runs through most of Royal Rumble 1995's undercard matches: ambition. As a whole, Royal Rumble 1995 showcases a field of upwardly mobile young professionals clamouring desperately to break their glass ceilings and cement their place on the next rung on the ladder. Hart and Diesel's encounter that night places their main event level of competitive capability inside of an elite class far beyond anyone else on the show. The restart of the Intercontinental Championship bout between Razor and Jarrett evidences a similar, if less intense, ambition-driven desperation for success, and the intention of the Holly/Kid vs. Bigelow/Tatanka Tag Team Championship encounter was to capture and evoke the emotional undercurrent of undying competitive spirit too.

This well constructed, thematically synergetic undercard lends the Rumble match a suddenly freeing context: an inspirational tale of an insatiably hungry Michaels and Bulldog seeking to prove they belong in the elite class occupied exclusively by Hart and Diesel. Furthermore, in this new frame of context, Michaels specifically writes the perfect middle act to his first career in WWE; his Rumble performance here is both a shattering blow to the ceiling forged for him by his bodyguard Diesel having eclipsed him in their respective paths to the World Championship, and so too is it a fitting prequel to the torturous final climb he would go on to face at WrestleMania XII just over one year later.

When watched as a complete entity, Royal Rumble 1995 is a night of athletic aspiration and clear talent positioning; an Olympiad of WWE. When reduced to its component parts, however, that quality fails quickly and catastrophically. There is little joy to be found in the Rumble match when watched in isolation, or in its undercard for that matter. Combined, though, they become far greater than the sum of their parts. In simpler terms, the thematic synergy that runs from evening's opening to evening's end elevates every part of the show, the strangely idiosyncratic Rumble match most especially so. Such is the key to understanding Royal Rumble's identity: it is not exclusively about one of its halves or the other.

Even successes like the 2009 Rumble match do not, on their own, adequately represent what it is that makes Royal Rumble such a special show. The sub-genre's less favoured efforts, such as #70, help to identify that for us instead. The undercard, while not more important to the show, is comfortably *as* important. When both halves of the show work together, the unique capabilities of the titular sub-genre become as diverse as they possibly can be and may even render it invulnerable to failure; such synergy affords the self-reflexive elevation found in the 1995 offering.

Ultimately, there is no other show quite as idiosyncratic as Royal Rumble, so to reduce it to its component parts is therefore unhelpful, misrepresentative and constricting. The lesson is clear: Royal Rumble, as a show, may be defined by its singular take on the perennially popular battle royal but by no means can it be, nor should it be, reduced to that term alone. It is limiting to do so.

#69
Brock Lesnar vs. John Cena
WWE World Heavyweight Championship

Summerslam
August 17th, 2014

Of the Big Four, the so-called "Biggest Party of the Summer" is perhaps the greatest oddity, and the most unfortunate in a certain sense. Even the withered Survivor Series continues to benefit from a clear idiosyncrasy: its stipulation match. Royal Rumble likewise. WrestleMania's reputation precedes it of course, but Summerslam has none of these things, and instead has languished for almost its entire existence in the cooling shadow of the Grand Daddy of spring time.

Survivor Series was created as a means to continue capitalising on the on-going Hogan / André saga. In that sense, its birth was the result of reaction and any ability to rival WrestleMania in prestige limited from the get-go. It was the spawn of WrestleMania, never intended to be a rival. Summerslam has, as the years have gone by, been looked to as a WrestleMania of the mid-term. It was not created as a reaction to another show but as its own separate self, opening up an ability to rival something like WrestleMania in creative scope if not in practical execution. Summerslam has been levied with the weighty responsibility of replicating, to some degree, the completely unrepeatable, and expected to transform into "WrestleMania Light." Does it therefore lack an identity all its own?

The answer is no. Though the majority of the time Summerslam may read on paper as "just another show" and, outside of its longevity, may sometimes struggle to justify its presence among the distinctively grandiose Big Four because of this, the most successful editions in the pay-per-view's library often capture a lighter version of the creative aspirations of a WrestleMania and, when watched, feel exactly like a WrestleMania Light for the summer months, when fan attentions are perhaps more distracted. The less successful, by extension, are the ones that categorically fail in doing so and remain simply "just another show." The culmination of long running blood feuds often help attain the necessary status, as do WrestleMania rematches, complex on-the-night angles and emotively powerful storylines that you might otherwise find punctuating the company's premiere event. 1997, 2002, 2009 and 2013 are all strong examples of this atmosphere being successfully created, each feeling like a slightly lesser version than their respective WrestleMania. In the cases of 1997 and 2013, Summerslam could even be read by the more dispossessed fan as apologies for the generally lambasted 'Mania offerings of those same years.

Emulation, then, is the word for Summerslam, a show at its best when emulating the *feel* of a WrestleMania without necessarily striving to rival it in scope. It is a show that benefits from the same kind of confidence and bravery that is often found on the Road to WrestleMania. When Summerslam shows gumption, when it shows guts enough to emulate WrestleMania, at a time considered among popular fan belief to often be a creative down period for the company, it forges its most celebrated moments.

#69 is one such moment. It shocked WWE fans across the spectrum because of its bravery and gumption. That bravery and gumption, that shock, allowed #69 to become a match as ominously large in its intention and as divisive in its reception as Lesnar's Streak shattering outing at WrestleMania had been the same year. Given the end of The Streak was the culmination of twenty-two years worth of work – both directly and indirectly – and that it was, by its very nature, only ever able to occur at WrestleMania, there is no way that #69, regardless of what its intent had been, could come to rival it on equal footing. What it did do, though, was successfully echo the same aspiration: to create an immortal moment in time that shook the WWE Universe to its foundations with a match that would be talked about for many years to come.

#69 was a complete departure for the company, a rare pessimistic embrace of the radical and, rather like the success of Bryan at WrestleMania, a vicarious opening for the more jaded element of the fan base to feel vindicated of their years-old criticisms. John Cena, be it fairly or unfairly, is attributed as a major reason for the rot at the heart of WWE that seemed to get increasingly worse as the Brand Extension wore on - in large part because of his dominance over the rest of the roster in real terms, but also because of his typically predictable story that played out in every other Cena feud for the longest time. #69 was the antonym to this sentiment, if not the outright antidote.

What's interesting is the video promo hyping the match doesn't vary from that typical Cena formula of the impassioned, heart-driven champion facing the insurmountably monstrous contender. In retrospect, that video closing on Lesnar's promise to leave Cena in a pile of blood, urine and vomit becomes haunting, knowing as we do what follows. This match is not just a squash match. Earlier in the year, Heyman said Lesnar would subjugate the WWE universe; *subjugate*. This match is an evisceration of the last hope of a universe already in bondage. WWE may never before have allowed room for quite as bleak a tale as they do on this occasion: the failed prevention of a bloody coup d'état.

Lesnar straight away gets the upper hand and takes the wind out of Cena's sails with an F5 in the *first minute.* As soon as it hits, there's a palpable shift in crowd response.

They become much more electric, much hotter blooded. Lesnar chants morph into the Cena pantomime which in turn transposes into a shapeless verbal awe. One minute in, #69 feels special.

Oddly, from that point on there is little that can be said for the remaining content. If you think memory of the match is too hyperbolic regarding the dominance of Lesnar, it may shock you to know you could not be more wrong. The slow pace and unvaried action, while usually negatives, in this case are the very reason for the match becoming the nightmare it is. Cena matches against monsters deplete his character's energy as quickly in most other occasions as in this instance, but usually Cena eventually wins the day in the most narratively jarring fashion. *It never happens here.* The fiction is denied such closure. WWE is a babyface's world that portrays its masculine heroes as borderline infallible, always winning out in the end. This is a match that lobotomises that philosophy without anaesthesia, and for that it deserves major props. Even the most cynical criticisms levied at this single stroke masterpiece cannot contend its audacity.

Cena gets a couple of very, very brief spurts of comeback, but they do not last at all, watching only as blinded, desperate bids for survival more than anything else. To see Cena crawling away from an imposing Lesnar marching relentlessly towards him is perturbing horror, Lesnar's ebullient approach to Cena's decimation harrowing. The way he traps Cena's hand under his foot for fun and watches him struggle is a humiliation, as is taking only seconds to recover after being hit by an AA, mocking The Undertaker with an offensively hubristic, spirit-shattering foresight into Cena's approaching doom. That Lesnar *laughs* before getting onto his feet and *warms up* transforms his character further into an ultra-human leviathan. He even dismisses Cena's last gasp of hope by breaking the STF with near lackadaisical ease.

The approach is simple; one dimensional even. Its effect, however, is apparent to even the most disinterested viewer. By the time Cena even manages to muster enough offense to get an AA, the awed crowd immediately launches from their seats in exhilaration - proof that a powerful story derived from established character will trump a content-laden approach; content is thin here, but the way that content is drawn from and plays off of character is the true achievement. By the end, Cena's face looks like one of defeat. Though he fights on where he can, his spirit seems to be in disbelief of Lesnar's invulnerability.

As stated, Summerslam is at its best, most memorable and most individual when it strives to emulate its bigger brother and, in #69, you have a very clear example of that philosophy in action. If ever one thing could come close to emulating the historical weight of The Streak being subjugated it would be taking the most prolific World Champion in WWE's history, its poster boy and the source of both its successes and failures of the entire preceding decade and defeating him in wholly convincing fashion. Traditional takes on professional wrestling have a term for #69's kind of match: the squash. It is a darker perversion of Cena's very first match in the company, and that it would come at a time when Cena's status in both the real world and WWE's fictional world was believed to be untouchable ensures that "radical" is the only fitting label.

As Summerslam should look to emulate WrestleMania – and has done just that when it has succeeded most - #69 sought to emulate the shock and awe of putting the 1 in 21-1. #69 is the kind of approach that can set Summerslam apart as special and more than "just another show." The squash of John Cena is the kind of moment that should come to define the summer's Biggest Party; though not WrestleMania moments, the next best thing. And Summerslam's ownership of such moments can comfortably justify its ranking among the Big Four and, perhaps more presciently, as second only to the Showcase of the Immortals itself.

#68
Brock Lesnar vs. Kurt Angle
WWE Championship
WrestleMania XIX
March 30th, 2003

So we come to The Show of Shows.

In the entire history of professional wrestling, only a handful of matches have the honour of saying they closed a WrestleMania. Which was the best?

A lot of people would immediately select Hulk Hogan vs. Randy Savage or Ultimate Warrior. Others may opt for Hart and Michaels in their sixty minute epic. The large majority would more than likely go for Rock / Austin II, headlining as it did what many consider to be the best 'Mania of all-time. Fans of a more recent generation may choose a match involving Cena, be it against Triple H, Shawn Michaels or The Rock. Now Daniel Bryan, after his night in New Orleans, has made his claim to the accolade too, as has Roman Reigns.

However, #68 is a match that goes grossly overlooked by WWE and grossly underappreciated by fans. Though there have been much higher profile main events, higher grossing main events and perhaps even been better quality main events at WrestleMania, there has never been a more fitting one. The entire set-up is everything it should be. After all, what word does the name for the Grandest Stage of All derive from? Wrestling! And *what* a professional wrestling match this is.

An early deadlock informs the viewer that this is going to be a tug of war from the get-go. High impact underlines what both men do throughout and you can hear skin slapping on skin at every point of contact, every suplex folding up the recipient with inhuman contortion. Everything feels stiffer than average, every set-piece aggressively exacerbated. You get a great sense of legitimacy; the realism so powerful it borders on the real.

The crowd isn't as constantly electric as they have been for some other 'Mania main events and that unfortunately takes away from this bout's standing somewhat. However, though not loud from start to finish, they are loud when it counts. Whether it's the fluid variation or the high impact tone, the crowd gobbles up every impact move thrown out; and there are a lot. At heart, this is an affair that may be as inherently a sadist's exercise as was #101's Regal / Benoit bout.

The majority of the work is crisp, but miscues are an issue on a couple of occasions; there are a couple of noticeable instances where a move is called too audibly or missed or, as we all know, botched completely. The Shooting Star Press remains a truly shocking moment.

Beyond that mistake, though, there's not a great deal to complain about. The counters are impressive and the exchange of finishing moves is mercifully compact. The performances of both men are genuinely among the best out of any single WrestleMania bout too. It is ultimately a match worth loving not in spite of its flaws, but precisely because of them. It proves an absolute war, and the competitive vibe is made all the more convincing by the icing on the cake: the handshake the two men share after all the dust settles. Knowing the wider context, knowing the battle scars both men left with, should by rights make this main event all the more endearing to the viewer. It is the perfect main event for a near-perfect WrestleMania.

There have undoubtedly been a number of matches out of the 'Mania closers with far greater appeal to a modern day fan than this one. In fact, compared to many of the theatrics we've seen over the years, #68 seems to get lost in the shuffle precisely because it is so straight-laced. It is because of that fact that it should appeal, though, and certainly why it could be called the perfect WrestleMania main event. The set-up was simple but effective. The psychology was intelligently, maturely crafted. The mistakes simply added to the fortitude of the performances, making it all the more dramatic and epic. In fact, if you are a fan of professional wrestling, then this match is exactly everything that you are a fan of. Brock Lesnar and Kurt Angle were two proud professional wrestlers who, on that night, went out and damn near killed themselves to tear down the house fighting for the WWE Championship in the main event of WrestleMania. What could better symbolise the show?

That is the mission statement this chapter is now concerning itself with via this selection. What match best symbolises WrestleMania?

It has been stated already that WrestleMania is perhaps the easiest to define out of all the Big Four. It is grandiosity in professional wrestling exemplified; a draw in and of itself that is a genuine pop culture event now, with a prominent social media presence to back itself up. In the eyes of the company, it is the centre piece of every calendar year, financially and creatively. This can be seen in how they deploy their biggest angles and moments, how they transform WrestleMania's past into a distant fantasia. WrestleMania is the premier event in the professional wrestling world. There is simply nothing like it.

When it comes to trying to discern its unique identity then, there is little task to be found. It does what it says on the tin. It is a mania of professional wrestling.

Return, then, to #68 and the word perfect. In Kurt Angle, you have the only gold medal-winning Olympian in WWE history and a man with a stake in the race to being named the greatest of all-time. In Brock Lesnar, you have a man as physically talented as Angle, if not more so; an individual who has attained an obscene degree of combat sporting success and whose natural gifts are unrivalled across the sporting spectrum. In the WWE Championship, you have the world's most prestigious professional wrestling championship. In WrestleMania, you have the world's premier professional wrestling event. In the closing match of WrestleMania, you have the rarest of air breathed by only a handful of other matches in history. Has there ever been a match that has so *perfectly* embodied the idea of a mania of professional wrestling? Arguably the two greatest amateurs to ever lace a pair of boots in WWE transition into headlining the pinnacle of the professional sphere in an effort that shatters their bones because of its impact; it is wrestling and it is manic. It *is* WrestleMania.

...or at least it would be. There is just one problem. This thesis is championing a new way of thinking about professional wrestling that distances itself from the traditional orthodoxy of simulated sport and / or sports entertainment. In these traditional views, there is little room, I feel, to debate the status of #68 as the definition of the biggest of the Big Four in WWE's pantheon of pay-per-view. However, if taking professional wrestling as a performance art, such a view no longer quite fits and the meaning of #68 shifts ever so slightly from being the perfect embodiment of WrestleMania as a sporting Mecca to being the perfect tribute to what WrestleMania *was* in the conformist view from which this book is attempting to move away.

#67
The Undertaker vs. Kurt Angle
World Heavyweight Championship
No Way Out
February 19th, 2006

So if professional wrestling is performance art, what then is the best example of a mania of professional wrestling? Oddly enough, one that never even occurred at WrestleMania.

The pre-match promo on this occasion highlights just how big a deal this meeting was. Hearing the line "When that bell rings…I don't have a soul either!" from Angle remains chilling even now. The promo pushes Angle as the best wrestler in the world, a soulless, relentless machine. It pushes Undertaker as something otherworldly, as a power that extends beyond the average pro wrestler. Then you see clips of them both taking other famed competitors out, including legends like Foley, Michaels, Triple H, The Rock, Austin, Nash, Sid, Big Show, Edge, Flair, Cena and more. This isn't just another throwaway monthly title defence; this is a big, *big* deal.

It's a fantastic set-up. Undertaker brings a big fight feel to any scenario. Couple that with the legitimacy Angle always brings to the ring, particularly during his closing days in WWE under the Wrestling Machine gimmick, and what you get is something that feels so much like a sporting main event but with that unique WWE gloss; the gloss of performance art. WWE shows here the unique world-exclusive product it supplies. In its pairing but also through its execution, what this match presents is a hybrid of fantasy and fact, at times documentary and others fiction; it is perhaps that potent cocktail that made Angle and Undertaker such a fascinating, acclaim-worthy duo.

The early tone is of the Striker against the Grappler. 'Taker, the striker, takes the early offensive, exploding out the gate and proving to be the quicker man in the first few minutes. Angle plays his role by showing a great deal more measure; it's important to note such measure is deliberate and not, as is so often with 'Taker opponents, trepidation. These two are presented quite clearly as equals and that pervades the larger discourse.

There are certain elements of this epic that do feel rather indulgent. WWE, though not pushing it overtly, show signs of their sometimes-fascination with "reverse psychology," as Undertaker, despite being established both by announcers and his actions as the striker, instead opts for submission; Angle vice versa. However, like most things indulgence is a double-edged sword and has its positives - it's interesting to see Undertaker's performance be so enthused in a manner not often seen from a predominantly character-driven author. It's almost out-of-character; an Undertaker that cuts loose and indulges in what he seems to love most: professional wrestling.

Angle, meanwhile, has a validating outing. His speed is insane and he maintains his usual crisp execution from start to finish. Of particular worth is his increased intensity. As a performer in WWE, Angle seemed to grow increasingly intense each year. By 2006, what you had really was a Wrestling Machine. Angle had an almost incomparable balance of speed, skill and intensity by the time he departed WWE and, had he stuck around, Shawn Michaels may not have enjoyed his comfortable lead as being considered the best ever in the company. That individualistic style is certainly on show in this instance; Angle at his best.

The pace is fairly even. Sometimes it borders on slow, but there's enough shifting momentum to maintain interest. They make complete use of their environment, not limiting the action to between the ropes, but at the same time not getting carried away and allowing most of it to happen outside. This is a balanced blend of theatrics, athleticism and psychology. Amidst all that, as if it weren't impressive enough, is the sheer amount of content. It's a hefty volume of a match; a weighty tome filled with a myriad of offensive and defensive moves and counters from both men. They dance their way through the thirty minute run time, masters of their craft in a visitation of a psychology that does not talk down to its audience, but rather trusts their ability and desire to invest.

Remarkably, the psychology that somehow feels so complex and demanding of its audience is actually pretty standard - Angle's focus on 'Taker's knee is a major plotting point, and Undertaker commits himself fully to it. There's also a wonderful moment where Angle tells the referee not to count out Undertaker following his crash through the announce table; another psychological aspect that plays up 'Taker's toughness, Angle's attitude as champion and the importance of actually winning a title match actively. The questions resulting from a simple couple of seconds are many. How much must a definitive victory mean to these two? Is that as a result of the fact that their respective opponent is who he is? When you ponder it, it's a moment that *brilliantly* contextualises the eventual finish.

#67 is an absolute masterpiece punctuated by a lead-in to the finish that consists of some of the crispest and most sublime counter wrestling ever put to canvas. Smooth, restrained and peppered with a number of finishing moves and near falls - including a trademark Undertaker sit-up, sold as it should be by the champion - it all has the crowd positively manic with excitement and pumped for that final bell. It is literally exhausting in its brilliance, concluding prose of Dickensian scale with a climactic pentameter of Shakespearian quality; a perfect closing match of a WrestleMania defined as performance art.

The key is the beating heart of this opus – the documentary of Angle's skill clashing with the fantasy of The Undertaker's character.

On the one hand, this dynamic informs the grand narrative. Angle portrays his Wrestling Machine character with aplomb. He has an answer for everything thrown at him, locks his Ankle Lock on out of some extraordinary positioning and with seamless fluidity. His level of endurance is not what necessarily keeps him moving inexorably forward towards eking out his narrow, debatable victory; rather, it's his grit. The Undertaker, on the other hand, has a character famed for his endurance in the fictional realm of WWE. His ability to absorb seemingly endless degrees of punishment and continue sitting up afterward often sees his work deploy an increased ante in the final act. The character unveils a new layer of his lethal retinue on this occasion, revealing the true extent of his own ring acumen as he, too, has an answer for everything Angle throws at him; the only difference between these two soulless characters is that Angle's effort is informed by his natural abilities and The Undertaker's by his unnatural abilities. It is a clash of two worlds, see-sawing back and forth, unpredictable and impossible to foretell.

On a more practical level, it comes to define the performance art theory's version of a mania of professional wrestling. Who is Kurt Angle? The most accomplished and competitively successful athlete WWE has ever recruited; an Olympic gold medallist. Who is The Undertaker? The most beloved, famed and respected fictional character WWE has ever created; a spiritual successor to André the Giant himself. They are two sides of the same coin; WWE's coin. What #67 then becomes is an invasive real world presence clashing with a fictional universe's height of fantasy. One for his athletic success, the other for his fictional character, both individuals embody the pinnacle of the two spheres of performance in WWE. Together, and specifically in the case of #67, they created art.

So not only is #67 a great example of performance art through its story, but also in its holistic amalgamation of WWE's many faces; of sport; of fiction; of art; of affecting success and of memorable entertainment. Contested over the Big Gold Belt – as prestigious a championship in its prime as the WWE Championship is today – were it handed the prestigious honour of closing WrestleMania, it would have perfectly defined the number one professional wrestling show on the planet; a mania of the many things professional wrestling is capable of in its transcended state.

In simple terms then, if #68 was a mania of professional wrestling when considering professional wrestling as simulated sport, #67 is a mania of professional wrestling when considering professional wrestling as performance art, perfectly, succinctly and successfully defining the performing arts Mecca that is WrestleMania.

Chapter 9

Post-Modernity in Professional Wrestling

#66
Shawn Michaels vs. Marty Jannetty
Intercontinental Championship
Monday Night Raw
May 17th, 1993

At this stage, it is important to clarify that this paradigmatic shift is not going to necessarily be suited to universal application. There are, after all, vast differences in professional wrestling culture across the globe and, as the title betrays, this thesis concerns itself exclusively with the pro wrestling culture propagated over the years by WWE. This is not to say, however, that applying the interpretive analytic wrought by the performance art argument to WWE matches alone cannot speak to issues pervading the wider industry as well.

I have already demonstrated how moving towards performance art unlocks the creative potential of pro wrestling in the age of information and betters our understanding of pro wrestling's functionality. From the detrimental effects of ego to the evolution of in-ring habits; from fan-bred stigmas to fan-led influence; from forms of memory to the challenges of the future; from new ideas for the industry to age old truths of the industry; viewing pro wrestling as performance art enables us to view matches as lenses through which to consider such a wide breadth of issues.

Considering this book is looking at only WWE matches, it seems quite a leap to suggest a single promotion's product can comment on such universal themes. Well, there is a reason why WWE has, within its library, matches that evidence such prescient themes: WWE has been a moderniser. Though labelled by many as a promotion irreparably damaging the integrity of the profession, in truth it has been, is and will continue to be a frighteningly powerful force for change. WWE has come to shape certain industrial habits of today so often taken for granted. When this occurs, WWE has helped move the industry further still, playing also the part of the post-moderniser. To support such a claim, this chapter shall now offer up two very prominent, very powerful examples that have altered the way professional wrestling promotions in the western hemisphere execute (or are perceived as executing) their ideas, thus moving the industry into a state of post-modernity; at least, from this fan's view point.

#66 - one of the first prominent matches of its kind - examples how WWE took their time in exploring the break-up of The Rockers, resulting in a memorable segment that lives in infamy to this day, a series of entertaining matches and, most importantly, an emotional connection. While Marty would ultimately fall by the wayside, initially it made both men matter and gave them a leg-up into the singles world. The fans cared massively that The Rockers had split up. They hated Shawn for it. They sympathised with Marty for it. One can only assume, as a result, that #66 won the achievement it did – Match of the Year – not just for content but also for the concept behind the match - what it led to, what it came from, the general idea that a tag team break-up could be armed into a longer-running storyline to build more revenue and birth more creative heft. All that potential began expanding to its fullest with #66. This match was noticeable. It was new; fresh; a post-modern reaction.

The pace is speedy; the moves showcased coming fast and furious, performed with ease and precision. It indulges in the flamboyant while averting the disaster of camp. Marty Jannetty, unfortunately, gives what feels like a somewhat forced performance, at best managing to strike only an adequate tone with his effort. Shawn Michaels is typically on form and plays up the cowardly villainous role in the pre-match scenario as well as could be hoped for. He comes off as the more nuanced character wrestler too. The emotional resonance of the rousing piece of work - the feud's original apparent conclusion - is impressive, the title change perhaps a little misguided in retrospect. In all, it's an incredible composition for its time and stands out now for its simplicity; ground-breaking for its day, reductive for today. Most important, though, is its background.

On the face of it, a formula was perfected that has been followed ever since and allowed any number of floundering talents, who otherwise were perhaps not tapped as future singles stars, an opportunity to shine. Look at The Miz; would he have gotten to where he got in the first quarter of 2011 had he not had his rehabilitating stint in a tag team before becoming the catalyst for its break-up? Many others across the years have enjoyed similar benefits. It does not always work, and there are just as many victims of splits happening too soon, being mistimed or ill imagined, but the method, it seems, is one The Rockers very much built the benchmark for that fans still use as the go-to comparison today.

That's the point: the comparison almost every fan now unfairly jumps to: "Which one is The Jannetty?"

It is a story that has transformed into a professional wrestling myth - a tag team star that fails on his own because he got "carried" in his tag team days by the attributes of his partner. Whenever a tag team splits today in WWE, the comparison is applied. In some cases, it's applied as soon as a team *forms*. Does this not condemn at least one half of a tag team to instant damnation, as well as the concept of said team itself to dismissal?

The fickle attitude WWE has of tag wrestling has already been explored in this book, but regardless of whether the division is in a boom period or a lull, there is clear intention from WWE through the years to utilise the tag team as a rehabilitation centre for the failed and failing. Main event talent without direction, upper mid card talent threatening to sink and lower card talent that the promotion has little idea how to use have all been both beneficiaries and casualties of this utility treatment. Though the second chances that have been afforded by this method are not to go without praise, it has two profoundly negative effects on both performers and industry. Firstly, it creates a sense of unfair predestination before the experiment even gets off the ground: one of the two talents will be pushed as a singles star at the far end and the other is doomed to obscurity. Secondly, it reduces a successful stint in tag wrestling to a means rather than an end, suggesting that a championship winning tandem is somehow less than a championship winning individual; the golden age of career tag teams seems to have long since faded away without fear of reprise. They are, today, much more of a rarity in the western hemisphere.

Philosophies as deeply rooted as this one now are, of course, too complex to be attributed to a single point of origin. #66 is by no means such a thing, but it definitely evidences the one feud to which the majority of others of the same ilk are compared. The Rockers' split was a watershed moment if not a genesis, and has led to a pervading, widening series of ideas that have reduced tag team wrestling to the state of a second class citizen within the minds of a great many fans. If that diminished state is the post-modern reaction to the modernised golden age of tag wrestling in WWE's Golden Age of Hulkamania, Americana and MTV, then it is an ugly one.

#65
Kurt Angle vs. The Rock vs. Undertaker
Triple Threat Match
Undisputed Championship
Vengeance
July 21st, 2002

WWE's influence as a force for change, adaptation and progression stretches far and reaches deep. It has not come to effect only foundational ideas, but has played a major role in the popularisation of active methodologies as well.

WWE, through its influence, helps to bring into mainstream thought ideas that can be deployed in almost any kind of match; some of those ideas are good, others not so much. A good example of the latter is the increasingly saturating method laid bare in the example of #65: deploying a deplorably lengthy sequence of signature and finishing moves, each followed by a near fall / kick-out, to generate a less creatively achieved, if no less potent drama.

#65 shows, quite clearly, that when this tactic is relied on too heavily - when it constitutes anything more than a closing sequence - it becomes a problem. Why? It means there's nothing *there.* Sure, it'll get the same reaction as the greatest and most complex story ever told, maybe even a bigger one, but it will also get praise heaped on it that other, more cerebral and mature compositions will not. #65 is an example of where the story just about has a beginning, definitely has an end, but doesn't really have anything else.

When you think of The Rock, Undertaker and Kurt Angle, you think of an unbridled amount of talent. So when you put those three names together and add the Undisputed Championship to the fold, you would think that the result would be an incredible thrill ride and a match capable of standing head and shoulders above most others in all of history. Some do indeed call this one of the best triple threat matches of all-time. I cannot agree.

The action remains pretty upbeat but incredibly simplistic given the level of talent involved, with all three limiting themselves largely to strikes. Anything more is disappointingly absent so, while still entertaining, the clash doesn't become quite as engaging as the effort put forth by #80's Triple H, Benoit and Michaels outing.

The Rock first uses a Chokeslam on Undertaker followed by an Ankle Lock on Angle. In turn, the sequence is followed quickly by Angle hitting The Rock with a Rock Bottom. The Undertaker soon enough floors Angle with an Angle Slam and the cringe-worthy self-awareness prevails for the remaining duration. All this within the first ten minutes; is it tongue-in-cheek wit or creative malaise?

The fall interruptions are timed with precision, but just as you dare hope for some tertiary interaction, the story reverts to the Triple Threat's originally prevailing method of rotating bodies in and out to keep the structure limited to one against one. Still, it does continue making time for everyone to start hitting everyone else with their own finishing moves again. True, there is something to be said for the method of which I am so critical: the action is fast and furious and the crowd is clearly enjoying it. As a matter of fact, so quickly do the twists and turns come that you can tell JR is struggling to keep up on commentary. The remissive attitude is inescapable even in light of these positives, though.

As the match progresses, it becomes increasingly evident that there is little story running through the larger discourse. Between the finishing moves, there's a lot of brawling and little of anything other. Even Angle's splash of red seems entirely random, done as if obligated to, lacking impact. In the latter most stages, JR is proclaiming the matter a dog fight but, quite frankly, the content is so water thin and the psychology so insubstantial that, in its worst moments, the bout barely constitutes artistic. In the third act, more false finish is rolled out as we witness ironic Angle Slams and ironic Sharpshooters, ironic Last Rides and ironic Ankle Locks. As we close on the finish, there is a nice sequence that finally shows some creativity as Rock counters an Ankle Lock into a victory roll and Angle misses a clothesline, running straight into a Chokeslam. That three-cog whir is the kind of substance warranted in its expectation given the three talents on hand. Sadly, it stands as a fairly isolated incident.

As a method, the extended exchange of finishers and signatures offers immediate satisfaction and a sense of escalatory drama, but on repeat viewings loses its magic. It doesn't grab like it may have done on the first time viewed. The best art – even just good art – does not need the mitigating circumstance of "A Moment" to succeed; it is timeless. In the same sense, the best professional wrestling matches should rightfully never age and remain infinitely re-watchable. #65 is not.

The drama of these kinds of matches is predicated upon a single facet: the fans' knowledge that a finishing move is traditionally *supposed* to finish a match. When someone kicks out, it therefore becomes "dramatic." Execute that ten times over in the space of five or so minutes and modern audiences will proclaim the work a masterpiece, it seems. An excessive surplus of near falls wrought by excessive deployment of finishers, however, is not substitute for complex storytelling.

Unfortunately, this opinion may be considered a minority opinion today. The method, that in the case of #65 is so brazen it is off-putting, is increasingly becoming the first port of call in today's professional wrestling to build drama. More and more, the industry plays off of traditional beliefs to generate artificial quick buzzes; it then smothers the work with those quick buzzes until nuance is suffocated entirely. The kind of matches wrestled by the likes of the New Generation in the 1990s – matches that would as often finish on something other than a finishing move – feel like a rarity more now than ever. Use and subsequent over-use of these extended exchanges of finisher mars the work of even the most talented professional wrestlers in the world – as it does so obviously with #65 – and has transcended long ago the status of habit to become a phenomenon.

It is not impossible to live with this phenomenon. Perhaps it possesses an expedient appeal necessary to ensure channels aren't changed by casual fans. It certainly requires much less patience that slower burning, longer building efforts demand; efforts today often criticised by fan bases as being "too slow." It cannot, however, create depth, nuance or the subtle touch. It is a heavily content-driven idea that may function effectively in more content-driven styles of professional wrestling – on the independent circuit perhaps, or the hyper-reality of puroresu – but in a company priding itself on storytelling, shouting in superlatives for extended periods of time fails to convince. #65 is the embodiment of an approach growing in frequency and popularity that talks much but says little.

Were it deployed rarely and only on grand occasion, it would work beautifully, allowing the creation of a unique sort of verbosity. Now, though, the method is employed with little discerning, as liable to be witnessed in television bouts as it is WrestleMania main events, homogenising in-ring approaches and rendering matches strong in their moment impotent with the passage of time.

It is a difficult idea to attribute to any specific genesis point. As early as WrestleMania VII, Randy Savage and Ultimate Warrior were travelling this road. While it may be unclear whether WWE started this post-modern reaction perhaps generated by the heady mix of increasing industry transparency and the frenetic tone that came screaming out of the latter end of the Attitude Era, it is very clear that they have most certainly exacerbated it. Just as the post-modern tag team in WWE has been denigrated to a means rather than an end, the post-modern match has reduced finishing moves to exactly the same. Finishing moves rarely these days seem to finish, and signature moves act only as cue cards and crowd prompts, threatening to script audience response as much as the show itself.

Both these phenomena are indicative of the post-modern, fully self-aware state professional wrestling now exists in. This is lived with rather quite willingly by most, which is ultimately the curiosity at the heart of this book's suggested shift in reception: in a post-modern industry, why does popular and critical reception still strive to remain distinctly pre-modern?

Chapter 10

Ego in Professional Wrestling

#64
Hulk Hogan vs. Shawn Michaels
Summerslam
August 21st, 2005

Matches like #64 are the intangible moments you live for as a wrestling fan; the excitement on commentary, the nervous tension in the crowd, the flash photography. After all, Hulk Hogan and Shawn Michaels truly is a dream pairing. The still active and much loved Shawn Michaels would challenge the retired but nostalgically sought after Hulk Hogan and, much like with The Rock three years earlier, time would come to a halt as generations collided.

The announcers playing up the names both men have defeated allows the big fight feel of this Summerslam main event to grow exponentially, as references made to beating the Undertaker, chopping down Vader and slamming André the Giant generate historical weight and give the match the sheer scale that it has when considering the body of work the two performers involved had crafted. Radically different as they may be, in both their instances they remain hugely influential.

The action in this one is limited, but any criticism levelled at lack of variety is excused by the classical psychology. The size differential is highlighted from start to finish and in various ways, becoming the composition's central realistic attribute. Michaels comes off as appropriately tenacious, which plays right into the hands of the familiar Hulk Hogan formula, and the blade job is used not just for the addition of blood, but to help even the playing field in favour of the Heartbreak Kid. Michaels can thus beat down a man much bigger than he is convincingly and with the acceptance of the viewer.

That beat down is the piece's highest accolade. The success of the Hulk Up as a storytelling tool is always directly relative to the quality of the beat down preceding it. The more intense and emotional that beat down, the more intense and emotional the Hulk Up becomes, hence why HBK cutting off the initial comeback is a brilliant touch and something rarely seen (if seen at all). It's a great set up for the coming finish and is the point at which the match reaches the next level that dream matches require so as not to become disappointing. It allows Michaels to extend the beat down with a transformative brutality. Seeing the great, powerful American hero reduced to a bloody, limping mess with pained expressions riddling his features is very striking, precisely because of the post-modern castration of the first Hulk Up. Hogan's old age does nothing but seem to add to the atmosphere too. Michaels beats on him and beats on him and beats on him, using submissions, foreign objects and every trademark and finishing move in his arsenal, all without attempting the pin fall. It lacks only an evil rubbing of hands to signify conclusion.

The resulting Hulk Up belongs in a dream match. The crowd goes crazy, Hogan goes crazy, everything begins to feel like a genuine adrenaline rush and it's hard not to get sucked in despite the modern judgments one can levy at the Hulkster.

Giving credit where it's due, Hogan actually performs admirably given his age and, if this had been his One More Match, it would have been a great way to bow out. In addition, Michaels puts on his usual sterling performance.

He portrays obnoxious well, as if he hadn't missed a beat since 1997.

In terms of it being a dream bout, it doesn't carry the same weight in star power that Hogan vs. The Rock did or that Hogan vs. Austin could have, but if you view it exclusively in terms of both men's respective industry redefinitions, it's perhaps unbeatable.

On the one hand, because the result wouldn't affect anything in any way, it stands apart from any time, era or periodisation. It is an event unto itself. As a result, the more time that passes since it took place, the more its magic and its prestige is added to. Its general contextual irrelevance is what ensures its standing as a memorial. Unfortunately, this also means its uses are none. #64 is not so much historical as it is mythical, the problem with myths being they count for little. The Rock, when he defeated Hulk Hogan, cemented his position as a legend for the ages. The intention was the same when John Cena beat The Rock some eleven years later, though to middling critical success. Even if the practical achievements of both efforts can be debated and disagreed upon, the symbolism of both count for a great deal. It is much more difficult to know what to make of Michaels vs. Hogan, especially happening at the point in time it did.

Most importantly, however, this match, despite being thoroughly enjoyable, is nevertheless paradoxically a debacle and a prime example of how ego can unduly affect the finalised product offered to the fans for their entertainment. Many know, of course, the rumours of Hogan escaping a rematch and return loss. We know the fact that Michaels deliberately over sells the offense of his opponent. We know there were politics and those politics leaked out into the ring. Is Hogan to blame? Is Michaels to blame? Are they both to blame? It doesn't matter. The point is animosity bred from ego unduly altered the product being sold. Though it may be a vein, perhaps even arrogant assertion, as the audience one would like to think our enjoyment would be the top priority of those performing, given we've surrendered money to watch their work; thus, dragging ego into the ring strikes as an unprofessional turn of events.

Luckily, the over-selling works in the situation, creating an accidental element of entertainment. Luckily, because of the positions both men occupied within the industry at the time, the lack of a pro-Michaels rematch did no harm whatsoever then, nor does no harm in retrospect either. Luckily, because of the unique position the bout is in, it perhaps does *more* good that they never had a return bout.

Nonetheless, #64 is the first of two examples in this chapter of how performers' egos have the capacity to unfortunately mar the experience of fans that paid hard-earned money for a good time. Professional wrestling, by the very nature of its unspoken hierarchical attitude, breeds ego and even our sentimental personal favourites might act in a questionable manner, if the stories fans hear are to be believed; we must always take them with a requisite pinch of salt of course. Nevertheless, there are times when the ego is undeniably present. #64 is such a time. It is therefore important to learn how best to pre-empt events mitigated by egotism from recurring.

Such is the lesson part-taught by the crashing and burning of #63.

#63
Brock Lesnar vs. Goldberg
Special Guest Referee: Stone Cold Steve Austin

WrestleMania XX
March 14th, 2004

For #63, the company booked two mega-stars to clash in a match that we were told by Vince McMahon could not even be controlled by the Air Force. On the one hand was Goldberg, the freshest and most popular new star to emerge with a World title out of a company riddled with the rheumatic joints of the 1980s. On the other was Brock Lesnar, a man who enjoyed a similar meteoric rise to superstardom by racking up victories over the likes of Hogan, Rock, Undertaker and Big Show within his first half year. Both were known for their incredible strength, intensity and decimation of opponents. Like #64 then, this was no doubt a dream match. It was built slowly and effectively with seeds scattered as early as the preceding Survivor Series, developed further at the Royal Rumble, reached boiling point at No Way Out before boiling over completely heading into the big one. With the inclusion of Steve Austin as a Special Guest Referee, you had the makings of a show stealing classic. What we got was a show killing farce.

Notable by its absence is crowd reaction as Lesnar makes his entrance. The apathy felt by fans towards a man they knew was leaving soon, especially in the midst of a savvy MSG crowd, is immediately apparent. Goldberg receives a slightly better reception, but one still noticeably lesser than what had come to be expected.

"Sell out" chants start from the very beginning thanks to neither man looking particularly interested in doing anything. The apathy felt by fans quickly turns to hostility, the two combatants getting a unanimous reaction. Professional wrestling fans feel spurned easily and, when one does nothing to endear oneself to them, that individual can definitely expect to feel their verbal wrath.

After minutes of nothing, things finally begin with a tie up and they jostle strength for advantage. Roughly ten minutes in, the two revert to the old clichéd exchange of shoulder blocks, in some ways comparable to the Warrior / Hogan match only with the fan investment completely flipped, the crowd not wanting either one to win. As the bout progresses – or rather as the bout should but fails to progress – there is a growing sense that there was not a great deal of interest from either man.

JR says it best, naming it pedestrian. The whole bout whiffs of indifference: from the wrestlers, the fans, even the action. The composition is void of drama. Best described as an irritating necessity of a match for those involved, it's a mercy by the time it finishes and Austin acts as the voice of the fans both in attendance and at home by giving the two men a Stunner for their troubles.

#63 is a testament to everything pro wrestling should not be: ignorant of the fans. Importantly, beyond the immediate circumstances surrounding the match's occurrence that no doubt played a major factor in why it unravelled the way it did, there is also possibly a wider issue at hand that one needs to dig a little deeper to uncover; a problem that has certainly bitten Vince McMahon and his company back more than once in the past, both before and after this event, and which is found in the early careers of both Lesnar and Goldberg.

"Superman" is a comparison thrown around a lot among the more cynically thinking fan bases and usually gets directed at those being portrayed as what might be considered too strongly. It is something of a pointless observation. When you look back on the history of the company's approach to their top tier title, most of the time it is around the waist of a top babyface; and if you're a top babyface in WWE, you are protected. It is a phenomenon not limited to today, stretching all the way back to Hogan and with the only really notable, sustained exception to the rule having been Triple H's runs in the Attitude and early Brand Extension Eras. The problem described with the term "Superman booking" is not just a problem after the push has happened, though; it is a problem in need of pre-empting before the push even begins.

When a guy is presented in an unstoppable manner, be it as hero or villain, and when he is written consistently as the pinnacle of the company over a prolonged period of time, and then a day comes when he has to deal with the fact he is no longer the pinnacle, it's going to dent the ego; that's only human. In professional wrestling, when such a day dawns things can become rather messy. How long did the stories, be they true or not, of the Ultimate Warrior - whose very name was designed to set him above everyone else - holding the company up for money the night of a pay-per-view dog the memory of the man? How many stories are there of some kind of Hogan politick designed to keep him on top? How many times have you heard about a 90s HBK throwing a temper tantrum, or read rumours of Triple H using his influence to deny younger talent a share of glory? Remember when Austin "took his ball and went home" or when CM Punk complained he wasn't being given his due by a company that gave him the longest title reign in twenty-five years? These are just the tip of the iceberg.

They might come off as presumptuous for any fan to discuss, but the degrees of truth or falsehood in these rumours are entirely beside the point, as is whether any of this played directly or otherwise into #63 or not. Rather, the lesson lies in the truth behind those rumours' mere *existence*: if you write a character to be invincible, could it be that eventually the man who plays the character might just start believing he should be? WWE has shown that it absolutely loves making people look like Supermen from the off, never seeming to learn. Not even from #63.

"Superman booking" isn't just tedious and emotionally obscure, but loaded with dangerous potential to massively backfire later down the line in one form or another, directly or by extension. Sadly, despite the stark warnings of the negative effect ego has, and the kind of treatment that does nothing but propagate such egos in the first place, WWE are liable to continue on with the same approach with some of the next big dogs of the yard. Hopefully they will remember that, when it comes to ego in professional wrestling, for the sake of the fans more so than anyone, it pays dividends to always tread lightly.

Chapter 11

Continuity in Professional Wrestling

#62
Bret "Hitman" Hart vs. Diesel
WWF Championship
Royal Rumble
January 22nd, 1995

As this chapter will show, continuity is conducive to greater success in professional wrestling – for long-term story; for character; for the world-building needed to create the "shared universe" utilised so well, at times, by WWE's Reality Era, and suited so well for the performance art theory of professional wrestling posited in this book.

The example offered by #62 to prove this claim takes the form of characterisation, here for both the Hitman and Diesel. Characterisation plays such an utterly vital role in making this bout the quiet classic it is; a match that pretty much gets nothing wrong, building off past events to better contextualise the present action and hint at an exciting, wild and unpredictable – though, importantly, not inexplicable – future course of events.

Heading into this bout, the feud had been pushed as a Hitman absolutely hell bent on regaining the belt he unfairly lost months prior. He upped the intensity and, as a result, Diesel upped his belligerence in retaliation. The result is an *incredibly* competitive match with a big fight feel generated brilliantly by McMahon on commentary as he contextualises the unstoppable force of Diesel's momentum – the only man to have won the WWF, Intercontinental and Tag Team Championships inside of a year - and the immovable object of Hart's drive – the first man, we are told, to have ever won the "Triple Double."

Within *seconds,* Hart amps up the tension when he goes for Diesel's leg, ignoring a rope break, shoving the champion and being the first man to use a clenched fist. He also begins cooking up a Sharpshooter in the early goings, using the ring post and transitioning into familiar sequences often unseen until a good fifteen minutes into a Hitman match. Essentially, this is a famed marathon runner coming in at a heavy sprint, evidencing Hart's intense expedience and singular focus while putting over just how high stakes a WWF Championship match really is.

It's quite an ingenious approach for the competitors, a tenacious effort from both men that shows off their best assets to their fullest potential. Oddly enough, Hart takes a cue from Perfect's borderline morality seen in #99's King of the Ring semi-final encounter. Hart's matches with Diesel often saw him showcase a more aggressive and edgier side of his character's personality. That's most evident in this outing especially, using the ring post as a weapon, refusing to break holds on rope breaks, tying Diesel's legs around the ring post and even introducing a steel chair. Such actions feel an organic evolution of the storyline – again, it's about Hart's aggressive drive to recapture the title, regardless of what it takes to do that. It's fascinating to observe Hart increasingly devolve into morally objectionable territory as the match goes on, until, by the lead into the finish, he's outwardly behaving like a villain.

The really brilliant thing about taking that kind of character progression and making it the focus of a title match is that it promotes Diesel as a seriously tough competitor. Here is a former two-time World Champion, arguably the biggest star in the company at that time, throwing absolutely everything he has with unheard of aggression at an essentially still fresh-faced champion…and the champion takes every bit of it before responding in kind.

There's a merciless cruelty to this composition that makes it feel putridly, violently competitive. Every time Diesel tries to get some breathing room, Hart - in the face of admonishment from the official - simply jumps right back on him. Similarly, Diesel evidences anger in his execution that would later manifest as a villainous turn following his loss at Survivor Series. As Hart relishes his aggression, Diesel seems to relish every single power move he executes, be it a simple strike or a stiff slam; his power was always the focus of his matches with the Hitman, but here it's more than just a superficial psychology.

The realism compels. Credibility is lent by treading that line of increased intensity without ever becoming frenzied. Whereas some wrestlers allow increased intensity to devolve into over choreographed set-pieces or melodramatic expressions, here champion and challenger maintain an even pace with timely escalation. The action is creative but realistic, and its execution is where the magic lies: confident, purposeful and, rather like the characterisation on show, focussed. The changes to both men's styles and the pervasive undertone are found in subtle nuances, not in galling overtures. Much like Undertaker and Angle in #67's No Way Out 2006 main event, Bret and Diesel stack this encounter with endless variety, forging a free-flowing epic. It's exhausting to watch and structured in a manner to make the viewer conscious of its duration. Altogether, #62 is a darkly beautiful myriad of power, speed, grit and ill will.

The interference run from Michaels, Owen Hart and Backlund would usually dampen affairs and scream of the kind of over-booked nonsense that once plagued the product. However, given the wider tone of the event, they instead simply help to thicken the *venom* that this match is dripping with. There's a surreal aura to events, a brooding atmosphere of bitterness and frustration that is so well crafted it threatens to infect. When the three illegal assailants descend on the action, it's hard not to be immersed in the rabidity and start barking at the screen for everyone to kick the daylights out of everyone else. The effect is frightening.

Everything that happens compliments everything else as it should. It's certainly tempting to proclaim it unfortunate that there's no solid finish, but it is tonally fitting. Listen to the words announced by The Fink when the match is thrown out: the official is unable to maintain control. That's not just a disqualification because of interference but rather because everything from the opening bell on watches as a snowballing escalation of events until, finally, enough was enough. Such a lack of a more solid finish may be the bout's most pertinent lesson.

Hart and Diesel met several times across 1994 and 1995, their feud eventually culminating in a No Holds Barred encounter that was as exhausting and as cold blooded as #62 eventually proved to be. Diesel's turn following his loss at Survivor Series would, in the traditional sports entertainment view, be received by fans in terms of its use and qualitatively judged in terms of its sense as "a booking move" – a move informed by the required logistical utility of a professional wrestling promotion. Taking this view makes the continuity harder to marry up and easier to criticise as inconsistent, considering the meetings Diesel and Hart had in the past.

Take the alternative performance art view though. Diesel's actions should rather just be seen as his character's heated reaction to the frustration of having been finally and indisputably bested by a veteran he had twice before taken to the limit in disparate instances in the past, all heightened by the hostile environment that any meeting of Hart and Diesel's characters always generated. Hart vs. Diesel was not an on-again-off-again feud with its own internal cause and effect, as would be tempting to label it in the orthodox take on professional wrestling. Rather, it was a series of three unrelated, different encounters between two intriguing characters from a single, shared universe that would eventually culminate in a moment informed not by their previous meetings or future feuds, but by the characterisation previously established through #62's conclusion. In simpler terms: because of unrelated, established continuity, not because of the nature of a single feud, Diesel reacted as his character demanded, and Hart his, to a specific set of circumstances regardless of who was involved.

It is a simpler, I dare say more accomplished method with clear application for WWE's shared universe.

#61
Hunter Hearst Helmsley vs. Shawn Michaels
European Championship
Monday Night Raw
December 22nd, 1997

Continuity has as many practical applications as it does creative ones and, as important as it is for character and story to have an acceptable level of canonical adherence, it is just as important that their motivation remain consistent in portrayal too. I am referring, of course, to the professional wrestling championship.

The concept of the championship is untouched, regardless of whether you take the traditional or the performance art view of professional wrestling. As either a sporting championship or narrative MacGuffin, a belt must be treated with appropriate reverence inside of the fiction. In this abhorrently must-see car-crash of a match, Michaels and Helmsley achieved one positive thing: showing exactly how *not* to treat a championship. At a base level, #61 is how one can devalue a championship in just four succinct minutes. It is another slice of WWE history that stands as a learning curve.

Instead of the great match they could have performed - the match JR and Cornette are making up for the viewer on commentary – what occurs is an obnoxious exercise in self-gratifying mockery. There's a collar and elbow tie-up which sees Michaels go down in Fingerpoke of Doom style, before Hunter runs the ropes and a three count follows. That's it. JR groans as it unfolds and Cornette seemingly breaks his own character, openly referring to them both as jackasses despite the fact that, as the heel colour commentator, he should surely be siding with the bad guys. The sense of irritation from the booth is palpable. As if the actions of D-Generation X weren't bad enough in robbing the viewer of a potentially great match, they proceed to continue their ingratiating actions by hamming it up afterwards, pretending to cry and be lost for words.

As many great things as professional wrestling can give us, there are just as many negatives. Professional wrestling is a delicate beast, as is continuity, and a single slip can tarnish and destroy the hard work of innumerable individuals. These miserly four minutes is an example of how to deconstruct a championship and how to bankrupt a MacGuffin of merit and worth. The European Championship provided a nice set-piece for any time the company found itself overseas in the titular continent. It was created and awarded through a spectacular tournament in early 1997 and had, until #61, been carried only by the likes of Bulldog and Heartbreak. In short, it had been constructed with reverence. Here, Michaels and Helmsley made themselves a driving force behind a four minute effort to tear down that hard work and shatter the positive, weighty continuity lent the belt.

By failing to treat the championship held up in this instance with the right amount of reverence, what D-Generation X manage to do is publicly affirm the idea that a championship is just a prop. This "match" is, thus, a reminder to WWE that their titles need to be treated properly; in other words, that a continuity of value is adequately maintained.

The problem is that creating such continuity is a long, sometimes arduous process. It takes time and a lot of hard work and effort to forge. Take the European Championship's closest cousin, the Intercontinental title. Many see it as having long lost its majority value as an accomplishment worth admiring, but consider how that value was created in the first place: through hard-fought matches between hard-working individuals that made every one of their title bouts look like they were the most important matches of their careers. Whether it was Randy Savage, Mr Perfect, Bret Hart, Shawn Michaels, Razor Ramon, Chris Jericho, Chris Benoit, Rey Mysterio or Dolph Ziggler, these were performers willing to make that championship look like it meant as much to them as the World title did to others. It was their epic classics and their reaction to wins and losses that created the belt's revered reputation. Of course, the longer this continuity of value lasted, the more the matches engrossed fans; and the more that matches engrossed, the heavier the championship's value to the characters vying for it was implied. It was a self-perpetuating process, as is its opposite.

Had DX decided to actually give the fans a timeless iteration of the untapped heel vs. heel genre (like the one that Edge and Orton created in #93), the European Championship may now enjoy an entirely different memory.

As a championship, it was anything but memorable. And why should it be? As early as its third champion, the title already became a joke – a statement that is meant literally, not passionately. #61 was more than likely intended as levity but that Michaels and Helmsley didn't want to actually wrestle to hold the belt seemingly implies that being able to call yourself European Champion means little; so go the narrative repercussions. If it was a grand achievement, surely Michaels wouldn't be so comfortable to lie down and ostensibly forfeit without concern, and surely Helmsley wouldn't be quite so ready to patronise the meaning of victory? And if it didn't mean anything to them, the characters vying for it, why should it mean anything to the audience?

Though performance art would posit that championships are merely plot devices to set a narrative into motion, for that idea to function effectively still requires the characters chasing that championship to act as if it has value *to them*; that this does not occur with #61 means not even the best interpretive efforts seem able to redeem it.

Without value and without merit, nothing about a title is memorable - not its champions, not their reigns and rarely their matches. For the longest time, this was a major concern. Fortunately, WWE has historically taken steps towards trying to re-forge some of the lost value in certain championships at appropriate times. Take, for the most obvious example, their top prize. The combining of both the World Heavyweight and WWE Championships in 2013 narrowed the field at the top of the roster and helped reintroduce a need to ruthlessly compete for a spot in the main event, rather than talent simply waiting a turn for the company to experiment with you as so often seemed to be the case during the Brand Extension. Then, placing that championship on the part-time Brock Lesnar in 2014 catapulted the WWE World Heavyweight Championship to the status of a serious mega-attraction; if familiarity breeds contempt, rarity breeds excitement. Also, the multiplicity of gold that was such a strong staple of the Brand Extension Era dissipated a great deal as the Reality Era grew - as rarity breeds excitement, scarcity breeds value.

The story of the European Championship should be all the impetus needed to avoid the mistakes of devaluing of championships through unprofessionalism, surplus or over-exposure. CM Punk, as WWE Champion, would often say it wasn't a belt he held but a championship title; Michaels and Helmsley managed, through the devolving effect of #61, to ensure that the European Championship wasn't a championship title but just a belt, simply because they acted as if they didn’t care.

#60
Owen Hart vs. British Bulldog
WWF European Championship
Monday Night Raw
Recorded February 26th, 1997

To undo the hard work put forth in #60 should be a crime. Another quiet classic, #60 is the antithesis to the preceding entry; the proof of how a promotion should, I believe, treat all championships, whether we take sports entertainment or performance art as our approach. #60 is the coda in need of deploying consistently to accrue the appropriate continuity of value for championships to feel a warranted driving force of both character and story. It is another "How to."

When you look at the artistry of #60 with a close and attentive eye, it possesses an intimidating deluge of worth. It is difficult to analyse and avoid making the inevitable comparisons to Bret's bouts with Bulldog, but actually that's not always a bad thing. The Intercontinental title match at Summerslam '92 is undeniably one of the all-time greats, but crucially leans heavily on its impressive content. #60 is a relation of sorts, but it's a far more cerebral affair that goes to prove both Bulldog and Owen together could write as affectingly as their more renowned relation.

An action-packed and hard-fought match with a lengthy duration would have alone made the European Championship look cared about by the fictional characters and something worth fighting for. Owen and Bulldog refused to stop at that level, though. Instead, they create an emotional resonance, a contextual relevancy to the championship that not only increases the title's own emotional importance while allowing it to slot immediately and seamlessly into the company's wider continuity. Most of this admittedly works only on a subconscious level, but that's precisely why it's so important to highlight, as well as precisely why this match is such a master-stroke.

The action is pretty standard, though the aesthetic is as smooth as you could imagine and the moves on show are impressive, even if they remain usual. The strengths of this opus don't lie in its physical content; the value of this match lies in its subtext. These two artists make you work for the reward, the result of which is a more engaging physical dialogue than has been seen from any comparable, higher profile encounter.

To make the obvious contrast to those famous Bulldog / Bret matches, in the opening ninety seconds the two go right to work setting this match apart from the undeniable fame of those earlier affairs. Whereas Bret often played the technician to Davey's power, what we get here is duelling displays of agility. While feeling slightly choreographed, that early chess game helps establish a foundation upon which the two go on to build their encounter. Lest we forget these two were bickering Tag Team Champions at the time – creating a complex dichotomy - and so we get the traditional angle of one-upmanship between closely matched partners. Note how such previously established depth to the background of this tournament final – growing personal animosity between familial tag partners - lends further substance to its action.

The opening act shows knowledge of how to effectively foreshadow, touching on the tones that the authors intend to weave in and out of the rest of the duration. The aforementioned displays of agility are followed by your usual stalemate, which transitions into the two finally mentioning Bulldog's power, with a test of strength seeing Owen bent in an impressively steady bridge. Not only that, but Owen tells the audience how that strength differential will be combated: through dizzying displays of gymnastic capability. The sequences through which these two lay all this out are far from over-stated.

The foundational construction continues as the two then begin playing on the deeper complexities of the set-up, with

Bulldog allowing Owen back into the ring off the slingshot and, importantly, not taking advantage of it, as an outright villain might. In three minutes, the two combatants inform us that they're evenly matched, they evidence for us the methodology they intend to follow - playing to one another's best strengths - and finally emphasise the unique background to this particular tournament final. There is no chain wrestling done because that's what lengthy matches should start like but rather different approaches utilised for specific storytelling purposes, all of which add substance.

Patience is a factor too, and any viewer needs a little to enjoy this affair as much as possible. The pace does become methodical, but the intrigue involved and the psychological complexity of its make-up is enough to cover up that one arguable flaw. Everything is as important as everything else. The pace is smooth, the tempo constant and the whole story fully fleshed out. Nor is the finish too sudden either and you can feel them constructing it as early as the fifteen minute mark. The high impact moves become more frequent; so frequent, in fact, that they develop into the match's norm for the closing act, establishing a legacy of realism that compliments everything that comes before. The actual final pin fall is, in itself, a suitable inversion of the final pin fall between Bret and Bulldog back at Wembley; a fan pleasing touch of historical irony.

This is, in a lot of ways, a match that enjoys making emotional and cerebral demands from its viewer and, when watched with brain engaged, is even more rewarding an experience than the far more famous Intercontinental Championship match from Summerslam 1992. Its profile is much smaller and its legacy far less celebrated, but relative to what each match *needed* to achieve this is inarguably the most indulgently successful of the pair.

The reason for the increased focus on content in this review is the same as to why it was included. There is as much artistry to this match in the traditional view as there is in the performance art view taken by this book. That is a fitting accomplishment. As the value of championships is an important common ground of sports entertainment and performance art theories alike, the match selected to best evidence how to generate such value is an incredible common ground too. To see a composition so unashamed to consider itself as important as arguably the greatest Intercontinental Championship match of all-time that headlined the biggest Summerslam of all-time, despite being recorded ahead of time and taking place only on a Monday Night Raw, is a labour of love all championships require.

To see two notable stars lay out their arsenal and capability so exhaustively for the prize of a newly minted European Championship is a self-validating method: the effort creates the very aura around the prize that allows the prize to explain the supremacy of the effort. As a foundation for a championship, it goes to great pains to provide stability and trust that this prize is one worthy of repute because the characters are shown, through their exacting performances, to genuinely care about winning it. In contrast to the criminal levity of #61, the maturity on show in this instance is admirable, disallowing room for *any* degree of dismissal or contempt to show through, no matter how slight.

Chapter 12

Memory in Professional Wrestling

#59
William Regal vs. Christian
ECW Championship
ECW
November 10th, 2009

The place was Sheffield, the city in which I was living. The year was 2009, the beginning of my third and final as a University student. News broke earlier in the year that the WWE's traditionally annual Autumnal UK tapings would be occurring in the Steel City's Motorpoint Arena that November and, needless to say, the stars had aligned perfectly. Tickets were purchased, my best friend visited from Loughborough and, soon enough, one packed tram ride later on a cold November night we were being encouraged to cheer as loud as possible for the evening's opening pyro. It was the night Chris Jericho wrestled The Undertaker for the very first time, and I am able to say I was there live when that happened. In our section of the throngs situated on the floor directly behind the announcers (thirteen rows back to be exact), the combating chants of "Let's go Jericho!" and "Let's go 'Taker!" never let up. When Kane eventually emerged to save his big brother from a JeriShow shaped beat-down, the roof almost came off, I swear. It was an incredible evening of which that historic meeting of legends was only the highlight.

I say "the highlight," but perhaps a more apt phrase would be "a highlight."

It should be said that part of the reason for the crowd's apparent exhaustion during the main event of Smackdown that week might be the ECW taping that came first, headlined by #59. The electricity that surged through that same crowd when our home grown own, William Regal, looked to represent Queen and Country was powerful enough to make hairs stand on end. The entire arena hung off of every move and, even though the pond may have been comparatively small, this was Great Britain's greatest having a go at that small pond's biggest fish. Regardless of any lack of stature, the reaction to this match in that building on that night was as if they were contesting for the WWE Championship in the main event of a WrestleMania. Every year, it seems the infamy of the idiosyncratic British passion grows, thanks in no small part to the party atmosphere of the post-'Mania Monday Night Raw, and I like to think our investment into this forgotten television bout on a largely forgotten brand is no less of a testament to why that infamy is so deserved. Christian was very much popular with sections of the crowd himself, but for obvious reasons Regal was far and away the fan favourite, with the passion of British fans voraciously taking centre stage with him.

They start off slowly, testing the waters, semantically informing the audience to settle in for the long haul. The crowd's duel chants start early, and I here proudly proclaim I was one of the men chanting for the dastardly Regal. The reason for his popularity in this instance is mainly a matter of patriotism, but it's an interesting idea to ponder how predisposed to the harder hitting style some older British fans may be because of the professional wrestling heritage in this country being so different; World of Sport is so many worlds away from what WWE is today that the expanse between the two resultant products is breathtaking. Comparing the whimsical nature of the former with the boisterous appeal of the latter is a comical comparison of British and American culture and, in my more romantic moments, I like to think that British whimsy continues to live on, at least in part, through the influence of William Regal.

While I think you can't deny the crowd are very much into the action, my personal memory is of an atmosphere more crazed. Perhaps that's my memory playing tricks; and don't expect anything ground breaking when you view it. In retrospect, it watches a good, strong television match; a highlight of the week, rather than of the year. As solidly entertaining as it is, I do not deny this is a very sentimental pick. It's a selfish inclusion to be sure, based on my own personal experience of the match.

It is such incongruity with my memory – in this instance but also with the Smackdown main event wrestled much later that night – that begins our inspection of memory's various guises in professional wrestling. Memory is an important element to the professional wrestling industry, being as it is an industry passed down from generation to generation through a series of cultural conceits. Whether through the guise of reverence or prestige, contempt or cliché, tradition, the unspoken rule or any given reputation, professional wrestling relies on memory a great deal to fuel its continued existence. This chapter will now take a look at some of the more predominant roles memory plays.

The skewing effect of my personal memory of the show perhaps mars any ability to execute a relatively dispassionate analysis of #59. On this occasion, that is no bad thing. It is a phenomenon experienced by the majority of fans lucky enough to attend a live event. For example, I have spoken to a number of fans who attended the lamentable WrestleMania 29 and all of them share an absence of the malice felt so profusely by huge swathes of the television audience. For some of those in attendance, the night was a magical one. That is because attending a professional wrestling show live – be it WWE or a local promotion in a sorry looking school gymnasium, as the cliché goes – is a strong reminder of why the addiction to wrestling shared by both life-long fans and successful talents develops in the first place: professional wrestling is *fun*, and a kind of fun against which nothing compares, nor can hope to compete.

And more powerful than the live experience is the romanticising memory of that experience; an overwhelmingly seductive narcotic if ever there has been one. Perhaps memories are what keep us fans coming back for more. Perhaps memories are what keep some talents active much longer than they have any right to be. Certainly such memories skew analyses like this one, which is precisely why they are such a vital aspect of the industry's character; a spiritual truth, if we were to be poetic, that cuts right at the heart of the matter. Professional wrestling: it is no forgettable thing.

#58
Shawn Michaels vs. Chris Jericho
WrestleMania XIX
March 30th, 2003

Since 2003, Shawn Michaels has encountered a wide variety of opponents at WrestleMania, which includes the biggest names in professional wrestling history, let alone WWE. At 'Mania alone, here we have a man who has wrestled Chris Jericho, Triple H, Chris Benoit, Kurt Angle, Vince McMahon, John Cena, Ric Flair and The Undertaker in a year by year stretch. That list is made up of some of the single most influential and contested figures in the history of the company and the industry as a whole. All of the matches have presented us with a memorable encounter to go down in the history books, but #58 may just be the best of the bunch.

The structure has all the marks of two men who understand how wrestling works best. The spurts of action come at all the right times and last all the right lengths. There's a sense of every move, every movement, every single second, mattering and helping construct the total package. Their timing could be no less perfect; the turns into moves, the jumps, the slaps; everything indicates "best in the world." There are teasers too, playing on unspoken but universal semantics; they'll telegraph a direction, counter into another, play that direction out with brevity before returning right back to the original idea (a veritable masterpiece of emotional manipulation). The eventual pin fall - a surprise from out the blue - is a wonderful finish of understated realism punctuating a flawlessly executed classic. Jericho then giving Michaels a low blow after their hug not only provides a personal favourite WrestleMania Moment of my own, but also makes the whole affair feel bittersweet. It's a beautifully told story.

If ever a match could be chosen to represent a symbolic memory of WrestleMania, this pristine affair would be a fitting choice, standing as a succinct explanation as to why Michaels earned his most famous nickname of them all – Mr. WrestleMania – and why Chris Jericho was always justified in being named the Best in the World at Everything He Does.

...well, perhaps it is not the *only* choice.

Randy Savage vs. Ricky Steamboat at WrestleMania III: expression as flawless in its execution as it is in its timing; everything about it shines and glistens. It is a beautifully crafted piece of artistry that holds up even by modern standards. What it has to do with #58 is simple.

Many say the success Savage and Steamboat wrestled with at 'Mania III could never be replicated. Many say nothing will ever better it. #58 could be seen as a parallel. The two performers involved have reputations similar to the ones Savage and Steamboat continue to enjoy in retrospect and, while there was no title on the line, it occupied a similar place on the card when you speak comparatively to the main events of the night. On a night when Hogan and McMahon clashed, when Rock and Austin tied up their trilogy and when two accomplished amateur and professional wrestlers competed in the main event for the WWE Championship, this match stole the show from right underneath all of them.

#58 is a match that should invoke clear memories of that 1987 pinnacle in any fan with a keen appreciation of success. The lack of wasted movement, the precision of execution, the palpably giddy atmosphere and the show-stealing personality recreate the spirit of the most famous Intercontinental Championship match of them all. It is these two factors that prompt me to deploy the term "spiritual sequel;" an intriguing concept with positive application.

As a shared cultural history, professional wrestling is held with exceedingly powerful sentiment, especially in a company so revisionist and obsessed with the grandeur of its past as WWE. This leads to a practically universal comparative reception of work – sometimes fairly, sometimes unfairly, sometimes for the better and sometimes for the worse. Regardless of outcome, this is a habitual trait of professional wrestling fandom. Indeed, it is one that has bled through into this very thesis which, in

Chapter Six: Judging By Past Example, actively encouraged seeking out the past for purposes exclusive to the present and future.

It is in such a sense that the comparative reception that often dogs professional wrestling exhibitions can be put to good use; a tool, in essence. Sometimes, instead of a tool, though, it can become a ghost. More specifically: a haunting. There are times when some professional wrestling bouts can be haunted by previous successes because of comparative reception. The response to Michaels' final match at WrestleMania, for example, was unfairly levied with the responsibility of living up to the reception of its direct predecessor the year before, the reception of which almost seemed to become mythical as early as the morning after. Instead of being allowed to exist as its own entity, wrestling fandom resigned itself at once to, "It won't be as good as the first."

This does not happen exclusively *before* affected matches either, but often afterward too. How much does the finishing sequence of Survivor Series 2014's Team Authority vs. Team Cena owe to the Team Austin vs. Team Bischoff bout in 2003, for example? Likewise, was the main event of WrestleMania XXVIII just a cynical attempt to recreate the timeless intangible of WrestleMania X8? Why do wrestling fans (including myself) rush to comparison whenever an obvious such comparison is apparent? That professional wrestling is no forgettable thing can easily mitigate reception to bouts that, individually, deserve the right of success in our memories, as well as a reputation unchained from that which came before.

That is not to say #58 is one such match. It is not. There is little popular comparison between it and that famous match wrestled in front of 93, 000. It is a match that enjoys a reputation all its own, but it is in its invocation of the spirit of its predecessor wherein lies an opportunity for us to combat the ill-effects of the aforementioned comparative reception professional wrestling fans are so eager to pursue.

At the heart of the matter lies the important task of defining "inspiration" as a concept in professional wrestling. This is not something quite so literal as a tribute, which should by rights be defined as a purposeful act with overt credit given to that being paid tribute. Nor is it anything as insipid as plagiarism, which should by rights be defined as a conscious copying of a previous success that refuses to recognise that being copied. Rather, it is a less concrete concept of memory: a piece of work that, while possessing clear similarities and / or exhibiting parallel traits to an event in the past, still strives to achieve its own unique success through its own unique purpose and should, therefore, by rights be afforded the opportunity to stand on its own feet as an individual idea free from comparative judgment of quality.

To simplify matters, take an example. As a group, the first version of Evolution that existed between 2003 and 2005 was clearly inspired by the exploits of the Four Horsemen. On a literal level there were, of course, four competitively active members. The presence of Ric Flair drew clear parallels. Their operations were carried out in not too dissimilar a fashion. Triple H living out 2003 as a "working champion" that was, nevertheless, the villain in a hero's world intoned the Nature Boy of the 1980s. Evolution, however, strove toward its own achievements. The name of the group was born from its theme and indicative of its purpose, all of which set it massively apart from the Horsemen. Evolution was not a modern reaction to a staple of the golden yesteryear as much as it was its own group worthy of its own recognition that drew only its *inspiration* from what had come before. It was neither tribute nor plagiarism; Evolution was the Four Horsemen's spiritual successor.

This is a principle that applies to groups, individuals, matches, even events. The heroic fairytale of Macho Man at WrestleMania IV is a spiritual successor to the villainous effort of Macho Man at The Wrestling Classic; John Cena is a spiritual successor to The Rock; Cactus Jack vs. Randy Orton a spiritual successor in form and achievement to Cactus Jack vs. Triple H. By framing memory in this third sense – not to fuel tribute or plagiarism, but inspiration – renders the more negative outcomes of the comparative reception of professional wrestling (which *will* continue) inert.

#58 may not have striven consciously to invoke the memory of Savage vs. Steamboat, but through its success it invoked that memory nonetheless without sacrificing its own ideas or identity. It is not a tribute, nor does it copy but, even if only accidentally, it remains a brilliantly entertaining, powerfully relevant example of a spiritual sequel – in this case to arguably the most influential professional wrestling match of all-time.

It is that idea of the spiritual sequel that is important to take note of; when applied to more consciously inspired efforts, it is the idea that enables us to marry up any conflict between a piece of work invoking vivid, over-powering memories of the past and a piece of work being able to maintain an individual identity free from comparisons to its inspiration, be that inspiration direct or otherwise.

#57
Mankind vs. Shawn Michaels

WWF Championship
In Your House 10: Mind Games
September 22nd, 1996

It is worth noting how excellent an effort both individuals exhibit with this precognitive attitudinal piece. The unforgiving journey pulsating at the heart of the composition is indicated no better than in the state of ringside come the final third of the match, by which point looks like an absolute warzone. It is no accident. Mankind and Michaels exert an immense amount of effort and passion to put on a show for the fans that will be remembered despite the fact that it takes place at only a run of the mill monthly pay-per-view and not one of the Big Four.

Yet, the really important factor is the way it all culminates in the interference from Vader, Undertaker and Psycho Sid. It is a conclusion highlighting the idea of a previously explored "shared universe" of WWE. Directly put: #57 is a choice based exclusively on the trend indicated by its lack of clear finish.

WWE first initiated a monthly pay-per-view series in 1995 to help combat the onslaught of WCW. The resulting concept was In Your House, providing a pay-per-view show every month outside of the then-Big Five. WWE has continued to host monthly pay-per-views ever since, despite the competition which directly led to them instituting such an idea long since fading. The market saturation that has resulted is difficult to contend. When each episode of Raw is the same length as a pay-per-view, when there are so many other shows on WWE's Network every week and when now there is 24 / 7 access to all content, storylines possess much less longevity and angles much less vitality. The result: an unbridled increase in linearity in their stories.

As the exposure of the product increased, WWE began to compartmentalise their product more and more. The artificial nature of the script was far more transparent. Sight of a larger picture narrowed. When two men feuded over a championship, that feud would run until exhausted, leading to an explosion in sequel wrestling, with the same performers clashing repeatedly over several consecutive months. The exhaustive nature of this approach also ensured a greater sense of sterility if those same two individuals one, two or however many years later down the line came to meet again. All stemming from the linear approach rested upon because of the increased prominence and availability of product, they were all massively damaging traits of the Brand Extension - especially as the era neared its expiration.

As mentioned in Chapter 11: Continuity in Professional Wrestling, however, this changed. Though the product remains as exposed as it has been for years – perhaps more so in fact – WWE re-energised their creative approach in the Reality Era with a stronger sense of "shared universe," even if stumbled upon accidentally. Especially at the time Brock Lesnar held the WWE World Heavyweight Championship and made only sporadic appearances, there was a return to the more holistic, sandbox approach to storytelling and the construction of feuds, which had been so effective during the In Your House days and is so clearly on show with the climax of #57.

During the In Your House years, there was a lack of linearity that saw feuds build off the back of longer-term personal animosity boiling away in the background, allowing championship matches to often be *exclusively* championship matches feeding into or off of larger issues. Again, this is just like #57.

In this instance, Michaels and Vader had wrestled only the previous month over the belt and had lingering personal issues, just like Mankind and The Undertaker too; so too were there lingering peripheral subplots involving Sid and Camp Cornette. All of these feuds were interwoven into the end of this championship match, which took place as an isolated quest for a legitimate, valued prize. When these moving cogs all collided together, it formed a naturalistic conclusion to a championship bout dictated by the logic of the growing narrative, feeding equally as naturally into the following pay-per-views.

WWE eventually went some way to actively executing #57's method in more recent years; they adapted rather effectively to operating a product around absentee World Champions, for example. Such is the point being driven at. This is not memory as teacher but memory as reminder, not necessarily of what WWE *should* do but rather that WWE *still can*. Storytelling is WWE's primary concern and there is a reason that WWE has become the number one professional wrestling promotion in the world. Even though there may be long stretches in the company's past, and will undoubtedly be more long stretches in its future, where we question why it is we watch their product, it is memories of bouts that exhibit the reflexive approach of the New Generation like #57 does - and memories in years to come of bouts exhibiting the shared universe ideal at the heart of the company's greatest creative stretches - that can answer such doubts.

Perhaps, more poetically, #57 is also memory as faith. Through bouts like #57, we find successes that justify the faith WWE loyalists have that WWE is the best at what they do; a faith they often come under fire for possessing. This is not exclusive to WWE of course, which remains just one example. So too will memories of WCW's grander successes justify the faith of WCW apologists, of ECW's justify the faith of ECW cultists, and so on and so forth for professional wrestling promotions of all sizes and nations throughout history and across the globe.

I am a WWE loyalist because I believe WWE do what they do better than anyone. #57 is, in its own small way, a prompt for me to keep that in mind, a representative justification of my faith if ever one is needed. Our faiths in our favoured promotions are always there for a reason and, if ever you might lose sight of that, seek out a match that is, for you, the kind of memory that reminds you just what that reason is.

#56
Eddie Guerrero vs. Chris Benoit
United States Championship
Vengeance
July 27th, 2003

The idea of tribute has been mentioned in passing and, indeed, this match was selected because of its nature as a tribute. It is a tribute to the late great Eddie Guerrero. There are few deaths that have affected professional wrestling fans quite as powerfully as Eddie's. The monochrome images of his "In Memory" video tribute, created by WWE following news of his passing, sit in the memories of all kinds of fans like a mural carved in stone. It pains greatly to think that his past, in the end, asked an impossible price of him no man could have paid. That his life touched the lives of so many across the world, though, washes any such pain away, and it was through matches as brilliant as #56 that he was able to touch those lives. As controversial as it may be, this is also a tribute to the ***career*** of Chris Benoit. His love for professional wrestling could never be in dispute and his physical masterpieces between the ropes are worthy of memorial.

You might not remember Vengeance 2003. It remains perhaps one of the most criminally under-appreciated shows of its era. Though it did admittedly have some trite nonsense on it, it started with a twenty minute tournament final for a workhorse championship between two of the greatest workhorses in the industry ever: Eddie Guerrero and Chris Benoit.

You might not remember their incredible natural chemistry so evident in #56, but they're very generous in the ring during this encounter. It is clear their first concern is to make the other guy look better. You might not remember their portrayal of such a convincing even playing field, each man having an answer for the other's questions and an ability to deploy that answer as swiftly as the question is asked; watching makes one nostalgic for the triad moves both men utilised so famously: the Triple German and Triple Vertical. You might not remember their stunning fluidity; their textbook build of tension; their explosively physical aesthetic. You might not remember #56 is an exhibition which pulsates with enthused zeal, offering up two master manipulators of space, time and emotion.

This is because, as good as #56 is, it might be you remember instead their better matches; their bigger matches; their more widely renowned matches. That seemingly raises the question as to why #56 was selected for this list, and more importantly what it tells us about memory in professional wrestling.

Both men had such an understanding of what it took to be good in the ring, of what professional wrestling could and should be. They were capable of such magic together that they deserve to have all their matches held up as must-see so that fans everywhere can watch at least one encounter between two of the best ever, and certainly one of the best pairings ever - be it together as a team or against one another as bitter rivals. #56 was selected because of its status as a personal favourite of mine – as my tribute - but no fan should go their lives without seeing at least one Guerrero / Benoit match, regardless of which it may be. In the vast pantheon of professional wrestling, this pairing deserves the place they carved.

Such is the most important role memory has to play in the professional wrestling industry, and such is its most indispensable responsibility. Even with the good intentions of this book, even with the cynical efforts of WWE over the years, even for all the apologists and all the prideful, professional wrestling remains now (and perhaps will remain forever) a niche interest and a marginalised industry. Though I am arguing that it should, by rights, be considered performance art – and that, when it is, can realise potential unlike any other similar form of art – mainstream popular culture will more than likely remain largely ignorant of it. This means that men whose lives were, in one way or another, taken by their love for professional wrestling will often have their work unrecognised because of societal contempt.

Fans are obligated to remember performers who have lost their lives in the pursuit of our happiness. More importantly, I believe fans are more than willing to remember performers who have lost their lives in the pursuit of our happiness, because it is the very least that we can do.

I owe a lot to the world of professional wrestling, least of all the dream I have realised in writing this book. I dare say there are many others who, in their own lives, owe a lot to the industry as well. It is an industry that transcends time, passes eagerly from generation to generation and envelops the lives of its most passionate fans. It is an industry as glorious as it is brutal and it is an industry predicated upon the willing sacrifices made by those who choose to endure its unforgiving demands for the sake of our entertainment.

So, #56 is not just a tribute to what the two men in that ring achieved on that one night and gave us throughout their entire careers. It is also a statement and symbol to let them and all the others throughout the years who have lost their lives know one thing: that while the world stands oblivious, we remember.

And we always will.

Chapter 13

The Future in Professional Wrestling

#55
Tommy Dreamer vs. D-Von Dudley
Monday Night Raw
February 24th, 1997

Home to the disillusioned counterculture too rebellious in its taste for the sanitised global corporations backed by millions of dollars of production value and international exposure, ECW forged a legacy that remains prominent even to this day. ECW transcended being a professional wrestling promotion; it was a family. Perhaps even a cult. However one may choose to categorise it today, and chose to categorise it then, ECW had influence.

When ECW chants surfaced on WWF television, the business savvy of Vince McMahon could smell an opportunity to cultivate, to boost variety and perhaps even win over the minds of a cynical few. #55 was chosen as one of three matches that took place as a result of Vince McMahon seizing an opportunity to cooperate rather than compete, forging a working relationship designed to boost the exposure of both promotions to two vastly different audiences by hosting sanctioned ECW matches on his own flagship television show.

All three of those matches, including #55, turned out to be entirely forgettable efforts that, even at their most forgivable, remain average at best and difficult to care for.

#55 is a match that suffers from haphazard discourse, with several cringe-worthy moments that shatter the fiction and drag you from your suspended disbelief. D-Von coincidentally happening to stumble into the steel steps propped on the apron by Dreamer in just the right position for them to be blasted into his face with a baseball slide, for example, puts a strain on your cooperative willingness as the viewer. The introduction of weaponry less than a minute into affairs does little to dispel the negative ECW stereotype – that it was a promotion fuelled by cheap stunt work – and the narrative seems to plod along through various kinds of spots, utilising a variety of weapons and furniture, entirely disinterested in telling the kind of story indicative of a WWE match. Admittedly, I am writing exclusively as a WWE loyalist, conditioned to expect from professional wrestling what WWE has conditioned me to expect, and so it may be unfair to judge an entirely different product by the same standards. Nevertheless, as a cross-promotional opportunity of national exposure, it is difficult to see any focus on winning new viewers on the part of #55. Its greatest asset is, throughout the entire duration, the aforementioned red hot crowd of cultists that the more cynical analyst may claim were more in love with the idea of ECW than they ever were with ECW itself.

What is done particularly well is, at least in terms relative to what actually occurs in the ring, the appearance of other talents. The design of this cross-promotion, of course, was to give the top ECW talent some international exposure on a widely viewed programme. We got the BWO, Taz, Whipwreck, the Dudleys, Dreamer, their World Champion Raven and, of course, The Sandman and Sabu. At least from that perspective, the enterprise succeeded.

Or did it?

Those talents were given exposure, but an uneducated viewer may be left stumped as to why Raven showed up in the first place and what he was all about. Sabu is unconvincing as a talent worth caring about when not only does he botch a swan dive off the set that carried little shock value as a result, but also didn't seem to catch Whipwreck off Taz's suplex properly either. Meanwhile, The Sandman simply looked like he'd gotten lost. More to the point are the events surrounding what goes on in the ring. Every time there's a match being wrestled, a WWE star appears over the action, giving a promo on some WWE related occurrence scheduled for later in the show, making ECW look second fiddle. Perhaps that would be expected, but it does seem to passive aggressively neuter the reason for ECW being there in the first place.

Jerry Lawler is the worst aspect of the experiment's pervasive sense of failure. His storyline hatred for the product was what explained away the extreme visitation, but his zealousness in selling the angle on commentary becomes counter-productively suffocating. He crosses from critical hostility into dismissive contempt which, combined with the lacklustre bouts offered by the ECW talents and the already distracting second-screened WWE talents, does more harm than good. Some degree of vindication comes in the form of Heyman outwitting Lawler yet, by the end, even Heyman is drawn into deafening, distracting bickering.

As a result, all three bouts – and especially #55 - sadly wind up tainted. However, it's not the matches that are the important factor here; it's where they take place.

It seems fans of professional wrestling from all spheres are clamouring for another Monday Night War. They claim it'll increase viewership, push professional wrestling once more into the mainstream popular consciousness, make it all "cool" again and, most importantly, improve the product through competition. There's only one problem. In this day and age of television and professional wrestling, competition is a redundant and obsolete concept. It can no longer exist.

We live in an age of instant access and instant gratification where anyone anywhere can simply log onto the Internet and learn about everything if they so wish. In that age, with the new WWE method now inclusive of the Internet Wrestling Community - and, at times, even encouraging of them - and with the advent of professional wrestling streaming services such as the WWE Network and NJPW World, professional wrestling is more readily accessible than it ever has been. The Monday Night War was predicated upon a single necessity: the necessity to choose. Two programmes on at the exact same time meant your loyalties were divided and you decided to watch whichever *one* of the two shows you happened to favour. While possible to watch both, it took perhaps a little more effort. This bred conflict, which bred competition which bred a wrestling boom. However, now there is DVR, streaming sites, social media, internet dirt sheets and more besides. To choose is no longer necessitated. Today, we can have our cake and eat it. We can watch one show live, record a second off TV, watch a third on our smart-phone and a fourth on our tablet, all at the same time if we want. How could choice ever be necessitated again?

Competition is inert and, in this age of instantaneousness, has left a gaping void. Division regarding the quality of products across all promotions is much deeper rooted and far harder to combat today than ever before, thanks to everyone now having a public platform to voice their opinion. This does not rule out another pro wrestling boom like the one forged by the Monday Night War, but it does comfortably rule out competition as a driving factor.

Simply put, competition is not the future. Co-operation just might be, though.

That's why #55 and where it took place is a must-see. If anything, ECW on WWE in 1997 was how *not* to cross-promote for a number of different reasons but, while the execution was flawed, the concept was nevertheless sound.

Often the claim is made that the professional wrestling industry is, like history, cyclical. This may have led to the mistaken belief that it is renewed competition and "another Stone Cold" that is required for the glorious success of yesteryear to be revisited. This is not so. The industry has gone so far one way and strayed so far into post-modernity, the only place left to go is back on itself – to a 21st Century version of a territorial system.

If those small-time indy promotions raved about by the countercultural hipster elite were to get one segment on international television to show what they can do, that's immediate exposure to an audience convinced it is starved of quality. Should one of the major international companies like WWE get one brief match in Japan or Mexico or in an indy perhaps they can use it to open some eyes and drill through the impenetrable opinions of the self-favoured few who like to think themselves "true" professional wrestling fans. It's like talents touring territories but always coming home; it just so happens they no longer tour territories, but instead they tour internationally televised promotional powerhouses.

The fact is if another war broke out – impossible, but to speak hypothetically - someone would inevitably have to lose. In the long run, the only losers in conflict between promotions are the average professional wrestling fans. Someone ends up without their favourite business.

Someone ends up without a quality product to back. Someone tunes out for a few years. Someone else tunes out for the rest of their life. By working together and seeking to help nurture opposing promotions, you simply reinvest in the professional wrestling industry. The days of attempting to hoard success are now long gone. NJPW World can reach as many homes as the WWE Network can. As many people can as easily watch Wrestle Kingdom as they can WrestleMania. The cyclical return professional wrestling is crying out for is the same mutually beneficial cross-promotion matches like #55 were intended to be; one that can now function far more effectively in as affluent a world as ours than it ever could before.

This book's primary focus in its development of the performance art mode has, throughout, essentially been on thinking about the future of the industry. There is a practical consideration to make about that future too though, and in that vein the future in professional wrestling is not, as the argument goes, in any kind of a war between promotions. It is, instead, through cooperation like that seen in #55; if not for the sake of talent and promoters, then most certainly for the sake of professional wrestling fans.

Chapter 14

The Audience in Professional Wrestling

#54
Triple H vs. John Cena
WWE Championship
WrestleMania 22
April 2nd, 2006

First of all, it should be stated that this is by no means one of the greatest WrestleMania curtain calls. Its greatest success is, instead, the beauty of its simplicity, made infinitely more effectual by a ceaselessly vocal Second City audience.

With the overwhelming support for Triple H, and with Cena at the time being at the very pinnacle of the initial backlash against his act, this match becomes one of those very rare instances where Cena genuinely *is* the underdog. JR describes it as Triple H schooling the champion; much like in Cena's matches with The Rock, the composition watches as if there is little fabrication in that statement. It is a narrative that feels genuine, naturally stemming from the vitriol emanating from the older generation of fans who already held nostalgic fondness for Triple H anyway.

Yet when you take away all the mitigating factors, it is incredibly clear that, for a twenty minute match framed as an education, the bout is remarkably thin on content. Triple H's act shows us nothing new, and it watches very much as a typical paint by numbers "Triple H Match," which for the main event at WrestleMania threatens disappointment. Everything from the methodical, arrogant offensive style to the use of the sledgehammer is a Cerebral Assassin cliché. Cena's own performance feels similarly familiar too.

JR bemoans those who claim that Cena cannot wrestle, stating in ingratiatingly euphemistic fashion that the man is just "unorthodox." Such a flippant answer to the most prescient question of the time feels in conflict with a Cena showing which betrays the man's relative inexperience in comparison to his polished opponent. This does allow the fashioning of a fun tale of "anything you can do I can do better," though, as the challenger has an answer for everything the champion throws out, performing a textbook vertical suplex in return to Cena's Fisherman. In mutually beneficial response, the champion thus shows himself as hanging with a challenger consistently talked up, and shown to be, the more advanced performer of the pairing. The work is therefore equal parts reverential and confrontational.

However, despite the strong performance from both men and the serviceable effort they compile, the real reason it's on the list can be expressed with a single word: Chicago. This is a match all about the audience.

The role of the professional wrestling fan in the professional wrestling industry has, just like so many of the other ideas so far explored among these pages, changed radically since the turn of the century. The IWC has been born as an entire subculture of the professional wrestling fan, and the growth in power and prominence of social media, along with WWE's obsession with capitalising on that growth, means the influence of the professional wrestling audience now reaches farther than it ever has before. This is an important change that must be considered in any appraisal of the industry, let alone any reappraisal. In the case of #54, we get an example of the immediately positive contributions professional wrestling fans can make through their voracious reactions and willing enthusiasm towards what is occurring between the ropes.

Often a live crowd makes or breaks a piece of a promotion's product, be it an event or a match, and through that power can directly shape the possible legacies such events and matches go on to possess.

There are other examples of this phenomenon scattered throughout WWE history. Look at the entire Attitude Era; main event matches often deemphasised surface-level scientific mechanics in favour of emotive roughhousing and remain perennially entertaining to this day - not for the diluted content that relied so heavily on adrenaline fuelled, heart pumping brawling but for the intense and emotional crowd reactions that came as standard. Those reactions made things matter, feel urgent and watch as real and fun. One prime example would be the fondly remembered Austin / Rock II from WrestleMania X-Seven; it justifiably remains one of the most critically acclaimed, popularly received, infinitely re-watchable matches in history despite its disinterest in technical exhibition, and that the crowd were blazing hot for its duration is in no small part responsible for that personality trait.

Conversely, there are matches lambasted because of disinterested live crowds and an apparent lack of reaction which should, by all rights, get far more praise in any level-headed critique than they do currently. Consider the Fatal 4 Way main event at Armageddon 2004: a match that provided a brilliantly synergetic end to the year as JBL was pitched against all three of his previous challengers – all of whom he had cheated, in various ways, to defeat - in a creative and character driven affair that carried a sense of chaotic, poetic justice. Despite its highly positive qualities, that bout proves a tough watch because of audience apathy.

The case of #54 between The Game and The Champ is an endearing exhibit to the importance of a crowd. Part of the reason for the bout being such a tonally fitting conclusion for that event certainly boils down to a live audience that makes its presence known from the opening tag match to the closing moments of the show; a trait, no doubt, Chicago is renowned for and one that makes any event set to emanate from that city an exciting prospect. On the night of WrestleMania 22 particularly, that audience made a lasting impression and allowed the event to become one of the more enduring editions of the Grand Daddy, which has and will continue to age very well, with a main event that should be regarded in exactly the same way.

Had the crowd been dead for this bout, it would've come off as poorly conceived. It obsesses with cliché through its focused desire for efficiency and so, at times, frankly, watches as void of originality. Regardless, despite all of that, you could sit down and watch it over and over again and feel exactly the same way the fiftieth time as you did the very first time you saw it. Thus, John Cena vs. Triple H at WrestleMania 22 is testament to how a crowd helps massively to make matches because, on that night, it was that crowd in that city making that match *that* good.

#53
Randy Orton vs. Triple H
WWE Championship
Championship changes hands on a Disqualification or Count Out
WrestleMania XXV
April 5th, 2009

The main event of the Silver Anniversary of WrestleMania is one of those matches proven contentious. It's widely remembered as disappointing, anti-climactic and one of the several reasons posited by critics as to why, on the whole, its particular WrestleMania simply did not function effectively. Amongst the fiercest criticisms, it is a match described as one of the most disappointing climaxes to a feud imaginable, void of feeling and "unworthy" of its spot.

These criticisms are unfair. Though a match with its fair share of flaws, it is also a match with its fair share of unfairly unrecognised positives too.

Among those positives is the same kind of fluidity seen in so many other examples in this book so far, with a plethora of excellently timed sequences of counters and countered-counters. The same commitment to character evidenced by Orton in #100's tussle with Shane McMahon is in full force once more, and Triple H comes close to matching it himself as the good guy desperately fighting against his overwhelming anger to ensure Orton does not take his WWE Championship and essentially leave him with nothing. There are few botches. The psychology is sound. Contact is never mistimed. The execution is pristine, as should be expected from the two artists in play. Beyond anything else, it is a textbook deployment of "WWE style," utilising both men's watermarks to tell a gruelling slog that, while not quite the intense fist fight the feud had hinted at, still feels suitably dangerous in its own sense.

Even the stipulation can be rethought. It cannot be denied that it may have worked better as a no disqualification match. However, throughout the season leading into the bout, Orton had the psychological advantage over his opponent and so, by rights, should have had the advantage during *the actual match,* if for no other reason than to ensure Triple H's eventual victory; that's not so much a professional wrestling mistake (as sports entertainment would claim) but storytelling intelligence (as performance art would argue). Indeed, it was a stipulation necessitated for the larger story to be suitably resolved emotionally, and to be more conceptually satisfying for the audience. Add in the fact that, at the time, the authority figure on Raw, Vickie Guerrero, was a villain too and it makes sense that any stipulation imposed would play more heavily in favour of the antagonist than the protagonist. As the pre-match video promotes, Orton's motivation here was to take Triple H's last vestige of happiness from him: the WWE title. As JR points out at the onset, Triple H therefore should, at all costs, prevent that from happening.

All in all, it was a professional wrestling match of the most classical variety…only the lack of crowd reaction leaves us to consider it something other.

Put plainly, the crowd simply does not care. That may be, of course, down to exhaustion: already this show - held curiously in disregard by fans still today - had offered a strong Money in the Bank curtain jerker, a nostalgically fun Steamboat vintage, one main event championship match, Steve Austin's Hall of Fame toast in the ring and, of course, that epic Shawn Michaels vs. The Undertaker match. It is easy to understand just why that live audience might feel exhausted; who could blame them?

It is that Shawn Michaels vs. The Undertaker match that is perhaps most to blame, of course. Heralded as one of the greatest professional wrestling matches of all-time – not just in WrestleMania history, but in history in general – it certainly exceeded its already high expectations. Such was its success that it made the front page news of local publications the day after and overshadowed everything else on the card. It is a match with a clear and deserving appeal. Experienced in the moment, it was an exhilarating, engrossing thrill ride that had this fan literally leaping from his chair in his friend's front room on more than one occasion. Regardless of any personal opinion on lasting quality, its popular reception dictates its meaning as a bar-setting bout that many other performers in years to come will strive to meet. At the end of a first viewing, when not knowing what to expect, it leaves the viewer utterly spent; that is without the added mitigation of the rabidity of a live professional wrestling atmosphere that amplifies any emotion by a factor of ten for those actively in attendance.

Compared to the main event then, it is a stark contrast that should prove the opposite side of the coin pointed out by #54: as a live crowd can help boost the status of any given match, so too can it drag down the status of any given match. At the 25th Anniversary of WrestleMania, 72, 000 fans expended so much energy during the engrossing account written by Michaels and Undertaker that they were left spent and confused by a main event levied at the last minute with a seemingly strange, apparently limiting stipulation. There was nothing left for them to give, and apparently not enough impetus within the match to draw it from them by force. As a result, they remained deafeningly quiet and emotionally remote for as long as #53 ran. Now, so many years later, #53's status has been marred and its legacy denigrated to one of the worst WrestleMania main events of all-time as a result.

It is an undeserved reputation. In practically every analytical sphere, #53 succeeds. Even in the wake of audience disinterest, the match was worked with tremendous skill. Had the crowd been as lively for it as they had been for matches that preceded it earlier in the evening, it is my ardent belief the legacy of #53 might be entirely different. Such is the power of the professional wrestling audience.

The reason why Randy Orton vs. Triple H at the 25th Anniversary of WrestleMania happens to be something you must-see before you die is simple: it proves that crowds help massively to break matches because, on that night, it was that crowd in that city that made that match seem *that* bad.

#52
30 Man Royal Rumble Match
Royal Rumble
January 26th, 2014

The effect that live crowds can have on the lasting reception of matches is only a small instance of a far wider, increasingly important question pervading the industry: just how much of a role does the professional wrestling fan play? Elements of the preceding two entries may read as a chicken and egg scenario. There is some truth in that observation. Though a lackluster crowd reaction may unfairly harm a given match, is it not the responsibility of the match itself to ensure the crowd reaction is *not* lackluster? The debate is obstructively cyclical.

It remains important that we attempt to account for the changing role of the fan in professional wrestling, though. The influence of an audience is not limited to the live event, and certainly not in the current age of the Reality Era, instant global communication and proliferation of social media. Now, with the ability social media has to mobilise disparate discontent into revolutionary movements, for all intents and purposes turning tools such as the hash-tag into weapons capable of intimidating even

WWE, never has it been more vital for the professional wrestling fan to understand their own power – the reach of it, the limitations of it and the responsibility that comes with it.

In the instance of #52, you have a match that accomplishes two very important things. First, it highlights the paradoxical debate as to whether fans influence the product or the product the fans. Second, as the origin point for arguably the plainest example in professional wrestling history of fan power being consciously exercised to attempt to affect change, it stands as both testament and warning to the issue at the heart of this selection.

To many, the pervading memory of the 2014 Royal Rumble has developed into one centered on the controversy of Daniel Bryan being omitted from the titular battle royal. It was, in retrospect, an odd turn of events; boiled down to the simplest description, the hostility of the live audience that night amounted to a crowd criticising a company for not including a talent in a match said talent was not advertised to be included in. Heading into the event, Daniel Bryan's white hot heat among the WWE Universe had convinced the majority of the fan base that he would not only compete in the Royal Rumble match but go on to win it; and that any other option would be both inexplicable and unacceptable. So, when instead it was the oddly misplaced Batista who emerged the victor – a talent representative of the toxic stigma of the long-damned Brand Extension Era – the result was perhaps inevitable. The entire final act following Rey Mysterio's entrance in the thirtieth spot is marred by hostility impossible to ignore or dismiss. It may seem easy to overestimate the ferocity of said hostility in one's memory, but any re-watch should prove such overestimations to be falsity.

So too should it prove to be an unfair mitigation of this Rumble bout's reputation. Until the controversy surrounding Daniel Bryan's absence – a controversy that, again, was solely the creation of a presumptuous fan base – the match itself was shaping up to be the best for half a decade. The opening stretch of the 2014 edition is a constantly moving narrative with a frequently rejuvenating excitement and a sense of progression that expresses the best traits of Royal Rumble as a sub-genre, outdoing any alternative such passage in preceding efforts by comparison. Roman Reigns is a breath of fresh air throughout and his record breaking number of eliminations, though feeling intrinsically synthetic due in large part to the fourth wall shattering knowledge of his positioning as John Cena's heir apparent, is overshadowed by more prominent controversies.

It is by no means a perfect Rumble, with various elements that do hurt the bout. Importantly, though, the live audience that night played a large part in tarnishing the quality of the show; a live audience more than onside with the pay-per-view in its first hour and a half before deciding they'd rather entertain themselves instead in the second. In front of a different, more willing and attentive audience, #52 may have earned the position its intention deserved: among the best ever. The best opening stretch of perhaps any single Rumble, a number of enticing teases between characters of parallel dispositions hinting at potential future feuds, deploying prototypical tropes and possessing record breaking efforts, it is a Royal Rumble that got everything right bar one little thing.

It did not give the people what they wanted.

The outrage felt inside of the building that night was but an example of similar outrage felt throughout the television audience too. Social media lit up when it became apparent Daniel Bryan was *not* going to main event WrestleMania (if the Rumble was anything to go by on that front anyway) and that discussion became even more frenetic when the live audience hijacked the show. This frenzied atmosphere continued in the weeks that followed. Events made the front pages of mainstream news outlets in numerous countries, and ensured that WrestleMania Season that year had a tense and electric atmosphere that simply felt different; somehow, perhaps, more important. And for the second time inside of a year, this gradated atmosphere converged into a wider sense of WWE being on the brink of the overdue maturation of its newest era.

The hijacking of Royal Rumble by the live audience led to the idea among fans that they held the power to hijack any show they wanted. The first Raw in Chicago following CM Punk's departure on January 27th was threatened in the build-up by #HijackRaw. The idea, however, in a brilliant, prime example of WWE's creative approach in the Reality Era, was in turn hijacked by the promotion to create a poignant and affecting segment wherein Daniel Bryan utilised the recently born #YESMovement – again, an idea that rose to prominence on the back of events surrounding #52 – to have his demands for WrestleMania met. The resultant duo of bouts against Evolution alumni at WrestleMania XXX saw the fruition of the chaos's promise.

These are complex issues; arguably the most complex since the Montreal Screwjob changed professional wrestling forever. It would be impossible to deconstruct and analyse them effectively in the space of a single review in this book. What this review of #52 should do, however, is point out the new fangled role and responsibilities – even rights – of the professional wrestling fan, post-Digital Revolution.

Hijacking shows is a dangerous thing, capable of being as damaging as it may be beneficial. For now, WWE have proven it knows how to combat the efforts effectively, with the aforementioned Chicago crowd merely cheering good guys and booing bad guys; unintentionally or otherwise, they ended up as one of the most complicit crowds in recent memory.

However, in such a world it becomes clear just how atomic one mistake by WWE might prove to be, and just how frightening a degree of power the average (and in terms relative to the industry, the uneducated) fan can come to possess. The 2015 Royal Rumble's own controversy a year later proved as much. Though this review and this chapter can give you no definitive answers to the questions they raise, it can hopefully at least prompt you, dear reader, to contemplate those questions, so you may arrive at your own conclusions to an increasingly important issue.

What is the role of the enabled pro wrestling fan?

Chapter 15

Chemistry in Professional Wrestling

#51
The Rock vs. Chris Jericho
Undisputed Championship
Royal Rumble
January 20th, 2002

The Rock was Chris Jericho's first ever singles challenger for his Undisputed Championship and I distinctly remember a memorable promo heading into the pay-per-view where The Rock very quietly, very intensely informed Y2J that he did not think him to be a joke; a paranoid thought instilled in the champion by endless main event talent informing The Rock that they'd see *him* at WrestleMania.

The idea was clear, and one promoted by JR during the opening moments of #51; Jericho was to enter as the underdog champion with little chance to win. That alone can deal damage to a man's position in the eyes of the fans if not treated with a fine balance; it was not. It is not the one-sided nature of the exhibition that has it listed here, though, as it largely fails to detract from the sheer entertainment of proceedings.

Chemistry is the name of the game in this instance, the element that facilitates the heart pounding success of the affair. Like any form of performance, be it artistic or otherwise, professional wrestling is often reliant on the right pairing to reach its best; where two of the best push one another to become even better by virtue of their respective talent. This is not necessarily about the pairings that have gone down in history as among the best because of the storylines fabricated around them, but the less obvious partnerships that simply clicked with one another in the ring and proved to have an incredibly natural physical dialogue. Seth Rollins and Dean Ambrose, The Undertaker and Kurt Angle, Bret Hart and Mr Perfect, Randy Savage and Ricky Steamboat; these are but some examples of pairings that, whenever finding themselves together inside of the squared circle, never failed to show professional wrestling in as fine a form as could be hoped for. Chris Jericho and The Rock rank among that number.

The reasons for that are highlighted with clarity in #51. It was their intensity; that's what Rock and Jericho portrayed whenever they were in the ring together. Their matches were fluidly performed, but because of how much they clearly enjoyed working with one another, because of how generous they were with one another in their performances together by giving the other as much as he was getting himself, the action felt genuine and immersive, intense and explosive. The result was a raucously enthralling success each and every time. The fact that, in this particular instance, The Rock and Jericho were able to still achieve that, even in the face of the kind of creatively lopsided approach that so easily offends older WWE fans in particular, makes it perhaps their greatest production as a tandem. Theirs is a partnership worth remembering, worth paying tribute to and a partnership that any WWE fan must absolutely see an example of before they die.

What is always fun about Rock / Jericho matches is that a viewer will always get the very real impression that the two of them enjoy the work they put on together and that enjoyment translates into their prototypical pace. This match is no exception to the rule; there's a high energy from the opening salvo onwards that refuses to relent. These two really knew how to build a match like a rollercoaster and it meant they had not just the live audiences eating from the palms of their hands, but you at home too.

A second of many mighty aspects is fluidity. Even in the down periods, when the pace slows as Jericho lays a beat-down on the People's Champion, everything remains in seamless motion. There is a gorgeously fluid transition to the outside leading to a table spot. The transition from the Rock Bottom through the table into a submission in the ring is similarly smooth and another example of how textbook a pair of performers these two were. The finish is smooth too and, before you know it, you've witnessed twenty minutes of action that feels like ten. Neither Rock nor Jericho needs someone to make them look good, but what is so admirable here and in their other matches together too, many as they were, was that they still decided to do just that. The result is professional wrestling at its most explosive.

It is difficult for any fan to know, of course, just what it is that leads to good chemistry between the ropes. It would be easy to assume friendship and willingness is key, were it not for Shawn Michaels and Bret Hart, in their primes, possessing arguably the greatest in-ring chemistry of any pairing in western professional wrestling history. It remains a vague idea at best, even in the wake of scrupulous analysis. It is an important idea, though. Too often are talents paired together – in practice or in theory, such as in "dream match" discussions – without consideration of the possibility that, though on paper it may look like a natural fit, in reality it may prove a struggle.

There may be no formula to defining good chemistry, perhaps being more a coincidence of nature than an applicable scientific theory – but there is an identifiable lesson. With chemistry, success is guaranteed, as it was in the case of not just #51 but of any Jericho / Rock encounter. Without it, even the greatest can struggle. We as fans, in our perceptions of the industry, should not be so quick to think so reductively of the art form as to assume success is guaranteed simply because two names thrown together are, individually, among the best that play the game. Jericho clicked with The Rock; not always with everyone. Undertaker clicked with Kurt Angle; not always with everyone. The Rock clicked with Steve Austin; not necessarily with everyone. Understanding this enlightens us to the fact that sometimes bad matches are inevitable, not because of the failings of individuals but the unforeseeable struggles of partnerships.

Chapter 16

Professional Wrestling is…

#50
The Ultimate Warrior vs. Hulk Hogan
Title vs. Title Match
WWF Championship
WWF Intercontinental Championship
WrestleMania VI
April 1st, 1990

To close the book's look at the state of the wider industry through a WWE lens, I turn your attention to prescient questions regarding just what professional wrestling *is*; and not in the same sense as the question I posed you in the opening pages of this thesis. For all intents and purposes, the following reviews will busy themselves exploring, to use a poetic turn, professional wrestling's soul.

Hulk Hogan and Ultimate Warrior are criticised heavily for their capabilities inside of a wrestling ring. A lot of the time those criticisms are fair enough. Few would disagree with saying that both had a number of limitations when wrestling, yet there was one particular instance in which they allowed those limitations to become an advantage.

#50 isn't a match between technicians or brawlers. It's a gladiatorial encounter between two behemoths looking to out-muscle their opponent. It's an encounter that, today, threatens to watch dated or feel cheesy. It certainly remains vibrantly colourful. There is no amount of hyperbole that can speak more volumes than the frenzied fever permeating the sixty thousand in the SkyDome that night; a reaction exacerbated by the taunt off between the two combatants as Hogan enters the squared circle.

The discourse unfolds as a long, hard grind, fuelled by a fatiguing aesthetic that communicates the narrative's dominating atmosphere of infectious exhaustion. Such exhaustion ensures that, when the comebacks of both begin in earnest, even the most ardent viewer will find themselves reduced helplessly to the state of a screaming child, absorbed by the magic. Hogan and Warrior portray a pair of equals. The tests of strength, taunt offs and face downs don't stop following the opening, as they often do. They very much become the *point* of the entire piece. That means no real prolonged down time. The crowd's excitement never fades out, like it sometimes can, and their investment makes the match feel like an exhaustingly amazing thrill ride by the time you reach the end. That sense of exhaustion plays well into the tone of the encounter too, again fitting the characters involved to perfection.

Consider that both the characters of Hulk and Warrior were based on their ability to endure; both can take huge amounts of punishment but still have something left. Their key, most effective character traits were essentially an over-dramatisation of that inherent factor of a wrestling story: the babyface makes a comeback. Understanding this, the two performers seem to simply accept what they are and are not capable of. They limit themselves to the likes of tests of strength, wear-down holds and other relatively simplistic offense, none of which is particularly complex and all of which allows them to conserve most of their energy as the duration increases. Nor, because of their character foundation, is the match quality sacrificed in favour of easier content; the simplicity plays remarkably well into the over-dramatisation at the heart of any Hogan or Warrior match. Their predominant methodology, drawn from their similarities, is very much a case of "anything you can do I can do better." It watches essentially as a strong-man version of #58's HBK vs. Jericho from 'Mania XIX – it is a radically different beast, but one that shares the same juxtaposing themes of one-upmanship and deadlock. Headlock for bear hug, clothesline for shoulder block, taunt for taunt, finish for finish, comeback for comeback; simple but beautiful.

This remains one of my personal favourite WrestleMania matches of all-time.

The real world role this match can be seen as playing, in historical terms, intrigues. It was the first to follow on from that Hogan vs. André dream match ideal, modifying it into being about the top two babyfaces of the day facing off as opposed to the biggest new star against the biggest declining star. It laid out a framework that most dream bouts of any variety have each in their own way followed. In other words, where Hogan and Warrior put on a dream strong-man match because that's what they did best, Rock vs. Austin realised a dream brawl and Shawn vs. Bret crafted a dream clinic in their own respective WrestleMania epics. This match, while not the first dream match, was the first WrestleMania blockbuster face vs. face main event to explicitly emphasise the symmetry between said faces, and then organically produce a rivalry from that fact.

It is the philosophical bravura of this classic that is most important, though. These days, professional wrestling fans seem to be increasingly obsessed with words like "realism" and "legitimacy" and "believability." We're no longer quite so innocent and we appear to be demanding that our professional wrestling product becomes ever-more complex. Professional wrestling fans seem to want cynical grit and realism over fun and flawless heroics; CM Punk was a performer who embodied all these concepts and, as such, reached a level of stardom that was, for a long time in WWE, unfamiliar to him. It may also be why there's an increasing rejection of stars like The Rock. Part of The Rock's criticism stems from his unique career path, but how much may also come from a modern day rejection of his character's generally quite camp nature? Nowadays, fans seem to favour the Reality Era soliloquies of a CM Punk more than The Rock's more old school hyperactivity and catchphrase-driven microphone work.

It is in that world, rooted in its demand for the real, that #50 becomes something truly special. It comes from not just another time, but so too another world. It would be all too easy, awfully repetitive and a little wearing to, at this juncture, again write about all the usual cliché points of the perceived detrimental effect of the internet and social media, but sufficed to say that the reason this match is must-see, and the reason why it remains a personal favourite of this fan, is because it just isn't self-conscious. It just doesn't care. It isn't a counter-argument to the criticisms levelled at this performance art, but an unafraid, passing dismissal of them. This book has, thus far, concerned itself with what questions the matches it lists ask; in this case of #50, that question could not be simpler. "Who cares?"

If you watch this match being a critic first and fan second the likelihood is it might not do much for you. If you instead allow yourself to be entirely dedicated to the fiction for just twenty minutes, you may just learn to love it.

What we have here is a guilty pleasure. It is a spectacle that's *so* unashamedly professional wrestling that it's a hostile dismissal to the cynics and critics. It's over the top and loud, but it's so grossly over the top and loud and so entirely unrealistic that it's a powerful reminder of how fun professional wrestling is if you buy into the ideal behind it. This is not a match well suited to the Reality Era but it is a match that speaks for a reality: professional wrestling's soul.

This match is *clearly* a staged performance. It's perhaps, given the two characters involved, the most obviously staged performance in WWE *ever*. The action is clearly drama first, documentary second. The characters clearly aren't factual, but vibrantly fictional. It is precisely because of all this that it's so much fun. At a time when defending professional wrestling is at its most self-conscious, this is a refreshing reminder that sometimes we just don't need to bother. This match isn't about criticism and objectivity. It's a gross self-indulgence in everything professional wrestling is: camp, brash, loud, cheesy, ridiculous and full of life. Where usually we get on our high horse and defend this industry to the death, this is a match that simply shrugs its shoulders, refuses to apologise for being what it is or what it does and then does it regardless. It is utterly fearless.

When it comes to watching, maybe once in a while we should be too. Not just with this match, but all of them.

#49
The Ultimate Warrior vs. The Honky Tonk Man
WWF Intercontinental Championship
Summerslam
August 29th, 1988

#49 is a contradiction. It's short in duration (31 seconds) but long in life; ugly to see but beautiful to behold; simplistically one-dimensional but so vastly multi-faceted that it's impossible to really analyse. While it may be one of the shortest entries on this entire list and far removed from the epic that was #50, #49 is poetic in its own right.

Initially scheduled to wrestle Brutus Beefcake for the Intercontinental Championship, the Honky Tonk Man, at this stage having held the belt in question since June of 1987, issued an open challenge to the locker room. In wonderfully nonchalant fashion, the villain comes off as deluded about his own abilities and, crucially, terribly over-confident. Having held the belt for so long, Honky Tonk seemed unafraid to meet any challenge. The narcissistic champion was about to get more than he bargained for.

To the credit of the producers involved, it takes some time for the Warrior's familiar riff to echo through the Garden, building anticipation to further hype the already guaranteed drama. When the music does hit, the crowd goes berserk. In typical fashion, our maniacal hero charges down to the ring and takes out the champion in short order. Honky is the consummate professional in his performance, coming off as cowardly and inept when up against the stopping power of this other-worldly phenomenon. Warrior's antics merely exacerbate the ecstasy of both the crowd and the viewer.

And what a crowd! It's remarkable to behold how popular the Warrior was in this instance. It's an arresting visual to see the fans in attendance jumping feverishly up and down in a deafening cacophony of excitement as the Warrior raises his new championship high in victory. But it's not just a moment at the end of the match. Rather, from the second Warrior's music hits, the volume is jacked to an ungainly loud decibel. That heat is infectious, bleeding through the screen no matter how much you attempt to remain level-headed and detached. Such is the ferocious emotion of the crowd that the age old cliché of having an out-of-body experience almost comes true. Such is the case for me, at least.

If I could take a more personal bent for a moment, allow me to say that I "mark" for the Ultimate Warrior. Such is the exact point behind why this match was selected. Do not mistake me; it isn't because I feel a loyalist's desire to ensure unduly favoured representation of Warrior. Rather, because it's all about the "mark out." After all, isn't it such moments that define us as an individual fan? There is no truer moment as a professional wrestling fan than when we "mark out." It is the so-called "mark out moments" wherein we expose ourselves to this world freely, and so entirely unashamed.

This match was chosen for my experience of it and for what the experience made me come to understand: the infinite regression of "marking out" is the poetic nature of being a professional wrestling fan.

It's a fascinating state of mind really. It reduces our sensibilities as adult fans to a helplessly maudlin infantile state. It's a complete alteration of self. This book's arguments are undoubtedly fuelled by my individual dispositions and, having read every entry on this list thus far, you will by now know my tastes all too well. I therefore freely admit that, if I were to look in the mirror when watching #49, my most enduring adult cynicism would recoil in disgust of the wide-eyed and awe-inspired child staring back at me.

Of course, this is not just a phenomenon isolated to myself. We all have these inexplicable turns with many of the enabling moments strewn through history, each one often contradicting everything we thought we were as a fan. One prominent example would be John Cena's return at the climax of the 2008 Royal Rumble, now living in infamy as the moment people "forgot to hate John Cena." Do not think of that as a pessimistic reality about Internet Wrestling Community band-wagons, but a poetic truth about the magical moments only professional wrestling can capture for us; when the world shrinks away and all our wearied worries vanish into thin air.

Perhaps all professional wrestling fans have some guilty pleasure; a talent they cheer for that might embarrass them, or a match reviled by many that they enjoy. The underlying point of it all is that, as professional wrestling fans and, perhaps more importantly as adult professional wrestling fans, very often we can forget why we're here. We can easily lose sight of the fundamental instinct permeating each of us when we tune in. Generally, this book and its author are pretty dismissive of the enduring negative stereotypes pervading older fans, most especially the IWC. There is, though, an element of truth that, in our desperate bid for knowledge, understanding and reputation, we might sometimes over-analyse, hyper-criticise and downright spout misinformed nonsense in our more zealous fits. Some of you reading may even think this book is a prime example of all three; and in some ways it is. It is precisely because of that the inclusion of this somewhat clownish squash match should be testament to the serious point being made by #49.

In its most fundamental form, professional wrestling is escapism, pure and simple; and, in that vein, consider that "to mark out" *is* to escape. Unfortunately, sometimes the phrase, as well as the term "mark" itself, can take on negative connotations. It should be the exact opposite. Being reduced to an infantile state of mind is no bad thing when it comes to this wondrous performance art. On the contrary, it should be its most absolute point; the one constant objective any professional wrestling match and every professional wrestling performer should strive to achieve regardless of any grandiose philosophies about the industry's place in the world in the years to come. Such an objective is, after all, essentially the job, is it not?

The preceding entry is a wonderful reminder of how sometimes it's perfectly OK for professional wrestling to be colourful and bright and a little bit ridiculous. It is a facet very much true of this thirty second squash match as well, because there is no better way than to describe that inexplicable process wherein we lose ourselves. "Marking out" is colourful and bright and a little bit ridiculous. #49's achievement is as infinitely complex as the greatest in-ring masterpiece. It is professional wrestling's purist truth; it's most naked beauty. It is not just must-see, but must-experience.

#48
Big Show vs. Kane
Monday Night Raw
May 8th, 2006

To call #48 an oddity would be a radical understatement. A chain wrestling "clinic," for lack of a better term, exhibited by two of the most infamous and enduring super heavyweights in the promotion's history simply had to be included in this book, and certainly had to be included in this chapter.

This is a match that shares an obvious common ground of subversion with the effort put forth by Big Show and Mark Henry's #95 Vengeance tussle. Where the two compositions differ is in their tone. The leviathan clash of Henry and Show evokes the sense of a conscious design of grander purpose. In this instance, Kane and Show instead express mere levity; they perform what could best be described as a whimsy.

As a match, this truly stands testament to the skill of both Big Show and Kane. It's perhaps too easy to forget just how genuinely *big* these two athletes are when they're performing with two hundred fifty pound guys every single week. This is an important point to make, as only by realising the nature of their size in the world away from professional wrestling does the awe-inspiring show of their agility and athleticism, evident in their interaction here, strike home its fullest impression. That impossible marriage of size and skill, by virtue of its excess, could even be placed above the more regular displays of acumen from performers we are more accustomed to seeing such acumen from on a weekly basis. Big Show's float-over is neither really any worse or better than one you might see performed by John Cena, for example, but the difference is Big Show weighs close to *five hundred pounds* and is around *seven feet tall.* Just as the man would perform a top rope elbow drop in years to come, he here decides to float-over and go behind as if he were bred from Olympian stock.

#48 is all about the context of size; it may not have consciously striven to upset stereotype, but it upsets it nonetheless. The size of the two competitors turns the most bog standard of technical exchanges into something incredibly entertaining to watch. That transformative philosophy is not only in line with the exposing nature of the preceding two entries in this chapter, but it also evidences a care for quality and a dedication to memory from both Big Show and Kane. JR says it best during the actual bout: Big Show and Kane were the last two people on the face of the planet you'd ever expect to go out and put on a show of technical wrestling, especially when it wasn't even a special occasion. Not only is it impressive that they were able to pull it off in the first place, but the fact that they did so and made it look convincing makes it all the more incredible a feat.

By working against doing what was expected, a simple throw away match on Raw becomes more entertaining than the majority of pay-per-view matches, if not all of them, wrestled between the same two competitors. In only five minutes, the two giants show off their athletic talent and their ability to perform with aesthetic realism. So impressive is the bout's various feats that, had it perhaps happened on pay-per-view rather than being nestled away in an unsuspecting corner of an unsuspecting episode of Monday Night Raw, it might just have come to enjoy a far more prominent reputation than the non-existent one it unfairly – but without complaint – today endures.

Consider again: a five hundred pound man doing forward rolls, float-overs, headlock takedowns and, not just chain wrestling, but smooth chain wrestling that looks good. Consider again: a three hundred and thirty pound man lunging down for drop toe holds and doing go behinds without ever looking outside his comfort zone. It should, at this stage, go without saying that the talent on show is rare and one of a kind; strong evidence to again prove pro wrestlers are the most elite athletes on the planet.

Big Show's natural gifts are one-of-a-kind and, athletically, he may even surpass his famous spiritual predecessor, André the Giant. He is a performer who has simply bettered with age; a fine professional wrestling vintage if there ever was one. Big Show, today, performs with more versatility between the ropes than he ever has before. Matches like #48 show that the World's Largest Athlete remains capable of a rare magic. Comparatively speaking, Big Show is, pound for pound, perhaps the most gifted professional wrestler to have ever been employed by World Wrestling Entertainment; and what he achieves in this short little bout is deserving of immortality born through recognition.

The tandem's other half, Kane, is a man sentenced to have his entire career overshadowed by that of The Undertaker, thanks to his gimmick of the younger brother. Arguments can be made – and strong ones at that – that Kane is perhaps the more talented of the two and was simply never afforded much of a vessel to show it. Across their careers, Kane has proven a more versatile character performer than most, and his longevity has avoided the same sense of failing fitness that has plagued so many in the latter most years of their career. Kane's talent is indisputable fact and no other five minutes might encapsulate that fact better than the five minutes of #48.

Beyond the natural talents of both men, the pervasive fact of the match furthers our introspection of professional wrestling's soul. This athletic miracle is something you could only ever see in this glorious business. There are plenty of sports that utilise big men and plenty of sports that show them to be incredibly athletic, but only the one – ours - has the largest athlete on the planet showing an inhuman level of agility. Professional wrestling is all about the astounding, and what could be more astounding than a few short minutes of simple chain wrestling from two men who, by all rights, should be beyond the size to execute it as well as they do here. The ridiculousness is a sight for sore eyes and an impossibly entertaining spectacle.

It represents another personality trait that ensures our love for the performance. Professional wrestling is a place where miracles happen. Where else might you see time stand still; men fly; boyhood dreams *really* come true; or two giants chain wrestle?

#47
Shane McMahon vs. Kurt Angle
Street Fight
King of the Ring
June 24th, 2001

This may be one of the lesser mentioned Kurt Angle performances of his time with the company, but it happens to be one of his best. From the utilisation of his amateur skills as a means to humiliate his opponent rather than combat him to his sell jobs portraying McMahon as an impassioned force of equal strength, this may be one of the most effective elevations of an opponent committed to canvas. Touches like Angle being too battle worn to do anything other than literally roll McMahon to the ring from the entrance way allow McMahon to appear as an opponent taking the Olympian to the absolute limit.

This may be one of Angle's earlier shows of the intensity that would eventually watermark his work in his closing months with the company. That trait would carry over into his battles with Austin in the latter half of the year and, though it would later come to manifest primarily through his relentless amateur skills and mat-oriented arsenal, it is the mitigated environment of a Street Fight that lets him express it to the fullest in this instance. Though Street Fights are now creatively sterile events utilising familiar spots and the same two or three weapons, this is a war that sees the immediate environment become as much of a weapon as any Singapore Cane or steel chair; the shattering panes of glass in the entrance will be seared into your memory from the first moment you witness it. This is the Street Fight that put the *fight* in Street Fight, looking real, feeling real and eschewing cartoon parody for outright viciousness.

This also may be Angle at his most villainous and morally deplorable; McMahon is not a professional like he is, nor an Olympian, yet Angle shows no mercy as he bad mouths McMahon, slaps him in the face and humiliates him with his amateur acumen. He suplexes him into a glass panel that should but doesn't smash. Then he suplexes him through it and it *does* smash. The bloodied Shane has already landed on his head once when Angle picks him up and suplexes him into a second glass panel that doesn't smash. McMahon lands on his head again. Angle, ever persistent, picks him up and suplexes him again; and *again* the glass panel doesn't smash and *again* McMahon lands on his head. Finally, Angle launches him like a human spear through the wall and, even after all that, even after they get back to the ring, we still get an Angle Slam off the top rope. That's damned impressive; even more so when you consider one of them isn't even technically a professional wrestler. Angle's character is entirely dismissive of good taste in the face of brute anger.

Shane McMahon's performance is not easily ignorable either. In the case of #47, McMahon proves just how good he could have been had he chosen to train fully as an actual professional wrestler and not follow in the corporate footsteps of his parents. He proves to have admirable range between the ropes, deploying arm drags, hip tosses and frog leaps with fantastic agility, exhibiting fierce grit and unrelenting determination; enough to match even the most ardent characters. He even performs a Shooting Star Press - a move most *actual* wrestlers can't perform (and even Brock Lesnar badly botched when it mattered most) - onto an aluminum trash can. He shows the kind of determination that professional wrestlers can be proud of; a determination not often found among the privileged athletes in mainstream competitive sports. Despite having suffered potentially serious injuries, and despite the serious likelihood of more serious injury once up, a professional wrestler takes the punishment and finishes what they went out there to do. That's what #47 represents.

Angle had already wrestled twice that night. Then he went out and wrestled another half hour match. He gets busted open early. He's eventually bleeding from the mouth; he gets slammed on an unprotected floor and clearly, from his facial expression, takes it badly. He winds up rolling through shards of glass that lacerate and slice. He ends up back in the ring cut like a stuck pig and showing perhaps genuine signs of total exhaustion. And what does he do? Voluntarily plummets from several feet in the air off the top rope to end the contest.

When putting that all down on paper and reading it back, it sounds as if it should be illegal. It is a shopping list of brutality that reads as so absolutely ludicrous only the most obscene words prove adequate enough a reaction to it. This is because the dedication that McMahon and Angle show here is inhumanly impressive and should be held up as prime exhibit of why professional wrestlers are some of the toughest, most committed athletes on the face of the planet.

Professional wrestling gets a bad reputation; all fans know that and have likely experienced the stigma that stems from it. Professional wrestling gets ridiculed and lambasted, which is most unfair to the men who put their bodies on the line to entertain fans. Mick Foley is a prime example, as is Terry Funk. But when a man who doesn't even count himself a professional wrestler takes part in a match - when he pulls out of the bag one of the grittiest and most excessive displays of fortitude in history - it shows dedication and passion unlike any found in any other sport. There's a reason moments in this match were once used on the Don't Try This video highlight reel. It's that kind of dedication that should make anyone pridefully extol themselves to be a fan of the men and women who jeopardise everything just to make sure we can turn around and say that it was worth it; because sometimes I'm not so sure it is.

The performances of both combatants in this war represent one of the very best, most important and most admirable qualities of professional wrestlers. If ever you could pick a match that was indicative of professional wrestling's gutsiest drive, then #47 would be that match.

#46
Bret "Hitman" Hart vs. The British Bulldog
WWF Championship
In Your House 5: Seasons Beatings
December 17th, 1995

For over a decade, Bret Hart created a body of work that is hard to rival for its consistent quality and this consistency can, to some degree, be recognised through the most persistent refrain of the Hitman's work. That refrain is the greater underlying issue at the heart of this stoic effort: realism. Some of the more modern and quick to react viewers of today might criticise Hart's work as too insistent; the over-long and laboured lethargies of a talent more inclined toward the marathon than the sprint. This is misrepresentative. Though Hart would often perform with a rigid aesthetic and slowly developing narrative, it was, by his admission, all in the name of realism.

In the 21st Cenutry, it feels that matches are much more impatient. There is often a lesser sense of build, rushing to a climax without prologue. The teasing whispers of complex, multifaceted storytelling are too often displaced with a barrage of athletic display; impressive in its own right no doubt, but lacking the resonance of older school approaches. Such was the approach of the Hitman. Hart's sometimes (and it is important to stress the word "sometimes") slower pace is representative of his realistic presentation in a professional wrestling ring, and it is that realistic presentation that best exemplifies his dedication to his craft. He strived to consistently present a match that people could believe was genuine and heartfelt. This bout is indicative of these ideas.

For the entire first half of the bout, in fact, it all looks to be the consistently recognisable Bret Hart formula, starting with chain wrestling and moving into a prolonged beat down, all punctuated with momentary blasts of spontaneous action and brief babyface comebacks. Nevertheless, it has the feeling from its opening minute that it's going to build into something far greater, and that ominous atmosphere eventually comes to fruition with exhausting effect. It is unashamedly gradual.

Where the match switches up a gear is clear to pin point – with cringing realism, Hart gets crotched across the top rope and tumbles to the outside, before being launched into the steel steps and raining blood from the resultant gash; a rare enough sight in 1995 on WWF television made even more impressive by the fact that it's nearly impossible to tell when Hart actually blades. It is when Hart begins to bleed that this so far standard Hitman outing turns into something of a memorable hidden gem. It stops simply being a title bout between two men who had previously encountered one another for a different belt and becomes so much more character-driven.

Immediately, the stakes are raised and the atmosphere alters palpably. The prototypical Hitman beat-down becomes twice as dramatic, despite not really being any different to the majority of his beat-downs throughout his career in its structure. Why? The perfectly fleshed out blade job, not simply done for the sake of adding blood to the match as other talents sometimes made too much of a bad habit of, but done instead to enhance the story with disturbing intonations of survival. It is a title fight altered remorselessly into a battle of survival against an enemy who has never been beaten by the hero. Bulldog is portrayed as the Achilles Heel in the career of Bret Hart, and the escalatory crimson advent serves only to punctuate that idea further and get the crowd even more behind the valiant champion. It fails wholly to recapture the sense of epic fun the first outing between Hart and Bulldog had back in Wembley, and this feels like a conscious choice, displacing rampant energy with draining fortitude. The peril is heightened, as is the risk and, fittingly, the reward. In terms of craftwork, storytelling and context, it far surpasses its more famous rival; a superior effort in artistry on a much smaller, more personable scale, where the make-shift victory of the good guy comes only with costly sacrifice.

Costly sacrifice is, in fact, the wider issue at the heart of this selection, highlighted by this match with unflinching bravery. In keeping with this chapter's introspection, here we have proof that professional wrestling does not get the credit it is due as an art form – perhaps even from professional wrestling fans - while other, more readily recognised forms of art receive more credit often times for doing less, simply because they are in a more acceptable mainstream industry.

Film stars are often times admired for their dedication to preparing for a role, for example, with method actors never breaking character even away from camera often being praised for their dedication to craft (whereas professional wrestlers never breaking character away from the ring are curiously looked at with bemused disdain), and other actors often lauded for their complete physical transformations demanded for a particular role. Some of the more famed artists in acting may do this multiple times across their career, and it is certainly nothing to downplay; often times it comes with frightful health risks and deserves the praise it conjures.

Similarly, professional wrestlers, no less responsible for crafting fiction when they stand between the ropes, have made an industry staple of willingly cutting themselves with razor blades all in the name of achieving essentially the same effect: realism. They do it on nights for performances that won't even garner major industry recognition – let alone mainstream applause – but simply for the live audience who happen to be watching; again, all in the name of realism. They break bones, suffer concussions and voluntarily launch themselves into a fifteen foot free fall without a crash mat waiting for them at the bottom; and all in the name of realism. #46 is a prime example. There Bret Hart is, slicing his head open for a single portrayal of realism that lasts no longer than half an hour.

There is no mainstream plaudits for Bret Hart though, nor this match, nor any performer or match achieving likewise. Despite all of what every single one of those professional wrestlers who have done and will go on doing what Bret Hart does in #46 – and on occasion to a far gorier extent, let it be said – they get no recognition for it. In the worst instances, they might actively and openly receive only spite.

Consider this to be recognition of another element of professional wrestling's soul. Realism is what many of those involved in the performance art strive for. It is through that striving that they sacrifice a great deal; their health, their blood and a little bit of their common sense. If #47's Angle / McMahon Street Fight represented professional wrestling at its most admirably gutsy, then #46 is the kind of match that provides the blood-soaked reminder of why that degree of fortitude must be recognised and remembered with the appropriate degree of superlative praise.

Perhaps recognising professional wrestling openly as a performance art may help us get one step closer to sacrifices of the kind made by Hart in the case of #46 – sacrifices, though, that are relegated largely to the past - being recognised, appreciated, rewarded and applauded by more than an educated few. If it is dedication to the artistry that is praised, admired and even adulated in other performance arts, why not in the business where men slice open their skin to generate immersion and the suspension of disbelief?

#45
Kurt Angle vs. Chris Benoit
Steel Cage Match
Monday Night Raw
June 11th, 2001

#45 is not so much intense as it is explosive, and that explosive style begins from the very opening with a series of impressive suplexes from Angle. Speed is another notable factor too. The execution of pretty much everything, from suplexes to runs to counters, is so swift that it's hard to keep up, with one's mind usually being able to comprehend only what's happened a second after the fact. The action exhibits a desire to exacerbate their usual dynamic, for the sake of putting as much content into their fifteen minute affair as they possibly can, and that exacerbation is the bout's most prescient theme. A German suplex isn't just a German suplex, but rather one off the top rope. The aerial offense isn't just aerial offense, but a series of suicidal leaps of faith. Even the runs off the ropes seem to be at an accelerated rate. This is Benoit and Angle, just so much louder.

It's nice to see them begin utilising the cage from the get-go, with the kind of simmering prologue usually found in their work absent. It's almost as if they felt a need to entirely skip the first act and one could be forgiven for thinking you've walked into the match half-way through. More importantly, use of the cage is kept simplistic and traditionally respectful. There's no superfluous intricacy and no over-wrought ideas that strain disbelief. Instead it is used simply as the wall it is or the platform it can be. They launch one another into it or jump off of it; it's reductive, eschewing creative faux-pas and focussing instead on resonance.

The level of physicality is quite frightening, maintaining further the theme of exacerbation. It probably goes without saying that the most important moments in the match are the two spots from the top of the cage. As moments, they are so visually striking that you'll struggle to forget them, and so physically high impact that they threaten to induce infectious nausea. Angle physically bounces off of the ring canvas upon missing the moonsault, and Benoit's own bounce off the diving head butt isn't far behind. We've seen so many aerial attacks performed from the top of that cage over the years that they threaten to become rather old hat, but the two here, perhaps elevated naturally by their very legitimate reputations, seem somehow much more impressive.

One of the more traditional and old school gimmicks for a professional wrestling company to host, the cage, when handled well, still remains one of the most fitting rubber matches any professional wrestling feud can be granted. In one sense, that may be what works so well with #45. There have been far bloodier affairs than this one, for sure - Flair and Triple H from Taboo Tuesday 2005, for example, contains a blood-soaked aesthetic amidst its barbarous overtures - but the crimson curtain is notable by its absence in this instance. That is, importantly, rather refreshing and goes to show that the cage can pivot on physicality as much as it can on barbarity. The conceptual regression at the heart of #45 returns the emphasis to wrestling over violence.

One downside to this rendition is that there are much fewer attempts at escaping than you might find in other iterations. A strikingly large portion of the match unfolds as if neither man is actually concerned with winning in that context, but again that simply serves to stand it apart from its brethren and helps it watch as a more confident and accomplished piece of work. Where Bret and Owen Hart placed the primary focus on the *concept* in 1994 with #82, Angle and Benoit prioritised the *setting* instead.

It may posit strong contention to be labelled one of the best cage matches of all-time, but to do so would feel like missing its point. This is a Kurt Angle / Chris Benoit match long before it is anything else. The fact that it is a Kurt Angle / Chris Benoit match amplified to the power of ten is the unique element of it; the bit to take away and feel more satisfied with than when watching some of their other efforts. The physicality, while dangerous and perhaps a little disconcerting, is perversely its most impressive characteristic; one that is allowed to take centre stage because of the absence of limiting preconceptions propagated by the bout's genre. That physicality highlights the better aspects of both men involved and the absolute zenith of professional wrestling, which is what this match speaks to the most.

It's not just about creative simplicity and the achievements of the artistry these two would so often engage in. It's about commitment. It's about drive - drive to succeed, drive to improve, drive to outdo. The creative character of #45 is secondary to the fierce commitment shown in its execution.

Professional wrestling features some of the most dedicated athletes on the planet. #45 states the fact outright. Given its curious nature as a performance art, professional wrestling can often demand so much more than legitimate sporting endeavours. It is precisely because it is scripted that, so often, it fails to provide its athletes with the same kind of safety measures allowed in sports. We're not meant to believe these men are breaking script because of an injury and, such is the commitment of those that perform, they often refuse to allow a chance of that happening by working through injuries that could so easily end the careers of sporting stars. It's an incredible personality trait that isn't shouted about enough with these men, and it is the lesson to be learned when watching #45. Like in the preceding entries, the commitment shown here speaks to all professional wrestling fans on a level that little else does. Matches like these emphasise work ethic, emphasise taking pride in one's life pursuits; it's not about guts or sacrifice but enthused dedication.

The dark end to Benoit's life is a poignant and thorny issue at the heart of all this. If you allow the end of his life to characterise his career (an approach this book has consciously chosen to avoid solely for the sake of historical integrity), then #45 becomes a vitally important cautionary exhibition. To ignore that warning would be irresponsible for a great many reasons. This match can also represent the better side of that line too, though, speaking to the short-term positives as well as cautioning about the long-term risks. This duality is why it's such an essential watch for any fan.

In either guise, #45 is a stark reminder as to why so many of us fans have such a respect for a business of performers that, by the very nature of what they do, *demand* respect. I think to varying degrees, all professional wrestling fans are in awe of the industry and of those that wrestle - these two men often times more so than most - and it's matches like #45 that offer the clear reason why. Efforts like those put forth in this cage match more than deserve respect; more than deserve adulation in fact. This is a match that, quite simply, inspires awe.

Does anything better represent professional wrestling than that?

#44
Alberto Del Rio vs. Dolph Ziggler
World Heavyweight Championship
Payback
June 16th, 2013

Harrowing: the word best suited to describe the disturbing tonality of this affecting Reality Era cornerstone. Its successes come in the wake of this discomfort, leading to a double turn that seems to, in retrospect, be inevitable.

The support for Ziggler is noticeable by its volume from the opening bell, but Ziggler himself acts no differently than his Show Off character's vanity dictated he should act. It does nothing to sway the dogmatic Second City crowd, though, nor do Ziggler's more questionable tactics which, in traditional definitions, would be classed as underhanded. The "RVD" chant that picks up in the early goings seems to clarify exactly the phenomenon occurring in the match's opening act: a crowd deciding to act on its own volition as opposed to the creative prompts offered by the composition. There is the same cynical distraction that has become all too frequent in the modern age.

It should go without saying that this does not take long to change once the pervading story of the match kicks in, both in cause and effect. An elbow to the head makes the narrative switch gears and, from that point on, Del Rio's focus is singular: target the head. Once the angle becomes clear, Ziggler's effort immediately adopts the sense of an underdog heroic turn, and it takes little time until a hush falls across an otherwise hot crowd as they apparently question what is unfolding. Is this all a work, fully aware and conscious in its attempt to turn knowledge of Ziggler's real world health into a confrontational fiction? Or is this simply a turn of poor taste?

The initial atmospheric boiling point reduces to an intense simmer when the initial drama settles following Big E's ejection from ringside. AJ's role soon transforms from a cunning distraction to a traditionally sympathetic support, while Del Rio begins to actively react to the negative reception of his cold-blooded methodology; that negative reception stems from the wince inducing refrain of a stiff kick to the head. It is a simple idea deployed with lasting impression. The sound effect that accompanies such kicks is nauseating, and Ziggler's performance is so convincing in its limp aesthetic that any Del Rio offense stops being a competitive effort to attain victory and increasingly takes on, as the run time progresses, more the intonations of a deliberate pummel.

Del Rio *pummels* Ziggler into defeat.

The narrative is simple, at times one dimensional and certainly repetitive. In that sense, this is a maiming that proves, with nightmarish emotion, that less is more. It is a minimalist form of storytelling that affords both performers plenty of room to create patient resonance. The pace is never break-neck, remaining even throughout, but the longer the bout goes, the more cumulative the effect of Del Rio's relentless onslaught becomes until even the simplest moves imply Ziggler's physical decimation. This was not just arguably Ziggler's first great show of heroism; it was perhaps also Del Rio's darkest show of villainy. Ziggler's defeat is total; an absolute route. Del Rio's victory is borderline gratuitous in its completeness. The promo the Mexican Aristocrat cuts following the match's fall-out – regardless of any questions it may raise regarding intent and design behind the composition's resultant double turn – feels wholly inappropriate.

Such is the relevancy of the entire affair. At the time that the work here was compiled, it resulted in many fans asking questions about whether what they had witnessed was excusable. There were concerns among the fan base regarding the danger entailed by pursuing the kind of story told by Del Rio and Ziggler, and whether it was appropriate to use the legitimate fears of the effects of concussion as a storytelling tool; especially given the stiff ergonomics and still relatively recent injury of the champion.

Confrontational storytelling like #44 always engenders this type of conversation.

Professional wrestling is a lethal industry, in often quite literal terms. As important as it is to defend professional wrestling against its detractors and lobby its case as a legitimate form of art worth far more than the contempt of the misinformed and to celebrate it, it is equally if not more important to at least consider condemning it for its bloodlust and carnivorous appetite. At its worst, professional wrestling devours those who make mistakes.

In general terms, WWE has become far more image conscious regarding the treatment of its talent and their concern for health and well-being. While the stringency of these measures can, and often has, come under fire from various circles, it is reassuring to have the faith that WWE is no longer as dismissive of the industry's dangers such as concussions. The Wellness Policy has been invoked publicly on numerous occasions since its inception. Rules have been applied that deny the practice of blading and attacking the cranium with weapons. However, the proliferation of dangerous genres like the Ladder Match has done little but increase exponentially, in the last decade particularly. Nor can the gravest of risks be eliminated entirely; by its nature, professional wrestling necessitates physical sacrifices.

Agree or disagree with any of these points, this is an important discussion to have; the industry makes certain demands on us, the fans, as well as promoters and talent to disregard certain morals we might otherwise hold. What #44 does well and with maturity is highlight these dangers in a metaphoric confrontation of what we fans demand perhaps too often without a second thought.

Fans knew Ziggler had recently suffered a severe concussion; fans knew how savvy WWE tried to come off as being about those kinds of issues; fans had already decided to dislike Del Rio. WWE saw this cocktail of ingredients and decided to run with it. They gave fans a reason to dislike Del Rio, played off their knowledge and their fears regarding Ziggler's health state and, most impressively, utilised the negative perception of company safety measures to invoke guilt. It stands as a testament to the skills of both competitors involved that the bout does exactly that, creating a sharp shock to the system that should, by rights, force a fan to confront the reason why they so brazenly and inconsequentially demand the sacrifices from professional wrestlers that all too often lead to disastrous results later in life.

#44 is a match that calls out the standard professional wrestling fan. It is a testament to the creative potential wrought by the Reality Era. Manipulating the kind of "forbidden knowledge" fans can now readily access in its fictional construct – in this instance, that Ziggler had been legitimately concussed – the composition reduces fans to the state many think they had long since left behind: the infantile helplessness of emotional vulnerability. It questions your nature as a professional wrestling fan, and your responsibilities in not asking too much for fear of consequence. Tonally, it stands apart from its contemporaries because of its confrontational bravery. Creatively, it exhibits the potential of professional wrestling not just as performance art, but also of the Reality Era's ability to reconstruct a 21st Century equivalent to kayfabe. Morally, it asks questions and refuses to provide clear cut answers. Was Del Rio in the wrong for targeting the head of an injured competitor? Was WWE right for pursuing that narrative line, so apparently against the grain of their safety-conscious PR? And by extension, are we wrong to lust for more, more, more?

It is important for each fan to answer the questions raised by #44 and matches like it for themselves. These are the matches that are necessary, creative expressions that remind us of the morbid results wrought by ignoring the omnipresent dangers entailed by professional wrestling. Some of us may be more encouraging of those dangers than others. Some of us may be resigned to the necessitated ills of pro wrestling, while others are confident that the industry can still adapt to dilute those ills even further.

There are reasons why professional wrestling requires guts and sacrifice, dedication and fortitude. For as much as it can give, it can take away even more.

#43
The Undertaker vs. Mankind
Hell in a Cell Match
King of the Ring
June 28th, 1998

#43 is a match that combines all the elements of professional wrestling explored individually so far in this chapter: the fun, the experience, its miraculous virtues and gutsy competitors, its sacrifices, its requisite determination and the moral demands made of those associated. In bringing these elements together, it transcends the status of a composition similar to those featured thus far; it becomes an affecting documentary capable of serving an important purpose.

One of the great injustices of being involved in the professional wrestling industry is suffering the full force of the ill-informed contempt that holds there is no ugly side to the profession; that they know how to fall. As you may have already presupposed, #43 is a singular example of undiluted violence that, planned or otherwise, proves even those who know how to fall will often push themselves to extremes no sport would dare reach. These are extremes that could quite literally kill in the name of entertainment and, by analysing them, we are unavoidably faced with the great moral contradiction of the pro wrestling fan: whether to cheer or condemn. The very existence of this contradiction, and the match that best exhibits it, provides a supremely effective defence against the dismissive cynic.

It is an unsure thing to know whether to label this composition a tribute to Mick Foley's dedication to the art form and to his fans or a damning indication of creative irresponsibility. The idea that he was all too aware of how difficult a job he and The Undertaker had heading into this match, thanks to the critical praise heaped upon the genre's originating effort from October 1997, makes the unnecessary danger of what happens feel borderline suicidal. This match is, at its most baseline form, escalation. It may not be as bloody as the first, it may not run as long as the first and perhaps it is not as well performed athletically as the first. It is, however, much more torturous.

It took Shawn Michaels and The Undertaker the better part of thirty minutes to find their way to the top of the Cell structure at In Your House: Badd Blood; it takes Mankind less than thirty seconds, and that The Undertaker willingly and enthusiastically follows him up means that, immediately, a sense of doom falls over their opening physical altercations. Watching in hindsight breeds a near-sickening sense of anticipation. To this day, I personally still get butterflies in my stomach during those initial exchanges.

Then it happens. Mankind falls his famous fall and JR calls his famous call.

In that single moment, this match was not just thrown beyond the memory of its predecessor but also beyond the memory of all its successors too. It seems almost inappropriate to dissect #43 because of the inescapable reality of the stunt.

Remarkable feels like both an odd word to use and a horrifyingly apt one too, as lightning quickly strikes twice in the same place. Once Mankind has fought off the medics and clambered his way right back up to the top of the Cell again, the impending doom that marked their opening swiftly returns and what follows remains genuinely shocking no matter how many times you re-watch the match. Coming off a Chokeslam, Mankind crashes through the roof of the Cell onto the ring canvas.

The duet of falls witnessed in this watershed event may very well represent the origin point of the Hell in a Cell mythology that demands, in the minds of so many long-standing fans, a desperate need to see unbridled carnage whenever the stipulation is broken out.

It is difficult to know whether one should condemn or applaud the bizarre desire to let the match go on following the second fall but, dispassionately speaking, that micro-match itself is nothing worth taking for granted. Though understandably a far cry from the best, most cerebral work of either performer, it presents a tour of vintage Hell in a Cell motif. So goes the great discrepancy at the heart of #43; it manages to be the best Hell in a Cell match of all-time because of its simple, single-minded adherence to the concept of a physical hell, but also, because of that same aspect, it simultaneously manages to be the worst Hell in a Cell match of all-time too. Perhaps this is not even professional wrestling. Perhaps it is just violence dressed up in the production values of a melodrama. Either way, it is one for the history books that continues to feel pioneering even today.

This was a night when wrestling was never realer, made never clearer by JR's cynicism following Mankind's plummet to the earth as he references those who criticise the industry as being illegitimate because its performers know how to fall. Therein lays the point of this choice. It is not on this list to be passionately defended as a showing of unbridled commitment to professional wrestling, or to be criticised as an unjustified indulgence in wrestling extremes for the sake of mere fleeting entertainment. It is on this list because it is the perfect dispassionate defence against those who seek to dismiss the industry due to its predetermined nature.

I dare venture my personal experience is not a unique one, but I get a lot of mystified looks from others when I tell them I am an avid professional wrestling fan. I get the same kinds of questions from the same kinds of people all the time and I know that no matter how well reasoned an argument I provide, the initial stigma and prejudice harboured against professional wrestling is something I will never be able to overcome. It is offensive, not because I cannot take the ill-informed assumption but because it refuses to acknowledge the sacrifices made by every man and woman who has ever laced up a pair of boots. So too does it entirely disregard the clear fact that some of the best professional wrestlers throughout the industry's history rank alongside some of the greatest competitive athletes in sporting history itself. Conditioning, durability, strength, athleticism and general physical fitness are all required, and in some cases to perhaps greater extents than anywhere else.

After all, there is no way to know how to fall fifteen feet through the air; twice.

For anyone unaware of professional wrestling's physical horrors that are sometimes all too real, this is the exhibit they should seek out. For anyone who believes themselves an ardent and life-long fan of the performance art, this is the dispassionate defence to deploy against those seeking to condemn you and your past time. As a matter of fact, the grimmest irony is that the only reason it is able to attain such status is precisely *because* of the staged nature of the performance art. Consider that The Undertaker did not throw Mankind off the roof by force, nor did he slam him through it by force. He did not inflict the punishment that followed on Mankind by force – did not slam him on thumbtacks or launch him face first into steel meshing by force. It was all done voluntarily; on purpose. There was no inflatable mattress or safety harness or chance of a retake. It was do or die and Mick Foley did it without hesitation and got up and carried on afterward as well. He free fell twice, had a tooth knocked up through his nasal cavity and had a gash sliced into his face so wide he could stick his tongue through it. But he got back up and carried on. He got thrown around an unforgiving ring canvas by a three hundred pound monster of a man and got slammed onto a sea of thumbtacks, which he proceeded to roll around in; and then he got back up and carried on.

Of all the must-see matches on this list, this is the one that proves wrong every critic and cynic who sees professional wrestling as anything less than completely and entirely legitimate; it proves them totally, wholly and undeniably wrong. It is a match that should perhaps be applauded, vilified, remembered and forgotten all at once. It stands apart as a testament to the demanding rigours this industry exerts on its performers. Most importantly of all, it is the undeniable must-see proof that, even if you know how to do it, falling still hurts.

Chapter 17

Men Out Of Time

#42
Bret "Hitman" Hart vs. Yokozuna
World Wrestling Federation Championship
WrestleMania IX
April 4th, 1993

To say WrestleMania IX is criticised would be an understatement. Alongside XI, it's remembered as one of the most underwhelming and rotten editions in WrestleMania history. How the main event went down certainly helps that criticism along with a hefty shove.

There is something of that special 'Mania feeling in the air for this bout, though; an electric intangible that crackles as the two men make their entrances. Even though it might curtail said electricity, the open air setting and the set design being deliberately modelled around the Roman Coliseum strikes a somewhat gladiatorial feel, adding further to the monster vs. underdog fable compiled in the wake of Yokozuna's initial push. It's an almost cinematic set up, with the shots of Hart from between Yokozuna's legs as the challenger conducts his pre-match rituals furthering the Hollywood veneer. There's some great creativity on show too that helps them get around the obvious problems provided logistically through the size difference of the two men.

Alas, the later the match goes, the more of the special intangible gets lost. Coupled with the short running time, the whole affair does begin to feel anticlimactic for a WrestleMania main event; it starts well only to rapidly thin out.

Then there is the radically disappointing finish; they had the crowd eating from the palms of their hands when Hart impossibly locked the Sharpshooter in, but Fuji's interference and Yokozuna pinning Hart without punctuating with a finisher leaves Hart looking a far cry from others previously in his poster-boy position. Effectively, Bret "Hitman" Hart, the best wrestler in the entire world, gets beat because he has something in his eye. It's a little silly and seems almost at odds with the wider story told, that of Yoko's size and mystery being his unbeatable advantage rather than the cunning of his manager.

Then comes the Hulk Hogan fiasco. Hogan's usual over-acting, Fuji's incoherence, Hart's humbling, Yokozuna's resultant humiliation - it ingratiates so much that it remains a wonder someone actually came up with the idea and, more to the point, thought it good!

To hear about it is surreal enough; to actually watch it play out is beyond words. It's the finish and the "match" after the match that earns #42 its spot among these pages. This was meant to be Hart's first WrestleMania main event; he loses, looks ineffectual and then has to encourage Hogan to go on and, in seconds, squash the man he just lost to. Indeed, it seems the curious precedent of Hart's run at the top of WWE being repeatedly curtailed by the promotion's apparent attention deficit can be seen to have begun that night.

Strangely enough, the fans in the crowd seem to eat the bizarre incident up, though this does not mean criticism is unwarranted. Hart deserved the spotlight that he had worked so hard to achieve. Yokozuna deserved a convincing and adequate start to the title reign he was meant to undergo as a monster champion. The company deserved a main event that could show the world that the WWF Championship – that the WWF - did not *need* Hulk Hogan. The world got Hulk Hogan.

Adopting a paradigm shift like the one this book suggests presents a prime opportunity to reshape our understanding not just of how we receive pro wrestling today and could come to receive it in the future, but also how we receive its past; how we think of its history. At this stage, history is an area of the industry WWE has a pervasive stranglehold on. This next section of the book concerns itself with the beginnings of a grassroots, fan bred rethink of that history, and will focus on developing new schools of thought slightly freer of (though by no means entirely uninfluenced by) WWE's sponsored representation of yesteryear. This rethink will consider two aspects: the most important and / or influential individuals and matches. We begin here with the former. Indeed, who better than to begin with than Hulk Hogan?

There is no denying Hulkamania was the force that changed the industry forever and helped make it what it is today; there may never have been quite as fierce a revolution. Nor is there any denying the man's charisma and talent for storytelling or striking an enveloping emotional note with his work. Sadly, it is that same exact talent and that same exact influence that has allowed Hogan to help popularise one of the most damaging and dangerous trends in professional history too; a trend perhaps more prominent at the end of the Brand Extension Era than it had ever been, and one perfectly represented by the way #42 plays out: men out of time.

Since the turn of the century certainly, talent wrestling well beyond their prime and occupying spots many fans and (apparently) talents alike feel would be better placed on the shoulders of younger, fresher stars has become in vogue. In the midst of that movement has been the Hulkster himself. That the man who headlined WrestleMania in 1985 continued to headline wrestling shows as recently as 2011 is, frankly, writing as a fan, maddening. It is not my intention to berate arguably the single most influential professional wrestler of all-time, but there can be little denying that the latter most stages of his career have proven as toxic in varying ways as the earlier stages proved revolutionary.

#42 is one small example of Hogan's longevity in the spotlight, and the lessons it teaches about ensuring talent do not stay around longer than they need to. There is a certain admiration to be had in Hogan's dedication to the industry that made him as much as he made it in return, and his earlier work as WWF Champion in the mid-1980s would surprise many for its far edgier tone to what would occur at the beginning of the subsequent decade. Having said that, instances such as #42 watch as inexcusable.

When restricting himself to an ambassadorial role with the occasional on-screen appearance to help promote pay-per-views or a given match, few can make as many excited as Hulk Hogan could; a testament to his lasting influence and penchant for hype. The fear, however, might be that, despite his continued popularity even in the face of dwindling relevancy, the predominantly recalled narrative of his career will be of the damage he dealt when past his prime as opposed to the world-altering magic he weaved during it.

#41
Ric Flair vs. Shawn Michaels
Career Threatening Match

WrestleMania XXIV
March 30th, 2008

Going into #41, the vast majority of people were aware that Ric Flair was going to lose and that they were about to witness the last match of the industry's biggest icon of all-time. Thus, one thing was immediately evident before anything even happened: this was history. What followed was one of the better surprises of history.

Flair evidences his veteran savvy as the antidote to the restrictions of his age, remaining one step ahead of his opponent and maintaining an advantage for the large part of the opening minutes. Things go rather awry when Michaels goes for a moonsault through the table, only for said table to not bust properly at the expense of his ribs. The result is, however, a criminally overlooked gutsy performance from Michaels working through the heat of agony to allow Flair his final moment in the sun.

Flair's offense is pretty admirable given his limitations and he seems to execute more moves in the course of #41 than audiences had seen from him since 2003. The result is nostalgia that has the viewer quickly forgetting HBK's injury. There are some neat counters performed by both men alike and Flair does a fantastic job, given his age, of keeping up a hasty pace that stays constant almost for the duration. Indeed, given the composition's logistical demands, there is remarkably little down time.

The result may very well have been a foregone conclusion – few professional wrestling stories have so obviously telegraphed their ending simply through their very nature - but the nostalgic appeal is overpowering and has the fans in attendance getting just as giddy over the near finishes as they do in any match with an entirely obscure outcome.

Perhaps some of those fans were simply clinging to a faint vestige of hope that they'd be swerved; that Flair would live to fight another day.

Michaels' quote at the bout's conclusion is as memorable now as it ever was, speaking vicariously for the fans as it did, and seeing Flair with tears in his eyes begging to get the killing shot continues to blaze its way into memory. Then, before you know it, the whole affair is over, along with Ric Flair's illustrious career, in all of just three quick seconds. It reminds you rather coldly just how fleeting our time in this world is.

Only that was not the end it was supposed to be.

As seventy four thousand gave the Nature Boy a rousing, standing ovation for the final exclamation mark at the end of an immensely admirable career, not one of them knew for certain that Ric Flair would prove unable to say goodbye to the business that had for so long been his entire life. Soon enough, Ric Flair appeared again on professional wrestling television and, for the next two years, would participate actively in the ring once more.

Ric Flair is a sixteen time World Champion who, some would argue, outstayed his welcome and achieved forgiveness and absolution through one final knock-out performance. How many fans of the youngest generations may remember Ric Flair primarily from their experiencing the more limited performer nearing the legally defined age of a pensioner rather than the world class, all-time elite talent who wrestled for sixty minutes every night against the best performers in the world?

The increased frequency we see today of professional wrestlers continuing to perform long after so many feel they should could be attributed to a number of reasons and, though Hogan and various of his era's alumni undoubtedly set a precedent, it is perhaps most accurately categorised as a generational phenomenon. In the 1980s, when you were a professional wrestler, you were only a professional wrestler and careers after having hung up the boots were perhaps not quite so meticulously anticipated as they may be now. It seems professional wrestlers of more recent generations are better prepared for life outside of the ring, if sensible empiricism and historical trend is anything to go by.

It is not a negative by virtue. Other talents who stayed longer than most were, are and still could be capable of contributing massively to the product in one form or another. It is just that the flip side of the coin is a severe extreme.

Hogan's longevity hurt his reputation among fans for the negative effects they perceived it to have on the various promotions he was active within. Ric Flair presents a different sphere; one that delivers unfortunately heavy blows to the nostalgic fondness of memory. If one phenomenon has presented itself as prominent in recent years among professional wrestling fans, it is the ease by which one can fixate on the negative and lose sight of the positive. Flair's own longevity threatens to prove such an example for many. Though he remained very generous in making others look good in his latter career, there was something increasingly uncomfortable as the years wore on and he continued to don the famous robes. Speaking empirically, his latter day performances became shadows of the gargantuan efforts they once were, and while his passion, dedication, skill and success can never be called into question by fans, the wisdom in continuing on for so long as a performer may be.

This is not an idea specific to Flair, or Hogan for that matter; the industry is littered with examples of it at play. The issue, nonetheless, is a serious one, and rather pervasive in this day and age. Though professional wrestling is addictive and all that some may know, there comes a time when to step aside seems, to this fan, almost necessary. Especially for talents incapable of wrestling at the level Flair wrestled in his last bout ever inside of a WWE ring: #41.

Chapter 18

The Man Erased From Time

#40
Triple H vs. Shawn Michaels vs. Chris Benoit
Triple Threat Match
World Heavyweight Championship
Backlash
April 18th, 2004

When it came to choosing the bouts worthy of inclusion in this book, it was an easy decision to include both iterations of this instantly classic line up, though the differences between them both remain stark. The first, already covered as #80, not only served to redefine its genre, but so too did it possess superior depth and resonance than what some might be tempted to consider this inferior sequel. Where this sequel succeeds in grand fashion, however, is in shying away from any attempt to replicate, focussing instead on being little more than a brilliant professional wrestling match. In its lack of critical concern, it may just surpass its more memorable prequel. #40, as a match, is already an extremely rare thing: a sequel that bettered the original.

Let us first explore just why I hold this match more fondly in my heart than its immediate predecessor, and the various reasons as to why I would rank it superior.

Consider first the location: Alberta, Canada. A crowd partisan in its hostility towards the otherwise beloved Shawn Michaels was guaranteed, shifting the dynamic away from the first match almost immediately; couple that with a similar degree of partisan support for the prodigal son, Chris Benoit, and the atmosphere becomes explosive. That level of emotion adds poignancy different to its

WrestleMania precursor, focussing instead on a validation of the champion to prove he was not just a one-hit wonder.

It is the crowd reaction that is perhaps the major difference between #40 and its predecessor, as any move committed against Benoit is met with a great deal of verbal hostility. Whenever Michaels has centre stage, the inevitable Montreal-fuelled chants of derision follow suit. The result of this extremely biased crowd is that Benoit's usual intensity and high impact moves become twice as effective. Lawler, in the booth, mentions a sense of uneasiness when Michaels and Hebner are both in the ring at the same time as Benoit; such uneasiness permeates the entire narrative. There is in this match a heart-thumping tension that was absent at WrestleMania; almost a sense of stress.

It's interesting to see the late '90s sneer present on Michaels' face on more than one occasion; I wonder if the reaction prompts him to tap into a part of his personality he had long since learned to put to bed? Michaels feeds off the more hostile reaction, arguing with ringside fans during the introductions and later locking Benoit in a Sharpshooter; a brilliantly constructed spot that sees Earl Hebner come charging down to the ring. To say the moment has the fans hot under the collar would be an understatement of the nth degree. By the time we're in the final third, as Michaels hits a Sweet Chin Music on Benoit instead of Triple H, it's looking evident that Michaels is actually relishing the opportunity to provoke the ire of the fans. Seeing a little more attitude from him on this occasion, alongside The Game's usual vitriolic performance and Benoit's intensity, makes for an infectious, immersive piece of art and a top quality character performance.

All three are afforded chances to express, in subtle fashion, their learning experience from WrestleMania XX. It is fantastic longer range storytelling, and the larger synthesis is evidenced on multiple occasions where the three men go to perform moves they hit at 'Mania only to miss their mark.

There is also an increased sense of urgency with #40. At 'Mania, the three settled into a steady pace and only started breaking out the finisher attempts fairly late in the game. Here, though, they start from the first quarter with a nice wary moment between Michaels and Triple H, and later an awesome sequence in which Benoit has Triple H locked into a Sharpshooter, followed quickly with Michaels in a Crossface. Such attempts at a victory come pretty frequently throughout and, in the case of submissions, never last long enough to feel overstated. All three had felt one another out a month prior and, recalling that hard slog, are willing to risk nothing, seeking to end it as quickly and comfortably as they can. The resultant frantic pace tastily compliments the uneasy, unsettled crowd.

The eventual finish is a genius move due to the number of levels upon which it works. Three are readily identifiable. The first is that said finish ensures the effort remains different from the match that had come before. The second is that the validation of Benoit – an idea that feels very much the concept underlying the piece - becomes unquestionable due to him having not just won twice but, between those two wins, beating both his two different opponents with two different submissions. The third, a nice added bonus for any Bret Hart fan, is that a Canadian champion was able to retain his World Heavyweight Championship by making Shawn Michaels submit in a Sharpshooter in Canada.

#40 is one of those matches where everything comes together just right and reminds you of just why this industry is the greatest on the planet.

There is, though, an issue with the memory of this match, as with WrestleMania XX's poignantly emotional masterpiece, regarding how the actions of Chris Benoit at the time of his death ruined his legacy for a great swathe of fans. Benoit's death may, at this stage, carry more historical weight than his life did, making #40 *very* important for the kind of fan that can separate the final actions of Chris Benoit the man from the work of Chris Benoit the performer.

Chris Benoit's ring work is worthy of remembrance. WrestleMania XX, in the light of events that occurred in 2007, may now represent the part of Chris Benoit's life deserving of memory; #40 represents his legacy. Coupled together, the two triple threats that rounded off the Road to WrestleMania in 2004 proved that whatever Chris Benoit could do, Chris Benoit could also better. WrestleMania XX will be Chris Benoit's most remembered, most celebrated hour, but #40 was undoubtedly his finest, when must-see was made preface and the greatest ever match of its kind reduced simply to Chapter 1. Regardless of whether you agree or disagree with WWE's decision to write Chris Benoit's work out of history in lieu of his final actions, #40 provides the symbolic representation of the legacy of one of the greatest of all-time; a legacy that is worthy of remembering.

Chapter 19

The Man Who Made His Time

#39
The Two Man Power Trip vs. Chris Benoit and Chris Jericho
WWF Tag Team Championships
Monday Night Raw
May 21st, 2001

#39 is quite phenomenal, and one of those rare instances where it's easy to forget just how phenomenal. In that same vein, in fact, it's easy to forget how historically significant a match it is also.

It's classic and it's old school and it works. What with the obvious calibre of all involved, one is able to get lost in the action perhaps a little more than usual when it comes to tag team bouts. So too is it refreshing to get a main event tag team exhibition between established stars on one side and rising stars on the other that's more than just a random show closer designed to combine feuds building to a larger pay-off. This match isn't part of a longer journey, but rather a destination in and of itself; and for it to be for the championships makes it even sweeter. It's a cerebrally crafted and intelligently executed story, with victory for the good guys looking constantly unlikely, but never so unlikely as to become unfeasible or hard to swallow when it unfolds.

The "five star" quality is not the reason for its placing on this list, though. Its under-estimated historical significance is. This is the match that saw Triple H tear his quad, which may have altered the entire course of WWE history.

Triple H has very much had an active career of three acts. The first was the career of any other wrestler. He worked hard, waited longer than he had initially expected in the mid card before finally reaching the main event – something he did *before* getting involved with the daughter of the boss, let it be stated. The latest act has been that of the part-time in-ring participant, full-time performer who has inherited the role of Mr McMahon, albeit with more accomplished artistic results, coinciding with his increased real-world responsibilities backstage. So what of the middle act?

When this match happened, something in the waters seemed to change. When Triple H returned from this potentially career-ending injury he was a lot bigger, and not just in a physical sense. His character became much more dominant and he barrelled his way towards WrestleMania to crush the champion. By the end of that same year, his run at the top of Raw, which lives in infamy among fans to this day, began in earnest. He dominated Raw with a title reign much longer than many felt healthy for the product. Such was the time many of the criticisms that dog his legacy truly synthesized too. Whether it be the perception of Triple H strong-arming his way into red hot angles to try and make himself the centre of attention, only to derail said angles in the process, or whether it be the incessant aggrandisement in WWE's hype machine, at every turn since his first return from the quad injury, his career has carried on its shoulders the accusation of nepotistic benefit. Indeed, many pervasively maintain Triple H is just not on the same level as his major contemporaries of Stone Cold and The Rock; that his natural gifts were a distant third.

It is important to recognise, however, that he was their foil more than their compatriot, and not just the best guy for that job then but, perhaps, better than any guy who has needed to take on that same job in their own time either before or since. Nor should we take away from his own incredible accomplishments; for example, when he turned villain again in 2013 and asserted himself as one half of the Reality Era's power-that-be, he helped to breathe much needed fresh life into a sterilising product.

Alas, the debate over Triple H's role within the company, following the quad tear he encountered in #39, is mitigated by the fervent, frequently unjustified revulsion of the jaded minority. It remains difficult for fans to defend certain decisions made regarding his career over the years; some felt his feud with Brock Lesnar was criminally over-wrought while others still have not "forgiven him" for the 2011 feud with CM Punk. It is occurrences such as these which cause people to categorise the majority of his career as an exercise in self-preservation and self-publicity.

Yet, regardless of whether the incessant accusations are close to the truth or otherwise – and it is important to understand that I, as the author, hold Triple H in great reverence - the point is that Triple H's career, before tearing his quad, read like the career of any other professional wrestler. However, in the interest of historical responsibility we must accept that, after the must-see historic moment #39 presents, the ferocity with which WWE promoted The Game, booked The Game and represented The Game seemed to explode. At its best, their promotion of him was heavy-handed, while at its worst it could become propagandistic. This shift in portrayal is traceable. Some call it a sign of nepotism; perhaps, though his rise to the top came prior to any romantic involvement with a McMahon and his talents in the ring are entirely undeniable. Some call it a sign of insecurity; given Triple H was at his height in the same era as the mega-stars of The Rock and Stone Cold, it is a seductively easy assumption to make, especially when coupled with the large shadow cast by best friend Shawn Michaels, however Triple H's earliest work in the company preconceived Attitudinal tropes before any of these men.

The continually raging debate has even wound up levying The Game, justly or unjustly, with such responsibilities as Jericho's middling success as Undisputed Champion in 2003; the struggles of important talent in 2003; the stalling of Randy Orton's babyface push in 2004; self-gratifying work with The Undertaker in 2011 and 2012; and more besides. I account for all these accusations – and the debate in general - not because I necessarily agree or disagree, nor because I have any definitive answers, but because they have solidified Triple H's place in history as one of the most important figures behind the changing nature of the world's premier wrestling promotion.

Indeed, regardless of the answers to the questions this debate raises, and regardless of how justified fan perceptions of "The Triple H Effect" are or are not, there is no denying that Triple H remains one of the most anomalous and influential figures in WWE history. For better or worse, that reputation is set to do nothing but exacerbate in the years to come. Nor is there any denying Triple H has done plenty of good for WWE, despite there being large contingents less ready to accept that; losing, rather quite frequently, to the next generation is only one example often dismissed, ignored or denied. Whatever side of this historical cult of personality you fall on – the ever-faithful or the dogmatically cynical - without #39 and the post-recovery change in portrayal of The Game, that cult of personality may never have existed in the first place. That makes this match history, and that history makes it necessary viewing for any fan of professional wrestling.

Chapter 20

The Men Of The Reality Era

#38
CM Punk vs. The Undertaker
WrestleMania 29
April 7th, 2013

Punk came into #38 as a character who had identified himself entirely by his success as WWE Champion; he was now denied that identity. So, what then did his intention become heading in to WrestleMania 29? He came to MetLife not only to challenge The Streak, but to hijack The Undertaker's entire world.

This match and the feud that culminated with it was about an attack on The Undertaker that no other man had ever had the audacity to attempt. Punk's mockery of The Undertaker's now deceased mentor Paul Bearer, and his theft of (and dismissive attitude toward) the iconic Urn, highlighted a desire to take for his own everything The Undertaker was: the closest character WWE has to a god. After all, a god is exactly how CM Punk's character now thought of himself thanks to the venomous, corrupting influence of Paul Heyman. Then, on the night itself, Punk took that attack to a whole other morally reprehensible level.

During the entrances, Punk emerges wearing The Undertaker's own legendary colours of purple, black and grey; little by little, he was proving a parasite transplanting the blood of Undertaker's legacy and stature into the body of his own career. The duelling chants of the crowd further this idea (albeit inadvertently) as the perennially popular Dead Man even saw his army of fans begin to switch allegiances to his tormentor; whenever Punk escalates his strategy by hijacking The Undertaker's own signature move set the split reaction becomes a unanimous show of support for the Best in the World. The effect is tremendously powerful, for once Punk has the crowd as well there was only one thing left for him to take in order to displace The Undertaker entirely: The Streak.

In the earliest stages, a Punk victory sometimes feels inevitable by virtue of the story being told. As Punk enjoys the experience so do the fans, and it begins to feel like a domino effect of evil – Heyman poisons Punk, Punk poisons the fans and the fans poison The Streak. By the final act, Punk's kicking out of the Tombstone is labelled as "a miracle" and "supernatural" by Cole; words often associated with 'Taker. It becomes increasingly clear too that Punk desperately wants to break the Streak with nothing less memorable than sickening irony; whether he mocks Undertaker's winning pose, steals Undertaker's arsenal or nails Undertaker with the famous Urn, it seems everything Punk does is specifically designed to not just win, but win in the worst way. And if he can't win ironically, he will win embarrassingly; he will get Undertaker to submit or be counted out. This is a brazenly smug attack on The Undertaker, both physically and spiritually.

As a traditional match, they do brilliantly and the whole thing is a refreshing reminder that Undertaker still had intelligent, cerebral efforts left in him following the increasing hyperbole of his Tetralogy of work against Michaels and Triple H in the preceding years. The match moves around the ringside area with fluidity; downtime is limited; counter sequences are laced with enough theatricality to create moments of drama, but not so melodramatically that they feel awkward - Undertaker's glare at Punk as he sits up inside the Anaconda Vice is a memorable visual, and the motion of him slowly, powerfully measuring his spot to counter into a Chokeslam comes off with exhilarating emphasis.

There is an issue beating away at #38's heart, though, that pervades the anathematic career of the Reality Era's foremost pioneer: was this result beneficial for CM Punk, coming out of two consecutive defeats at the hands of The Rock and a third against John Cena?

Seeing Punk inevitably lose to The Undertaker undoubtedly further soured fan reception of the product at the time. Punk would go on to lose to Brock Lesnar later that year at Summerslam, and being slated to wrestle Triple H at WrestleMania XXX made it feel as if he was returning to what had once been characteristic of his career: being over-looked. This is a gross misinterpretation of the path his career was apparently taking. His losses to The Rock did start a chain of events for CM Punk but, far from being a descent, I feel it actually represented a gradual ascension. I understand that sounds like an unconvincing statement in lieu of his number of losses in big match environments, but look at the names he lost to or, in the latter most case, was slated to still wrestle.

After spending 2012 playing second fiddle to John Cena and paired with talents such as Alberto Del Rio, The Miz, Kane, Dolph Ziggler, Ryback, a still-to-peak Daniel Bryan and, on television, Mark Henry, in 2013 CM Punk would go on to feud – however briefly - with The Rock, John Cena, The Undertaker, Chris Jericho, Brock Lesnar, Paul Heyman and The Authority, headed by Triple H; a retinue consisting almost exclusively of the blockbuster elite of WWE's roster. Few get to wrestle any one of these men;

fewer get to wrestle all of them. CM Punk, prior to his walk-out, was making his way to doing just that.

Losing to The Rock and John Cena made possible Punk's match against The Undertaker; losing to The Undertaker made possible his match against Jericho, which eventually made possible his match with Brock Lesnar; while the feud with Triple H would have largely been unrelated, his performance against Brock Lesnar surely did him nothing but favours in the eyes of a promotion that felt he was a fitting dance partner for the heir to the throne at the company's biggest event in history. So, the chain of events Punk's feud with The Rock set in motion saw the Second City Saint firmly elevated from a main event full-time roster member to only the sixth member of the most elite upper echelon.

That sounds rather unlike demotion. The successful, brilliant encounter CM Punk created with The Undertaker in #38 can only help cement this argument further. His mere presence in the top half of that card – otherwise occupied, once again, by those same names of The Rock, John Cena, The Undertaker, Brock Lesnar and Triple H – affirms his new found status. In fact, being booked in the top half of the card and succeeding critically in wrestling Undertaker to a classic match helped shape the entire reception of WrestleMania 29 as an event; a clear indicator of how integral he was to the product at that stage.

These are important points to make, and #38 is a match that represents the fiercest conversations a fan can currently have regarding CM Punk. Was he justified in leaving the way he did? Should he be commended, condemned or simply remembered for his positive contributions? Did the company value him as it should have done?

The circumstances surrounding Punk's departure remain controversial, and the truth behind them may never come to light in as close to an objective manner as can be hoped for. His legacy should not be denied, though, nor mistakenly perceived, and his positive contributions were of a rare, great breed. Whether you agree or disagree that CM Punk was given a push appropriate to his stature, the Reality Era was catalysed by the Second City Saint's infamous Pipe Bomb in 2011 and, without the high emotion of the ironically prophetic angle worked that summer, the entire course of WWE would be different; I dare venture, even worse.

#37
Chris Jericho vs. Daniel Bryan
NXT
February 23rd, 2010

One of the Reality Era's most synonymous names and greatest successes is the individual who made his WWE in-ring debut with #37. Daniel Bryan has certainly become central to the historical narrative of the Reality Era, with fan support for him having grown naturally and exponentially over the Era's earliest years. Indeed, the night CM Punk won his first WWE Championship to usher the period in, Daniel Bryan won the Money in the Bank contract that would lead to his first World Championship victory the following December; and, by extension, the beginnings of his explosion in popularity following the infamous eighteen second loss at WrestleMania.

So too has Bryan been central to the greatest controversies of the Era. The Yes Movement proved the first time WWE utilised social media hostility to weave a fiction in 2014, leading to a phenomenal WrestleMania in New Orleans, and similar controversy sparked because of him the following year on the road to Santa Clara too. Only history shall prove whether he is remembered as a prominent WWE World Heavyweight Champion or as consistent a 'Mania closer as some of his famed forebears, but it is guaranteed to remember him as centric to some of the most salient Reality Era experiments and, therefore, as one of its most important pillars. A performer need not hold championships and close shows to be the most important part of the product, after all.

This is the kind of light his debut effort sheds, being one of the first experiments that hinted at the Era soon to unfold. Pairing Bryan up with a reviled talent like The Miz was done to purposefully provoke fans, being a metaphorical representation of the conflict between the then counter-cultural Indy training grounds and the media-friendly factory line of the commercial WWE. That pairing might even mark the beginning of a shift in product that saw WWE more readily embrace the aforementioned counter-culture, of which a large part consists of the same sphere I, myself, have come from: the Internet Wrestling Community (IWC). Such an embrace began just as Daniel Bryan's career began; like John Cena before him, Daniel Bryan debuted on WWE television by wrestling one of the most respected World Championship contenders of the age in Chris Jericho (who was even reigning at the time).

At a time when Bryan should rightfully be considered a successful WWE headlining talent, it is striking to see the strange youthful vigour in his face as he enters the arena at the start of #37. Compared to the likes of Jericho and, yes, even The Miz, when Bryan makes his entrance in his underwhelming red and white coat he looks fresh from the so-called "little leagues" and there's no shame in admitting, to a certain comparative level, he very much was. Add to that the further comparison of the heights he would reach by mid-decade and Bryan looks even more starkly like an unfurnished product.

#37 is a strong debut that leaves a lasting impression. Jericho, as World Champion, sensibly is allowed to work his own magic in the opening moments, which gives Bryan the space to land the first offense and start strong. As a performer, Bryan had something to prove heading into the commercial world of WWE and the two men do a grand job working that real life fact (another early sign of the pending Reality Era) into their own story. The World Heavyweight Champion comfortably weathers the storm and soon has the upper hand once more, as rightfully the World Heavyweight Champion should, but not before the opening minutes successfully generate an atmosphere of credibility that lasts for the entirety.

One particular moment is worth highlighting. With Jericho outside the ring, Bryan comes hurtling off the ropes with impressive speed, lunges into a suicide dive and Jericho goes to counter. Things go unfortunately awry and Bryan gets slammed kidney first into the announce desk, giving himself a lovely red raw scar to work through. Given the circumstances and the wider context, it oddly works in favour of everything. Bryan, as mentioned, had something to prove: that his reputation was warranted and his mould-breaking statistics far from the hindrance some feared them to be. Being on the receiving end of something so brutally accidental in his first televised bout and getting right back up to work through it speaks volumes for the man's toughness and, more vitally, determination. What's even more impressive is the swift transition into his placing the World Champion in an impressive submission hold that most WWE-centric fans had likely never seen before, showing innovation, ring presence and skill all in one.

It is certainly worth me pointing out that, like Cena in his own debut years before, Bryan loses. That loss, however, is wrought out of the World Heavyweight Champion needing to utilise almost every tool in his arsenal. The Codebreaker and Walls of Jericho are both called upon, with this *rookie,* in his first ever WWE match, withstanding one of the two.

The result of all of the above is, simply put, one of the best thought-out and well-executed televised debuts of a rookie WWE has ever given us. It is a master class of construction and a lucky example of all the stars aligning to leave the viewer and the live audience with a lasting impression. It's an impressive origin story for a man who will go down in history as a landmark in company history and a major cornerstone of the Reality Era. The whole affair reeks of the kind of effort that, at the time it occurred, was seen to be lacking from weekly WWE programming. That effort highlights something that has never been more important to consider.

WWE was behind Daniel Bryan from the beginning.

How many times are they willing to give a guy ten minutes of in-ring television time with the World Heavyweight Champion and let him get plenty of offense in, come close to getting a victory and emerge looking strong all in their *debut* match? The most obvious example of this having happened previously had been with John Cena. Surely most fans would agree there's little doubt WWE were behind both John Cena from the very earliest days of his career.

This realisation makes #37 representative of WWE's faith in Daniel Bryan as a major component of the company; something of a landmark match that, due to taking place on a show now long forgotten and overshadowed, has drifted from memory. Nor was this incident isolated either. Daniel

Bryan would go on to be apparently fired from the company following the impactful debut of The Nexus on Monday Night Raw months later. His return would come at Summerslam, in the main event multi-man tag bout in which he proved to be, again, a major centrepiece. Only John Cena lasted longer than him on that winning team.

Then, as already mentioned, when the Reality Era was ushered in on the night of Money in the Bank 2011, Daniel Bryan won the Money in the Bank contract that would begin his ascent to the company's highest echelon. He was booked to be successful numerous times over much larger talents that, so folklore goes, "WWE much prefers to push." His eighteen second squash at 'Mania saw his popularity *explode*. His reign as Tag Team Champion in Team Hell No provided a television highlight almost every other week, some barnstorming bouts and, of course, saw Bryan involved in another of the biggest, most important debut matches in WWE history: Team Hell No and Ryback vs. The Shield. Not only was Daniel Bryan eventually one of extremely few men to hold a clean pin fall victory over John Cena without doubt or shenanigans of any kind – seeing him capture the WWE World Heavyweight Championship at Summerslam 2013 – but he became, largely, the primary protagonist set against The Authority since the moment of their debut too, before opening and headlining WrestleMania XXX.

His popularity has proven invulnerable against the ravages of time and fan-bred disbelief. And it started from day one, with #37.

#36
Ryback vs. John Cena vs. CM Punk
Triple Threat Match
WWE Championship

Survivor Series
November 18th, 2012

Both Punk and Bryan are incredibly important figures in the history of the Reality Era. In the clamouring support for both from fans, though, there is a danger that we may lose sight of the fact that, while both individuals were cornerstones of their age, it was really elsewhere that said age's greatest pinnacle of success lies. Punk pioneered a new age, but managed to build only its bare foundation – a vocalised desire for change. Bryan became synonymous with that vocalised desire, at times outright symbolic of it. Though not "The Hogan," "The Austin," or "The Cena" of his day, his presence was no less vital, and his career the one perhaps most largely affected by the new found power of the fans lent by such elements as social media. In such an interpretation, it becomes clear Punk was a cause rather than a result and Bryan a by-product rather than The Product; neither proved to be quite the force #36 presents.

Nobody could have known just how much of a mile would be taken by the three men who were lent an inch at the end of Survivor Series 2012. The door cracked open for them and the phenomenon that resulted came crashing through with fervour, enthusiasm, passion, dedication, drive, legitimacy and more besides.

It seems quite ironic that the debut of The Shield adds the exclamation mark at the end of what is predominantly an unoriginal piece of work, given how it is The Shield who would go on to be the Reality Era's second great unapologetic force for change after its pioneer, Punk. Unlike Punk – and indeed, rather unlike Bryan too – The Shield would also prove to be said Era's highest pinnacle of achievement.

The Shield did something incredibly important for WWE that neither Punk nor Bryan was able to do; they brought a dogmatic, *unrelenting* fight for the top spot to those already inhabiting it. On multiple occasions since their debut on WWE television, the Hounds of Justice have all individually gone on record by stating that their intention upon debuting was, without any ambiguity, to become the number one talent in the promotion. That dogmatic zeal was evident from the first moment; their eagerness in even as short a moment as their interference in #36 impresses. Importantly, it too seemed this attitude proved infectious, spreading throughout the locker room in a manner that translated clearly on screen. As the Reality Era progressed, matches grew less lethargic, watching as if all had something to prove. The result: an improved product all round.

This shift really seemed begin in earnest the night after Summerslam 2013, at least in a visible manner apparent on screen, when it became obvious that the Cena-shaped glass ceiling *could* be shattered (evidenced by Bryan's enduring growth in popularity and the continued success of The Shield, even when drifting aimlessly). It was furthered too by the unification of World Championships; a move that proved divisive among quarters of the fan base at the time, but that contributed by thinning out the field at the highest level and forced individuals to compete with cut-throat aggression to reach said level. The Authority, as a group, lent greater synergy and mobility across all levels of WWE's roster, and brought The Shield out of the one period in which the group seemed to be meandering creatively. Even during the group's brief babyface run, their unapologetic desire to replace the current crop of increasingly dated talent was obvious, as documented by the metaphor found in #96's WrestleMania six-man tag against Kane and The Authoritarian Age Outlaws.

Since the group's split, their ascent still did not recede. Seth Rollins proved in 2014 that, with the right amount of talent and desire, any man can climb the ladder of WWE to usurp Cena's spot that had, for so long, been needlessly considered sacred. Though Roman Reigns did not come to enjoy the same ease in his own climb, he at least maintained the legitimacy of his candidacy for becoming "The Guy," refusing to flinch or apologise even in the wake of overwhelming negativity from fans during the Road to WrestleMania 31; though some would contend this to have had a poisonous effect on the product, such gall is to be admired at least. While Dean Ambrose seemed to be the only one of the three to be placed on an initial back-burner, his popularity proved to be as enduring in its growth as Bryan's, and his return to the main event repeatedly played out as an inevitable matter of time.

Such a brash, swift and enduring shattering of the status quo going beyond even Punk's best efforts and Bryan's strongest support could not have been possible without their natural gifts either. Rollins: a talent as capable of being the smarmy, cerebral heel equal parts cunning, cowardly and callous as he is at being the aggressive, multifaceted babyface that can blend speed, tenacity, technique and intelligence with surgical precision. Ambrose: a poetic, soliloquising, unlikely hero able to draw both humour and emotion from his perceived lunacy, leading to work that can be comfortably read as darkly tragic, darkly comic or equal parts both; the fact that this could be just as easily deployed to villainous degree tributes the character's Shakespearian quality. Reigns: a quietly charismatic, crushingly good-looking, intensely brooding and quickly taught leading man capable of compiling top quality work with talents of all varieties, appealing to even the most stringently critical fan base, while carrying the potential to be moulded into the image-friendly, muscle-bound, vanquishing protagonist that can fervently appeal to all demographics alike: old or young; casual or hardcore; male or female.

As a group, The Shield was one of the most successful in professional wrestling history, with a strong claim to being *the* most successful in WWE history. If history proves the singles careers of all three Hounds to be as equally successful, that debate will no longer *be* a debate; it will be a fact. Punk ushered in a new age that the plight of Daniel Bryan came to symbolise. The most enduring legacy of their age will belong to neither of them, though; it will belong to Rollins, Ambrose and Reigns. Following their interference at the end of #36, Michael Cole claims that The Shield might have altered the entire future of WWE with their debut. Whether it is because of their old school, unabashed drive to negate the John Cena Equation, their unrivalled natural talents in the ring or their unflinching influence on the consistent brilliance of their deployment by the promotion, rarely have there been statements that have proven to be quite so prophetic.

#36 was a formulaic composition that introduced a reformulating value. That is not a matter of belief; that is a matter of fact.

Chapter 21

A Phenomenon

#35
The Rock vs. Mankind
"I Quit" Match
WWF Championship
Royal Rumble
January 24th, 1999

While this was at the height of an era when WWE far from shied away from what could be considered a rather adult-orientated programme, much like the Mind Games match in the midst of a family friendly era, #35 takes everything to the next level; and the degree of sheer violence really is quite incredible. Ringing a bell on someone's skull could cause permanent damage, for example. Nor do the two combatants waste time in getting so violent. They don't beat about the bush, immediately indulging in the stipulation without worrying about steadily escalating the tone.

The match very much shows signs of its time, the difference in performers then and performers now especially. The same can be said of the content too; Rock and Mankind are able to do things which, at the time, were pretty fresh, whereas today entries in the same genre often consist of a plethora of recycled spots, perhaps because of so much over-exposure to these extreme match types. The violence witnessed in #35 is thus amplified by the simple fact that most of it is the first instance of its kind. Such originality compliments the action in harrowing fashion.

Most of the action takes place on the outside to add extra impact to even simple wrestling moves, such as Rock power-slamming Mankind over the barricade onto the floor, or even giving him a DDT on the concrete. There are also a lot of little touches that make it all the more unique: dimming the lights when Mankind hits the "amps" makes the incident all the more believable, and for Shane McMahon to come out afterwards and act genuinely concerned, only for The Rock to refuse to let the whole thing stop, emphasizes not only Rock's aggression but also Mankind's grit.

By the time of the finish, following a nice little underdog moment where Mankind fights back despite being handcuffed, the brutality becomes nigh overwhelming. Hearing Mankind's uneven gasps for air into the microphone, and The Rock even snapping viciously at the referee, lends an atmosphere of quickly escalating pandemonium. Simple aesthetics intonate a genuine lack of control, with an inordinate number of chair shots to the skull rounding off this draining exercise of body horror. The reality of the danger in the climactic sequence is especially apparent in a post-Benoit industry. The Rock doesn't just hit Mankind lightly either; these really are forceful, borderline disregarding chair shots, so stiff that eventually the steel is bent totally out of shape and Mankind is genuinely busted open the hard way. It truly is difficult to watch by the time Mankind is face down on the concrete. A match's conclusion has perhaps never been so genuinely relieving; even the previously electrified crowd is left in something of a stunned state.

The Rock and Mankind were able to piece together a great match with #35. It most definitely stands as the benchmark for all other "I Quit" bouts to aim for. None have quite achieved the same sense of realistic, believable brutality that this one did, nor have any of them been able to recapture the sense of intensity or heightened emotion. The performances of both men are so immersive one could almost be fooled into thinking the on-screen hatred their characters felt towards one another had spilled over into reality. This Mankind match is on the same level as the Hell in a Cell with The Undertaker. Indeed, if that barbarous conflict could ever be given its own spiritual sequel, this would most definitely be it. That Hell in a Cell was real; too real. This "I Quit" match threatens to become very much the same by the time of its conclusion.

Matches like #35, and the Cell documented in the case of #43, are cringe inducing testaments to Mick Foley's commitment to his art form and, perhaps more impressively, his commitment to his peers. Nobody has given quite as much back to the industry they took from as Mick Foley, in both the conceptual and literal sense of the phrase. I need not run through a list of Mick Foley's injuries; they've become something of an urban legend in professional wrestling lore. This commitment and sacrificial nature was not in vein, though; they are the characteristics that make #35 the generous benefactor it proves to be for The Rock. It is the kind of transformative, demanding effort that made Mick Foley into the star-making phenomenon he proved to be.

This is a phenomenon by no means limited to The Rock, though. Many attribute Foley's programme with Triple H at the front end of 2000 to be a similarly star-making turn, with The Game becoming that much more validated as so-called "World Championship material" following that infamously bloody rivalry. Years later, Foley would prove he could still cast the same spells even in retirement. His work alongside Randy Orton prepped the Legend Killer for his initial World title victory over Benoit later that year, and dealt the same legitimacy to the pretty boy antagonist as it had Evolution's leader beforehand. Two years later still, Foley repeated against Edge. These four are the most obvious examples, but Foley was capable of further legitimising stars already considered to be at their peak too. His, again, transformative efforts with Undertaker in 1996 worked wonders for the already fabled main event star – more so than *any* feud previously. That very same year, Foley's work alongside Shawn Michaels at Mind Games, documented earlier in this book at #57, did for the Heartbreak Kid the very same thing it did so brilliantly for the Viper eight years later. He was even Stone Cold's first championship contender in 1998, and Kane's first ever in-ring opponent in 1997.

In general, Foley's work seems to go *under-appreciated*, though not *unappreciated.* Not only was he great at creating other stars, he created an impressive star all his own. He was involved in a number of classics, and many of the matches coming out of the Attitude Era that could contend for that fabled (if ultimately asinine) accomplishment of "five stars" involved one of the Three Faces of Foley. His promos were often the most complex in professional wrestling his side of Bray Wyatt. Even his in-ring skills were superior to the humble claims of the man himself; the aforementioned Mind Games match with Michaels and feud with Triple H proved Foley could hang with the best.

Mick Foley can comfortably levy a case for the greatest of all-time thanks to his library of work and the proven quality of his skill. In terms of giving back to the industry, none can supersede. Foley could be relied upon to put in a star-making turn whenever he needed to; not for himself, but for the man he was working with. #35 is one such powerful turn; one of many. No talent has been able to replicate this ability since and it is hard to think any will. The lack of upwards mobility and progression among the roster was a notable facet of the later years of the Brand Extension Era that, perhaps in part because of the void left by Foley's retirement and the lack of a replacement able to match him, marks a perfect example of not realising how a great thing one has before one loses it.

Mick Foley, because of his skills, accomplishments and his legacy of creating feasible, legitimate new headlining characters, was not just a world class professional wrestler; he was a phenomenon all his own.

Chapter 22

The Phenom

#34
The Million Dollar Team vs. The Dream Team
Survivor Series
November 22nd, 1990

Two men in WWE history stand on a level all their own, above even the likes of Hulk Hogan and Steve Austin. One is André the Giant; a man as much a pop culture icon as he was a professional wrestling force of nature. The other is the talent who, it could be argued, has fashioned himself, through his hard work, success and aptitude, the modern equivalency of the Eighth Wonder of the World: The Undertaker.

Whenever assessing the most important and anomalous performers in WWE history, it would be criminal and asinine to not take account of the Phenom. The Undertaker, like André really, should need no explaining to professional wrestling fans; I dare say even to some non-fans. His character has been labelled in some quarter as Vince McMahon's greatest creation, even if it has come to be more so the creation of the man under the trench coat. The longevity of The Undertaker's career and relevancy is remarkable in itself. Add to that his plethora of achievements throughout his career – multiple World Championships, feuds with legends of all eras (from Hulk Hogan and Ultimate Warrior to Bret Hart and Shawn Michaels to Steve Austin and The Rock to John Cena and Randy Orton) and, of course, the greatest undefeated streak in professional wrestling history – and it becomes clear that it is no hard case to argue his status is equal to that of the

Giant. Some talents could be classed as once in a generation; The Undertaker is one of a kind.

His library of work is uniquely varied. From borderline farcical, character-driven compositions like his Casket Matches with Yokozuna to more traditional, physically demanding intonations of competition in matches with the likes of Hart, Michaels and latterly CM Punk, The Undertaker is a character – indeed a talent – that has reinvented himself time and again to ensure endurance and worth of place. Like a fine vintage, in fact, some would contest that the best work of his career has come in its twilight years when the shackles of character that chained his earlier pieces with abundant limitation was willingly shed whenever the situation would benefit.

Whenever afforded the opportunity to flex his athletic muscle alongside his character muscle his success has been, at times, borderline obscene. His feuds with Batista, Edge and Punk all stand apart as highlights, as does his monolithic Tetralogy of WrestleMania matches against Michaels and Triple H between 2009 and 2012. The frequency of his successes and relative failures are almost beside the point, though, because his status has rarely edged away from that of beloved, respected or admired (sometimes all three at once). It is in the scale of his contribution and the extent of his willing generosity – to opponents and the company – that makes him the natural selection to succeed André the Giant as WWE's second great myth.

It all started with this match. Tellingly, the moment Undertaker steps onto WWF television for the first time he has what he continues to have to this day: presence. Though the presentation finds many of the later theatrics absent – the lights don't dim, there's no smoke, or a gong –

and though the odd choice of manager, Brother Love, feels incongruent, there is no denying that the outfit and the manner in which the character is portrayed both create the atmosphere of an event that carries on throughout the match's duration.

In the beginning, The Undertaker gimmick was built like many monsters, with limited facial expression, slow movements and a deal of no-selling. In retrospect, his does not feel quite so homogenised, perhaps in part because of the format at hand. Debuting in a Survivor Series match proves advantageous, as it allows him to evidence his invulnerability to a range of characters across the roster, while his first ever altercations allow him to exhibit the range of his athletic abilities. He out-powers Jim Neidhart, out-maneuvers Bret Hart and proves swifter than Koko B. Ware, who is quickly despatched.

The Undertaker's debut is the story behind the match; a little slice of history that now sits as a monolithic event in spite of its unassuming execution. It's interesting to know that Survivor Series homes the debut of one of the greatest forces in WWE history; even more interesting is the fact that it homes the debut of The Rock and The Shield too, the latter of which may eventually prove to be of similar historic significance. Given how singular The Undertaker has grown to become, it is an odd thing to consider that he debuted in a genre characterised by its collaborative demands, amidst a cast of heavily established characters and names. Even in such a heady roster, the different nature of The Undertaker's character stands head and shoulders above his compatriots and opponents both. This was the introduction of a character to take note of. That, within a year, he was defeating Hulk Hogan for the World Championship – and that he would one day be defeating the likes of Steve Austin and Batista for World Championships too – would indicate people did take notice of him. His legacy stretches beyond the more recent predominance of The Streak and transcends any number of World title wins or WrestleMania main events. His work is not subject to the same critical demands as that of his colleagues through the years.

That's because the Phenom was different, and there may be no way to define that difference other than to quite simply state the fact of the matter.

He is The Undertaker.

Chapter 23

The Prodigious Sons

#33
The Rock vs. The Hurricane
Monday Night Raw
March 10th, 2003

On the surface, #33 seems an entirely pointless waste of time designed to fill air space; the kind of match that is there to occupy television between important events that actually matter. It turns out to be something quite different, instead a powerful defence for a man still lambasted because of his career decisions. That man has had as unique a career as anyone. His successes across mediums of entertainment position him, arguably, as the dream talent for a man like Vince McMahon, whose vision is exactly such an all-encompassing form of entertainment orbiting the world of professional wrestling. I write, of course, about The Rock.

The Rock, here, plays his role as the smug, ingratiating villain with verve, his every move exacerbated by the then pervading popular opinion of him having sold out to Hollywood. Indeed, the condescending contemptuousness that Hollywood Rock composed himself with marks him as an early blueprint for the Reality Era philosophy, taking real life feelings of fans and moulding it into his grander fiction. The humour of the piece is derived from such contempt, with Rock's disgusting dismissal of his enemy confounded by that enemy's unexpected prowess. Through moments such as putting on Hurricane's cape and pretending to fly, Rock crafts a revolting showing that remains consistently entertaining; his was a talent that meant fans loved to hate him and saw them adhering strictly to the voluntary pantomime of the professional wrestling show.

His Hollywood character was a transformative turn for the legend who, had he stuck around after hitting such a hot streak, might now have to his name the strongest argument posited for Greatest of All-time. It was a character that was truly well ahead of its time. His manipulation of live reactions, his interaction with fans and opponents, his character touches; his performances exuded confidence and, in the case of #33, that confidence transferred to his work by osmosis.

It is a shocking result when The Hurricane earns the biggest win in his entire career. Such is the point that returns us to the anomalous nature of The Rock's career. For a long time defined by the question, "Did he sell out?" it is now an issue, following his return to the company in 2011, perhaps better expressed as "Has The Rock given enough back?" Simple historical empiricism suggests that the vehement criticism that The Rock has suffered for his career choices is largely unwarranted.

The professional wrestling audience is one of the most demanding and petulant audiences of any product; we are a difficult bunch to please and, more often than not, a little too willing to act like spoiled children. If demands aren't met in an immediately forthcoming manner or precisely according to the blueprint we often design for ourselves, it is common practice for conclusions to be jumped to. In the Reality Era, it was taken further with the advent of social media enforcing the will of fans with palpable hostility and outrage. This kind of petulance has dogged the legacy of The Rock since 2002. The "dissenting" tendency among his cynics to refer to him by his real name rather than his stage name, for example, marks clearly how much of an "Other" he came to be considered by a portion of bristling fans.

When The Rock left, he provoked fierce negativity. He was still young, he was still one of the best (even having hit a peak better than his preceding work up to that point) and he was still capable of performing in a more entertaining fashion than most of his other contemporaries. These reasons meant many felt he owed it to WWE to give back or continue on rather than move to Hollywood to pursue a movie career and treat WWE as a platform to success in other fields. When he understandably proceeded to distance himself from his professional wrestling career to forge a movie career free of presumption and type-casting, many fans took it personally.

It is a strange attitude to have, even if an understandable one. The Rock's career was relatively short; very short in contrast to others considered to be at the same level. In the space of under seven years, he accomplished a career as legendary, if not more so, as the likes of Hulk Hogan - a man whose active professional wrestling career spanned over twenty years. The Rock accomplished everything there was to accomplish in the company and, instead of staying and suffocating younger, fresher talent – though motivated by his own desires – he moved on. In any other profession, it would be a sensible, logical career decision.

A question: why does the number of years The Rock spent as a full-time WWE competitor determine the degree of faith in his passion for the industry? It is easy to empathise with those frustrated by his early departure from professional wrestling as a full-time performer, especially given the roll he was on at the time, but it is important to question a) just what it is The Rock is expected to give back and b) whether he ever has.

Using an established position to help build successive generations is a professional wrestling tradition from which no performer, no matter how extraordinary, is considered to be exempt. From André the Giant to The Undertaker, so goes the expectation and rightly so. Self-made success or not, The Rock is no different. What is less recognised is just how much he *has* given back; a fact trampled by the cynic stampede toward protestations of "selling out." This fact, though, is clearly evident with even a brief look back at The Rock's career path in WWE.

He became a main event, World Champion star in 1998. His popularity had already sky-rocketed and the World title wasn't his path to being a top star, rather the recognition that he already was. From day one of his main event success, he helped to make new stars. To use the most traditional quantitative measure deployed by those involved with professional wrestling when determining how much a performer has "given back," just look at the names The Rock helped make and / or strengthened in *losing* to them.

Mankind; might the fans have gotten behind such an unlikely World Champion if The Rock were not such an ingratiating antithesis?

Triple H; The Rock had been an established top tier talent for almost one whole year prior to The Game, and had helped mutually elevate the Cerebral Assassin during their Intercontinental wars too.

Kurt Angle; a man who won his first World Championship within a year of having debuted, but doing so credibly by virtue of The Rock's performance in defeat.

Chris Jericho; his chemistry with The Rock ensured any effort put forth by the Great One in losing to Y2J would do the Ayatollah of Rock 'n' Rolla a world of good in winning his first World Championship. And his second.

Hulk Hogan; when Austin refused to wrestle the Immortal One, The Rock stepped up with a willingness to sell a decades old gimmick.

Brock Lesnar; when Austin refused to lose to the *Next* Big Thing without more hype, The Rock stepped in and made sure Brock Lesnar became *The* Big Thing with a losing effort in the main event of the second biggest show of the year.

Jeff Hardy; during one of his darkest periods, he was made to look world class by The Rock in a match not too dissimilar to #33 itself.

Goldberg; WCW's mightiest powerhouse was in need of making a forceful, impactful debut on WWE television. The Rock made sure he did just that.

Quite a list, to be sure, and a brief one at that; we might, for example, now add John Cena to it as well.

So, despite his deceptively short, incredibly successful run, The Rock has given a great deal back to the WWE; in the sense of generating money through tickets and merchandise; in the sense of making new stars and legitimising others; in the sense of never failing to entertain audiences that were never anything other than lively when he was in the ring or on the stage. He just did all of this – and in the process ensured legendary status – in half the time as most others.

#33 is testament to The Rock's willingness and generosity as a talent and performer, showing the kind of attitude and ethic that has earned him the right to be in the position he is in. #33's very existence proves Rock's selfless nature as a pro wrestler. Though he never turned down success, nor did he ever fail to help forge it for others. Losing to Hurricane gained him nothing. It did result in a fun time, entertainment for the fans, and relevancy and increased legitimacy for the Hurricane, if only for the briefest time.

Any professional wrestler with that kind of work ethic in the face of the kind of overwhelming success that happens usually only once in a generation is a professional wrestler that should rightfully have the ability to choose to wrestle whenever he wants, whenever he can. Granted, of course, whether The Rock "sold out" is a judgement each fan will either eschew or buy into individually. History makes it hard to contest, though, that, if he did, he had certainly earned the right to.

#32
Daniel Bryan vs. John Cena
WWE World Heavyweight Championship
Summerslam
August 18th, 2013

When The Rock did return from his long hiatus in the beginning of 2011, it was to inevitably set up the feud that seemed to be screaming to happen. Being (arguably in the case of the People's Champion) the standard bearers of their respective eras chains Rock and Cena to comparative reception and, regardless of whether such comparisons are logical and fair, the prospect of a bout between the two was tantalising.

Their feud was actually an issue directly related to the one explored in the preceding review, where Cena claimed The Rock was disingenuous regarding his proclamations of love for professional wrestling because of his career path. When considering the amount The Rock did for his contemporaries and employer during his active years, such cynicism on the part of Cena feels unwarranted. When comparing The Rock's work to John Cena's, it threatens to become outright hypocritical.

Consider that John Cena ruled the roost for the vast majority of the Brand Extension Era, and few could touch him. His merchandise sales eclipsed all those of his colleagues prior to the onset of Reality. For the majority of this period, though, he was often levied with responsibility for the gradually increasing sterility of the product's creativity and, when considering the number of opponents that Cena failed to elevate, it becomes hard not to levy such responsibility on his shoulders. At the very least, John Cena can be said to be a performer nowhere near The Rock's level at elevating those he works with. Compare Cena's brief interaction with Zack Ryder to The Rock's with The Hurricane for a succinct example; Hurricane defeated The Rock where Cena's character, despite being a babyface, smugly made it abundantly clear Ryder had no hope of beating him. Following his work with Cena, Ryder's hot streak failed to ever rekindle.

Some never recovered from the damage dealt. For others, said damage was only fleeting and some others still took months, sometimes years, to get their careers back on track. It cannot be argued that feuding with John Cena proved detrimental to their upward trajectories. Umaga, The Miz, Mark Henry, Wade Barrett, Alberto Del Rio, Dolph Ziggler and Ryback are just a few that suffocated to varying degrees during Cena's run; almost an entire generation.

Frustrations with him in that sense can be understood. They may even be justified. As time wore on and the Reality Era began to kick into gear, these victories from Cena became increasingly unacceptable, bordering on morally outrageous to the fan base. When new stars saw their popularity explode naturally in a way that never happened for others before them in the preceding age, John Cena's position could no longer afford to go unjustified. His legacy might have become irreparably toxic if he did not do something to redeem his run up top. In professional wrestling terms, that meant something very clear and extremely unbending: he had to lose in categorical, undoubted fashion.

2013 began with a clear indication of the fan sentiment towards Cena's position when he main evented WrestleMania with The Rock for a second year straight and defeated the People's Champion; many felt it was an indulgent display. It turned some away from WWE. This confirmation victory, however, was not of *who would be* the guy for the coming period, as such inter-generational battles have come to represent. Rather, it was confirmation that Cena *had been* the guy of the Brand Extension Era. Consider that the early departure of The Rock from the company in 2003, followed in short order by the early departure of Lesnar from the company in 2004, meant not only did Cena have to step up to the mantle of "The Guy" much sooner than he might otherwise have needed to but that also there was no forbear to do the so-called "favour" for him either. So instead, it was upon the culmination of The Rock's return run in 2013 that Cena received said favour; at the end of his stint, rather than the start.

An unusual, perhaps even entirely unique incident in history better contextualised with what followed. If the first half of 2013 was confirmation of Cena's status throughout the preceding age, the second half was the validation that status was deserved. At Summerslam, with #32, the time had come for John Cena to lose in categorical, undoubted fashion and live up to the endgame responsibility of any performer carrying the weight of being "The Guy."

How does one loss justify as lengthy, to some even as damaging a run as top dog like Cena's? Consider the loss was against Daniel Bryan: the most naturally popular wrestler in WWE since perhaps even before John Cena. It was a match that carried a sense of event, and rightly so; it lived up to promise and really marked the maturation point, the coming of age, of the Reality Era; and it resulted in the Reality Era philosophy's real first masterpiece of a feud between Daniel Bryan and The Authority, which was felt palpably and harshly enough to combatively divide fan reception.

The match plays off of the vibe of moral ambiguity that beats at the heart of both character performances. Contempt is felt from both competitors; Cena exhibits it with a resentful expression when Bryan kicks out of a sit-down powerbomb, while Bryan exhibits it in attempting to off Cena ironically, with his own STF. The motivation for this contempt on both sides is even more interesting. For Bryan, it's Cena's status as a parody of professional wrestling. For Cena, it's Bryan's grand claims being unsupported by a lack of real notable achievement.

Explosive is an adjective that applies for the duration. The crowd investment is palpable, as is the energy. The pacing is pristine and lends a sense of athletic relentlessness that only the best in the world could hope to compete with. Fluidity is the name of the game; moving from holds to impact offense, sometimes then to trademarks and finishing exchanges, is all seamless. This is not a sweeping narrative linked with stand out set-pieces; it's physical poetry. If the aim was to portray a war of two men equal in their ability – one through acumen, one through experience – then the flailing ebb and flow manages that with beautiful exhaustion. Just when it seems both competitors are at a stalemate as the action pauses, it erupts like a dormant volcano anew.

The action is as clinically executed in the final moments as it is in the first minutes too. There are no slips. Their work is tight, well timed and, frankly, flawless. As an achievement, that perhaps sees it rank higher than the Punk / Lesnar masterpiece that preceded it earlier in the evening; though, it may not be quite as emotionally affecting.

The point remains clear, though. When push came to shove, John Cena recognised his time had come to take a step back. Without protestation or contestation, he lost to Daniel Bryan and validated both his prolonged run as the alpha performer in WWE and the gross, borderline overbearing achievements of his career in general. He may not have been as naturally capable of elevation as The Rock was, nor be as naturally athletically gifted as Brock Lesnar, but unlike both The Rock and Brock Lesnar he was there to do what he had to do at the time he had to do it. Daniel Bryan defeated John Cena cleanly, not in the twilight of his run as a main event star in WWE but at its beginning.

The Rock and John Cena are two of a kind. Theirs is a debate that may rage for years to come. In the end, the fairest conclusion is that, though their methods were both different, both questionable and both controversial, they both validated their places in WWE history as warranted by, sooner or later, living up to their most important responsibility as "The Guy."

Chapter 24

The Father and Godfather

#31
Hulk Hogan vs. Mr. McMahon
Street Fight
WrestleMania XIX
March 30th, 2003

The career of the progenitor of sports entertainment himself, Hulk Hogan, against the owner and innovator of WrestleMania itself, Vince McMahon, in a Street Fight - the scale of that is almost unbelievably huge.

Throughout the years, ever since Vince McMahon decided to turn himself into a regular on-screen character following the aftermath of Montreal, he has placed himself in increasingly high profile matches. It started with him facing his greatest nemesis, Steve Austin, in the main event of a weekly instalment of Monday Night Raw and, within a year, Vince was winning the Royal Rumble and headlining pay-per-views. Throughout pretty much the entirety of 1999 and certainly the first half of 2000, as well as the Invasion angle, the McMahon family were all over the televised product. At times, it worked greatly to the detriment of the WWE television shows and many notable critics seemingly frowned upon it.

Vince's own involvement, specifically, has been persistent and, throughout, he has placed himself in marquee matches against an extremely impressive list of all-time greats. Indeed, given his limited number of matches, Vince McMahon's in-ring record could rank amongst the most impressive in terms of the quality of his opponents. "Stone Cold" Steve Austin, Ric Flair, Hulk Hogan, Brock Lesnar,

Bret Hart, Shawn Michaels, Triple H, CM Punk and even The Undertaker all fall onto the list.

The difficulty many have with Vince McMahon wrestling, though, is the simple fact that he is not a wrestler. As WWE's Chairman, and the most successful pro wrestling promoter of all time, he can naturally do what he wants. While, courtesy of empathy, reverence and respect, we should not condemn him, we should recognise the difficulty in excusing the apparent self-indulgence any McMahon bout carries with it. The matches are often awkward, often last too long and often hog air time better spent on more relevant affairs. This Hogan match, then, is perhaps an exception to that.

This match does not shy away from sinfully indulging itself in a manner that could so easily be criticised if the opponent were anyone else. Be it nostalgic fondness for Hulk Hogan or not, this match is more than acceptable as a main selling point for WrestleMania, both financially at the time and qualitatively in a historical context. It could be called so bad it's good, but the truth is it just really isn't that bad at all.

It plays well in Hogan's favour that Vince is allowed to uncharacteristically get a good half of the offense in the match. The Street Fight stipulation, of course, adds to the quality and allows two pretty limited men at this point to make things better than, on paper, they should have any right to be. The chair shots throughout are disgustingly high impact, like gun shots rattling through the rafters. The blade jobs, love them or hate them as a principle, make things even more dramatic. This extra shade of red is very much appropriate, adding something to the already highly emotional proceedings.

Then there's the Hulk Up. If ever there was a perfect Hulk Up, this was it. It might even have the most cynical fan "marking out." It's a fun, epic and emotional end to a fun, epic and emotional match. The historical scope of their story is wonderful, its excitement palpable and the action oozes pure, visceral emotion.

Without a doubt, this was Vince McMahon's best match; one of the best worked Street Fights of all-time and possibly a runner for the best match of Hulk Hogan's career, as well; certainly a contender for his best WrestleMania match. The question, however, at the heart of this entry is, "is it really a Hulk Hogan match?" It seemed, both at the time and now looking back on it, that somehow it was more about Vince McMahon than it was the Hulkster and, perhaps, that is partly the reason why the added stipulation that Hogan's career was on the line gets pretty lost amidst all the fever. This isn't a Hulk Hogan match at all, in truth. It's a Vince McMahon match.

That truth, in turn, presents the affecting symbolism #31 takes on: for all his hype, all his impressive matches, all the historic moments he has been a part of both internally for WWE and externally for professional wrestling as an industry, this is a match that reminds of one quite simple, quite plain and quite inarguable fact: essentially, Vince McMahon has become the world's most successful backyard wrestler.

That is not intended to imply any reductive disrespect; it is actually written with a great deal of affection for the unmitigated success of Vince McMahon: pro wrestling's very own Alexander the Great. As the father of WWE, Vince McMahon is, to some degree, the father of the modern Western professional wrestling fan. His company is the leading force in professional wrestling today around the globe, after all. As fans, it is important we recognise the importance of that attribute.

Vince McMahon's actions as the leader of WWE are frequently controversial, often leading to many of the disillusioned fans, and even more of the old school thinkers, calling him "out of touch." It may be that he is; why is that necessarily a bad thing, though? It might sound overly reverential, but Vince McMahon has proven to be a pioneering forward-thinker. It has been stated already that he was a moderniser in professional wrestling courtesy of his leadership of, and influence over, WWE, and now he can be called a post-moderniser too. Vitally, this has only happened because of his ability to adapt his product with the times, contrary to the pervasive criticisms he suffers. Professional wrestling could not continue to function in the 1980s as it had twenty years prior because the world had changed, so McMahon changed the game. He is on record as saying his competitors drove themselves out of business by not reinvesting financially; I wonder how much it might also be because they failed to reinvest creatively too.

Under Vince McMahon's leadership, WWE may make odd choices from time to time, but it continues to exist and lead the way in professional wrestling for a reason: Vince McMahon's openness to change. That is the very issue at the heart of this book's grand design – to rethink the equation; just as the industry had to change its game in the 1980s, so should it again today. Regardless, the question in #31 is answered by its own symbolism: Vince McMahon created Hulkamania, because Vince McMahon led the charge to modernise, and later post-modernise, professional wrestling.

#30

Macho Man Randy Savage vs. Ricky "The Dragon" Steamboat
Intercontinental Championship
Maple Leaf Gardens
July 26th, 1986

How can you ever not be impressed by a bout pitting these two legends together? Before their WrestleMania III encounter, these two would wrestle across the country and, in doing so, create a library of work impressive by its own right. Checking out any of these matches is worth the time, so why is #30 on this list over any others?

In the early stages of conceiving this list, news broke regarding the very sad, very untimely passing of Randy Savage. As a fan, I had not expected this to hit me as hard as it did and so, in order to pay tribute, I picked for this list the first match that came up on an internet search of "Randy Savage vs." #30 was the first hit.

Sitting and watching this bout made clear just how brilliant Randy Savage was on any night of the week at any event he was performing at, whether it was at WrestleMania or something far more unsuspecting (like #30). Picking an unheralded, random composition from a dusty corner of history is a tribute in itself to Savage's uninterrupted brilliance for all the years he spent between the ropes.

The magic of a Savage match was never derived from an abundance of complex content and jaw-dropping visuals. He was known as an aerialist in his time, but one defined differently to how one today may be defined. Instead, Savage was able to use the simplest of moves in exactly the right order to create something truly affecting. He used just the right blend of action and placement to morph a fluidly told, gripping narrative. Realism may not be quite the right word, but believability is most certainly fitting, as is simple and gritty too. Savage was a master chemist, and his ingredients all the basics. He was infamous for practicing his matches beforehand until perfectly ironed out. Such micromanagement allowed his matches to exude confidence in their execution. Margins for error were always tiny, so when coupling that attention to detail with the preciseness of a talent like Steamboat, the result is an economy of movement dismissive of trepidation.

Prototypical at its heart, #30 is a match indicative of the wider leviathan importance that the Macho Man has in WWE history: it is well ahead of its time.

There are moments in the confines of the action that make the match feel as if it would be more at home in the late 1990s than in the late 1980s. The brawling on the outside, the brief moments in the crowd, even the unexpected blade job all made the work feel, at times, like it was matching the structure of a Rock vs. Triple H World title match, not an Intercontinental title contest from a decade prior. #30 even takes the time to work in a referee bump, complete with an uncounted pin attempt; a hugely over-used staple of professional wrestling throughout the decades, particularly prominent at the turn of the century. Not only is this a match that few seem aware of, it is a match that, if not pioneering because of its lack of influence, is most certainly prophetic in its form.

Macho's career as a whole, in fact, has the fingerprints of creation all over it. Randy Savage helped draw grand designs, fathering the "WWE style" used still to this day at WrestleMania III and blueprinting the modern main event style prescient throughout WWE history – again to this very day – at WrestleMania VII with Ultimate Warrior. So too was he a professional wrestling soothsayer. In the confines of any given one of his efforts on any given night, you can find tropes that are now held up as being indicative of ages much later down the line. It was not just in his matches either; he would often be a part of hard-hitting angles that maintain their sharp edges even in the desensitised internet age of the world, like Jake Roberts' attack on Elizabeth documented by #78.

This is the very reason it is looking at Randy Savage that closes out this section on the most important and anomalous individuals in WWE history. From Phenoms to phenomena, from cornerstones to poster boys, without a doubt two figures tower over all others in the promotion's past, and will continue to do so in the future. That is because there can always be other phenomena, there always will be other poster boys and there may yet be a third Phenom, but there can only ever be one *first*. Vince McMahon created WWE as we know it today and, arguably, by extension modern Western professional wrestling as we know it today too. He is the father of it all and his towering stature needs neither explanation nor justification. Only one man stands shoulder to shoulder with him in historical significance and that is Macho Man Randy Savage.

Professional wrestling is an industry that takes the issue of respect very seriously. Many of the performers who make this proclamation may owe more to Savage than anyone. Hogan popularised professional wrestling and catapulted it into the mainstream. He deserves recognition for leading the pack with a charisma and energy few others could match. His role in ensuring the WWF could exist in the MTV world of the late 1980s is a vital one. But while Hogan ensured the WWF had an immediate future, Randy Savage ensured, consciously or otherwise, that professional wrestling had a long-term future. It is precisely because his work was so ahead of its time that renders the term "timeless" more relevant in application to said work than to that of any of his contemporaries, forebears, or even successors.

Put succinctly, if Vince McMahon built the stage Randy Savage wrote the play. In that sense, he is the Godfather of WWE to Vince McMahon's father, despite never having been "The Guy" of his era. As the promotion is identified through a combination of both its philosophy and style, together McMahon and Savage are the progenitors of the company as we know it today and, together, the two most important men in WWE history.

Chapter 25

The Intercontinental Championship: The Best of a Personal Favourite

#29
British Bulldog vs. Bret "Hitman" Hart
WWF Intercontinental Championship
Summerslam
August 31st, 1992

Like Steamboat vs. Savage, Warrior vs. Hogan, Austin vs. Rock and Cena vs. Punk, this is a wrestling match in the WWE history books that stands as more than just a match. It has the same aura and emotive significance as its life-blood; this is an historical event. That you can watch it decades removed and still get the same feel good sensation at its conclusion should stand as a tall testament to the achievement of Hart and Bulldog on that fateful summer evening.

Even with sentiment aside, this may be the greatest Intercontinental Championship match of all-time. If you take the Intercontinental title as representative of a division in professional wrestling (from the perspective of simulated sport) or if you take it as a piece of genre television defined by its MacGuffin (from the performance art perspective), either way you have a defining match at hand. For all the thirteen years of the Intercontinental title that came before this match, and for all the years that have passed since, nothing may have quite beaten this well-crafted and superlatively performed opus. If you want to romanticise the Intercontinental Championship then what better match than this?

The action starts slow, establishing a steadily unfolding pace while carefully clarifying the dynamic that characterises most matches between the two combatants: it is swiftly established as a battle between Bulldog's power and Hart's technique. Intrigue soon follows the caution of their first scenes, as Bulldog neutralises Hart's technical advantage with an explosion of agility all his own, putting the champ on notice; while the power belongs exclusively to Bulldog, the technique far from exclusively belongs to the Hitman.

One of the most enjoyable aspects of this epic is its purely athletic focus and such emphasis facilitates Bulldog's win watching as all the more impressive. He very much feels like the genuinely better competitor and, thus, as a British fan myself - and for the British crowd at the time - his big win goes from being a personally inspiring one to a nationalistically prideful one. Yet, unlike bouts wrestled before more millennial crowds, while an emotional match, it remains good humoured.

The later the match progresses, the clearer it becomes that the Bulldog is struggling. Fortunately, there's enough left in the Brit's tank to be able to lend his comeback enough emotive credence to keep the roller-coaster narrative fluid and bring his power game back to the forefront. In the third act – the bout's most effective - the frenetic storytelling dims with a double clothesline that marks a point of exhaustion so terrible Hart has to apply his Sharpshooter literally lying down; a rare occasion of the Sharpshooter being applied outside of the work's conclusion. It's a nice prelude to the actual finish that comes out of nowhere and provides a naturalistic conclusion to this purely athletic competition – an exhausted counter of a weakened sunset flip.

Naturally, when claiming #29 the greatest Intercontinental Championship match of all-time, the elephant in the room becomes the fabled WrestleMania III Intercontinental Championship match. While #29 may represent a grand achievement, it hasn't had anywhere near the lasting historical significance that its more beloved predecessor has enjoyed. But such is the grandiose historical fact lavished upon Savage and Steamboat that it really should stand apart of *any* comparison to *any* match (another reason why #58's Michaels / Jericho 'Mania match is best viewed as only a spiritual sequel). To place it within a comprehensive tome of related title defences almost seems to rob it of its most significant personality trait. In other words, the exceptional circumstance of WrestleMania III deservedly makes that match exempt from comparison.

That should not allow the significant abundance of quality in #29 to look slight; that would be unjust. Truthfully, it's hard to imagine that any other Intercontinental title match will ever top this one. Think about the conceptual definitions at play: Summerslam is the second biggest show of the year; the Intercontinental Championship was the second most important championship in the company; Hart and Bulldog were originally going to play second fiddle to more heavily established main event talent; quite literally, then, this is a match that was actively designed to be second best. Yet this match exceeded such expectations, outright defied conceptual definitions and cast a very long shadow over the Intercontinental Championship out of which no match may ever step forth.

Perhaps, though, my adulation for this personal favourite defence of a personal favourite championship is a little skewed because of my nationality; I am, of course, British myself.

British WWE fans are confronted by a multitude of obstacles to their ability to follow the product. Consider that, traditionally, WWE tours our shores only twice a year and most people get only to see the equivalent of a house show in that time frame. Only once each tour is there a television taping, and those tapings always take place down in London during the April visitation. That leaves only one viable chance a year for many fans to get to attend a WWE show with some deal of significance. Then, focussing solely on the television aspect, following events remains tricky; having to stay up until 4am to watch a generally lacklustre edition of Monday Night Raw demands a great deal of dedication. When it comes to pay-per-views, the only real option for a working individual in full-time employment is to watch it the following evening, risking spoilers in the process, or to book a morning off of work to catch the action when it matters most: when it's live. Similar pragmatically difficult circumstances no doubt apply in other nations across the globe too, in some degree or another, who may not even get a visitation to their shores.

This is not intended as embittered lamentation, though, and is all stated with complete dispassion. WWE is, quite understandably, an American enterprise and, quite understandably – perhaps justly – prioritises its American fans first. The reason these elements of the British WWE experience are highlighted here is simply that they play actively into why #29 is a personal favourite of mine, and should be a personal favourite for Brits too. It is an optimistic match, an airy delight, the historical significance of which should rightfully pull on the heartstrings of any proudly British fan. It seems difficult for many to envision the British contingent ever getting a shining moment of glory again on the level #29 provided. Thus, it becomes more than just a match and more than a historical event even.

It is a vindication of the British fan base and a notification that we are, indeed, valued. It is a hug; a pat on the back; a love letter to the British WWE fan. It is one of the most important matches in WWE history for any British fan as a result, and a perfectly fitting choice to kick off our look at the promotion’s most vital compositions through the ages.

Chapter 26

Sports and Entertainment: The Best of Both Worlds

#28
Brock Lesnar vs. Kurt Angle
60 Minute Iron Man Match
WWE Championship
Smackdown!
September 18th, 2003

At this stage, you are more than familiar with the intention at the heart of this book: to move the reception of professional wrestling towards one that makes more sense in the world today and that allows us to view it in its transcended state of performance art. Nevertheless, even when doing this we cannot ignore history and, for the longest time, WWE has rightly characterised itself sports entertainment. Though my opinion is that such a mode of thought is ineffective in this day and age, I fully embrace that it was not always so. There is, therefore, a historical responsibility to account for WWE's sports entertainment past; this chapter will succinctly do just that, looking at the matches that best represent the greatest efforts of both halves of that equation in the promotion's history. One has already been dealt with in Chapter 8's #68 WrestleMania XIX main event match and the theme continues now with #28. If Angle and Lesnar put the wrestle in WrestleMania, so too did they put the sports in sports entertainment with this sixty-minute epic of an Iron Man Match.

Legitimacy is what this one's all about: two of the best qualified amateur wrestlers to ever walk in a WWE ring clashing in the most wrestling-orientated stipulation in the company for the top prize available, with each holding a past victory over the other.

Dissimilar to other bouts in the genre, the action starts out like any other match without making special room for a different opening designed to compensate for the elongated run time. That's to be admired for its confidence in conditioning, performance and in ability – a confidence that stretches end to end. Bar a little showmanship to help thicken the psychological dynamic, Angle and Lesnar literally wrestle for sixty minutes. As hyperbolic as it sounds, it is a peak of human athletic capability. Refreshingly, Cole and Tazz fall in with the sense of legitimacy too courtesy of an impressive sports-style commentary.

The pace is pretty steady until the closing minutes, with such evenness allowing the discourse to unfold in what feels like an organic dramatisation – nothing comes out of nowhere and nothing feels displaced. So too is there a nice variety of falls. It's not just all pins, as in some others. There is an example of each of the four most common methods of victory: submission, pin fall, disqualification and count-out all make an appearance. It's an exhaustive match as a result, quite literally a stroll through the very substance of a wrestling match, draining to watch and indicative of the industry's sporting side. If that were not enough of an embodiment of *sports* entertainment, a good 75% of the action takes place within the ring and between the ropes. There could be no other way to end the purest wrestling rivalry WWE has ever seen in as fitting a fashion.

That they simply do not run out of steam – it feels very much like they have plenty more left at contest's end – is worthy of remembrance alone; how they use that to prevent crowd disinterest in the all-important middle section is masterful. Just when you think there's nowhere left for them to go entering the final twenty minutes, they start to form a more stylised drama, beginning to quite expectedly break out closer near falls and exhibiting more pained expressions of frustration. Lesnar starts utilising increasingly impactful power moves, with an impressive powerbomb and equally striking superplex looking especially painful. The final quarter hour is the most dramatic of the lot, as frustration and desperation gives way to frenetic urgency. The entire final straight tells a story almost isolated from the rest of the match. Angle is down 5-2, against a man proving to be invulnerable. Lesnar's power, toughness, aggression and cunning have all taken centre stage. With his opponent having such a commanding lead and well-rounded offensive arsenal, Angle needs to utilise every fibre in his being to be able to force a draw. Even that aspect on its own - that the champ turns his sights to forcing overtime as opposed to gaining an out-and-out win - sets the piece apart from others of its kind.

We see the effectiveness of a submission finish as the final minutes eke out. Seeing Angle on the cusp of forcing the bout to a draw with Lesnar on the verge of tapping out, the legitimacy of the action has you entirely suspending disbelief. This is real emotion at play, and the closing moments play out almost as a sick perversion of the finish to the first ever Iron Man where Shawn, the noble sympathetic challenger seeking validation, held on while in the Sharpshooter. Here, the cunning and despicable challenger seeks to stick it to the crowd by holding on while in an Ankle Lock. The fact that he does, even after the entire final two minutes have been Angle locking Lesnar in submission after submission, is a finish to this superlative achievement of a match that'll leave the viewer winded. This brave and uniquely dark ending is very much the crowning achievement.

That achievement reminds again of the sports in sports entertainment; in the latter, the good guys always win, but in the former that might not necessarily be the case. WWE has always been a place where good guys are likely to win the day more often than not, but here it's a rare example of the "bad" ending we receive, because the bad guy was the better competitor when it mattered. This difficult-to-beat Iron Man match becomes an hour long tug-of-war, with the advantage in the opening resting firmly with the challenger but increasingly shifting the other way as the match progresses, until it rests firmly in the corner of the champion for the final five minutes.

The performances of both individuals are remarkable, the believability of the match all-consuming and the content is a master class of professional wrestling. Quite literally in every conceivable way, this match is an absolute unadulterated success. It is the rubber match to WWE's purest wrestling rivalry in its entire modern history. It's a monument to the athletic achievement of professional wrestling, in spite of its fiercest critics. It is the greatest sporting achievement in the history of sports entertainment.

#27
The Rock vs. Stone Cold Steve Austin
Special Guest Referee: Shane McMahon
No Holds Barred Match
WWF Championship
Backlash
April 25th, 1999

So what about the equation's second half; what about sports *entertainment*? What match best exhibits the latter of those two infamous words?

The feud of which #27 was a part is to be revisited later in this list; for now, sufficed to say there is a reason Austin and Rock are two thirds of WWE's personal Rushmore and the financial, popular and critical success of their work together has seen them go down in history deservedly as one of, if not *the* most entertaining pairing in WWE. Unlike #28, #27 was not the rubber match of this famous feud, though. As a matter of fact, it was one of the earliest matches in the years-long programme. It is because of this relative lack of history and the lack of weighty responsibility lent by the absence of WrestleMania fever that it is able to become the finest embodiment of entertainment over its various prequels and sequels.

Actual wrestling is minimal at best. Yet the intensity evidenced in both men, coupled with the visceral emotion of performers and fans both that bled through this entire age, helps keep things engagingly entertaining. This is a match that doesn't take itself too seriously, nor concern itself with pretentions above its station. It's plain and simple and aimed at achieving only one thing: a fun time for the fans.

Both characters are shown going to extreme lengths to walk away with the WWF Championship and that tone of "extreme" is what makes the affair such transfixing entertainment. The Rock, in particular, shows why he was so much fun to watch, talking trash on a Spanish commentator's headset, stealing a camera and inserting a certain degree of slapstick comedy to proceedings. Even Austin's response to a lot of Rock's antics takes on a comic tone of its own, simply by virtue of association. The moment in which a Rock-operated camera turns to see a standing Austin giving him the middle finger, and hearing Rock's resultant expletive on the directional microphone, is a classic.

Very much a match of its time, this is twenty minutes of shameless, confident action that watches like less of a wrestling match and more of a Hollywood fist fight. These are two evenly matched gladiators quite literally tearing down the world around them in their quest to defeat one another. What's not to enjoy? The refreshingly honest drama of the Golden Age and the strikingly competitive athleticism of the New Gen had been traded in for visceral emotion; a visceral emotion that also shows little concern for the psychological complexities that the Brand Extension Era would insist upon, and which the Reality Era would so fearlessly experiment with. Like the general product of its Era, #27 was a thrill ride.

For all the criticisms the Attitude Era receives, the historical truth of it being the most successful period in company history cannot be denied, nor the historical circumstances in which it boomed. Today is a day in which WWE obsesses over its own lineage and future legacies, while in the days before Austin 3:16 it was a company led by Vince McMahon's competitive obsession to progress. In the Attitude Era, however, everything was much more reactive. In the midst of a war they were losing, it watches now like WWE were essentially "booking for the moment" and, as a result, the pace of the general product was more intense and, I dare say, more liberated. Here, Rock and Austin watch as performers concerned only with the immediate task at hand: to put on a good show and bring the viewer back the next night. This is not a composition trying to pioneer or fulfill promise; it is a composition trying only to entertain. The matches of these poster boys of a generation should be remembered as the artefacts of truth that they are, proving the hyperactive, unconcerned flaws of Attitude were also, paradoxically, its greatest advantages.

Rock and Austin were two men in a much larger field, wrestling at the top of a deep roster. While various levels of that roster provided different ideas and match design, needless to say what was happening at the top often cascaded down. It was an unrelenting and chaotic time period, providing an intensity we'd never had before and haven't had since. Shows would often provide much action with little staying power, but the moments that are remembered are, arguably, more memorable than any of their counterparts from other periods of company history. While it rarely got anything unforgivably wrong, when it got things right it proved more memorable by virtue of, at times, its lunacy and, at others, its intensity. The Rock / Austin feud was one of the things it got very, very right, boldly embodying the second half of the sports entertainment equation better than any other programme ever has.

That did not apply just to their work one month out of the year in their WrestleMania bouts but any time they met, whether on Raw, at Survivor Series in 2001 or here. Pound for pound, this match at least deserves to be rated above their first two encounters at the Grandest Stage of All; a controversial assertion perhaps, given the popularity of their X-Seven main event particularly. #27 is more foucssed than 'Mania XV, more succinct than 'Mania X-Seven and free of the heady creative intention of my personal, sentimental 'Mania XIX favourite; such apparently free-spirited intention only favours the piece all the more.

Thus, it becomes not only a historical artefact, accidental in its design to speak in deference of the Attitude Era as a whole, but also becomes the pinnacle of *entertainment* in WWE's history of sports entertainment; not because it was their final encounter, or their grandest, but simply because it was their *most fun.*

Chapter 27

Coming of Age in WWE

#26
Edge and Christian vs. The New Brood
Tag Team Ladder Match
WWF Tag Team Championship
No Mercy
October 17th, 1999

The first bouts in this chapter were held back from entry in Chapter 7's coverage of gimmick matches as genre because, historically, they are such strong examples of watershed moments; turning points we are able to identify in history, which introduced paradigmatic shifts away from a then-orthodoxy.

The three concepts to be dealt with over the following four reviews do not represent any kind of exhaustive list of the most important historical waypoints by any means, but they tackle three more folkloric aspects of how WWE has operated over the years. Identifying, then, their respective coming of ages – easily done when utilising our new understanding of pro wrestling matches as performance art genre - becomes not only an interesting exercise, but a necessary one to shrug off the inaccurate popular assumptions perpetuated by WWE's propagandistic attitude to its own past.

The multitude of Ladder Matches on this list should show just how intrinsic the concept has become to how WWE elevates its talent and obsesses over successfully established tropes. It is, therefore, the first of the aforementioned concepts to be explored at this juncture, and such exploration leads to an intriguing conclusion.

Unlike in other cases, the Ladder genre matured over a pair of matches spaced a couple of months apart, with the latter-most exhibiting clear signs of what this over-exposed genre would become by the end of the 2000s. The first part of this coming of age came in the guise of #26; a vitally important match in company history without which ideas like Money in the Bank and TLC may never have come into existence.

There's a nice sense of tradition to this match – the prize is a bag of cash and it's the final of a Best Of series between two solid tag teams to determine who wins the services of a famed manager. Such tradition is in juxtaposition with how genre-defining this would eventually prove itself to be; that contrast proves a wonderfully whimsical paradox. It is a match that reads in its set-up as quite traditionalist yet watches as a historically important piece of progressivism.

If occurring today, the word that should apply to #26 would be tame. In this day and age, running up a ladder to deliver a dropkick is decidedly orthodox. Tipping a ladder backwards and crushing the athlete beneath lacks expected superlative effect; so do the moves that #26's combatants execute from atop relatively average-sized ladders. For the time, though, we must remember these were spectacular spots with fans rightfully amazed with the feats of athleticism. This is cutting edge work and, while today the match lacks the same sense of exaggeration courtesy of its dense library of successors, it remains an entertaining watch. It's an inherently contradictory piece of history. In its contemporary setting, this is a match that stood apart because of its ground-breaking accomplishments while, in the modern era, this is a match that stands apart because it feels refreshingly simple. In both instances, it's something that stands with its head above the crowd and, as a result, despite showing its age, it remains perennially relevant.

Psychological synergy has a greater, more consistent presence with #26 than many other later iterations of the stipulation. The match's story is more cohesive by virtue of the role that the ladders adopt, limited to that of a platform off of which moves are executed. Occasions do occur wherein the ladder is used more proactively as a weapon to debilitate, but these moments are demanded organically by the logic of the narrative; the target of such an attack may have only just attempted a run up the ladder to retrieve the money required to win, for example. In such context, the ladder is a weapon of prevention over destruction. The greatest virtue of such an approach is maintaining the focus: the story revolves around the simple but inherent principle of trying to climb the ladder to win, and is never distracted by unnecessary sub-plots jarringly imposed.

This ultimately results in a staggered psychology that allows the action to progress at a steady pace instead of decaying into an unfocussed kinetic assault on the senses. It is also well suited to the idea that this is still a tag match. All four men take a lion's share of the work. There are no supporting actors - only four leading men - giving each performer a spotlight to show what he can do; and it pays off. Guts and athleticism are aplenty in this match and, if ever there was a true ensemble cast assembled for a professional wrestling match that complimented one another instead of competing, this would be a top contender.

There's clear competency among these four in how the more outrageous stunts are performed. The over-zealous execution that has come to mark modern interpretations of the genre is notable and admirable by its absence. If anything, watching this match in today's context goes to show just how comfortable the Ladder Match would go on to become with its own clichés; this was when it was still taken seriously, before grit was replaced with glitz.

This was a genre-defining effort from four future foundational stars of the company, three of whom would eventually find their way to World Championship gold in WWE. #26 marked all four out as a potential future megastar - a destiny met by half the field at least - and provided performances that are remembered for their creativity, as opposed to their lunacy. This was a landmark for professional wrestling as an industry and a benchmark for the Ladder Match itself. This is another slice of WWE history.

In fact, #26 carries the rights to the tagline given to one of its predecessors. Shawn Michaels vs. Razor Ramon at WrestleMania X is described by WWE's promotional machine as the match that redefined the Ladder Match. That claim should be strongly disputed. The use of the stipulation remained few and far between after 1994's MSG mega-show, and the style of the Mr. WrestleMania classic itself adheres very closely to the more psychological style Hart and Michaels wrestled years prior in the *only* iteration of the genre to have occurred before 'Mania X (and to much less celebration I may add). The Michaels / Ramon effort was a definition before it was anything else; it is really #26 that *redefined* the genre some years later. That its redefinition persists to this day as the genre's predominant philosophy - even if it was added to and developed by the majority of later efforts - transforms the composition into the coming of age story of its genre; the Ladder Match would never, ever be the same again.

The truth is that before Edge, Christian, Matt and Jeff took to using two ladders in one match, the stipulation had only ever featured one-on-one encounters. This match was the first step on the Ladder Match's descent into madness; it would eventually lead to the Triangle Ladder bout - the second half of this two-part tale - at the following 'Mania, which in turn provided the clear blueprint for the TLC Match. #26, nevertheless, first introduced fans to a new stunt-oriented performance, heavy on bravado and light on subtlety. Many of those stunts are pretty tame today but, without them, it is difficult to believe that the kind of increasingly dangerous efforts by guys like Benjamin and Kingston many years later would exist.

#25
Edge and Christian vs. The Hardy Boys vs. The Dudley Boys
WWF Tag Team Championship
Triangle Ladder Match
WrestleMania XVI
April 2nd, 2000

Growth and change don't occur overnight, as it is sometimes tempting to believe. These things happen gradually, and so can it be said about the transition of the Ladder Match from WrestleMania X through to TLC and, most latterly, Money in the Bank. #26 began a process of redefinition by introducing increasingly dangerous spots and the idea that more than two competitors could work inside the same environment at the same time. A beginning was all that it was, though; a pilot episode that may wane under superlative comparison to today. #25, then, is the match that turned outline into portrait, pilot into series; not only did it prove the workable longevity of the ideas presented in #26, but took those ideas further to show the more competitors, the more stunts and the more props the merrier. In doing so, it completed the two-part coming of age of a genre now so often integral to any changing of positioning in WWE's talent pool.

The participants quite literally jump right into their cause, with the first stunts coming only a couple of minutes in and largely consisting of aerialist verbosity. These earlier stunts help quickly mark this match as requisite viewing too; when you get a "Holy Shit!" chant in the first five minutes, you know it's going to be a crazy ride. The further the match progresses, the more frenzied the apparently initially disinterested crowd becomes, proving #25 a supreme achievement of narrative build toward crescendo; not always easy in these hysterical environments .

JR calls the composition an amazing offensive display and that is perhaps the best description for it. He also says it's very untraditional; if only that were still the case. That's probably the most #25 has going for it. Like in the case of #26, the composition cannot quite stack up next to later examples of its kind, but the offense shown is creative, innovative for its time and, given how most other matches with this level of hype and attention of that era were limited mostly to brawls, to watch some of this comparatively unusual offense is refreshing and a nice break from the norm; a fitting attraction at the year's biggest show.

The ring does get cluttered a little too much and a difficulty that still dogs the genre is present: there's occasionally too much downtime amidst the action, wrought by setting props up. Moments such as these are the genre's primary, most inherent flaw; it sacrifices immersion and pace for the sake of synthetic drama.

A result of this flaw is that #25 finds itself needing to degenerate into stunt man pantomime at points, lacking greater depth of reasoning as everyone climbs ladders and fist fights until they all fall down. In that sense, #25 is a dangerous enabler that set the first bar. #25's historical responsibility supersedes that of #26 as a result. The narrative of the evolution of the Ladder genre is one watermarked by greed; its habit became an addicting one that demanded more, more, more. The genre's coming of age story started that trend, which is exactly why said story comes in two parts rather than one. If #26's Tag Team Ladder Match showed what Ladder Matches could be, this prophetic Triangle Ladder Match showed what the Ladder Match was due to become.

Prior to this and its older brother from No Mercy 1999, Ladder Matches were few and far between. Since that event, though, fans have, more often than not by now, been getting more than one a year. They come out on television for the odd occasion, WWE have had more than one pay-per-view dedicated exclusively to the concept and that's not even mentioning the genre's regularity on other big shows too, such as WrestleMania and Extreme Rules. The market is saturated and, as a result, the quality has suffered immensely, and the danger has been raised to a level that is now often unnecessarily unsafe.

If any of the participants of these two redefining moments were to regret raising the bar quite so high, it would be hard to disagree with them. Centrally, of course, that's because, by the law of averages, it's only a matter of time before something seriously bad is going to happen to someone in such an environment. The more recent version that, in its unmitigated bravery, launched the fiercest reductionism of the genre *ever* – Seth Rollins vs. Dean Ambrose at Money in the Bank 2015 – was met with a lukewarm popular reception, no doubt propagated by its attempt to thankfully change the game by consciously doing less when more was expected; the nature of that reception threatens, if future entries into the genre want to be received with greater acclaim, the resultant effort may inevitably involve an unjustifiable degree of risk.

Together, in #26 and #25 we have a very important but overlooked, gruesome piece of professional wrestling history. They are very rare examples of when the term "redefined" can actually and genuinely be applied. That redefinition should be morally divisive; traditional powerful, affecting professional wrestling – like that seen in the aforementioned Rollins / Ambrose version – was thrown aside in favour of an instantly gratifying assault on the senses suited to the impatient society of the 21st Century. However, regardless which of those approaches you may personally prefer, this two stage coming of age tale that saw the Ladder Match alter its method, reshape its purpose and cement itself as a perennially profitable attraction (financially at least) remains an absolute must-see.

#24
30 Man Royal Rumble Match
WWF Championship
Royal Rumble
January 19th, 1992

The 1992 Royal Rumble is, quite possibly, the single most important iteration of the event in its history. That's not because it featured the first victorious single-digit entrant in the Rumble match, nor for any of the impressive iron man performances. It's certainly nothing to do with the fact that the title was on the line. It's because the 1992 Rumble marked the year in which it stopped being a novelty; 1992 was its coming of age story.

When the star of the show, Ric Flair, enters at #3, one of the most entertaining runs in Rumble history begins, with the single most entertaining Rumble soundtrack of all-time accompanying, composed by Bobby Heenan. The match hinges off of the Nature Boy heavily with a focus that rarely strays; every time someone new comes in, the story remains Flair-centric and, if the new entrant doesn't immediately blood their performance with a fracas with Naitch, Heenan and Monsoon still contextualise said entrant through their relationship to him.

The extent to which the 1992 Royal Rumble is a Ric Flair match is indisputable when you begin breaking down the bout into its composite parts, to discover Flair's integral role in most of the 60 minutes' highlights. Consider Piper's entrance, for example, which sees the action reset at around the halfway mark. After the ring has emptied, Piper and Flair are left to perform a great little combat before Jake Roberts follows, flitting from side to side with moral sterility; while it may be a Flair match, it is performances like Jake's that can help make the Rumble such an enthralling platform.

The pace inevitably slows down but the match is kept fresh by its interspersed points of narrative emphasis - Savage's entrance and immediate targeting of Roberts with the involvement of Undertaker; the entrance of the Hulkster; the inevitable coming of Sid Justice. Indeed, there are a number of points of interest littered throughout this marathon run worth their own notation.

The British Bulldog is allowed as frightfully entertaining a showing as he was the preceding year, if not getting a greater share of the stage, remaining in the thick of the action following his number one entry for quite some time. So too are there a number of impressive iron man runs. Michaels, having drawn number six, holds on for a notable period of time. Piper, IRS and Savage all clock in impressive run times of their own as well. Naturally, Flair's is the one that'll stick in the memory the most. The fact that none of these men spend any particularly lengthy period inactive though, constantly involving themselves in the thick of the action, remains ever more impressive.

Flair's performance itself is worth at least a paragraph, especially considering my labeling #24 "a Flair match." What really entertain are the examples of every single classic villainous trope throughout. Beg offs, low blows, flops, double crosses, eye pokes, walks on the outside, unsporting double teams, underhanded capitalisation; he reads from the Book of Heel so much it's like a sixty minute advent calendar with the pay-off of a sweet, sweet victory for fans of the pro wrestling bad guy. The 1992 Rumble becomes infinitely re-watchable as a result of this tongue-in-cheek exhaustiveness. So too, of course, did he wrestle over an hour in the WWF in 1992 which, at a time when Warrior and Hogan remained the company's biggest names in its modern history, really was a rare thing.

Rarity is perhaps the key word for #24. When thinking of transitional years in WWE history, minds may often first think of 1987, 1997 or, more recently, 2014. WrestleMania III, the Montreal Screwjob and Royal Rumble 2014 are all of incredible significance. Certainly 1992 rarely enters that conversation, but it too was a major moment of change in the company.

The return of the Ultimate Warrior and his evidently diminished popularity; Hogan's first major leave of absence from the company since becoming "The Man;" the final WrestleMania to actually take place in a stadium until 2001; the first majorly publicised over-seas WWE event in Summerslam; and, of course, the ascension of Bret Hart to a main event level culminating with his eventual World

Championship victory; they all meant that the WWF on Rumble day in 1993 was *radically* different to the WWF on Rumble day in 1992. It all started with #24.

Since its original inception in 1988, up to this point the Rumble had been rather akin to what King of the Ring once was. While winning it would be an impressive feat and look pretty good on any character's CV, it didn't really amount to anything directly in either kayfabe or reality. Testament to that are the winners that came before Flair – Duggan won the first in what now feels like inexplicable fashion, Big John Studd won perhaps because of his stature, and Hogan won twice running because he was Hulk Hogan. Then 1992 rolled around and, for the first time, WWE lent the Rumble greater importance.

1993 would capitalise on the idea of the Rumble match rewarding a prestigious prize outside of "a win" by becoming the first example of the winner receiving a title shot at WrestleMania. That stipulation then became the reasoning behind the bout's importance and drama permanently. 1992 was, therefore, key; the coming of age. After it had been and gone, and after Flair had showed the world how hard one had to work to attain a prize at the end of such a 30 man slog, the Royal Rumble went from being a novelty to one of the most important matches in the promotion's calendar, as well as throughout its history. If one wanted to go to extreme lengths, the argument could even be posited that, if it were not for 1992 - had the Rumble remained as nothing other than "something a little bit different" - it may not be here today. The resultant changes to WWE's historical progression would be catastrophic to even suggest.

As a result, #24 is a seminal moment in history, even if few are liable to realise or remember why. 1988 saw the birth of the Royal Rumble; 2014, with its Bryan centred controversy, evidenced its continuing importance; but 1992 was the first year of the rest of its life.

#23
Randy Orton vs. The Undertaker
WrestleMania 21
April 3rd, 2005

Rather like The Undertaker character itself, The Streak was something that could only, in kayfabe, generate the aura it generated in its day because, rather like The Undertaker character itself, there was something inherently farcical about the idea; especially in a post-kayfabe world such as the Brand Extension Era. That it became the leviathan, divisive, controversial and enthralling WrestleMania tradition that it did casts clear light on the Dead Man's unique place in professional wrestling history and WWE lore; everything he was involved with, by his career's twilight, was "Event." Both The Undertaker and his Streak – which ended the same year the Reality Era's first masterpiece of a storyline in Bryan's ascent peaked – may have been the very last vestige of *traditional* 20th Century kayfabe WWE will ever see. A grand claim, to be sure.

But regardless of such a sweeping historical idea, it is important to clarify that, though inherently not of the same elevating ilk as the Ladder genre or Royal Rumble, whether The Streak should have been used to elevate a young talent was an intrinsic part of the debate that raged in its heyday. In some quarters, it continues to rage even after its conclusion. In a manner of speaking, it did do just that though, and more than once. It has already been explored in this book that a valiant, close fought defeat can serve more wonders than a decisive victory; simply having come close to ending The Streak elevated performers from generations following The Undertaker's to a position only a handful of professional wrestlers can claim to situate.

Ultimately, the most vital aspect of The Streak is this: it was a big deal. It remains a big deal, and that speaks for its weight as a concept in the minds of the popular fan base. Rightly or wrongly, popular opinion transforms it into one of the big issues in WWE history; The Undertaker's version of a phenomena such as Montreal, Hulkamania and Austin 3:16. As a result of that gravitas, it becomes pressing to have a grasp on The Streak's individual history, just as it is on the Ladder genre and the Royal Rumble.

In essence, The Streak started way back at WrestleMania VII against Jimmy Snuka. In all honesty, though, those first few victories watch more as a coincidental accruement of unrelated wins; a far-cry from the synthesised epics of later years. Thus, it seems almost redundant to involve them. In fact, anything up to WrestleMania X8 is something of a hard sell. Why X8? Undertaker signals his delight at having gone ten and zero as he leaves a bloodied Flair behind him – the first true to life recognition from the man himself that this was becoming something more than a paper achievement.

In more recent years, there has been talk of "The Streak within a streak" – an idea born from the need to more carefully define The Streak as a historical happening. In "The Streak within a streak" we eschew the disparate victories of The Streak's earliest years in favour of the more consciously stylised matches from WrestleMania 21 onwards; we might even include the matches at WrestleMania X8-XX in a longer version.

In accordance with this new concept, The Streak's identity transcends a mere mathematical measurement to become the phenomenon it grew to be by its final days. As such, the question of "beginning" becomes instead a question of *birth*: something entirely different. The Streak *began* with Jimmy Snuka; it was not truly *born* until Randy Orton. WrestleMania 21, therefore, is the first match of what is truly referred to as The Streak; it is another coming of age.

Watching this bout back, post-Streak, sees it play almost as a Punk-lite encounter. Where Punk was sadistically disrespectful in the case of #38, Orton is simply brash. Where Punk was condescendingly mocking, Orton is dismissive. Where Punk tried to get in the Dead Man's head, Orton concerns himself with simply getting in The Undertaker's face.

This is not to take credit away from the Legend Killer, because he does put on a career highlight performance, at least amidst his earliest years. A number of times his offense watches as stiff; there's a wonderfully impactful clothesline in the first half which sees both combatants go down, for example. There's a nice aggressive counter to Undertaker following a Snake-Eyes, and Orton's final RKO coming out of the Chokeslam is a tremendous exchange that shows early signs of how brilliant he has since become at pulling his famous finisher "outta nowhere."

While Orton is clearly giving it his all both in his in-ring work and his character performance, Undertaker seemingly plays it much safer. Curiously, he appears more conservative and performs with less energy than he did in later years. It does, therefore, feel a bit sterile at points. He watches a little more lethargic than the Legend Killer, which is a shame. This assumption may only be made because of the influence of his five penultimate Streak matches between 2009 and 2013, in which the Dead Man would wrestle with more verve to take the show home with his name stamped all over it. In conjunction with "The Streak within a streak" concept being argued, was #23 a Dead Man simply getting started? Settling in? Could the bout with Mark Henry the following year be described as teething problems, before hitting his stride with the difficult threequel opposite Batista? Was *that* the true beginning of The Streak as it would come to be known? They are all interesting questions to ponder in the debate of The Streak's true birth.

It is pleasant to see a big match situation not devolve into the bad habits of recent years, with endless finishers and kick-outs. Instead, the composition opts for a pretty classic and ever-effective method. The ref bumps, Orton Senior runs interference and Undertaker lets Orton have a long two count. Orton's aforementioned RKO counter to the Chokeslam gets an amazing reaction and, in line with the general story, he tries to win with a Tombstone as his vanity gets the better of him. Unfortunately, the Legend Killer fails grimly and proceedings conclude with a nice lean finish trimmed of any fat.

With that finish, The Streak first appeared. As the term "The Streak within a streak" intimates, there are really two sides to it; the streak and The Streak. The Streak started with #23, in a sleek match between two incredibly talented performers with a career-vaulting performance from the younger star; elevation in defeat if ever it has happened. Meanwhile, the streak started at WrestleMania VII and ended at 22-1.

If professional wrestling were a sport, even a simulated one, it would be easier to agree with that number. But, as this book has consistently tried to argue, professional wrestling is not a sport, and the time has come for it to no longer be seen as a simulated one either. It's a performance art, and it is actually only The Streak that WWE and the popular fan base really talk of. That Streak isn't 22-1; it's actually only 10-1. Interestingly, 10-1 watches as infinitely more impressive inside of the ring despite being numerically inferior. If no other argument here has you convinced that, because of #23's coming of age, it is my posited short history that fits better with our perception of Undertaker's greatest phenomena, take up the empiricist's challenge of watching it as 10-1; you will discover a far greater critically acclaimed beast in it than you ever will in 22-1.

Chapter 28

Generations: When Worlds Collides

#22
John Cena vs. The Rock
WrestleMania XXVIII
April 1st, 2012

It is a match with a great many cynics, but few show-closing bouts at WrestleMania through the years ever captured the same sense of festival, carnival atmosphere and magic as the first Cena / Rock epic did in 2012. The live music preceding either combatant's entrances, the visuals of the stadium at night, the crowd in an open air building, the two legendary performers set to face off; it is a match bottling up the essence of WrestleMania's glitz and intention and serving it up in a manner that, as cliché as it may now be to say, transcends time. The presence of that main event match is tangible; you can almost feel the warm Miami evening air on your skin as you watch both first ballot Hall of Fame talents make their way out to the ring.

It is easy to forget that, using popular periodisation to be explored in a later chapter, this was the first WrestleMania main event of the Reality Era; it certainly played on the reality of past comments made particularly by Cena. As a result, vindication is a prescient theme permeating The Rock's performance for fans of older generations. The boiling, personal issues behind the reasoning for this affair add an intangible to every look either man shoots the other, every passing grin and every physical exchange, in spite of the script. These men aren't just locking horns to see who is best, but to prove the respective points both men had been making heading into this epic affair. The issues at the heart of the story are personal, but the intentions on the night were to prove and disprove, rather than simply beat.

Though The Rock's performance is by no means perfect, it is more than admirable for being his first singles effort in close to a decade. And, even though there is a surplus of finishing manoeuvres throughout the composition, there is no lack of variety among the content. In fact quite the opposite; the trait caps off an otherwise exhaustive account of both men's retinues (The Rock even utilises the cross-body he had not deployed in regularity since his earliest days when using the surname Maivia). The resultant sense of never-ending story ensures that the finish – seeing The Rock nail a decisive Rock Bottom in the midst of Cena's arrogant misstep – comes off as truthful a conclusion as you're liable to find in any match; that is to say, far from having been routed, Cena was simply knocked off guard for only three short (but no less decisive) seconds to facilitate The Rock's victory; a victory key to the issues #22 presents when seen as performance art.

Explored already in preceding entries, the symbolic changing of the guard between The Rock and Cena would come a year later at WrestleMania 29. That was not the apparent point of WrestleMania XXVIII. The traditional, literal take on this intergenerational two match rivalry would therefore be that Once in a Lifetime was a mere prelude designed to reestablish The Rock for new generations of fans while allowing both combatants to walk away from their feud with a placating win to call their own. The possible performance art interpretation, however, exacerbates #22's historical significance a great deal, transforming into something much less mundane.

As the Reality Era has progressed, WWE has figured out an effective means of operating in the social media age. The

Reality Era has redefined kayfabe to mean something unique to the 21st Century, playing off of "forbidden knowledge known" to once again generate doubt in the minds of fans as to what is fiction and what is fact. As a process, this has necessitated, by default, a greater embrace of the volatile, often contradictory Internet Wrestling Community that had previously felt ignored and, at its most impassioned, actively spited. Consider that the Reality Era kicked off with an IWC folkloric hero in CM Punk overcoming the machine's manufactured superhero John Cena; Daniel Bryan became an epicentre of conflict between corporate intention and popular desire; NXT featured a future generation littered with the IWC's so-called "Indy darlings" that many said could never make it in a size-obsessed World Wrestling Entertainment; this alongside the blindingly bright futures of previous "Indy darlings" such as Seth Rollins and Dean Ambrose. When fully underway, the Reality Era ensured that the older, internet going fan was no longer a leper shunned on the outskirts of professional wrestling influence; they had become, arguably for the first time in the IWC's existence, inherent to many of the decisions made by the world's premiere professional wrestling promotion.

The outcome of #22 indicates this transition. The Rock vs. John Cena was billed in a manner not too dissimilar to the obviously parallel Rock / Hogan piece a decade beforehand. What this comparison does not account for is the mitigating circumstances in play, though; most importantly, the unique moment in time in which the match took place.

The Reality Era's onset really came the preceding summer in 2011 during CM Punk's Pipe Bomb feud heading into Money in the Bank in Chicago, making #22 the first WrestleMania main event of said Era. Already mentioned in the review is how #22 successfully manipulates beliefs in real world animosity harboured between Rock and Cena to benefit its tale, but the more important facet is the symbolism that comes with the performance art interpretation of that tale. That interpretation concludes that #22 is more than a generation vs. generation dream match. It is mark vs. smart mark; innocent fan vs. internet fan; child vs. adult. As the match plays out a game of equals, it metaphorically represents the equality of importance both major elements of the fan base had grown to be considered with in WWE's most recent age.

Thus, The Rock's victory, while vicarious in seeing the omnipresent haunting ghost of Cena despatched by the nostalgic favourite of the disillusioned, can also be seen as WWE reassuring older fans that the Reality Era would be one inclusive of them; the exact opposite of pervading sentiment throughout the Brand Extension. Knowing now that this silent, symbolised promise would be faithfully adhered to by the promotion in the years after cements the gesture as a historically meaningful one. For the first time, WWE had the favourite of the more aware fan base overcome someone indicative of their child-oriented PG marketing machine, and when it was least expected to boot. Meanwhile, CM Punk would go on to hold his championship until the following Rumble; Daniel Bryan would both open and close WrestleMania XXX; The Shield would be pushed as the harbingers of change - but a few examples of how WWE altered its method to be more accessible and palatable for full-time professional wrestling enthusiasts over the age of sixteen.

It should be clear then that, taking an interpretive performance art view, The Rock's defeat of John Cena at WrestleMania XXVIII was not just a victory but a symbolic promise of change that was, on the whole and in spite of the odd unsure stumble, lived up to with enthused vigour. Historically significant for it, the first WrestleMania main event of the Reality Era is beautifully indicative of the then still developing creative renaissance that would strive to increasingly include a demographic feeling too long under-represented; even under-appreciated. Of all the Reality Era's mightily forward-thinking accomplishments, these ideas – including #22's succinct expression of them – are among its finest.

#21
Hollywood Hulk Hogan vs. The Rock
WrestleMania X8
March 17th, 2002

It's something of a dangerous presumption, but #21 shows just how easily the so-called "Dream Match" can generate an almost guaranteed red hot crowd thanks to the power of nostalgia involved in invoking the concept. As a piece of work, #21 is an incredibly diluted affair and eventually spirals into decades-old familiar territory courtesy of the Hulkster. The Hulking Up matters, but it matters because it is the very fact that Hogan's routine *is* decades-old that gets the crowd as excited as they get. Absence makes the heart grow fonder and certainly Hogan was not just the sentimental favourite; he was *the* sentiment. The work thus proves even the weakest in-ring affair can become something spectacular, earning a rank amongst the very best bouts of all-time because it brings back a hero of years gone by. It seems, therefore, no real riddle as to why the 'E tried to replicate the scenario at WrestleMania 29, at varying instances throughout the Brand Extension Era and, more than likely, will try again in years still to come.

There is also an interesting comparative note to make. As explored in Chapter 12 with #58's Michaels / Jericho spiritual sequel to Savage / Steamboat, fans love historical analogies and comparative response in which, for example, they compare one star to another from times long gone. The second Rock / Cena match, whether seen as spiritual or direct sequel, provides an interesting empirical opportunity in its crowd response. Cena has received the kind of reaction The Rock receives during the match against Hogan for the majority of his career – extensively so in instances like #22's Once in a Lifetime - and, much to his credit, he has always remained calm and collected. In comparison, it's clear the crowd response throughout #21 gets into the head of The Rock. More interesting still, and far more relevant, is the fact that, while Cena took the reaction and chose to incite it further by effectively refusing to acknowledge it through change of character, The Rock took it and turned it very much to his own advantage. Cena never reacts; The Rock always does. In this instance with Hogan, for example, the longer the match goes, the more villainous he becomes, feeling the emotion of the crowd and reacting accordingly. In that sense, it's a far more organic performance than what fans have become used to from Cena.

It seems ironic, then, that beyond the unexpected crowd reaction to him there's little worth noting about The Rock. He exhibits a lot of aggression and plenty of trash-talk, but he always had that kind of a persona regardless of whether he was playing good or bad. And there's no doubt the fan partisanship comes from nostalgia; it certainly doesn't stem from the usually smart mark favoured "work rate," because it is The Rock, after all, who does a great deal of the work, selling somewhat dated offense enthusiastically and making a man very much out of his time still appear more than capable when competing with a current generation. Rock has always been a very giving performer in the ring though, so even this is no exception. Hogan matches him in that generosity, impressively. He actually loses twice; once in the final outcome, which of course was the right decision, but also once in the midst of the match when he taps out to a Sharpshooter when no referee is there to call it.

As much as Hogan remains the antagonist early and The Rock the protagonist, as Hogan becomes more in favour with the crowd reaction The Rock becomes more resentful. Whether it's planned or an outcome of the unfolding crowd reaction is hard to tell, but it certainly allows the two men to do something different to what they're usually accustomed to. It could have very easily become another example of a double turn not too dissimilar to Hart and Austin five years prior should WWE have chosen to go down that route. Furthermore, it's interesting to see a pre-cursor to Cena's weekly reactions flare up, and it feels fitting that it's The Rock that causes it.

This is a match that's all about reducing oneself to the rawest form of fandom and just sitting back to experience the emotion of an impossible time warp. This is because, as a match, the composition is far from the most intricate. The psychology is effective in its simplicity, with both Hogan and Rock testing one another in the early goings and representing their Eras with their respective trademark taunts. The moves are nothing astounding and, generally, the two combatants play quite a safe game for such a huge scenario. If one thinks on that too much, there is a danger of being left feeling a little disappointed with its orthodoxy. Even the finish feels noticeably sensible; for it to take three Rock Bottoms and a People's Elbow to put Hogan away is arguably the only fitting way to defeat the first wrestling mega-star in history and to pass along the torch.

That passing of the torch idea is at the heart of #21's selection, in fact. #21 was essentially a template for a very rare kind of match occurring only at generational crossing points; "Torch Matches" we might call them. It is a template we can retrofit on to André vs. Hogan at WrestleMania III. It is a template that Hogan vs. Michaels would follow years after #21 at Summerslam 2005. Further still, it is the template that the Rock / Cena Rematch of a Lifetime would revisit in 2013. The concept is fluid enough to even potentially apply to matches later still, such as Cena vs. Bryan at Summerslam 2013 or perhaps even Bryan vs. Reigns at Fastlane 2015.

Then consider the symbolism in the results of these matches that adhere to #21's template. Hogan beat André and Michaels but succumbed to The Rock; The Rock eventually fell to Cena, who was in turn beat by Daniel Bryan; finally, Bryan was displaced by Roman Reigns. Framing these results as the results of "Torch Matches" creates a mythological equivalent of WWE's factual past.

Hogan took over from André as pro wrestling's pop culture icon in the 1980s, and helped lead WCW to dominance during Michaels' struggle of a run at the top in the mid to late 1990s. The Rock would eventually help topple Hogan's WCW in the Monday Night Wars by rivaling Hulkster's popularity, only to leave and be succeeded by a John Cena resentful of Rocky's departure. Cena would be dethroned by Daniel Bryan as the first true star to break the so-called glass ceiling of the Brand Extension, and Bryan would go on to be unexpectedly, controversially displaced quickly by the company's preferred leading man, Roman Reigns.

Together these Torch Matches and their symbolic results form a performance art representation of the so-called passing of the torch throughout history. They create a WWE Mythology; a pocketed history; professional wrestling's answer to the Epic Poem, all written in the style of the template laid out by #21.

Chapter 29

The Injuries Felt Throughout Time

#20
The Undertaker vs. Shawn Michaels
Casket Match
WWF Championship
Royal Rumble
January 18th, 1998

It is well known that WWE is a promotion that chooses to exercise a tight control over the representation of its history, as well as attempts to manufacture its biggest stars for the years to come. This has sometimes proven to be a centre of controversy, with many fans feeling such moves towards tomorrow should be less orchestrated, developed instead through organic judgment of fan reaction. There are, in the annals of WWE's meddling, however, two matches occurring within a six month period that irrevocably altered the course of WWE history. These matches - hardly talked about at all in WWE's propagandistic presentation of its yesterdays but vitally important historical artefacts - eventuated in circumstances well beyond the control of the company. #20 is the first of them.

Shawn Michaels breaking his back doesn't often get mentioned alongside the other significant *moments* in WWE history, such as Hogan's first title win or the Montreal Screwjob. As an event in history, it's rather underplayed and perhaps rightfully so. The wheels of the Attitude Era were already beginning to turn before this particular match and, when Michaels left after WrestleMania, not a great deal actually changed. D-Generation X is often credited for starting the trends that came to fruition in the Attitude Era, and D-Generation X continued in the absence of the Heartbreak Kid; in fact, D-Generation X as the influential stable it is remembered for being today only really came to exist *after* Michaels' departure. In 1998, Michaels would have, quite rightly, gone down as being more of a New Generation talent than anything other, far from defining the era that was about to dawn despite the representation afforded him years on.

It was actually his absence from WWE that may have had a much heavier impact, bizarrely, on the product today. His time away from the ring brought on by that one fateful moment in #20, and his continued decline into the vices of being a professional wrestling Rolling Stone, eventually led to his rebirth as a born again Christian, his return to the company and the birth of Mr Wrestleamania, who would be at the centre of many Grand Daddy events to come. Michaels has gone down as one of the greatest of all-time, if not the single best, because #20 led to a series of events that eventually caused him to "clean up his act," as the saying goes.

It is easy to become too fatalistic about these ideas, so look at a potential world wherein #20 never happened. Essentially, without this match, the Heartbreak Kid's back would never have broken and he'd have never disappeared for four years. While Austin would have still become "The Man" because of the undeniable course he was already on and, while The Rock would still have shot to superstardom because cream rises to the top – both, by extension, meaning the Attitude Era would have likely gone on largely as it did anyway – the Brand Extension may have been a different matter altogether.

Without the post-redemption Mr WrestleMania, Cena would have never gotten "legitimised" at WrestleMania 23,

Ric Flair would have never wrestled one last awesome match, Undertaker's Streak would perhaps never have been exacerbated into the immortal entity it became and this entire book would read in a radically different fashion. D-Generation X would never have reunited, the Montreal Screwjob may never have gotten patched up and the entire philosophy of the product during the Brand Extension may have been completely different. What really opens things up is considering what may have happened - or rather, more appropriately, not happened - to Triple H. Had Michaels not vanished, would Triple H have ever become the leader of D-Generation X? And who knows how that might have stunted his character growth; the ripple effects of Triple H never becoming Attitude's foremost villain are frighteningly extensive to consider. Had Shawn Michaels not been forced from the life of a professional wrestler in the unforgiving manner he had been, who knows the effects it might have had on both the personal and professional lives of so many.

These are all impossible questions for a fan to answer and, maybe, even impossible questions for the man himself to answer. What we can say, though, with confidence, is not only may fans have been denied many of the awesome matches and feel good moments Heartbreak would eventually create if that were so, so too might they have been denied perhaps the greatest half of a professional wrestler's career to have ever been composed.

Fatalism aside, this entry is a very simple one. This match is simple. Its importance is simple. So far-reaching are the possible effects of this match *not* having happened – or having happened without injuring Michaels' back - it could be seen as directly having an influence on the shape of WWE not just through the Attitude Era, not just through the Brand Extension but also up to this very day. #20 is the origin point; the ground zero of not necessarily the most important butterfly effect in WWE's history but definitely one of the most relevant.

It may be a dud of a match, bloated and bored as it is, but in both its historical and fateful sense, it is most definitely a must-see for any existing WWE fan.

#19
Stone Cold Steve Austin vs. Owen Hart
Intercontinental Championship
Summerslam
August 3rd, 1997

Shawn Michaels injuring his back and being forced into what everyone thought would be early retirement was a massive fork in the road of WWE's history, if one not often spoken of nor obvious in its implication. It is incredible to think that mere months earlier, at the preceding Summerslam, Steve Austin fell victim to a broken neck that changed the course of history in WWE in similarly gargantuan fashion.

Like #20, #19 is an important historical document in the history of professional wrestling, the unique importance of which is contextualised by seeking to understand the reasons why Austin's career was so vital to the prosperity, perhaps even survival, of professional wrestling at the turn of the millennium. Such an understanding reveals #19 to contain within it a single move that changed everything.

Where Hogan revolutionised professional wrestling in the 1980s by helping to bring it in line with a wider social consciousness, Austin revolutionised the industry by creating a specific superlative that shifted existing public perceptions and damned any of the years to come to suffer handicapped comparative studies to the infamous Attitude Era. His career coincided with a noticeable shift in the wider philosophies underpinning professional wrestling, which went from being a vehicle to explore old fashioned notions of good against evil into a modernised expression of social anxieties, pushing the creative envelope beyond the boundaries that previously had been more than just boundaries; they had been outright taboos.

While various other factors were at play during this historic alteration, Austin is held up and revered today as the poster boy of the change. He was the enabler of a movement that brought about the buckling of old vanguards under the weight of a growing phenomenon that had, until that time, been limited to the status of counter-culture. If nothing else, it's important to recognise Austin's place in WWE history as the first man to create that winning formula on television, ignoring any pleas from higher-ups, fabricated or genuine, to tone down. That winning formula went on to become standard in the company and the wider industry. If the character of Stone Cold was not a genesis for something huge, it was certainly an internal tipping point.

It is important to remember, however, that the Rattlesnake's career is not exclusively an origin story. Austin continued to have a pervasive effect throughout his entire tenure, creating some of the greatest and highest drawing feuds in memory and maintaining the new status quo by burning twice as bright and twice as hot as any torch bearer had before him.

Any meditation on the career of Stone Cold Steve Austin requires asking some very big questions, the most notable of them being what might have happened had Austin never broken his neck. Like in the case of Shawn Michaels, that question leads to a domino effect that can so easily occur when changes to something as complex as WWE history are considered. Had no neck break occurred, Austin would not have required a year long absence between 1999 and 2000. Had such an absence not have occurred, what would have happened to the now stellar career of The Rock? Once again, that not only directly impacts the Attitude Era, but also the Brand Extension too. Without his own stellar success, would The Rock have gone on to become such a huge Hollywood star and, if not, what affect does that have on the movie industry, along with the history of a number of high earning franchises and the studios to which they are attached? While considering how the career of The Rock may have been affected had Austin been around, it is important also to note how adversely different Triple H's rise to prominence may have looked; and the consequences of that are, just like in the prior review, mind-boggling to comprehend. Perhaps most importantly, though, would the buy-out of WCW have been enabled any sooner, or later for that matter, than it eventually was?

It continues further. It's interesting to ponder on whether or not Austin's disagreements with WWE in 2002 may have unfolded how they did. Having been around much longer, and in a manner even more established, would the proposed Hogan / Austin bout have gone ahead, without a second thought being given to who the victor would be? Or would Austin have lost ground, as he did in the wake of the successes of The Rock and Triple H, as well as the company's indulgences in both those individuals? With Austin no longer wrestling against doctors' orders in lieu of neck issues, would better health have lent upward motion to Austin's willingness to do favours for others? And what about Brock Lesnar; how might that career path – and by extension the history of UFC and the Reality Era - have been altered had Lesnar been granted a pay-per-view rub over Austin?

Would Austin's matches watch differently had his ring game not needed limitation? Would his feud with Mr McMahon have occurred without the segment hosting that famous first Stunner? With the careers of The Rock, Triple H, Brock Lesnar, and even John Cena having been altered to unfeasible extents, it's frightening to realise just how much Austin himself is woven into the very fabric of pop culture; more so than might first meet the eye, with WWE, WCW, UFC and even Hollywood all hinging their own make-up, to varying degrees of course, on the path that Stone Cold's career took.

All of it is because of this one match. As a match, #19 stands as an entertaining bout in an entertaining storyline that was nothing more than a single part of a much greater whole. #19 is a composition that sadly, in some ways, could be seen as missing out on its full potential. Instead of the possible classic fans may have gotten, they got a trade-in. That trade was for what is perhaps one of, if not the single most far-reaching historical consequence in WWE history; maybe even in professional wrestling history. Austin is, in many ways, a figure unlike any other. What happened in #19 changed the world forever. Not just the fans' world of professional wrestling but the worlds of men, companies and entire industries.

Not even Hulk Hogan can make that same claim to the same extent.

Chapter 30

Questioning Popular Periodisation

#18
Bret "Hitman" Hart vs. Diesel
No Holds Barred Match
WWF Championship
Survivor Series
November 19th, 1995

One of the most intriguing issues when refashioning a history of WWE as a promotion is that of periodisation. There is a tendency to think of WWE in terms of "eras," like Attitude for example. While, at times, this obsessive need to categorise can damage our understanding of the company's growth by threatening to involve too much retrospective imposition, it remains a popular method of thinking about WWE's past that even the promotion itself indulges in. There is no denying its importance as a result. There is, however, a need to question popular opinions about what these periods are and where it is we draw the lines of each. For example, one popular opinion holds that the Attitude Era began at either WrestleMania 13 or Survivor Series 1997. It is nigh universally agreed it concluded at WrestleMania X-Seven. Another opinion suggests that ECW was heavily influential in the Attitude Era's inception. It is the purpose of this chapter to call some of these ideas into question and ask whether or not they accurately represent WWE's evolution.

Change is often a slow grind, making it curiously at odds with the natural pace of the professional wrestling industry that, thanks to the advent of weekly television and the famous absence of an off-season, moves at an incredible rate. Periodisation offers up a temptation to ignore this idea and think of change as a more immediate alteration. It is never quite so. The first three reviews in this next chapter will show that changes which, in popular thought, are often presupposed as having been fast moving and confined to narrow passages of time were actually in motion long before, or in some cases quite some time after, the opening and closing of any given era.

For the sake of argument, and in keeping with the previous example to expand this point, let us take the one period in WWE history the boundaries of which are perhaps most widely agreed upon: the Attitude Era, beginning at WrestleMania 13 and ending with WrestleMania X-Seven. The underlying point is simple. If the Attitude Era began at WrestleMania 13, it does not necessarily mean that the period's first Raw is War of March 24th 1997 watches anything like the final Raw is War of March 26th 2001.

Periodisation should not lead to thinking of WWE's past as large chunks of homogenised product that suddenly shifted overnight. The seeds of the Attitude Era were being sewn years before 1997. This was not a rapid transition spawned solely by the momentum of ECW. Not to deny the influence of Paul Heyman's brainchild; it certainly galvanised the speed of change to a great extent. The idea that it was solely responsible is not necessarily an accurate one, though, as ground was being broken within the confines of WWE before "E C Dub!" chants erupted in their front rows. Professional wrestling has always functioned best when it pioneers and alters taboos. #18 is just one tiny example of how a greater degree of violent edge was gradually seeped into the pores of McMahon's own brainchild quite naturally.

#18 – in November 1995 - features, for the first time ever, a Spanish announce table bump. The now infamous, at one time even over-used concept originated in the confines of this very match and would go on to become a staple element of big time bouts throughout the Attitude Era especially. It continues to this day, albeit mercifully with much less frequency. In the instance of #18, though, it is clear that this innovative idea would never fail to leave a lasting impression. The crowd certainly reacts in genuine shock; quite the opposite to the gleeful cheers of later eras.

It may seem daft to include the match for this reason now, but take a moment to consider the brutal innovation during its time frame. The WWF was a company orientated heavily towards children in an age that was only just beginning to witness the rise to prominence of ECW and the hardcore style that would eventually become omnipresent throughout the later Nineties and early Noughties. Certainly in the WWF of the time, something as simple yet as high impact as being launched backwards through the air eventuating in you snapping a wooden table in two was new, fresh and different. Now, though, fans don't give such moments much of a second thought. Worse than that, going through any kind of a no disqualification bout *without* some kind of spot involving the announce table threatens to leave fans feeling let down and / or deflated.

It is an incident that goes to show how forward-thinking Bret Hart could be in the ring when he wanted to be. He was, for all intents and purposes, not only the first man to introduce the concept of the Ladder Match to the WWF, but three years later would effectively introduce the now infamous table spot to the company as well. While the ECW alumni will, rightfully, continue to preach the importance of their role in the shift in product that culminated in Attitude, truthfully the professional wrestling business was already slowly starting to lean that way. This was no isolated occurrence. Only the following month, Hart would wrestle a bloodied composition with British Bulldog that would prove evenly brutal with #18, if not more so. In 1996, the trend went on still, with Michaels and Diesel jostling for the championship the month after WrestleMania in a No Disqualification environment bearing a striking resemblance to the kind of hardcore matches being performed by the close of the following decade. Mankind's rookie year led to matches perhaps more closely related to Attitude than the New Generation with the Buried Alive Match and Boiler Room Brawl both debuting in 1996. His match with Shawn Michaels that same year was, again, very Attitudinal in its design. Even as early as the summer of 1995 the Kliq were sharpening the edge of the WWF's shows.

Professional wrestling, like most things that live as long as it has in the world of entertainment, was evolving from day one. As the production level grew and as fans became ever hungrier for more action in the ring, the imaginations of the competitors did too by necessity, if not just for pleasure; for a man as creative in the ring as Bret Hart was, something as simple but as eventually ground breaking as taking a bump through the announce desk now seems inevitable.

#18 is one small piece of a large number of hints that the professional wrestling world was perhaps heading in the direction it eventually headed during Attitude anyway, regardless of the countercultural phenomenon of that famed promotion down in Philly - the influence of which, while entirely undeniable, has perhaps benefitted somewhat from the myth memory can afford. Talents were becoming more athletically focused and creatively minded and, as a result, the options for guys in the ring, and especially in no disqualification environments, were multiplying; only natural, then, that a guy as intelligent and as wily in the ring as Bret Hart would come up with something that so many would go on to imitate.

It may not have made history but it most certainly broke ground, and that's the important point. Regardless of where you place the opening moment of the Attitude Era historically, the change that the Attitude Era imbued did not come overnight in 1997, nor halt overnight in 2001. That process was slow on both sides of the age.

#17
Kurt Angle vs. John Cena
Special Guest Referee: Daivari
WWE Championship
Survivor Series
November 27th, 2005

I believe that there are five discernible Eras with which we can periodise WWE history: the Golden Age; the New Generation; the Attitude Era; the Brand Extension; the Reality Era. It is not the intention here to fashion a prescriptive history, but merely suggest a school of thought based upon careful empirical scrutiny. For example, some might argue the Brand Extension requires separating further between Ruthless Aggression and PG.

So, why the five Eras named above? No single Era begins fully formed, nor remains homogenous throughout its tenure. An Era's product in its final year is liable to be largely different to that in its first and the reason is the same as explored in the preceding review: change is a long and arduous process that never ends. On the whole, WWE's product is always reshaping, meaning any single Era will begin with a hangover from its immediate predecessor and culminate in taking increased steps toward the character of its successor. Periodisation is not a search for creative uniformity; it is the analysis of paradigmatic shifts wherein we are able to identify prolonged periods of time in which the *basic core functionality* of the product remains largely consistent.

In the preceding review, for the sake of its argument regarding the slow nature of change, the popular opinion of the Attitude Era's chronology was followed – beginning in 1997 and ending at WrestleMania X-Seven - but this view may not be entirely adequate. 2001 was dominated by the Invasion angle for its majority and, during that angle, famous Attitude tropes were still consistently applied. The difference was the increased roster, the lack of a number two promotion, the new proliferation of championships under a single roof and, eventually, the official onscreen absorption of the final vestiges of WCW's memory at December's pay-per-view Vengeance.

Nevertheless, change was brewing. The expanded roster and proliferation of titles wrought by the buy-out of WCW eventually led to the Brand Extension in 2002. By Summerslam, the product felt wholly refreshed. The Rock wrestled his last match as a full-time member of the roster in a losing effort to Brock Lesnar, the man tipped to carry WWE through the coming years. Michaels returned to in-ring action in what would eventually prove the beginning of his second career in the ring, Mysterio made his pay-per-view debut and Edge and Guerrero staked their claims for a future spotlight. In the weeks that followed, Triple H became the Raw-exclusive World Champion, Lesnar the same for Smackdown, and the blue brand went on to introduce its own Tag Team Championships to boot.

It seems Summerslam 2002 is a better choice to mark the final end of the Attitude Era then, with the infamous period's tenants watered down in the face of the growing change wrought by the Brand Extension. Elements that would come to dominate that period were becoming more prescient; from the talent pool – Lesnar, Edge, Guerrero, Mysterio, a returning Michaels and departing Rock – to the introduction of championship brand exclusivity in the weeks that would follow to the confirmation that Tazz and Cole would permanently call all Smackdown pay-per-view matches moving forward. The basic core functionality of the product had changed quite exceptionally by the end of the year.

However, as already covered, the Brand Extension and its defining characteristic did not arrive fully formed by any means. Lesnar would depart in 2004. The Benoit Tragedy in 2007 shifted the overall tone of the product. Brand exclusive pay-per-views would come then go. Perhaps most interestingly of all, though, the divisive nature of Cena's career would not begin to evolve into its final form that came to characterise the later years of the Era until late in 2005. Enter #17; an intriguing historical artefact that further supports the arguments posited by #18, albeit for the second half of the equation: just as the footsteps toward change begin long before the final transition into a new Era, so too do they continue long *after* said Era is first ushered in.

As the Brand Extension finally waned into the past in 2011, perhaps its biggest talking point had become the perceived detrimental nature of Cena's continued predominance as "The Guy." This talking point originated early on in the Era and simply grew in its veracity as the years progressed. The loathing felt for Cena's tenure at the top of the company among older fans came to be characterised by the familiar pantomime of combating chants that, in self-defeating fashion, ensured every match Cena wrestled was only ever about Cena and never about the man he wrestled, perhaps building the very glass ceiling fans claimed the Doctor of Thugonomics was responsible for. “Let’s go Cena!” “Cena sucks!” became the Era’s most recognisable audible refrain.

This is why #17 was chosen as the evidence to support the statements being made. It is a strange thing to take in the reaction for Cena in 2005 a decade on from the event. Not only is there a *thunderous* chant for him prior to his entrance in the instance of #17, but his reaction remains largely unanimous, as well. It is a far cry from the immediate division that would come to characterise his work as soon as a year or two on.

The angst grows, though. Soon chants for Angle pop up to combat the chants for Cena and there is an early hint of animosity as Cena hits his first shoulder blocks of the contest. As soon as those Angle chants begin, the difference in key is noticeable: deeper for the adult males backing Angle and higher for the children backing Cena. Importantly, the chants against Cena are not orientated around him; this is not yet active hostility ensuring that the affair is Cena-centric as his work would become by Era’s end, but more a choice of loyalty to the man perceived as the more talented, certainly more experienced performer.

The story active at the heart of this momentous atmosphere is simple and functional. Daivari is Angle’s personal referee, exhibiting all the actions typical of such a biased official. This is a composition prototypical of its genre, as Daivari continually obscures the natural flow of action to favour the Olympic Hero by preventing Cena from capitalising or refusing to count when the champion has the challenger down. In that sense, little is unique. However, the idea of the biased referee automatically disqualifying the babyface - a typically contradictory element of psychology resting at the heart of the genre – is circumnavigated by virtue of the fact that the villain is the challenger, unable to attain gold through a disqualification win. More so, the majority of less convincing elements of the Special Guest Referee genre have their negative effects naturally countermanded by the whimsically rebellious live crowd, who cheer as soon as Daivari kicks Cena's hand from the ropes, for example.

It is around the halfway mark that the first "Cena sucks!" chants flare up as the match shifts closer to what later Cena matches would become. While, in later years, this routine became a formulaic pantomime, in this instance it feels consciously rebellious. While these chants are not predominant like they would come to be, remaining interspersed with outright support for Angle, their initial occurrence is an important moment to witness. This hostility is at its most vocal when Cena begins his typical routine in the ring; and the disgust is palpable.

As a match that highlights the most important change in crowd reactions to Cena's ongoing predominance, it happens to, quite considerably, fully evidence just why that change occurred in the first place too. The rush of the opening minutes means that, the longer the match goes, the more anti-climactic, obvious and simplistic it feels, and that disappointment continues through the finish too - Angle is comfortably defeated by an FU, climaxing a match in which the champ landed embarrassingly and frustratingly little offense. The storytelling is poor, the genre largely left as an irrelevancy and the overall sense of achievement lacking.

At its core, this is a poor match. It is also a vitally important one. Indeed, it has a great deal in common with #18. Cena's divisive nature as champion began early, but not overnight. #17 presents the first noticeable incident of the now infamous "Cena sucks!" chants. Cena had been booed previously, but crowd chants had centered as much on his opponent as on him. #17 saw that begin to change until, eventually, the only name cropping up in the rabid combative chanting during Cena matches was Cena's own, thereby making him the only talent in such matches receiving a reaction and perpetuating his apparently damaging run as top dog that so heavily characterises our memory of the Brand Extension.

This occurrence of "Cena sucks!" is only a passing moment of hostility here, but one that would go on to become a monkey on the character's back, dogging both career and legacy and forming one of the Brand Extension's most curious and defining traits; that formation, it is important to understand, happened gradually.

#16
Daniel Bryan vs. Triple H
WrestleMania XXX
April 6th, 2014

This more progressive approach to history is naturally more complex and therefore demands a more complex micro-understanding of WWE's progression. In other words, beginning and end points to periods are important but not the full story; it is equally important to identify a period's internal moments of progression, maturation, peak and dilution. Once again, due to restrictions of space, it is my intention to offer up only an example of these ideas: a more recent, emotively affecting example hosted by the Reality Era.

Selecting moments, matches and storylines from the Reality Era indicative of some of the concepts mentioned in the paragraph above is a difficult task without the objectifying space of time but, even so closely removed, it is clear #16 was a major tipping point for Reality. Perhaps not the peak that many assumed it was (the crowning of a new poster boy) it was nonetheless a vital instance of maturation. Daniel Bryan's path to WrestleMania XXX was the first programme deliberately crafted by WWE that could have *only* happened in the Reality Era, thanks to the unique circumstances through which that era came to evolve.

To manipulate the more informed portion of the fan base is to play with fire. If fans believe themselves to be fully aware of how WWE want them to feel through a self-consciously distanced reaction to the product (that many would presumably think of as analytical) and if WWE are able to pull the wool of kayfabe over the fans' eyes to manipulate their emotional reaction as efficiently as the promotion could manipulate the emotional reaction of the most *uninformed* fans, the resulting creative could very easily be misinterpreted and lead to legitimate disenfranchisement. When Daniel Byran's months-long feud with The Authority arose following Summerslam 2013, this is exactly what happened for many fans; interestingly enough, it's also a prime example of the damaging effects that the continuing, ill-suited sports entertainment mode of professional wrestling has in an age of such transparency as the Reality Era.

Time and again, despite his presence in main events and his overwhelming share of the weekly television time on Raw, fans accused WWE of doing their best to legitimately suffocate Daniel Bryan's career; to "bury" him. This idea stemmed from the Authority's continual beat-downs and screwjobs of the Yes Man that those involved in the storyline have since admitted were often the very idea of Daniel Bryan. Essentially, the fiction took advantage of fan knowledge and IWC folklore on more than one occasion – such as ideas like the "B Plus Player" that played off perceptions of the promotion's favouritism toward larger athletes, along with comparisons to workhorse talents like Edge and Jericho. It was so effective that the fiction was entirely immersive. The results speak for themselves; the first babyface in over a decade universally supported by the entire fan base.

The return of Batista and his victory in the Rumble, along with Bryan's absence from it, exacerbated this immersive storytelling even further. The Animal was "turned" by fan reaction quite naturally, and Bryan having to fight for entry into the main event of WrestleMania positioned Batista and Orton – two of the "company's chosen" of the Brand Extension - as natural antitheses; not just to Bryan but to the change he symbolised. When CM Punk departed the company in controversial fashion leading to the Hijack Raw movement on social media, another element was added into the melting pot. Instead of weathering the storm and carrying on, WWE instead embraced the rebellion and used it as a plot twist on television to draw fans even further into the deepening tale.

Whether proactive or reactive, deliberate or accidental, the fact is Bryan main evented WrestleMania in an emotive culmination of the plot threads started at Summerslam. The Road to WrestleMania in 2014 was special because of WWE's masterful use of Reality Era ideas to create one of their most enrapturing stories in memory. The main event against Batista and Orton would prove Bryan's greatest vicarious victory, but #16 is more representative of the Bryan vs. Authority storyline's full, unabashed embrace of the age-specific philosophies being explored.

The reaction to Bryan and his famous chant as he makes his entrance to wrestle Triple H is an awe-inspiring visual. Cole contextualises Bryan as "the proletariat" to add further poignancy to an already emotive issue, surmising beautifully the atmosphere of the time. Vicarious truly is the best word to describe the piece. Bryan's career path months beforehand had proven infinitely frustrating for many fans swept up in WWE's masterful manipulation of internet sentiment and it is remarkable how solidly and universally behind every strike of Bryan's the capacity crowd is as a result; this is a far cry from the rebellious reaction to the carefully selected heroes of the Brand Extension.

Even under the heavy weight of the chaotic mitigation of both the night's atmosphere and the events leading up to this climactic confrontation, the two masters of their craft weave an interesting story apart from everything else. That is to say, even without the very unique foundations and meaning of this match, it still functions as a sublime effort. The action is as lean as its competitors, possessing not a fast pace as much as it does a *concise* one; Triple H's minimalism combined with Bryan's variety leads to an engaging kaleidoscope of content that wastes little movement. Triple H is afforded opportunities to be both the merciless and cowardly villain – two roles he has always taken to like a duck to water – while Bryan is allowed to breathe as both the sympathetic underdog and combative rebel.

The way the match watches invokes the spirit of the Hart / Michaels dynamic that proved so effective for that particularly special combination of talent eighteen years prior in their epic Iron Man encounter. The slower, cerebral and grittier Game contrasts sharply with Bryan's aerial moments and, as soon as the Cerebral Assassin begins surgically altering Bryan's capability in the most heinous fashion, he begins breaking out aesthetically uncomfortable offense; the way he hones in on Bryan's arm following a brutal moment on the announce table will draw more than one physical grimace from the viewer.

In the midst of the bout's circumstance, one factor has gone unfortunately under-played.

Consider that the quality of this curtain jerker is right up with the best WrestleMania *main events* - including that of XXX itself – essentially meaning Bryan wrestled two main events in one night! A tremendous achievement to be sure, but perhaps one that unfortunately has cast a shadow over the phenomenal outing of Triple H himself; one of his career's best, undoubtedly. Though his presence in lists of the greatest ever is contentious in some corners, performances such as this argue passionately for how justified his inclusion in that debate is. For a part-time, semi-retired performer well into his 40s, not only does Triple H hang with the younger, fresher Bryan - as driven to put on a stellar performance as he had ever been - but an argument could be made for him outshining the Yes Man to boot. After all, it is precisely the Reality Era foundations of this encounter that mean Triple H had as much to prove as Daniel Bryan did; that his presence at WrestleMania was justified; that he was out to make stars for the future and not derail them; that he was the right man for the most important job in WWE for a decade. As Bryan proved superlatively exactly what he needed to, so did Triple H.

Of course, Triple H brutally assaults the victor following the powerful victory, so as to ensure there remains some doubt as to Bryan's chances in the Triple Threat main event. When reviewing #16 in isolation, this has little meaning, though does reflect a very important point at the heart of discussing it: the ongoing stacking of odds and unfair treatment of the Daniel Bryan character at the hands of the Authority and the borderline inexplicable reaction many informed fans had to it.

Unfortunately, the storyline may have proven to work *too* well; its resultant, almost accidental symbolism a little *too* effectively. The affair had become so symbolic and indicative of change among a fan base disillusioned by the still lingering bad tastes of both the Brand Extension's creative sterility, and CM Punk's embittered departure, that many, including myself I must admit, took Bryan's big night at WrestleMania XXX to be his crowning as "The Guy." Thus, when he again failed to win the Rumble in a triumphant return from prolonged injury the following year, lightning struck twice and fans rebelled against the Roman Reigns victory offered up instead. That rebellion was nowhere near as successful, though, in large part because of the unique successes the Daniel Bryan vs. The Authority masterpiece had enjoyed. Where in 2014 Daniel Bryan felt like he *had* to main event WrestleMania, in 2015 it was much, much less of a necessity. The revolution had already happened; and thanks to the high artistic achievement that is #16, it had happened with inarguable success.

Not so much the final composition to throw off the last vestiges of the previous age, then, as it was the first to embrace the aspects of the new age in their fullest, #16 is a match indicative of the first storyline to result entirely from the Reality Era's unique creative philosophies, making it as intriguing an historical article as the two matches reviewed before it and ensuring its status as a major maturation on the road to its Era's peak.

#15
Mankind vs. The Rock

WWF Championship
No Disqualifications Match
Raw Is War
January 4th, 1999

This rhetoric of maturation and functionality is important to define in itself, of course. When boiled down to its essentials, it is not just an issue of chronology but also of identity. In the same way we can define the identity of pay-per-views like the Big Four, such as in Chapter 8: Abstract Genre: Understanding Ideas, so too can we apply similar methods in our attempts to define the identities of the five Eras of WWE's modern history.

It is not always the easiest task to define such identity. Even when we can, rarely is it the case that a single match is indicative enough of the period's character on its own. However, in the case of #15, we have perhaps the match that comes closest to such a thing. Though Attitude was a long time coming thanks to precursory moments like those in #18's Hart / Diesel Survivor Series encounter, the foundation upon which it was built was the Monday Night Wars; indeed, that foundation may be exactly why people mistakenly attribute WrestleMania X-Seven, and its indication of that war's end, as the close date for the Attitude Era entirely.

By 1999, the industry was knee deep in conflict. #15 marked the all important turning point when WWF retook the advantage and never again let go, pinpointing it as a vital and historic development for the company. And so too does it encapsulate within its run-time the most essential spirit of its age, transforming a short television match into a succinct historical definition of its Era and, by extension, a source from which to draw inspiration in our analysis of the entire Era's growth and recession.

The match follows most of the standard Attitude Era conventions. Most of the action takes place outside and, as soon as Rock gets on the headset, the older viewer is reminded of what made him such a special performer in his heyday; little creative touches from outside the box that seem sadly lost in the wake of legitimacy's assault on wit.

The two combatants take full advantage of the stipulation, as steel steps, ring bells and wires are all introduced without hesitation. Nor do they waste any time in bumping through the announce table. It's quite surreal; a sort of match without a match. No start, no middle, just an end, watching as if they took the final ten minutes of an epic and stuck to it without the preamble to facilitate emotional investment. This peculiar trait is what makes it feel so utterly frantic – a tone furthered by the camera work being so haphazard. The action literally watches as totally chaotic; the situation dangerously out of control.

Interference soon starts between the Corporation and D-Generation X and the tale descends into the overbooked mess that proved the norm for the Attitude Era; this does little favours for #15's susceptibility to aging poorly. With the growing trend towards criticising the Attitude Era in some circles, this susceptibility is by no means a phenomenon unique to this case either. It's not long before Austin shows up, the crowd goes absolutely crazy, Rock gets a chair shot and Mankind gets the title and, just as the interesting action gets started, it's all over.

As a match, #15 showcases everything that was wrong about the Attitude Era. It was overbooked, there was excessive interference, no clean conclusion, table bumps for no real reason, Austin became the central highlight despite not being in the match itself and as a wrestling match it is poor; very poor, in fact.

It remains a contradiction because of this. Though there are parts of the work that leave much to be desired, there are others that remain indefatigable successes. #15 is crazy, manic, *fun*. It's not the best example of professional wrestling in the world, but it was no less effective in achieving its goals. Perhaps it was more effective. There was an entire generation of fans reared on this very product and the elements so heavily at play. I am one of those fans, in fact, and though I have changed massively in my tastes, there is a sentimental place for this care-free approach to the industry that put the experience first and the achievement second. Like the time in which it sat, #15 ensures it maintains a frantic pace. It's distinct and obvious lack of patience is no bad thing, representing a blinkered focus on entertainment eschewing self-conscious effort to forge something monumentally historic, as more recent turns in the product seem to concern themselves with. #15's story is impatient, not waiting for the crowd to become excited because it just wants to throw everything into the pot and see what happens. It is one giant thrill ride; pure adrenaline. By today's standards, this entertaining onslaught on sense and context is a forgotten formula, but a no less enrapturing one.

There were times when more might happen throughout one episode of Raw back in the high years of Attitude than would often happen in a month of content leading to a pay-per-view in the worst doldrums of the Brand Extension. When Attitude's famed auspices took the last boat into obscurity, they left behind a product comparatively more patient, comparatively striving to be taken more seriously and, comparatively of course, much less intense. Some call the Attitude Era an age of clustering ideas and overbooking matches. Perhaps it was. It was crazy too, though, and crazy was fun. The approach transformed "Raw Is War" from being a name to being a *nature.*

When Raw was War, the product – the Attitude Era - preoccupied itself with vice over virtue; much the opposite to the PG years that rounded out the Brand Extension in its final days, for example. #15 is the kind of vice that was absent from WWE in the years that followed 2002. Such absence could make the product at its worst moments feel slow, cumbersome and almost afraid to do anything dramatic in spite of its solid qualities as a pro wrestling show. Perhaps it went too far in the opposite direction, becoming *too* patient and *too* self-conscious.

Regardless, #15 is the Attitude Era in a nutshell. From the perspective of a historical school of thought, it's a whimsically succinct exhibition of the predominant traits of its Era and, in that sense, may offer up a conveniently bottled definition of Attitude's identity. It is a best of and a worst of all in one, dominated by the tropes that, following #15, would be deployed in full force on a consistent basis. 1999 was a year rife with championship changes and over-booked nonsense from top to bottom. These ideas may have been attributed a degree more control by the end of the Monday Night Wars, but this was their peak.

This brash, unashamed indulgence of the contemporary is not the only reason as to why #15 is a strong contender to mark as the best badge of identity for the Attitude Era. There are other factors in play, not least of all that this was the night WCW made the mistake of giving away Foley's title win. That tactical miscalculation would prove fatal for a company that would soon enough be out of business. WWE's victory in the Monday Night War, though not the be all and end all of the Attitude Era's legacy, would obviously come to define the post-war professional wrestling world and affirm WWE's status as the longest running, primary and most powerful professional wrestling promotion in the world. #15, thus, becomes a match when WWE went from being the pugnacious underdog to the increasingly likely victor.

There is also a simple but intriguing observation to make: though talent positioning is not, alone, an effective enough means by which to draw the borders of a historical age, #15 sees the presence of the majority of Attitude's longest lasting legends; men most synonymous in the minds of many with this powerhouse of a time. Austin; Rock; Foley; Helmsley; McMahon; D-Generation X; the presence of these children of Attitude caps off an already strong argument for its legacy as the key expression of its Era's identity.

There were other matches, close in proximity and at a chronological distance, which had equal prominence in establishing Attitude's unique identity and setting it apart from the phases that it both succeeded and preceded. Few, however, had the same heady cocktail of historical timing, synonymous talent and creative philosophical expression as #15 did. This truly was The Match of Attitude.

#14
Hulk Hogan vs. The Iron Sheik
WWF Championship
Madison Square Garden
January 23rd, 1984

Regardless of any in-depth analysis of how long the unique products of the five ages in WWE history took to develop, and regardless of any acknowledgements concerning the complexity of periodising a company as ever-changing as

WWE, eventually a chronology must be arrived at. Questioning the popular borders of WWE's Eras is important, but ultimately pointless if not at least temporary answers are arrived at (temporary because it is important to keep in constant motion the method of reappraisal).

Given the nature of this book's central thesis – the performance art paradigm – it seems only proper to take, as an example of such chronological development, the beginning stage of WWE's modern history: the seed of birth of sports entertainment, as found in the guise of #14.

The Golden Age that saw the then WWF become a mainstream pop culture goliath, thanks to the traditional American values of Hulk Hogan, kick-started a process of change in professional wrestling spearheaded by Vince McMahon and his empire that continues to this day. It is arguable that, without Hulkamania, professional wrestling as we know it – as sports entertainment - may never have come to be.

While, in a lot of cases, WWE looks back on the past with the rose-tinted glasses or misleading blinkers of selective memory, there are some historical moments the significance of which simply cannot be debated; moments that have helped shape the professional wrestling world as we know it today in such a clear and decisive way that they simply cannot be contested, even with all the propaganda in the world. One such moment is the birth of Hulkamania.

In order to create as transparent an analysis as possible, let us first question just what is meant by the term Hulkamania. To many, it's something to print on a t-shirt and, to WWE, it was nothing more than a marketing tool to emblazon on everything from stuffed toys to foam hands and beyond. To many professional wrestling fans, it probably remains little more than a buzz word, a phrase that was part of the emotive gimmick of the Hogan legend. For the purposes of this analysis, the term is used in a much less literal and far more abstract sense. This is about Hulkamania as a concept, what that concept represented and what it would come to mean for the WWF and the industry at large.

Most are at least aware of how professional wrestling once worked in the United States, with the territorial system, National Wrestling Alliance affiliations and talent shares. Before Hulk Hogan came to prominence, sources indicate professional wrestling to have beem considered much more of a sport, focussing on feats of grappling acumen, physical conditioning and strength and grit rather than the over-stylised spectacle later generations have become more familiar with.

Hulkamania was, thus, at first a stranger in a strange land, taking ideas already partially instigated by a minority and achieving such success that it became the aspiration of a majority. Hulkamania, as an abstract, refers to the popularity boom brought about by the radical, sometimes resented changes that Vince McMahon instigated (and actually continues to instigate today) and what it all led to. Whether or not such changes were for good or for bad is, of course, for each individual to decide, but it is #14 in particular that began the prioritisation of spectacle over athleticism, where stylistic fiction became the focus to displace the portrayal of legitimacy. Under these terms, Hulkamania arguably may have led to the tidal waves of stigmatisation professional wrestling fans now suffer from – the reason that the wider world so easily misunderstands our passion, and why it exists.

Professional wrestling often doesn't age well in periods of vast change, and age is written all over this historic event. Hogan enters without any music - which is an idea that now seems so distant it watches as almost alien - and there is a deal of foreshadowing in how the announcers introduce Hogan as he heads down the aisle, discussing his knowledge of how important a part the spectators play; an interesting and fitting coincidence hinting at a promotion fully aware of what it was pulling the trigger on.

On the flipside of matches that age poorly is the crowd. Though older matches to modern fans can generally tend to come off as dated and lesser in quality compared to the kind of action fans get spoilt with today, almost diametrically opposed to that is the fact that, the later the year, the more apathetic the general crowd of the age can often seem towards at least some parts of a product or match. In the case of #14, for example, the crowd goes insane for every single move their American hero performs and their passion becomes increasingly prominent as matters progress. They really are rowdy, at times borderline surreal (Hogan sees fit to physically spit on the Sheik and they still cheer it) but, most importantly of all, they are universally willfully complicit.

The match itself is so simple that notable by its absence is the Hulk Up and, when a one trick pony decides not to do its one trick the action threatens to become a redundancy. Hogan simply counters a Camel Clutch by driving Sheik into the corner and goes straight for the Leg Drop.

Then, suddenly, he's the World Champion, Hulkamania comes screaming into existence and the world of professional wrestling never looks back; far from redundancy. In content, #14 is a diluted simplicity. In execution, it lacks imagination. Yet, it gets more of a reaction than many main events of the later Eras ever did. Why that might be is an issue to be explored in the next chapter, intrinsically linked with one of Hogan's most important matches and, by extension, one of the promotion's too. For the time being, the important factor to take away is that Hogan's popularity, at this stage, was inevitable. His being given the championship and a shot at the top changed the world forever. Never would there be quite as clear a turning point in WWE's history books as in the case of #14; a crystal clear marker, not just for the beginning of the first of the five modern Eras of the company but for the very sports entertainment mode of thought this book is campaigning against.

Hulkamania: the Intelligent Design from which all modern and post-modern professional wrestling life as we know it today can perhaps ultimately trace its heritage back to.

Chapter 31

A Trilogy of Change

#13
CM Punk vs. John Cena
WWE Championship
Money in the Bank
July 17th, 2011

All of the arguments made in the previous chapter regarding the slowness of change are not to say that, though one match cannot change the world, the world cannot change through one match. In three particularly unique instances, this has happened. The three matches in this chapter may not necessarily be the most significant to WWE's grand history, but they remain three of the most influential on multiple levels. To round off this book's brief start to reworking of WWE history, these three matches require accounting for.

The first of these compositions is also the most recent and stands as a clear marker for the beginning of the Reality Era. The last vestiges of the Brand Extension were on their way out the door (the very last Brand Draft took place earlier in 2011) and the product in the immediate was on the brink of changes for the better; Bryan won Money in the Bank and started a journey that saw his popularity skyrocket in incredible fashion; and most importantly, CM Punk transitioned permanently into a major main event role. Money in the Bank 2011 gave birth to some of the earliest unique elements now characteristic of the Reality Era and #13 was the night's crowning jewel. If the Bryan vs. Authority feud perfected the Reality philosophy of Neo

Kayfabe, CM Punk, John Cena and Vince McMahon drew out the blueprint.

Importantly, #13 does not deserve to have its qualities as a match ignored in the face of its weighty historical responsibility, and one of the most prominent positives #13 has going for it is, quite obviously, the extremely partisan home crowd. Punk is a talent that has always inspired fervent faith from his most die-hard fans and, in Chicago, his popularity eclipsed even that of some of his famous forebears, let alone his contemporaries. Never is that a clearer article than in this landmark affair. Much like in Cena's battle with RVD at the Hammerstein Ballroom in 2006, the sheer overbearing hostility of the environment is immersive on its own, regardless of the captivating, original story beating at the heart of the action.

In the midst of this partisanship, it is easy to lose sight of just how stellar a showing Cena has; this is, after all, a two man performance. Consternation about the quality of Cena's run as the top talent in the promotion was at fever pitch during the lacklustre first half of 2011. The tropes that had watermarked the Brand Extension felt increasingly stale to an increasingly disenchanted critical audience. Punk was a talent indicative of the frustrations felt by fans, and some performers alike, of Cena's apparent inability to elevate those he worked with and the impenetrable glass ceiling that it created. #13 becomes representative of the overdue challenging of these issues, as the most vocally frustrated victim of that ceiling defeats Cena for the WWE Championship in a big match, high stakes situation.

Those high stakes are brilliantly portrayed. As Punk's theme plays out across the electric, pulsating crowd chanting his name, Michael Cole on commentary talks about how WWE faithful have called him a demagogue and a traitor and mentions that his contract expires at midnight without him having signed another. Framing the context as the clock ticking on a potentially fatal hostage crisis creates expediency, urgency and pandemonium. Indeed, “pandemic” is the word best placed to describe an atmosphere that, even years removed from the fact, still feels enrapturing. Even John Cena himself does an uncharacteristically effective job of selling the situation by entering without theatrics or a smile; no salute and no talk to the cameraman. He walks with purpose and grim visage into enemy territory, while Punk stands surrounded by his loyal followers. Were this more a case of Punk being one man’s terrorist rather than many men’s freedom fighter, never would the odds have felt so genuinely against WWE’s contemporary walking dynasty.

The keys to the gross success of this encounter lie in many of these mitigating factors. Even the most historically notable aspect of the action is not the expected competency from the Second City Saint but the unusually dense variety of content from the perceived-to-be-limited John Cena. The routine of his that often provided the majority of his actions in any given match, while rolled out, is far removed from being the refrain it often was. Instead, Cena’s performance feels as if it is out to prove something more passionately than before. The quality of the acumen he exhibits can be debated all day, but that he made the effort to exhibit it in the first place counts for a great deal and kick-started the critically acclaimed reputation any Punk / Cena match would go on to be met with in future clashes. Theirs was a feud that felt more organically epic than the manufactured Cena / Orton feud ever did.

This is not a match chosen specifically because it began the Reality Era in earnest, though. Larger strides towards maturing the Reality Era’s creative philosophy would be taken later down the line with shows such as WrestleMania XXVIII, Payback 2013 and WrestleMania XXX. Instead, #13 was selected because it is perhaps the earliest indicator of said creative philosophy: casting doubt upon a fact by actively utilising it as a jumping off point for one's fiction, thereby successfully manipulating, to great effect, the tool fans have used to tear open the curtain previously shielding the workings of the business - the internet. It is a philosophy that has resulted on more than one occasion in an extremely effective reconstruction of a new form of kayfabe; an idea referred to earlier in this review as Neo Kayfabe.

Neo Kayfabe does not function in the holistic way kayfabe did years ago; such totality would now be impossible. But when wielded carefully enough, it can do more than "make do," instead actively combating the damage the internet was perceived as dealing during the Brand Extension, when fan rebellion became so frequent that it bordered on outright tradition. CM Punk vs. John Cena is the earliest example of this Neo Kayfabe being deployed. Fans could not be sure which elements of the progressing storyline were genuinely real or not; that is because the answer was those events were both fictional and factual all at the same time. This is a feud that took a real world situation, covered it with a layer of fiction and offered it back to fans; fans who then ate it up ravenously. It is a risky method that constantly threatens to backfire in a sports entertainment world – as perhaps it did on more than one occasion in later years with Daniel Bryan's various programmes – but with that great risk comes great reward, and #13 was certainly a great reward.

The Voice of the Voiceless; McMahon telling Josh Matthews he did everything he could to placate Punk's frustrations to keep him in the company; shades of

Montreal; Cena as a dynasty; Punk being an absentee champion following the broadcast; even the t-shirts with the unique date printed upon them indicating a self-conscious awareness of this match being of historic proportions; to include all of these ideas in the feud and culminate them with this match examples a paradigmatic shift that, if adhered to, can allow professional wrestling to do what many thought was impossible – function effectively in a world of instantaneous connectivity. This very book is concerned with embracing that new paradigm even more than it already has; this is, after all, not a finished process, and WWE continue to figure out how best to wield their new fangled philosophy.

Regardless, that #13 changed the professional wrestling world in its success is undeniable. If the ideas this book has argued as underpinning the Reality Era are accurate, and eventually perfected permanently, then professional wrestling will have survived the biggest threat it has ever faced in its continued existence.

#12
André the Giant vs. Hulk Hogan
WWF Championship
WrestleMania III
March 29th, 1987

The beginning of Hulkamania is, quite naturally, the second of the all important trilogy being examined here. Its birth has already been covered of course, with #14's Hogan vs. Iron Sheik bout. However, Hulkamania as an idea would not come of age until much later. That important maturation is best represented by #12; the first instalment of the streamlined mythology of WWE's history, documented earlier in Chapter 28: Generations: When Worlds Collide. Until #12 happened, André the Giant had been the biggest pop culture icon professional wrestling had ever seen, undefeated for fifteen years and, by some distance, the pinnacle of the industry. For him to pass all of that over to this new moralistic bleached blond hero was quite the event.

It is worth mentioning the stare down during the opening. It has perhaps become the most recognisable moment in all the clips of WrestleMania shown on a regular basis and is one of those images that stays ingrained in the mind regardless of how long ago it was first seen. The electricity in the crowd is phenomenal and the moment builds anticipation until the Silverdome is ready to explode. Then comes the opening salvo, working the fans into an emotional frenzy before anything is even really attempted.

The story is the important factor, though, not the content. Like many matches of the time, this is an effort that does not just survive by its emotion, but succeeds exactly because of it. For fifteen years André was undefeated, and now aligned with the most hated man in the promotion. For three years Hogan had reigned as champion, and thrived off his ability to overcome the odds. Now, with renewed faith in himself and in a higher power, Hogan's family-friendly appeal was even greater and his popularity soaring. There is a reason the Pontiac Silverdome was successfully filled out. That emotive foundation was propagated bell-to-bell by the always effective underdog effort. The live crowd is invested and, because of these factors, #12 is quite rightly remembered very fondly. Many have even attributed it responsible for inspiring them to pick professional wrestling up – as job or hobby – in the first place. The content may be wafer thin, but the emotion is immortal.

Above all else, it is its legacy that matters most, and #12 is a match with a complex legacy.

#12 raises interesting questions about Hulk Hogan and whether or not he was simply the right character at the right time. The 1980s was, after all, a time in the American social consciousness of healing and rebirth. Why did Hulk Hogan draw so much emotion from his crowds? Why was he a "Real American" and why did that hit such an emotional nerve with American fans, despite later failed attempts to replicate that magic with characters like Lex Luger? Was it Hogan's showmanship or McMahon's understanding of the wider world outside of the professional wrestling bubble?

There is a truth to be had in the claim his character had impeccable timing; an idea that changes the very context of this match's success. After being betrayed, emotionally exhausted and facing impossible odds, in front of ninety thousand fans Hulk Hogan conquered the evils laid before him before celebrating victoriously with "Real American" blasting out into the air; America as the hero; America as righteous and moral; America as standard; America recovered. This is a composition that met a social need for a victorious hero who represented the purest of American foundations and reaffirmed the nation's right to self-belief; a Reaganite main event.

The most important facet of its legacy, however, is one much more relevant to the turning point the professional wrestling industry was teetering on at the time.

André was the icon of WWE's pre-modern history. His unusual physical stature was the very foundation of his appeal. Both stature and appeal were the foremost explanations as to the believability and reasoning behind his fifteen year winning streak. Put simply, the Giant was popular and credible; defeating him, neither.

Heading into #12, André's popularity was negated by association with Bobby Heenan; a storyline plot twist pragmatically required. After #12, André's undefeated streak had come to an end at the hands of Hogan; an outcome, as we know, predetermined. That defeat was lent further purpose by its personable and morality-driven circumstance; circumstance transforming Hogan from champion to role model. A fifteen year undefeated streak ended, with a previously unrivalled popularity now fully displaced, with the torch held by the icon of yesteryear passed to the icon of the future; taking into account all of these ideas results in #12 being wholly representative of McMahon's confessional vision of pushing professional wrestling away from believability towards theatricality.

#12's legacy represents it as Vince McMahon's final, irreversible embrace of fiction over fact. Hulkamania and its coming of age with #12 are indicative of the ultimate choice Vince McMahon ever made: we're going to go with professional wrestling as theatre, not with professional wrestling as sport. If #13's Cena vs. Punk bout has the potential to become seen as the genesis point of professional wrestling defined by fan demand, then #12 should be seen as the genesis point of professional wrestling defined by Vince McMahon's.

#11
Shawn Michaels vs. Bret "Hitman" Hart
WWF Championship
Survivor Series
November 9th, 1997

And then there was Montreal; a word every professional wrestling fan will (or should) know.

The Screwjob remains to this day one of the most divisive, emotive, angst ridden conversations among professional wrestling fans. Was it a work or a shoot? Who was to blame? Should it be applauded or condemned? Did it begin the Attitude Era? Did it kill kayfabe? Would fans have ever felt justified in their vocal and social media revolts if Montreal had not proven that "The Result" in professional wrestling was anything but sacred?

It is with Montreal that we can now return again to the core of this book's purpose: professional wrestling's transcended state of performance art that, here, proves the industry has lessons to teach us about life and how we live it. #11 is the *most* transcendent example of this; a match that did not change the world but the results of which teach the power to do so is our own.

To arrive at that conclusion requires asking, "What is the historical truth of Montreal?"

There are a number of glaring inconsistencies when it comes to the retelling of this story among the available source material. At the same time, however, there are also a number of extremely important consistencies as well. The majority of both are found in the description of events throughout that specific calendar year. These include, but are not limited to: the flaws in Shawn's retelling of his February knee injury, along with the clear indications that said injury was widely doubted; consistent recollections of conversations between Shawn and Bret determined to put an end to bad feeling; Shawn's "Sunny Days" comment being a turning point in relations, spoken in retaliation to a perceived slight from Bret the previous week in which Raw went off the air before Shawn could Superkick him; Bret's dealings with WCW, and Vince's exacerbation of them; and, perhaps most interestingly, Vince's own haggling between the two individuals as a middle-man being a large cause of friction.

The problem in identifying both consistencies and inconsistencies alike lies in the reliability of the sources readily available to the mass public. One thing becomes increasingly clear upon assessing the reliability of these sources; only the match itself can provide our most honest clues, and certainly those closest to being unprejudiced, as to what happened that night. Yes, other sources provide us with a number of consistencies, undoubtedly, but overall the scene they paint is a confusing one. As a result, the match needs to be a prism through which to focus our haze of information, hopefully clarifying some degree of truth in the process.

As a primary source, the video footage of this match is vital. It has its limitations, but those limitations tell us something themselves. The camera work provides little clarity as to what was occurring on the commentary side of the ring. We can just about determine where Vince was sitting once the match-proper begins, but conveniently placing himself off camera means it's impossible to track his movements beyond the early happenings of the bout. Certainly we can't see how he acts when the time comes for the bell to be rung. It's also vital to note he is in no rush to immediately leave ringside as Earl, Shawn or Brisco were. The fact that the match is a WWE product limits its ability to give an accurate and unbiased account of events, but it does highlight concerns raised by others through the years. How was the music ready to hit? Why were they so quickly capable of going off air early? How did Vince know where to place himself to avoid being seen by all except the eagle-eyed, avoiding raised suspicions? Do the match result and the efficient conclusion of the production indicate that knowledge of the event was perhaps not quite as limited as certain accounts would lead to believe?

There is another piece of video footage linked to all this: the worked interview performed by Vince McMahon on Raw in the weeks following the event. While the interview itself is intensely limited as a source, it does have an interesting moment when Vince expresses regret that Bret didn't do the "right thing" for either the Federation or himself, despite the fact that it would not have cost the Hitman a dime to do so. This point is a vital consideration in seeking the answer to, "What is the historical truth of Montreal?" because it proposes a second question that might strike truer as to why the Montreal Screwjob teaches us the lessons it does. That question completely foregoes the obsession over who was involved, what they did and how they did it and focuses instead on the victim. That question is, "What did Bret actually *do*?"

January 4th 2010 is a night that is going to be etched into the memories of many fans for the rest of their lives, if ever they had thought that the Hitman would never again be a part of WWE beyond his Hall of Fame induction. By the time Hart did return, the Montreal Screwjob had become an all-consuming event. It over-shadowed the career of Shawn Michaels, defined the career of Bret Hart, informed the Mr McMahon character almost in its entirety and riddled an entire nation with the same chant: "You screwed Bret!" Bret's refusal necessitated the Screwjob (in the opinions of some) which, in turn, threatened to devour the memories of all those involved. For thirteen long years, nobody could move on from it. So to put it succinctly, what Bret did was risk legacies.

The Screwjob tarnished Bret Hart. He missed only two shows in his entire career, never injured the man he wrestled and, most importantly, provided a library of complex storytelling in the ring that few can rival. No one can deny the seemingly innumerable top quality efforts he put in through his years. Instead of these things, though, he was remembered, for the longest time, primarily for his perceived resentment (understandable in itself, if an accurate accusation) and, through that, his legacy was diminished to the status of one event: the Montreal Screwjob. It was an event that became a phenomenon overshadowing the work Bret Hart put into becoming a legend.

With that said, though, we must remember that Montreal is an event involving many players and Shawn Michaels is also a victim of sorts, albeit to a different degree.

In the DVD release *Greatest Rivalries*, Michaels describes, with a deal of genuine emotional pain in his expressions, how Vince said he would take the heat for the Screwjob, though Heartbreak knew McMahon would prove unable to stave off the overwhelming negativity resulting from it. His regret is clearly genuine. His eyes become glassy as he recounts the match and the events leading up to it. He states simply that there was no fun in being that guy in that ring at that time. Another idea at the heart of Montreal's historical truth: everyone suffered. In Michaels' case, thanks to his second career post-2002, luckily that suffering was confined to vocally hostile crowds in certain cities or in certain feuds. Even that, especially given its veracity, must have taken its toll. There're only so many times you can be attributed with responsibility for the ruination of a man's career before it begins to hurt.

Perversely, there is an argument to be made that Vince McMahon was the only one to benefit, thanks to the fruition of the Mr McMahon character that provided the all important antithesis to Austin through the company's financial resurgence at the turn of the decade. In the wake of the Screwjob's destruction, Vince McMahon's new villain would go on to become one half of the reason many claim we now watch Monday Night Raw instead of Monday Nitro.

The toll the Screwjob took on its three key players, thus, asks whether or not the Screwjob was worth it. If this was a necessity, the suffering the Screwjob resulted in might be excusable.

Unfortunately, it was far from necessary.

The transition from the family-friendly product of the New Generation had already begun in earnest in the earliest months of 1997. The WWF was already moving almost irreversibly to the tone of the Attitude Era. To simply give the Montreal Screwjob the status as sole catalyst for said transition is irresponsible.

Similarly, were the Screwjob not to have happened, the Mr McMahon character may still have come to be. Throughout the continuing switch to a more adult product during 1997, Vince McMahon was increasingly involved in the fictional events on WWF television. By the time the Montreal Screwjob happened, he was well on his way to becoming more of a character as his status as owner of the Federation was shied away from less and less.

Both of these assertions simply scratch the surface, but already dispute heavily the idea of the Screwjob as a necessity, in turn ensuring we can confidently claim that it was *not* worth it. The cost it demanded – that of the legacies of perpetrators and victim – was far too high. Understanding this revelation and the others covered in this review together lead us to the answer to our question, for there is another legacy that Montreal has had a direct impact on: your own. Shawn was right when, in his promo in 2010, he said Bret wasn't the only one who carried Montreal around for thirteen years. We all did, in a manner of speaking.

The real historical truth behind it all is that the Screwjob stands as a cold hard reminder, not to wrestlers or to promoters or to those involved, but to you and I as fans of professional wrestling not to allow our memories to splinter into realms of reality we will never truly know about. It's not about history, but responsibility; we have a responsibility to ensure things are remembered for the right reasons, not the wrong ones. The reason you should remember #11 isn't because Bret Hart got screwed – whether that be by Vince McMahon, by the referee, by Shawn Michaels or by himself – but because Bret Hart and Shawn Michaels created an in-ring product that stands apart from any other.

Like any Shawn Michaels and Bret Hart match, #11 is a blend of showmanship and reality that perfectly complimented one another to create a match that felt like a fight. Granted, perhaps there was a little too much reality in the end, but in an ugly way that presents the zenith of the pioneering creation these two were responsible for; this is professional wrestling as documentary, a cross-breed of genres that evokes real emotion. In remembering that this issue is as much about our responsibilities as a fan base as it was about the legacies of those directly involved, #11 is a match for every fan to watch and write their own review of, being sure to maintain its context as a professional wrestling composition and nothing more. Any fan doing this may find that instead of a dark, disturbing and definitive event, #11 is a match possessing a genuinely innovative aesthetic. She's one of a kind.

The Screwjob remains to this day one of the most divisive, emotive, angst ridden conversations among professional wrestling fans. It is time for that to change. Putting aside the Screwjob does nobody a disservice. If anything, it does a service. It's time Bret Hart and Shawn Michaels stopped being "those guys." They have taken the step, and if the people who it actually really did affect can, so can we; the humble fans.

When history is about learning from our mistakes and when professional wrestling teaches us lessons about life, together these ideas reveal the ultimate historical truth behind the Montreal Screwjob: moving on. The Montreal Screwjob, as a historical event informing a conscious artistic interpretation of the fiction that the match is intended to be, teaches us that we have the power to shape our world; to change it, if we want to, and define for ourselves who we are. CM Punk did this through #13. Vince McMahon did this through #12. We can too, if we heed the important lessons of #11.

Chapter 32

The Magnum Opus

#10
Shawn Michaels vs. Bret Hart
60 Minute Iron Man Match
WWF Championship
WrestleMania XII
March 31st, 1996

What is a magnum opus?

The literal translation means "great work," but what defines a work as great? More importantly, what defines something as being *the* great work of any given entity? Must it be definitive; crucial; affecting; pioneering; special?

In the case of WWE, that great work is a match that represents the very fabric of what the promotion is about.

Whether taking a more traditional take on professional wrestling or whether you, by now, subscribe to the performance art theory being fashioned in this book, WWE's style emphasises heavily the story over the content. The best WWE matches tell emotive, powerful, visceral stories laden with innumerable intangibles that hit nerves, touch lives and, in doing so, stay with fans forever. WWE matches are the arenas through which we live out our dreams vicariously through our heroes.

In searching for WWE's magnum opus, it must be asked which match, out of every match in company history, gave fans the most emotive, the most powerful, the most visceral story of them all. Which match allows fans to make pretend their dreams have come true? The answer is found with

#10; a match that puts that emotional story first and foremost before any other trait. More importantly, #10 is a match that tells a story every single professional wrestling fan on the face of this planet should find utterly appealing: a boyhood dream coming true.

Such everyman appeal is perhaps ironic, given this is a bout executed by two of the most elite performers in the history of the company. The focus of #10 remains largely on their status as equals. While their ring games differed, their results were one and the same: unrivalled competitive spirit. Bret Hart and Shawn Michaels' story is one of competition, and #10 is perhaps the purest and most untainted moment in that story.

Obvious is the fact that the composition's mightiest trait is its minimalist psychology whereby the sixty minutes end without a single fall. It's easy to miss the emphasis that the announce booth place on how winning the first fall will essentially win the match and, not only does that underlying theme create greater urgency in the closing moments, it also carries a sense of irony that, quite literally, it remained "one fall to a finish."

Many critics address #10 as being dull or boring, largely because of how long the two take to actually allow the action to grow. Certainly, the first ten to twenty minutes are methodical, so it can be understood how many would take that view. The truth is, however, that easing into this sixty minute bout isn't just an ergonomic choice allowing them to pace the action evenly enough to match the clock in their timing, but it ensures anticipation simmers slowly to a boil. By the time the two are unleashing more impactful moves, the audience has waited so long for it that their ecstasy is all the greater. It lends more credence and realism, that two evenly matched athletes in their prime would wrestle conservatively in the first half in an attempt to save energy for the deep fourth quarter.

It's intriguing to analyse the greater psychological picture. Around fifteen minutes in, McMahon almost points it out to the viewer, stating that, if the match were to be awarded on points, Michaels would, thus far, have the advantage. Indeed, the first two acts of this one see Michaels maintain the greater offensive possession and, while Hart has a number of answers for most of the questions Michaels asks, it's usually the Heartbreak Kid that comes out of any given set-piece with the advantage. Allowing the challenger to be presented in that manner for the first half allows him to become a threat, shattering preconceptions perhaps established the year before at WrestleMania XI and ensuring that the underdog story which unfolds in the bout's second half feels all the more enticing. They show Michaels holding success at his fingertips early, before drawing it further and further away as the sixtieth minute closes in.

Similarly impressive is how tightly the two work together. Many Hart matches are admired for their realism, and here that trait never wavers despite the marathon duration. The term "Excellence of Execution" is more than just a nickname in this instance; it should be a tagline by which this bout is remembered. And, if anything, it's even more impressive from Michaels' perspective, considering his are the flashier and more flamboyant moves possessing a greater margin for error.

The end of the second act proves a vital turning point. It is the moment that Hart firmly grasps the advantage that, until this point, had perhaps belonged largely to Michaels; and the viewer sees the brutal aspect of the Hitman character come to the fore. He begins a *merciless* beat down on the challenger, with all his focus on the lower back. With the announce booth hyping up the idea of Michaels being historically resilient, and Hart having withstood everything Michaels had dished out to him in the first two acts, there is almost the idea of a rope-a-dope tactic in motion from the champion; take everything you can and come back, when you can, with something twice as hard. And while Hart avoids actively acting like a villain, he does feel uncharacteristically malicious in the execution of his onslaught.

It really is an onslaught too. As the clock passes forty minutes, the pops Michaels receives from his kick-outs become noticeably and gradually louder. Now that the two men have established in the minds of their audience that Michaels is more than capable of attaining victory, it feels all the more cruel for him to go on such a distant back foot for the final twenty minutes. Added to his failed effort the year prior in the same spot, it becomes an almost necessary catharsis for the audience to see the hero of the day overcome the adversity in front of him. In short, the dramatic character of the closing minutes is doubled in its effectiveness because of the precedent created before it.

Vitally, at the latest stages, neither man's finish has made an appearance. There's no Sweet Chin Music in the midst of the action to create a dramatic near fall, nor is there a Sharpshooter to get the crowd hollering. These two save their respective finishers for the final conclusion. When that Sharpshooter is locked in, it genuinely feels like Michaels is in legitimate danger of having his dream being ripped apart at the final hurdle. When Michaels hits the Sweet Chin Music, it benefits from not having been deployed already. It's a less is more approach, one vital to allowing the integrity of the greater story to survive an excruciating amount of critical analysis. It's a characteristic respectful of the unwritten laws of kayfabe, beneficial to the story at hand and a lesson to learn from.

This is so effective a method that the deployment of both world famous finishing moves feels like an almost out-of-body experience if engrossed as wholly as any fan should be by that point. When that Sharpshooter is locked in, there's a level of emotional transference that threatens to overwhelm. When that final Sweet Chin Music connects, the relief is like a tsunami. Actually, perhaps relief is the wrong word. It's not relief. It's an emotional release, for which the viewer was made to wait over an excruciating hour for. That's the most vital point of all.

Many critics will claim this is a boring match that lazily plays out its narrative in a manner that just *expects* you to care. For fans to whom professional wrestling appeals as entertainment more than it does art, this certainly isn't the kind of match to seek out. Said critics may be too used to the contemporary style of professional wrestling in WWE. #10 may be boring to those who prefer more obvious emotional prompting and that's fair enough, because this match makes the viewer work. It's not going to tell you how to feel, as more modern takes on the genre might. It's more subtle than that.

For fans convinced of the performance art theory among these pages, and for those that have an appreciation of intelligent professional wrestling - of emotionally informed performance art - this match should rank highly for them. Looking for WWE's magnum opus means looking for a visceral, heartfelt story through which fans live out a dream vicariously via the hero of the hour; doesn't that mean WWE's magnum opus should be *our* greatest catharsis? If so, what better suits that than the boyhood dream of a professional wrestling fan coming true?

Chapter 33

The Most Historically Significant Match in WWE History

#9
Bret "Hitman" Hart vs. Stone Cold Steve Austin
Submission Match
WrestleMania 13
March 23rd, 1997

This book has endeavoured to select a number of the most historically important matches in WWE history. Sometimes, it has agreed with the revisionist company history that, indeed, these matches carry the weight on their shoulders of having altered the world. In other cases, the revisionist history has been called into question and alternative, more dispassionate points of view suggested. But the question still remains entirely unanswered: what is the most historically significant match in WWE history?

#9 is a match that gave WWE its redemptive reward of unprecedented success for its strife in the 1990s. In less than thirty minutes, the quiet alterations to professional wrestling that had been whispered about time and again exploded into an industry-wide dominating tone. The rebellion of counterculture experiments turned into an all-out mainstream empire, and this match is the ultimate loud, unapologetic, visceral expression of it. This is the firing of a starting pistol that would lead to the WWF sprinting away at a breakneck pace it had never managed before and has categorically failed to match since.

This match is the most historically significant match in WWE history, it is an achievement unlike any other and it is my favourite match of all-time.

In the first five minutes, the composition is set up as an everyman narrative that plays further into the hands of its animalistic spirit. It may not consist of the most high impact offense you'll see, but it's the kind of street fight you like to imagine yourself being capable of; like #10, we're allowed to live through the action, albeit viscerally rather than vicariously in this instance.

On a more basic level, their approach to the action allows the fans to get the best of both worlds. Starting off in a brawl plays to the strengths of Austin's character. Eventually, the piece transitions into a more traditional Hart match before finding itself dragged right back into the theatre of the brawl. It's a seamless blend of the styles of both men, reflecting the most wonderful aspect of the entire Hart / Austin feud. At Survivor Series in the preceding November, they created a clinical masterpiece more in line with Hart's famous precision, while here they fashion a precursor of what would later become the identifiable Attitudinal style led by the red hot charge of the Rattlesnake.

#9 is very much a strikingly visible experimentation in a new field thanks to this blending of styles. Essentially, by the time Hart is utilising the chair, the match has transformed into prototypical Hart fare tainted by the increasingly influential edge of the attitude Austin's character was a harbinger of. If the New Generation created a strong in-ring foundation for the company, Attitude took that foundation and introduced it to a world of vice. That's exactly what this match is – the strong foundation of a standard in-ring Bret Hart story introduced to the world of steel chairs, hard fists and blood that would watermark Austin's own eventually favoured in-ring story. It's evolution as a snapshot.

A notable facet of this encounter is the fact that submission moves are actually few and far between for a Submission Match. On the surface, that may be considered a forfeiture of purpose in the face of intended stylistic achievement. It's very much a positive, though. Through the scarce use of submissions, the two performers place a level of faith in the audience by creating a piece of work that is an affirmation of their confidence in the viewer instead of one that spoon-feeds them.

They must have known that it would have been jarringly out of character for Austin to suddenly indulge in the submission game and that a mat-based affair would have emotionally castrated the match, turning it into a laborious effort rather than the insanely brisk one it is. As a result, beating the living hell out of one another would provide the reason for one of them to submit instead. It deepens the semantics of the stipulation – this isn't so much a Submission Match as it is a match about submission. Including a few submission moves reminds of the method needed to acquire victory, but the larger focus on a bloody fist fight indicates the preferred method by which the two characters involved would want to emerge victorious; they want their opponent to submit because of a beating, not a hold, and that makes the famous finish all the more effective.

#9 is most fondly remembered for the exhibition of grit from Austin. The moment the blade job occurs, the match shifts its focus from an evenly matched brawl into a disturbingly dark beat down in such sneering fashion that, rather than being notable for a lack of energy some beat downs find themselves suffering from, it escalates the intensity. The presence of Austin's crimson mask catapults him toward greater aggression, like a wounded animal frothing at the mouth because of its masochistic enjoyment of the fight. In response, Hart's own offense becomes necessarily more intense. When he does have the advantage in the closing act, his beating down of Austin becomes almost frightening and, by the time Austin passes out in the Sharpshooter, it feels like a final insult rather than a heroic exhibition of durability from the Hitman.

That finish is legendary. The immortal visual of Austin's blood-soaked scream and guttural roar of agony will sear itself into your mind for as long as you live. It's a brilliant way for Austin to retain his status as the bad ass while moving firmly into the territory of the protagonist.

The way Hart takes Austin down - viciously and relentlessly snatching his legs from under him as Austin staggers for space to recover from Hart's shot with the ring bell - feels fittingly cold-hearted. His final decimation of the Rattlesnake comes from a darker interpretation of his Excellence of Execution character. His black-hearted intent is dangerous and repugnant and as excellently executed as his most heroic and memorable comebacks. As Austin lies unconscious in a pool of his blood looking extremely undignified, Hart parades around the ring in a shameless show of self-gratification to a notable absence of adulation from the crowd. By the time he renews his assault on Austin the work is firmly in double turn territory.

Austin Stunners the referee attempting to help him in the aftermath and limps to the back on his own power; a footnote to the larger story, it's an important affirmation that the Austin character is still as the Austin character had always been. If anything, it's a wink from the WWF that, while fans were now "allowed" to cheer for Austin, they could rest assured it was still the same man.

The rest, as they say, is history. Austin would go on to become the most profitable star of all time, leading the way for what would eventually become the most profitable period in WWE history and its finest hour of victory. Why it is the most historically important match in the history of the company should, thus, be apparent.

#9 is a gatekeeper; a match that allowed what had so far been something of an unspoken taboo in the WWF product to take centre stage: edge. Austin was not the progenitor of an overnight 180 in the creative approach of the company. The changes so often attributed to the late 1990s can actually be traced back much further than that. His performance here, an oxymoronic successful defeat, simply broke down the protective layer that had, to that point, isolated the New Generation from the maleficent influence of phenomena like ECW. It overtly made the unacceptable acceptable in the still relatively conservative WWF creative.

Bret Hart, the hero of the New Generation and wrestler most representative of the pervading style employed by that generation, is irredeemably doomed to the status of an embittered, resentful and malicious bad guy rejected because of his adherence to traditional principles and long-held social expectations of good guys. At the same time, Steve Austin, who would go on to become the hero of the Attitude Era and the character most representative of the pervading style employed by his generation, is embraced with open and waiting arms, not in spite of his vices but precisely because of them.

#9 is important for more than the fact it marked the beginning of the most financially profitable and successful period in company history. It proves a monument to history, commenting on the evolution of the world and standing as a figurative representation of the related shift in the WWF fan base and their views on the preceding and incoming eras. New Generation and Hart was out; Attitude and Austin were in.

Chapter 34

The Great Metaphor

#8
Shawn Michaels vs. The Undertaker
The Streak vs. Career
No Disqualification, No Count-Out Match
WrestleMania XXVI
March 28th, 2010

The Tetralogy is a term to describe four specific matches from a specific part of The Undertaker's legacy. It is a term borrowed from the literary criticism of William Shakespeare. Shakespeare's famous Tetralogy spanned a long history of Royal Succession, beginning with the overthrow of Richard II and ending with the patriotic reign of Henry V. Four plays, epic in scope and perhaps unparalleled in terms of quality and achievement.

What better analogy could there be for the four Streak matches between the 25th Anniversary of WrestleMania and WrestleMania XXVIII's End of an Era? They are matches that stand far apart from all others and very close together in themselves. It began in 2009 at the 25th Anniversary when Shawn Michaels challenged The Undertaker to tear down one of the great wonders of the professional wrestling world: The Streak. It is a match that lives in infamy; no doubt a histrionic effort that reshaped the way the promotion approaches its annual premier event.

What many thought could have been an end actually turned into a beginning; a beginning of a story that would take four years to tell. What followed was a professional wrestling fable that pondered upon the fragility of human success. Shawn Michaels developed an unhealthy obsession that resulted in the end of his career. The Undertaker developed an unhealthy hubris that risked everything he had built because of the blinding ego of his monolithic achievement. Triple H developed a spirit of Nemesis, a divine retribution fixated on the evisceration of another's relentless quest for greatness already attained. And, in a final hellacious chapter, the three came together in a raw collision of emotion as all sought their own version of closure to an era that had grown to consume everything that defined them. That era that ended wasn't of the company; it was of Tetralogy; it was of The Streak.

Of these four efforts, two stand above and beyond their counterparts as performance art compositions. One remains to be analysed still; #8 was selected because of its specific relevance to the grand design behind this very book. At its beginning, this book explored professional wrestling's transformative potential when viewed as performance art, including how a good professional wrestling match can function as metaphor. As this analysis shall now hopefully prove, #8 is the greatest – more accurately, the most fitting - metaphor a WWE match has ever provided.

The fragility of human achievement – a prescient theme of the Tetralogy - comes into play through the visage of the untimely consequences that revenge can breed, and just like with the other encounters involved in this over-arching four piece, Shawn Michaels and The Undertaker begin telling that story on their way to the ring. As Shawn Michaels makes his entrance, the impression is given that this is a match more about the challenger than it is The Undertaker; perhaps it is the only example of that switch of focus in the entire Streak, making it all the more unique. It is the announce booth's narrative rhetoric of setting suns and the measured demeanour of the Heartbreak Kid that creates an initial wave of bone-chilling fatalism, a near undeniable impression of inevitability that is being helplessly marched towards by a vengeful man.

Michaels is, of course, followed by the ethereal Undertaker. The entrance is one of the more muted WrestleMania efforts from the Dead Man, but perhaps it is also one of his most purposeful. The preceding year, Shawn Michaels descended from the heavens before dancing his way to the squared circle with all the usual boisterousness. For the second go around, it was a more standard affair – the Heartbreak Kid, off of his previous failed effort at The Streak, now stood robbed of his divine intention, instead relying on simple mortal aspiration. When the previously victorious Undertaker enters, however, rising from the pits of the stage and bringing his hellish intent with him, he remains as superlatively powerful as he was in 2009; it's almost a direct replication from the year before, in fact. What's more, he does so dressed in the style of an executioner. No mere stylistic choice; statement of dreadful intent.

As The Undertaker makes his long, cold march to the ring, Shawn Michaels' expression is a picture of serenity. His face isn't one of focus, it isn't one of nervousness; it is a statement of intent all its own. *This* Shawn Michaels is a man willing to live with the consequences of his actions. It is such peace of mind and unity of purpose that makes Michaels feel as dangerous this time as The Undertaker.

There is admittedly a great deal of signature offense utilised very early on, but that is in keeping with the aggressive voice both men give this properly escalated sequel. The Undertaker is able to gain an early advantage despite the Heartbreak Kid's intentions, and shows signs of a learning curve himself. Utilising his more recognisable moves so early is indicative of a man respectfully aware of how close to defeat he had been the last time. Playing into the underlying psychology, it relates as a competitor looking to finish this affair early and deny it a marathon run time that so dangerously invigorates as deadly an aspiration as that of Mr WrestleMania.

Yet, despite the respectful wariness of each, both men are entirely confident in their own seemingly inevitable victory. Both men already know they can withstand at least a single salvo of the other's best, courtesy of their epic already in the record books. As a result, they have no intention of killing time or waiting for an opportunity to present itself. #8 evidences men that are going to outright force their issue. Every move is designed as an endgame, from the blistering knife-edge chops to the myriad submission holds to the desperate moonsaults. Even seeing The Undertaker throw aside a medic checking on Shawn Michaels after a Tombstone Piledriver on the outside expresses the same urgency – rip open the other's offensive, force your issue, impose your opportunity and nail the final move whenever and wherever you can.

It's also important to realise that every plot twist comes, by virtue of their indulgence in false finish, as an explosive shock rather than as a result of a more measured constant motion. Never is that more apparent than the first Sweet Chin Music that acts as a sudden reminder of how this high stakes poker game can end in so brief a flash; it's not a finishing move, it's a revelation.

But even when used as transitional moves, they still continue to act as important plot twists – the superkick that lands The Undertaker on the table is a moment that allows Michaels to capture enough of an advantage to land an all-or-nothing moonsault, followed by a further kick to the chin inside the ring as he finally manages to overwhelm the

Dead Man with the physical onslaught he had lined up from the onset. The entire sequence, from the Last Ride inside the ring to the out-of-body near fall off the third superkick, flows beautifully.

It is, however, their final scene together that is the most impressive; the one wherein the great metaphor lies.

When Shawn Michaels kicks out of the Tombstone, Undertaker sensibly avoids expressing the same disbelief he expressed the year before. Instead, what the viewer gets is an expression of outright frustration. His more urgent and high octane game was still being withstood, his own adaptation being rendered inert by the adaptations of his opponent, whose promises had not yet been broken. The masterstroke of Michaels trying to turn The Undertaker's familiar WrestleMania state of cut-throat, relentless intent back on him seemed to be working, and such is the lack of Undertaker's own certainty that he fails to complete his signature throat slash - one performed so eagerly by Michaels during the opening stand-off, no less. Is that an expression of respect from the Dead Man, or of trepidation? Certainly, by the time Michaels crawls his way up The Undertaker's singlet, we get perhaps the first and only instance of the Dead Man showing hesitation and remorse for what he felt he had to do.

Then, even in the face of his inevitable failure, Michaels finishes what The Undertaker couldn't, slashing his throat again in the face of the Dead Man to signify his acceptance of what was about to happen and, at the same time, neutering The Undertaker of a true sense of achievement. When The Undertaker hesitates still, Michaels breaks the hearts of fans worldwide one last time by slapping the Phenom and challenging him to pull the trigger. Even the final Tombstone is given respectful forethought – 'Taker goes so far as to jump in the air to deliver the killing blow, knowing a standard execution had, thus far, failed to do the job.

Like in the case of each Tetralogy entry, this is a match with something to say, wanting to comment on the flawed nature of revenge and the pitfalls that chasing such revenge will inevitably lead you to. Shawn Michaels believed that he had no career if he could not end The Streak; Mr WrestleMania had transformed from nickname to primary means of identification. The title now defined the man's entire career, and he became obsessed with finding out whether he could answer, in the affirmative, the most demanding question that could be asked of him. It was a corner he could have only ever died fighting out of.

#8 reveals itself as professional wrestling's take on the famous tale of Ahab and his whale. If his chest had been a mortar, no doubt the Heartbreak Kid would have burst his hot heart's shell upon the Phenom. Ultimately, Michaels' fixation with hunting down the Dead Man and killing The Streak would consume his career, and the ending is the great metaphor behind the composition.

Heartbreak slapped The Undertaker in the face – an act that will forever remain his final act as a professional wrestler.

Who is The Undertaker? He is perhaps the true face of the company, the character most synonymous with WWE. In a lot of ways, no professional wrestler better represents the industry and respect for its traditions than he does. He is a man verging on a level of myth, as well as perhaps the only individual anywhere close to rivalling the eternal legacy of André the Giant. The Undertaker represents the tradition, fiction, respect and integrity of professional wrestling in WWE.

Who is Shawn Michaels? He is a man that has made a career, rather controversially, of flying in the face of every possible convention he can. Whether it was his breakthrough as a major singles star in spite of his size, his controversial influence on the product as founder of D-Generation X or his return to sobriety and in-ring competition following quite literal career-ending spine surgery, Shawn Michaels made a career out of slapping professional wrestling tradition in the face.

Shawn Michaels let his career die in exactly the manner he had allowed it to live, then, as he defiantly taunted the professional wrestling industry and slapped it unapologetically and defiantly across the face in his last gasp. There could be no more fitting a conclusion to the career of the man who may just be the greatest, and one of the most influential, of all-time. Indeed, it might define this match as the single most fitting end to any professional wrestling career.

Chapter 35

The WrestleMania Vision

#7
Floyd Mayweather vs. Big Show
No Disqualification, Knockout or Submission Match
WrestleMania XXIV
March 20th, 2008

In 1982, Vincent Kennedy McMahon had a vision of a world of professional wrestling that was greater than the sum of its parts. As a man with an ambition impossible to temper, he became the undisputed king of the professional wrestling world, with a reach spanning the entire globe.

WWE is what Vince McMahon designs it to be. His vision: a seamless blend of sports and entertainment; a clash of titans as the niche world of professional wrestling meets popular culture on every level possible; a phenomenon that would turn what was once a carnival sideshow into a worldwide industry with inconceivable profit margins, unique aesthetics and an appeal as global as its name.

It should come as little to no surprise that it was one year at WrestleMania the world saw the purest fruition of Vince McMahon's vision – one time when a well-known public figure participated against an athlete only professional wrestling could be home to in a successful match that generated twice as much income than was predicted for the host city, broke the attendance record for the host stadium and, for a second straight year, eclipsed 1 million pay-per-view buys.

Notably, and perhaps why this bout works so well, Floyd Mayweather actually comes armed with a pretty impressive and well-rounded gimmick for his one and only professional wrestling match. His entrance is grand, the presence of an entourage hints at ego, his theme music feels fittingly presumptuous and even his in-ring attire testifies the character be from the otherworldly grandiosity that pop culture celebrities so often exhibit. As a performer, Floyd is a natural, and should be applauded.

Simply take a look at how the opening exchange comes to an end: Mayweather arrogantly begins to brush himself down, allows himself a lopsided smirk and drinks from a rather ludicrously ornate chalice. They are the actions that would be exhibited only by a character so rich and successful that he could afford to remain oblivious to acceptable social behaviour and, when Big Show interrupts the Mayweather Entourage's sass with the frightening zeal of a giant locomotive, it is angled as him taking exception to Mayweather making a mockery of the contest. This is a match with complex semantic meaning substantiated by tremendous character work.

Mayweather performs his role vibrantly. The fear in his eyes as Big Show eliminates the first member of his entourage is entirely believable and, when Show finally begins to get the advantage, toying with the boxer like a doll, Mayweather throws himself into the performance. He shows no fear in taking a couple of impressive bumps for a man that doesn't wrestle for a living, and his screams of pain as Show begins to manhandle him are actually better than those elicited by the professionals that wrestle with Show on a weekly basis; though that may be due to the possibility of these cries being legitimate!

It's also nice for his entourage to play an active role in the story. They're not just there because boxers have entourages. They become participants, believably attempting to defend their man by becoming his human shield. Seeing Show simply plough through them with ease is a satisfying experience and elevates the sense of danger that Mayweather is actually in. Their admirable willingness to take bumps and express ignorance as to how professional wrestling differs to boxing is similarly in keeping with the context of the fiction. Seeing them flail their arms around and shout in panic as Show begins to literally walk all over Mayweather provides the vital percentage of wit that a blockbuster like this should possess.

The actual content is predictably thin, but it was always going to be in a match of this kind. Despite that, it remains far superior to the action in similar bouts of the guest celebrity genre. There is a sleeper hold from Mayweather and some of the usual trademarks from Show. By the time we get Mayweather's escape attempt, there's definitely a tone of schadenfreude coming to the fore, Show looking to a maliciously baying crowd for encouragement to continue his beat down. Big Show himself looks to be having a great deal of fun and relishing his first big bout following his return a month prior. It's also nice, perhaps again inevitable, to see them mould the no disqualification stipulation into a believable final act that masks any flaws in the set-up, allows Mayweather to get in some hard-hitting offense to put the giant down and protects the Big Show as well – he can forever say it took a number of chair shots and some brass knuckles for Mayweather to knock him out.

Vince McMahon, with this match, proved that the vision he had in 1982 was one that could work sublimely when done right. #7's critical and popular success mark it as the absolute, even literal, fruition of the original WrestleMania concept; perhaps so too is it as pure an example of sports entertainment as we are likely to ever get.

This is ironic to me because it also happens to be another powerful instance of the creative power we unlock with the interpretive performance art view as well. #7 is a composition that speaks very much of professional wrestling's place in the world, more so than most of the other matches on the list; hence it's high positioning. This metaphorical interpretation sees the piece symbolise the constant battle against willful ignorance and innocent misunderstanding professional wrestling fans wage on an almost daily basis. Mayweather's character is a larger-than-life celebrity, living in a world apart from ours where what we understand to be the rules of good taste and respect – the rules of regularity - don't apply; he has an entourage, a manager, rains down money, drinks from an ornate chalice, cannot be disqualified and doesn't even need to win by pin fall or submission. Big Show's character, in contrast, is the prodigal son, not wandering into a world unfamiliar but returning home from a stint away, aggressively asserting the nature of professional wrestling, its legitimacy and tradition on an opponent apparently not taking the situation very seriously. The finish then transforms into a galling comment: that the war we fight to defend the industry's honour against the wider world's contempt is one we very easily lose.

A fitting and inevitable end, I feel, for the fruition of the sports entertainment vision.

Chapter 36

WWE is…

#6
Stone Cold Steve Austin vs. The Rock
WrestleMania XIX
March 30th, 2003

If you could put WWE and everything it is into a match, which do you pick? In a list of 101 WWE matches to see before you die, it feels necessary to select one match that acutely – perhaps best - represents the organisation beloved by millions. To do that, we turn towards feuds and pairings that are the building blocks of any given professional wrestling show and the catalyst through which we identify, historically and in our individual pasts, a particular promotion's worth.

These feuds are the core of a product; our quantifiers of quality that make the sizeable assumption that the greatest matches more often than not stem from the greatest feuds. When they do, the emotional resonance of a match is as significant as the action itself, both acting in sync with the other. They become symbiotic and only during times that they have perfectly coalesced can we truly distil into thirty minutes the very essence of a product; in this case, of WWE.

So, what is WWE's greatest rivalry? WWE's product, as previously explored, is all about stories, pulling at the heartstrings and evoking raw emotion from the pit of your soul. WWE's essence, therefore, is a superlative of life. As you will come to see in the review that follows, this feud, and this match that saw it culminate in a final ending, is exactly representative of just that – a superlative of life.

Stone Cold vs. The Rock is one of those few rivalries that transcended its time, and for the closing chapter the two men returned to their original dynamic – The Rock as antagonist and Austin as protagonist. More importantly, this was The Rock as good as The Rock has ever been. His Hollywood character was executed with incredible intelligence and a level of creative complexity that's difficult to comprehend, and that character was never better than at this point in time. And while Austin may have been far beyond his prime, even suffering hospitalisation the night before the event, that simply makes his performance arguably the most superlative of his entire career. While it may not be the best exhibition of theirs and, while many others would claim their encounter two years prior to be a great deal more fun, no other match these two wrestled achieved quite as much as their last.

This was Austin's homecoming after his walking out the previous year, while at the same time it was The Rock's search for validation by searching for that one big victory that would crown his full-time WWE career – defeating, at WrestleMania, the Rattlesnake in whose shadow he had always performed. This may not have been for the title, but it was most definitely a battle to decide whose legacy would become the defining one. That it was booked second only to the WWE Championship match that night speaks for the importance the company considered those stakes to have.

When receiving the composition as performance art, we stumble again across a revelatory new potential. Chapter 30: Questioning Popular Periodisation already covered the change in functionality between the ropes throughout WWE's various ages in history; perhaps barring the now historically distant style of the 1980s, #6 is a match that exhibits faint traces of each era's unique philosophies. The New Generation's technical foundations; the Attitudinal tone; the Brand Extension indulgences; the recognition of Reality; combining these together creates a work that rises above chronological type casting.

The Rock is entirely in-character, and that's an important factor to understand. It is his work that makes what could otherwise feel dangerously standard instead far more emboldened. His vanity and ego is relentless, escalating further and further until you fully expect it to prove his undoing. From tapping his head after a counter to wearing Austin's own vest, The Rock is an enraging individual to watch. He takes on the age-old role of the egomaniac you hate to love and can't help feeling drawn to. If Austin's state of health led to any flaws in how these two men performed, The Rock's exhibition of charismatic bravura more than makes up for those.

Not to underrate Austin's own performance, but his health issues dominate much of how we might receive his effort. He is more limited than ever because of them, though that creates a sense of escalation all its own – because of his slower execution and handicapped starting point, it means he's constantly on the back foot. Thus, as The Rock's advantage becomes ever stronger, Austin is allowed to portray himself as the grittiest, toughest talent to ever step into a ring. Much of the Austin character's success relied as much on his physical fortitude as it did his misanthropic brutality. By the time he's kicking out of the second Rock Bottom and his face is red raw in its grimace of genuine and seriously legitimate physical anguish, the awe that you hold the man's pain threshold in is undeniable.

It is the final physical exchange that impresses the most. Austin's loss feels inevitable. Refusing to stay down, Stone

Cold kicks out of an ironic Stunner, a People's Elbow and the first Rock Bottom, but all without hope of a comeback; in turn, The Rock exhibits an appropriate emotional response, looking as shocked as he does angered. As he gets to his feet and stalks the recovering Rattlesnake so valiantly battling on, the close-up of his hardened gaze makes clear his ill intentions. This is a man possessed. By the second Rock Bottom, Austin is in visible physical pain and his expression can't help but remind of the same ardent grit he showed in 1997 when locked in that bloody Sharpshooter. This time, there's a palpable degree of failing energy and the emotional turmoil at play is drawn more from our desire to see The Rock fail than to see Austin succeed. As Austin helplessly clings on, The Rock's anger increases further, pacing the ring and mouthing off before he stops still. His expression of rage is replaced by intense intent. Austin staggers right into position, his fight long gone. And The Rock holds him there, pausing, relishing (or is that regretting?) what he is about to do. Then he hits the Rock Bottom for a third time, which gets his three count and realises the man's final objective; not only had he defeated Austin, he was the last man to ever do so.

Austin's final walk from the ring feels poignant, and his last salute as an active performer a humble one. It's too easy to allow ourselves the vanity of a victorious farewell; for Austin to be victorious only in defeat and, through that, doing a favour for the man that for so long had performed in his shadow makes it one of the greatest farewells of all-time. It is one final testament to the professional generosity both Austin and The Rock were never afraid to show to their opposite number.

As well as a mighty practical success, #6 also is a story of contrasts. One competitor is a straight-laced, no-nonsense Texan redneck with black trunks, no hair and a sense of function that makes him strike at the heart of his objective. The other is a tanned, verbose Hollywood actor straight out of the LA lifestyle, adorned with tattoos and unique ring gear that vainly proclaims his own name in tasteless font, and who is willing to put his mission on pause if only to appreciate himself. One had become known as the most profitable star in the company's history, the progenitor of a new kind of professional wrestling product that took the company to heights it didn't even see under the leadership of Hulk Hogan and who, even when absent, continued to dominate the entire product. The other was a man of similar talents who picked up the slack when the former wasn't there, catapulting himself to mainstream success despite having to languish in a Stone Cold shadow. Even the commentary was one of opposites, JR preaching passionately about the wrestling involved between two of the greats while the King instead focusses on the outside accomplishments of The Rock, now a hit movie star with renewed vanity and an exponential sense of narcissism.

Like WWE then, this match is a superlative of life. Austin's success was often attributed to the fact that fans lived vicariously through the man who got to beat up his boss, drink on the job and still succeed. While that may be an overly simplistic explanation of his appeal, it's nevertheless true that Austin always represented an accessible everyman. Most fans drink, swear, dream of being able to lash out at those they don't like, but all of it is done in the mundane moderation a good society demands. Austin dismissed the society, trusted nobody and did it anyway. He had the life that many inner-anarchists dream of. Austin, in short, was us. Opposing him here was Hollywood Rock: the representation of society's modern obsession with fame and the fake sense of superiority that comes with it. He was a man that turned his back on his roots and allowed his new found success in a world no average fan could ever know to ensure he returned as a stranger. When he challenged our greatest hero, he challenged *us,* and our world, to an out-and-out fight. Hollywood Rock was the kind of sickening superficiality general fans can't touch, but that considers itself (and actively crusades to prove itself) our better. #6 is, thus, a battle between two states of existence that very much define how many people see the world.

Just as Austin fails in his match here, Average Joe will never be able to shout as loud and appear as successful as the famous and fortunate, and will no doubt always fail to convince the world that it's perfectly fine being perfectly fine. But while The Rock leaves with the lasting legacy, the adulation and the fame and fortune his character considers to be success, Austin leaves with his dignity intact and the respect of those around him. Precisely because of this metaphorical take, if WWE is a superlative of life, there is no choice better than #6 to represent it.

Chapter 37

Etymology: Language, Psychology and Synergy

#5
Ricky "The Dragon" Steamboat vs. "Macho Man" Randy Savage
WWF Intercontinental Championship
WrestleMania III
March 29th, 1987

WWE's in-ring language is the means by which stories between bells are written, employing a series of pre-rendered semantic constructs any fan will instantly both recognise and identify the unique values of. If WWE is storytelling, then it becomes a vital enterprise to investigate the origins of the language through which those stories are told.

At some point in its history, this language had to have an origin point. This goes beyond the lexicon of blueprints and pioneers and instead focuses on zero hour; on a match so utterly vital to WWE that fans know today it is practically biblical in its efforts to create, be those efforts self-conscious or not. In an age where the variety of match types in WWE offered every year is perhaps greater than it has ever been, the single overriding lexicon, necessarily operated by all, is stretched further than it ever has been too. Without that shared consistency, fans would be lost for meaning in an eternal sea of conflicting semantic equations. In other terms, though every genre possesses its own dialect, that dialect has to develop from a single mother-tongue.

Such is #5; the origin point from which the present day mother-tongue seems to have evolved. This review will attempt to be more than just an appropriately distanced admiration; it must, instead, strive to be the first part of a surface level empiricist's investigation into the etymology of the ever-referenced but rarely defined "WWE style."

Their content is simple. As to why, the answer is simple and stems from the idea established in Chapter 24 with #30's other Savage / Steamboat encounter. Macho Man was a talent all about the structure of his story. His matches would often seem loathe indulging in melodramatic verbiage, fixating instead on constructing all the most basic words in exactly the right way. Not only would he do things you'd never seen before, he'd perform the oldest of tricks in a new way too. He was as much a revisionist of the old as he was an originator of the new.

In #5, there is a reliance on monosyllabic offense no more complicated than arm bars, leaping chops and knee strikes. What they do with those ingredients, however, is cook up a storm; the fluidity of the action has to be seen to be believed. This is a high speed chase of a match that, if anything, feels in danger of expecting too much from its run time. The result is an appropriate feeling of immediacy to everything they do. Such immediacy of pace is never more obvious than when the capacity crowd is chanting for Steamboat within only minutes.

Steamboat's individual outing is his stereotypical pro wrestling hero's performance: the consummate athletic hero who overcomes the perilous cheap shots of his enemy. Steamboat always did a great job in the role, though, so it is by no means a negative. Savage provides the antithesis, his own night that of a stereotypical professional wrestling villain. He cheats, he takes shortcuts and he does all the things very much expected from an antagonist.

What's interesting is to see a more nuanced and complete character performance in play from the Macho Man, though. At differing times, he plays the athletically capable heel, the charismatically overbearing heel, and the smart and conniving heel. While Steamboat remains, throughout, safely inside the box he always performed in, Macho Man watches far more holistically.

An easily missed, but no less genius stroke of creativity is in the understated restraint of Macho's beat-down on Steamboat. The devil is in the detail, with small touches creating a grand picture that the audience is entrusted to feel for rather than spot. Steamboat's ringside ally, George "The Animal" Steele, has to help Steamboat back in the ring to avoid a count-out, for example, while Steamboat himself continues to stagger around on his feet, helpless thanks to so much of his martial-art orientated offensive routine being predicated on his balance and precision. Macho Man is relentless in his pursuit, but doesn't suffocate the challenger which, in turn, lends credence to his vanity. He doesn't need to bay at the crowd or argue with the referee to come off as an over-confident champion lazily expecting victory; he just feels like one.

A similar methodology is relied upon in the way Steamboat slowly begins to claw back an advantage despite never seizing one definitively. As Macho Man's beat-down feels so quietly complete, Steamboat's comeback feels helplessly back-footed. The pace remains constant, but Steamboat begins to connect with an increasing amount of offense, the chess game devolving into an exhilarating cat and mouse chase. The resulting flurry of near falls effortlessly amplifies the feeling of nail-biting exhaustion in an organic frenzy that is so dangerously close to a finish that the crowd, at one point, actually pops for thinking Steamboat had pulled it out of the hat.

That flurry of near falls that so violently drags you to ferocious emotional outbursts is followed by the relief of downtime. Through a ref bump and an exhausted counter-offensive from the champ, the relentlessly constant pace slows to a grinding crawl as it teeters on the precipice of conclusion. The resultant believability makes the poetic justice of the finish feel cathartic. Not just emotionally but physically too, the relief following the final exclamation mark is positively palpable.

#5 is a fourteen minute walk-through of everything any WWE fan recognises as commonplace today.

It is a trend that bleeds through their entire screen time, with a whole list of tropes found to be relied upon through the ages that followed. A brief traditional psychology from both men focussing on a single body-part; the heel taking a break on the outside, leading his opponent on a wild goose chase inevitably designed solely to allow said heel to regain the advantage unfairly; the fierce flurry of near falls via a series of pinning combinations and counters to them; Steamboat skinning the cat; an attempt at a cheap count-out win to retain the championship; the heel pulling on tights for an unseemly victory; the referee bump; the heel champion, in a moment designed to protect his own credibility moving forward, having the challenger down for a comprehensive three count; the heel's attempts at cheating backfiring thanks to the presence and interference run by the babyface associate at ringside; and the winning pin fall is something in constant use – a simple and unexpected counter. Even if #5 was not the creator of these ideas, in lieu of WrestleMania III's standing as a major maturation point for the Golden Age, it certainly popularised them into becoming formula over option. This bout is a walkthrough of pretty much every single commonplace set-piece or frequently employed structural shade seen still today.

The reach this match enjoys was far beyond the imaginings of any bout that preceded it. Precisely because of that, it acquires a heavier sense of responsibility; it has become an amplified exhibition of professional wrestling language informing the "WWE style." #5 is more than a match; it's WWE etymology. The complexity and density of in-ring offerings today owe as much to this bout as they do to any modern day classic. #5 was where the essential devices of in-ring competition now taken for granted were, if not originated, for the first time coherently brought together in major view to form a popularised dialogue that the world saw and came to be influenced by.

#4
The Undertaker vs. Triple H
No Holds Barred Match
WrestleMania XXVII
April 3rd, 2011

Author's note: this review considers the bout in its original form; DVD and Blu-Ray copies edited out the unique choices of entrance theme, which were vital elements to #4's comprehensive approach to the art form.

If #5 wrote the dictionary, then, #4 is a complete and wholly exclusive alternative. The alterations created mark #4 as one of the mightiest pieces of professional wrestling as performance art ever committed to screen; a sweeping psychological epic that brings together every facet of the theatre that constitutes the final whole of a professional wrestling match with comprehensive depth.

It is the divisive reception to #4 that transforms it, in fact, into a poster-match for the performance art theory. Its successes or failures, depending on which side of the argument you fall, are determined by one simple idea: how you interpret it. The more cynical fans may still thumb their nose at this masterpiece because of its perceived indulgence at a time when the increasingly epic Streak matches were beginning to feel arrogant to some. The retcon performed on their WrestleMania X-Seven encounter irritated some. The apparently recycling of ideas from the two Michaels matches indicated a lack of creativity, many believed. The sheer amount of broadcast time occupied by #4 hindered encounters featuring fresher, younger talent, it was claimed. For certain, these ideas are hard to avoid when taking an orthodox sports entertainment view.

Taking the performance art view, though, defines #4 as the bleakest of all Streak matches – including 21-1 – and the most powerful instalment of the Tetralogy mentioned in #8's Shawn Michaels retirement bout.

Regardless as to whether or not WWE stumbled into the Tetralogy's tale entirely by accident, fans wound up with four matches linked closely together in visual, conceptual and emotional terms. Great storytelling is capable of being many things to many people, regardless of authorial intent. It is in disregarding authorial intent and developing a separate consumer's interpretation that treats those four famed matches as a single entity which returns us to the idea put forth in this book's first section: professional wrestling's transcended state.

Perversion is the name of the game these two men play. As fans reach the third chapter of the Tetralogy, the story has taken a turn for the worse. Following his victory over the increasingly obsessive Shawn Michaels, The Undertaker's quiet confidence had become ingratiating arrogance. A man already great now vainly obsessing over immortality, who before would respectfully accept or decline his WrestleMania challenger for professional reasons, was now so arrogant he would sympathise with the fool daring to step into the ring with him before a single punch was thrown, responding to unasked questions with a mocking smirk and an unconvincing gesture of theatricality. His wins in the preceding two years were now so career-defining that the Dead Man had come to believe himself to be absolutely untouchable, and allowed that arrogance to blind him to the reality of his new-found situation. Triple H, meanwhile, was prepared to become a monster, knowing that his cold blood and absence of conscience made his eventual killing strike inevitable. It is upon such a foundation of both men's arrogant certainties that their eventual respective falls from grace become so utterly perturbing to witness. Both occur in perfect synch as this entity, now known as The Streak, takes as much a hold of them as it had Shawn Michaels beforehand. If the Tetralogy is a didactic fairytale of obsession, this match is its corruption into nightmarish tragedy.

It all begins with the usually dramatic pre-match promo. With Mark Collie's "In Time" providing a haunting musical backdrop, throw-away lines become perilous warnings as themes of mortality, the passing of time and the vanity of human achievement (just as in #8) take centre stage, all while an ironically placed memorandum of both men's achievements plays out like professional wrestling's answer to a thousand-yard stare. The viewer sees how the match came to be, witnessing the mocking smirk of The Undertaker in the wake of Triple H's grim visage that silently obscures The Game's ill intentions. Incidentally, the Cerebral Assassin just so happened to be shown approaching Undertaker as Collie warns he can hear all of your thoughts, doubts and fears.

It is then that the fable begins unfolding, its defining characteristic the perversion of the familiar that turns the safety net of the expected into an uncomfortably dark mirror image. This perversion starts the moment the first entrance begins. The lights black out and the familiar gong sounds, only this isn't The Undertaker as might be expected. It's Triple H, sending a statement to his opponent by adopting the famous tropes of the Dead Man and turning them to his own use for intimidation, punctuated by that threatening promise of a one-night-only theme tune: "For Whom the Bell Tolls." It is not for The Game.

However, The Undertaker, the master of all mind games, is never to be outdone and assures Triple H of his own promise of pain in response. Odd, was it not, that just this once The Undertaker utilised Johnny Cash's "Ain't No Grave" as his entrance theme? Just as The Game uses Undertaker's signature entrance as a weapon against him, promising that the bell tolls for the Dead Man, Undertaker responds by promising Triple H there is no grave that will keep him in the earth. He punctuates that promise with a distinctly simple and average walk to the ring, betraying that he feels no need for a superlative entrance this year; the reductive nature of Undertaker's entrance flaunts the ease with which he perceives the pending fight in his predator's face.

Essentially, these two men are in the thralls of war before they've even reached the ring.

Note the positions adopted prior to the bout's official beginning. Where The Undertaker had stood in the preceding two years instead stands Triple H; an easily missed but pertinent representation of how the hunter had now become the hunted. Once the bout does begin, the threat that The Undertaker faces becomes increasingly obvious. Where previously Shawn Michaels' attempts to gain an advantage felt careful and hesitant, Triple H launches into a full frontal assault. The Undertaker's immediate responses are exacerbated in turn, the Tetralogy's third chapter threatening to escalate into something far more all-consuming than the preceding two entries within seconds.

Distorting the familiar remains a constant as events hurtle out of control, creating the harrowing punctuation of this sweeping epic's psychological complexity. By the time the two enter the very final act, for example, The Undertaker has become the underdog in his own story, as Triple H - the political liability so long invasive of fans' comfort - closes in on what seems like an inevitable, fatalistic win. The Game flippantly disregards the choke hold synonymous with an Undertaker comeback, mocks Undertaker's taunt and utilises Undertaker's finishing move. Even the usually articulate JR is reduced to sounding like a petulant child, with his ability to condense emotion into unique sound-bites perverted to a simple childlike cry of, "No!"

The sickest of all these alterations comes as The Undertaker closes out the dark fairytale with Hell's Gate, a move to which he turns to here seemingly more for its familiarity as a safety blanket than an overtly aggressive attempt to win a match; it's an instinctual flinch of survival, nothing more. The small touches make it the powerful ending it really is; Triple H lasts longer than anyone had at that point in the hold, worryingly demanding every last dreg of the Phenom's ebbing strength; the lifting of the sledgehammer is symbolic of Triple H's internal struggle, his dropping of it as much a conclusion to his own internal emotional turmoil as it is to his nightmarish assault; his final vague touch of Undertaker's face a deflated and defeated goodbye to something he had come so close to ending.

Then he taps out and viewers are given the most spine-chilling visual of them all, with the awful cinematography designed to emphasise the complete absence of The Undertaker. Yes, he had gained a win in the record books, but the celebratory pyro, grand stage and booming music feel sickeningly out of place as the viewer finds themselves confronted only by the still and motionless corpse-like remains of the two combatants. What should have been a glorious and exuberant moment of victorious relief is dragged down to the depths of a still world, revelling in the consumption of its all too mortal inhabitants.

The theme of escalation compliments this warped story of perversion too; after Triple H clarifies through his aggressive game that he is here not just to defeat The Phenom but to devour him entirely, The Undertaker's indignant outrage pushes him to overreach and try to do likewise to his new found nemesis. The match becomes emotionally out of control as both men, so sure of their victories, pursue their fatal goals with relentless malice. That feeling of relentlessness is partly built upon the foundation of the zeal in both men's performances. The combatants don't hold back in their execution. The emotive inflections of the opening two bouts of this Tetralogy are disturbingly displaced by a quietly brooding stiff aesthetic.

The action itself, though largely limited to signature offense and finishers, serves to continually support the unspoken psychology of this performance art interpretation of perversion and the sudden absence of the familiar. Bearing in mind the narrowly focussed ill intentions of both individuals and the escalating sense of emotional outrage, it makes sense that neither warrior would be hesitant in their efforts for victory. They have not come to wrestle but to kill or be killed, and it is in the attempt to tear their opposition apart with their most fearsome tools that the escalatory tone lays. The action may be thin, but its perverse alterations mean that a word like urgent doesn't quite fit; it's more than that, *worse* than that. It leaves the viewer feeling helpless, with the tiny, easily missed details usually taken for granted in an Undertaker match – and, more specifically, an Undertaker WrestleMania match - turned upside down. As a result, the certainty of The Undertaker at WrestleMania suddenly morphs into a frighteningly unfamiliar stranger.

The performance art theory would call the resulting pace steadily and exhaustingly relentless. It is methodical, perennially threatening and feels like it absolutely will not stop, ever, until one man is done. The bout's minimalism is intended to further substantiate the frightening reality of their unfolding torment. The overriding tone is an apocalyptic one, evidencing a new obsessive style of professional wrestling that hones in immediately on success without frills and dismisses a need to entertain with a purely character-driven obsession with victory.

Both men's performances exhibit the same totality of character wrestling seen in #100's Orton / McMahon 2009 bout. For example, The Undertaker's frustration in response to Triple H kicking out of the Last Ride shows an Undertaker fearful of his chances, having realised how dangerous his opponent really was; his bravado is distilled into a weak veneer trying to cover an overwhelming sense of doubt, which escalates further as Triple H kicks out of the Tombstone too. Where there was shock at the resilience of Shawn Michaels, now there is fearful anger at the persistence of Triple H. Suddenly a standard, business-as-usual WrestleMania match for the Dead Man was becoming a personal exorcism of both his own myth and his loathing for what he could not fathom – that he was not as invulnerable as he thought. This is an Undertaker learning that pride comes before a fall and that he could still be humbled. He becomes increasingly prepared to utilise darker and more disturbing means to put his challenger away but, ironically, the more he taps into his darkest intentions in order to maintain control, the more control he loses. Triple H is thus allowed to seize the momentum.

Triple H's own performance mirrors that of The Undertaker sublimely. What is an exorcism of myth for The Undertaker becomes a discovery of conscience for The Game. Where Undertaker grows to increasingly fear defeat, Triple H grows to increasingly fear victory as he realises just what is required to overcome the otherworldly nature of The Streak; an idea exhibited perfectly as Triple H crawls fearfully away from an Undertaker who just kicked out of a perversely ironic Tombstone. Triple H's cries of "Stay down!" are the sign of a character now entirely afraid of his own disturbingly violent potential. So powerful is this realisation that he takes longer and longer between moves as the bout winds to a close, such as his flurry of chair shots on the Undertaker that he fails to follow with a cover, instead continuing to wrestle with his moral self. His expressions switch frantically from numb apathy to resigned malice to reluctant sympathy until the turmoil floods his sense of reality, leading to him almost praying on his knees in the corner, unable to face the ramifications of an attack he committed too freely in the wake of his obsession with ending The Streak. By the time Triple H is reaching for his sledgehammer, the viewer sees a man filled with dread for what he is about to do. He moves achingly slowly, not necessarily out of spent exhaustion but because of maligning this necessary final end. His death sentence of, "It's time" is one spoken from a man now a stranger to his own amputated morality, resenting his own objectives rather than openly embracing them as he once had.

Ultimately, The Undertaker fears that the hype he himself had come to believe was nothing more than a fleeting moment of glory, and Triple H fears that either he is capable of becoming more monstrous than he ever thought possible, or he was not quite the monster he had convinced himself he was. This is a match whose outcome is not dictated by the opponent's fear of one another, but the fear of discovering who they themselves really are. This tale of obsession twists what fans know and turns everything into chaos. It consumes its two competitors and becomes an existential exploration of self-worth.

A poster-match for the performance art theory indeed, this complex psychological epic naturally demanded something beyond the traditional means of the "WWE Style" to see it play out on-screen. To criticise this match for its lack of focus on the physical aspect of professional wrestling storytelling misses the point. #4 brings together *all* facets of theatre involved in this wondrous performance art; the pre-match production, the music, the physicality, the expressions, the commentary, the cinematography and the post-match production all contribute to creating the ultimate story this review has attempted to convey. Following sports entertainment rules, which fans assume WWE matches must adhere to for fear of being seen as sub-par, would not have sufficed.

To tell this amazingly dense story, The Undertaker and Triple H tore up the rule book fans assumed was necessary. They instead tread a path much closer to the storytelling of cinema or literature than of professional wrestling. The result is the viewer being confronted by a strange beast they can't quite recognise. In other words, rather fittingly, this match is a perversion of the language we understand as fans. The tragedy is that the more cynical fans of sports entertainment have written it off as a lazy and indulgent effort, failing to see just how deeply rooted an exploration of human nature it truly is.

It does all depend on how you choose to interpret it. This entire book has tried to exploit professional wrestling storytelling as the complex and multi-layered creature it is. There is no greater example than this. This is the day when what fans would call The Streak truly ended. It is WWE's psychological odyssey, its creation of an entirely different style of professional wrestling language. It is the darkest chapter of the Tetralogy and a scary testament to the effectiveness of perverting the familiar.

#3
The Ultimate Warrior vs. "Macho Man" Randy Savage
Retirement Match
WrestleMania VII
March 24th, 1991

Having investigated two alternative ways of conducting a professional wrestling match, each utilising two diametrically opposed lexicons to communicate with the audience, the resulting and logical question would be if the two had ever come together to form as equally an affecting narrative. The answer is yes, and it happened twenty years before #4.

With direct parallels to #4 and clear influences from #5, #3 is a perfect linguistic amalgamation; a one-of-a-kind anomaly that is both reactionary and anticipatory and birthed the main event style still ardently adhered to. Importantly, and like all great matches, it speaks on multiple levels. Inclusive of almost every issue this list has touched upon (from guilty pleasures, to WWE-specific storytelling, to even the overuse of false finish), it is a seemingly all-encompassing tale.

We start with an unusual degree of adaptation from Warrior, who treats the situation as a weighty encounter. Instead of a speeding train hurtling towards the ring, he looks focussed; intense in a different way. In a world where villains are often treated as the cowards, it's important to establish a sense of unpredictability and genuine equality between the two in order for the drama to feel real. They do so successfully; as Warrior is doing his usual predatory circle on the outside of the ring apron, Macho is right up in his face, showing Warrior that, what many saw as an unstoppable force, was to him just a load of blunder. It's a great visual that, coupled with the audible heat from an excitable and giddy crowd, helps create the sense of an impending typhoon of drama and physicality.

Continuing the adaptation, Warrior develops an edgier attitude for this heated encounter. There was always a sense of dark aggression to his character, a feeling that he might be a little bit uncontrollable and always on the cusp of becoming a monster instead of a hero, but here that ultimately manifests into the guise of an anti-hero that would, a decade later, become the predominant stereotype for WWE's chosen leading men. Whether it's going mercilessly after the ever-interfering Sherri or simply placing Savage down for a slap to the face rather than powering him through the air with a fall-away slam, this is a Warrior now actively embracing his role as the conquering hero and complimenting it with the outrage that was always in him. Where, twenty years later, Undertaker and Triple H would craft something unashamedly apocalyptic, Savage and Warrior craft what could be seen in comparison, continuing the metaphor, as a crisis. From a storytelling perspective, they both indulge the idea of saturating finishers while still somehow, and paradoxically, utilising the age-old adage of less is more.

Warrior's ascendance to anti-hero helps perpetuate the nobility of Savage's own effort, managing victory in defeat. Throughout the match, there is an unusually relentless effort from the antagonist. Savage acts the coward in small degrees through his continual efforts to cheat his way to victory, but he never tries to walk away. The most uplifting interpretation of his performance is that it serves as a mirror image to Triple H's internal war years later in the instance of #4; it's just the flip side of that coin, as Savage tries to shout down his inner-hero only to find that, in the end, he cannot stop being heroic.

In this interpretation, Sherri's role becomes a central one. She is the corrupting influence; the poison that leads Savage down the wrong path. As the action unfolds, it is notable that Sherri, more times than not, is the means through which Savage could be seen to be cheating. Her constant and relentless presence corrupts the match as much as it does Savage and, when she turns on the Macho King after the bout is all done, turning her back on the now vanquished and redemptive villain turned hero, her character becomes more than a manager; she's a symbiotic parasite looking for a host upon whose success she can feed. Queen Sherri is the devil on the shoulder of Savage and her own banishment is the real success story; her performance, a real treat.

Then there is the infamous finish. Savage drops no less than five of his patented Diving Elbows to go for a definitive and unassailable victory. Only the victory doesn't come. Fans see the look of shock on Savage's face that they would come to see on the face of an Undertaker witnessing Shawn Michaels kick out of a Tombstone in 2009. The story continues after Warrior nails his familiar comeback. What had previously put away challenge after challenge proves far from enough, though, with Savage kicking out of the familiar press slam / body splash combination. Warrior now looks on in shock, peering to the sky and asking his Warrior Gods why they had so seemingly abandoned him. In that moment of high drama and frenzied hysteria, Warrior's zany act works utterly beautifully. Interestingly, and perhaps as a tribute to the creative intelligence of Savage, they only kick out of a finish once respectively; they did it right, years before anyone would ever think of doing it wrong.

Twenty years after #3, The Streak would take on a life of its own and possess two men to the point they were questioning their own identities; in 1991, Savage and Warrior were already doing that - Warrior confronted with the possibility that he wasn't invulnerable, and Savage confronted with an unfamiliar valour he had once exhibited a lifetime ago. Warrior's heroics looked increasingly unconvincing as Savage's heroics gained increasing prominence. One hero devolved into the state of an anti-hero as, conversely, another hero was resurrected from the grave that his immorality had dug at the command of his parasitic manager. Warrior's self-doubt compliments Savage's self-discovery and the crowd eat up every last drop.

Just like with #4, what happens after the bout is finished is just as important as the bout itself. The reassertion of the old Warrior is complete as he goes disappearing to the back, clad fully in his blindingly garish coat. Savage, who had accepted defeat and the end of his career to avoid complete annihilation, continues to slowly recover in the ring despite a surprisingly valiant effort for a man fans were, at the time, labelling a villain. As he does so, that parasite Sherri, now aware this retired competitor could no longer feed her any further glory, begins to assault the broken body that could no longer host her poison. She, in turn, is vanquished by the same woman she displaced: Miss Elizabeth.

What follows is one of the most genuinely emotional and poignant moments you will ever see in professional wrestling.

Once Sherri finally disappears, and after a tense moment of uncertainty, Savage relents to losing the fight with his inner-hero and, surrendering to the affection he felt for the woman who had so courageously and loyally stood by his side, the two hug in the middle of the ring in a criminally ignored, but no less powerful WrestleMania Moment. Their hug feels almost tangible, the emotion threatening to choke-up even the most objective viewer twenty years after the fact. As Savage hoists Elizabeth on his shoulder, his forced retirement and monstrous corruption is completely forgotten, displaced by the circumstance of the moment - a cathartic celebration of reunification.

#3 argues that a victory isn't always as literal as we may think it is – something that, twenty years later, The Undertaker and Triple H would discover for themselves through a far darker experience. Sherri's actions, Warrior's questionable moments and the poignancy of Monsoon's introduction to the match itself all make Savage's eventual defeat feel somehow all the more heroic. This is not an uncharacteristically valiant bad guy; it's a suppressed hero led astray trying to reassert himself, which he fully manages during his reunification with Elizabeth. Where Savage's character arc mirrors that of Triple H, his victory mirrors that of Undertaker – one was defeated in victory, the other victorious in defeat.

Everything done in #4 was done in #3 twenty years earlier. More so than that, most of what is done in every match listed before this one was done in this emotional twenty minute classic. The language used is a comprehensive amalgamation of the innocent rehearsed simplicity of that Intercontinental Championship match at WrestleMania III - a match so many think exhibits the best of professional wrestling - and the sometimes ingratiating superlatives of that Streak match at WrestleMania XXVII - a match that so many think exhibits the worst of professional wrestling. To have achieved that and, at the same time, be so all-encompassing of so many other issues about this wonderful performance art means this isn't a match before its time; it is simply timeless.

Chapter 38

The Starkest Warning

#2
JBL vs. Eddie Guerrero
WWE Championship
Judgement Day
May 16th, 2004

The topic as to how far professional wrestlers should be expected to go in their pursuit of conveying realism in a ring is always a hot one for discussion. Of all the questions pervading professional wrestling as an industry, it is this one that is the most humanistic and will reveal just how inhumane a professional wrestling fan we each very well may be.

It is because of its human importance that this match was rated the second most must-see in all of WWE history, highlighting in gruesome and undeniable fashion the dangers involved in professional wrestling and raising important moral questions. Is the horror of such a cannibalistic profession necessary for its true potential for greatness to be reached? Are the physical and emotional sacrifices, so monolithic in the lives of the performers yet so dangerously remote to those of the fans, prerequisites for this industry's greatest pieces of art? Is there a degree of necessary repugnancy for professional wrestling to be so emotionally relevant to its audience? The issues at hand with #2 are grander and much less myopic than specifics covered previously among these pages. It is about the ill-willed foundation of professional wrestling as a performance art, the questioning of its morality and existence as an industry and our responsibilities - not as fans, but as human beings - to those who opt in for such brutal practice.

Eddie Guerrero, who was so very well loved and respected amongst his fans and, perhaps more importantly, his peers, has been one of the most resonant, painful and deeply tragic losses the industry has sadly endured. As a result, I felt a responsibility to turn to this match in 2004 to explore the incredibly important moral questions posed by professional wrestling.

Never has it felt more important to scrutinise a match than in this instance. If you have a demand to see professional wrestlers give it their all each and every single night, you may find this uncomfortable affair something of a necessary spirit-dampener.

Regardless of their achievements elsewhere, what is most memorable is the chair shot that splits Eddie open, causing his profuse bleeding that turns #2 into the frightful composition it becomes. It sounds like a gunshot to his head, so pronounced that there is an audible gasp of shock from the thousands strong in the arena. The impact is perhaps most horrifying in lieu of Eddie struggling to take the bump; there's a visible pause before he slumps to the side. What happens next, simply put, is blood. The first gasp is followed by a second when, within moments of the impact, Eddie has already turned into a scarlet curtain, his blood pouring down his chest like water.

The chair shot is replayed twice like some kind of twisted Ludovico technique and, with each showing, it becomes increasingly horrific. The buzz amongst the crowd had been there from the opening, but where before it was an innocent enjoyment of storytelling, it suddenly feels far more visceral and far more real.

Whether Eddie's decision to continue, especially when he allows JBL to target his wound with right hands and even steel steps, was admirable or misguided could (maybe should) be debated. It is undeniably effective, though. JBL's next Clothesline From Hell really is as aesthetically shocking as it ever was and JBL's brutal aesthetic continues to play with uncomfortable effectiveness into the blood soaked visuals staining the television screen; Eddie eventually stumbles into a stiff powerbomb that makes the ring mat literally shudder.

It is in the dangerously unwelcome reality suddenly omnipresent that the final act feels so consuming. Every kick out feels like life or death and, the longer the match goes, the harder Eddie finds it to stand up; again quite literally. With referees having been knocked down twice and the ring canvas stained red and grey thanks to Eddie leaving himself streaked across it, everything becomes darker both metaphorically and in actuality. The previously airy arena feels claustrophobic. The enthusiastic crowd feels rabid. The entire match feels like it has transcended professional wrestling in all spheres. The shock on JBL's face as Eddie has his own Hulk-Up moment - made grittier by virtue of the deep crimson image of his skin - is probably the same expression on the face of any first time viewer.

The term "blood bath" has never been more relevant. Once it's all said and done, you can almost taste iron in your mouth. Like the industry this match is a part of, it feels like a carnivorous match. It's wholly concerning just what might have happened if this story had gone on any longer. Yes, its subtleties are impressive. Yes, its successful inversion of heroic prerequisites speaks volumes to the abilities, generosity and competency of both Eddie and

JBL. Yes, it's an exhilarating experience that draws the viewer in and, like the best of matches, leaves them feeling utterly helpless. But if there is an element of conscience within that viewer, they may find themselves feeling that the meat-market of WWE has never looked more naked, more exposed or uglier. Take that blotchy red ring canvas as an industry flashing its teeth at the professional wrestlers and the fans alike. This is a warning; a very real warning that asks a very demanding question.

Is it worth it?

When scrutinising the issue, suddenly any excuse for moments like #2 happening feels fragile; pathetic, even. It is amazing how fans – and I include myself in the number - can so consciously accept what's happening on their television screens every week knowing that these men and women are putting their lives on the line every single time they lace up a pair of boots.

This is not a moral condemnation, nor a plea to "change our ways," as fans or an industry. Professional wrestling is safer now than perhaps it has ever been and the stereotype of the business propagated by more mainstream media outlets is recognised among those who would know as being largely dramatised. Fans – including me - will continue to sleep at night and continue to watch professional wrestling and probably continue to rather impetuously demand these men and women work harder, wrestle better, and utilise more vicious means to perform. Unfortunately, there seems to be nothing to bridge the gap between the business's heinous demands and the brutal results. This time there is no definitive answer being suggested to the questions being asked. There is an inescapably necessary element of physical damage in the industry of professional wrestling and, while promotions can work towards negating the extremes – and have done so extensively - they can never wholly eliminate it. It is the nature of this very ugly, very aggressive beast; a beast we do nothing but enable through our endless complaining and demands for more. Professional wrestling is a rather morally ambiguous animal despite its sharply defined black and white morality stories; #2 and matches like it can at least raise awareness of such moral ambiguity.

What's the alternative presented if we do not at least discuss these things?

#2 is difficult to watch, but watch it you must. The most tragic thing of all is how enjoyable it may prove to you. In a testament to the amorality that grabs this fan every time I watch and discuss professional wrestling, it rates as one of my personal favourite matches of all-time because of how striking it is. It probably shouldn't, but I won't castrate my instincts in the name of outrage. Having said that, don't watch it because of the blood, or because it might prove fun. Rather, watch it because of its warning; because of its demands you answer unavoidable, arguably unanswerable questions.

#2 shows that professional wrestling demands respect. Its nature cannot be altered, nor perhaps should it. But every now and then, matches like #2 might have to happen to splash cold water over the faces of fans, promoters and professional wrestlers alike to remind us all that, if we fail to respect professional wrestling as an industry and all the rigours and tasks that come with it, it has the power to consume.

Chapter 39

Not to be Continued: The Most Must-See Match in WWE History

#1
Shawn Michaels vs. Kurt Angle
30 Minute Iron Man Match
Monday Night Raw: WWE Homecoming
October 3rd, 2005

This book has attempted to sway you on a number of ideas; refresh how you approach, think about and receive professional wrestling matches; evidence the transformative qualities of the performance art theory's interpretive capability; reframe the lexicon we use when talking about professional wrestling to fall in line with and better understand these ideas; utilise the opportunity therein presented to begin generating a grassroots history of WWE that asks about issues in need of discussion; ultimately, to present a new, revised way for professional wrestling to function in an age of instant communication and transparency. The common theme throughout all sections of this process was key: as the author, I wanted to ask questions.

I have attempted vigorously to do just that. Whether it was exploring the basic principles behind professional wrestling genres, trying to discover historical truths surrounding influential matches or recognising the anomalous nature of the careers of certain WWE employees both past and present, the questions this series has tried to ask you as a professional wrestling fan have gradually grown increasingly specific and, at the same time, paradoxically grander.

So, we have come to it at last: the number one most must-see WWE match of all-time. The key to this selection is its ending; or rather the fact that it does not possess one. As a result, this selection focusses on what I believe to be the most confident and respectful display any art form can show its audience. Indeed, therein lies the tragedy of its obscurity: the single time WWE placed the most confidence in its audience – be it by accident or not - is now long-forgotten. It is through its denial of closure that #1 does the very thing this book has attempted to do time and again: ask questions.

This review will, unlike all others thus far, be separated into sub-sections for ease of digestion if you wish to read it in more than one sitting. The review needs to tackle many things; storytelling and its facets in both professional wrestling as a whole and WWE as a promotion, the relationship between author and audience, the two-fold issue of why #1 *is* #1 and, of course, why it is those reasons constitute must-see.

I
Fairytale, Fable and Mythology: WWE and Storytelling

Ask many WWE personalities and they would likely tell you that they are in the business of storytelling. But have you ever stopped and asked yourself the important question of just what "storytelling" is?

Storytelling is social conscience. It is the voice inside your head weighing up pros and cons as defined by your culture at a safely remote distance to maintain a degree of invulnerability, with an emotional significance that ensures the lessons being taught are infinitely accessible and, more importantly, personally relevant. Storytelling is the eye through which you can learn the inherent truths of a society, entity or individual in any given historical snapshot; it is the mind's eye. This is a phenomenon that crosses all boundaries, be they geographical, metaphorical, philosophical or otherwise. In its most pragmatic form, storytelling becomes an anthropological tool. But how does this relate when considering storytelling within the confines of a professional wrestling ring?

This entire list has attempted to show that professional wrestling extends beyond the imitation of sport for the primary objective of fun. There is creative viability to the industry as a performance art, capable of exploring concepts as sweeping and emotionally provocative as international political realities down to the most intimate of personal narratives. Professional wrestling exhibits a composition of many traits from more antiquated forms of storytelling that have fallen out of popular thought over the centuries. It can be as far-fetched as a fairytale, as moralistic as a fable and as dense as a mythology.

The first and most important of three requisite acknowledgements to make when viewing professional wrestling as storytelling is that there is an internal continuity to the grand fictional reality referred to as kayfabe; a fictional natural order, if you will. When I talk of WWE's kayfabe reality, I talk of the *quintessential rules* of professional wrestling that, while for better or worse are being increasingly broken in the modern product, are still more often than not largely adhered to. This infrastructure's most basic but most important element is the setting of one entity upon another to drive forward a narrative; in professional wrestling's case, the conflict between good guys and bad guys.

Professional wrestling largely leans towards a reality that is wholly black and white in its existence and while over time the division between good guys and bad guys has been blurred almost to the point of invisibility (or worse yet complete non-existence), and while professional wrestling fans increasingly decide they have the agency and authority to ignore this division altogether, the fact that there *is* a division made, with opposing forces standing on either side, remains concrete. Whether or not you do, you are meant to cheer the good guys and boo the bad guys. Despite historical periods of experimentation such as the Attitude Era, this divide is the constant – the very foundation of WWE's world upon which it builds its stories.

The second acknowledgement to make is that, upon this absolutist foundation of good guys vs. bad guys, the stories within which these characters are cast remain steadfast in their tropes too. Most steadfast of all these tropes is storytelling's golden rule: the good guys win. This may be due to very practical reasoning – send the core audience home happy – or it may simply be because that's just what happens in stories. Fiction is there to allow us to escape reality, whatever that reality might be and, while its execution lends insight into the society from which said fiction emerges, its ultimate purpose is to entertain and, on a deeper level, make us feel better about ourselves.

Thirdly, in its most daring moments, a fiction may choose to turn all preconceived notions, whether they are spoken about consciously or not, on their heads. Daring pieces of work won't exist simply to make you feel good or allow you to have fun; they will make you ask questions and have the unmitigated temerity to doubt your moral centre and the principles by which you choose to live your life. The most daring may even call into question whether or not it is possible for someone subjected to the human condition to even have principles in the first place. Art work like this may have the bravery to allow the bad guys to win; may make it unclear as to whom the bad guys are; may deceive you into rooting for who is ostensibly the "wrong" character; ultimately, it will muddy the waters of every concept you ever thought you knew. Sometimes this may be done unconsciously – again, perhaps as in the case of the aforementioned Attitude Era – but the truly great fiction will aim to do it consciously and purposefully.

Professional wrestling, specifically in WWE, prefers usually to play it safe, sticking ardently and unflinchingly to its strict rules of world-building. Examples wherein feuds end purposefully with bad guys winning are extremely rare and, when they do happen, are often met with emotional confusion from an audience conditioned for simpler things; confusion that too easily escalates into outright rejection. It is precisely because of such reactions that WWE in particular, more often than not, opts for safer methods, and what we may consider to be its more daring moments are oftentimes examples of a company stumbling into something good as opposed to crafting something truly extraordinary.

All of these ideas were a part of the very complex reasoning behind why number one was always number one. That reasoning, in a nutshell, is this: #1 is a brilliant example of WWE, being a creature of absolutes, constructing a daring fiction to challenge its audience rather than spoon-feed it.

Let us expand on that latter point.

II
Ambiguity and Thinking like the Author

There is a major difference between a story's conscious absence of resolution and a story's inability to conclude appropriately. Ending and closure is in no way, shape or form the same thing. Mature storytelling recognises this. Mature storytelling confident in its execution is, on its best day, totally fearless – the previously noted example of stories wherein the bad guys are allowed to win is merely one chosen to illustrate the point.

This recognition of what indicates brave authorship is why authors of any kind should not be afraid to make demands of their audience. To be challenged is to be *involved* and being a participant in events is far more entertaining, memorable and impactful than being limited to the role of observer. Inclusive fiction is attained by varying means and can often depend on the most inconspicuous choices. From the wording of narration to the dissemination of exposition, to craft a compelling story is to master the art of creative disembodiment – to think like your audience. It can feel like a tired, worn-out cliché, but that's because it is perennially relevant and cannot be stressed enough. Every word, note or action has a meaning and every meaning a connotation and it is only through the proper composition of connotations that an author can truly achieve something transcendent. More often than not, the great storytellers achieve more through what isn't said than through what is.

Therein is the inclusivity. If it is paramount for a work's author to think like their audience when crafting their tale, it is equally as important for the audience to be able to think like an author when interacting with it. It is an expression of trust you won't find in less capable works, including the majority of those offered by WWE over the years. While the majority of modern audiences seemingly reject any effort made for them to be included in the creation of a greater meaning as being lazy, unimaginative or indicative of wider flaws, there are those who instead relish the opportunity to craft meaning for themselves. When open to interpretation, artistic endeavour achieves a whole new deeper level of social consciousness, as the underlying / over-riding values of the collective comes to shape, fashion and form the context in which a given story is received or concluded.

This can be achieved through different means, but for the purpose of this chapter and the match selection at its heart I must focus only on one: the ambiguous ending. It is the most divisive methodology that any story-teller could employ to engage their audience to the greatest degree. It runs the risk of alienating as many as it includes, but those that it does include gain so much more from the work in question that it is always a risk worth taking. These are the most trusting authors, giving more to their audience precisely because they provide them with less.

This is where #1 comes in and how these concepts apply to the world of professional wrestling. There is an incredibly important distinction to be made between purposefully executed ambiguity and the mere failure of narrative. When it comes to professional wrestling, the latter is rife. Characters can frequently find themselves being denied closure to arcs that would otherwise facilitate incredible growth and development. These turns of events are always unfortunate. Unlike any other performance art, professional wrestling is so visceral that it finds it incredibly easy to make the line that divides reality from fiction disappear entirely in the minds of its audience. Suddenly and without warning, even those that consider themselves informed can lose all sense of perspective, especially today given the ideas explored previously about the functionality of the Reality Era's unique product. It is because of this visceral nature that it becomes all the more important to ensure characters and storylines receive appropriate emotional completion. When they do, WWE are heralded as being among some of the greatest storytellers in the world. When they don't and WWE's trademark tendency to lose sight of narrative clarity strikes hard and fast, the audience is left bereft of closure, heightening animosity and furthering resentment. This may be yet another reason as to why WWE's kayfabe reality has always been non-relative; it's a comfortable safety measure if nothing else.

Taking all of this discussion into consideration, #1 is the only moment in time I could think of where WWE - usually storytellers who are paranoid about and patronising towards its audience - decided to irrefutably trust and respect that audience. #1 is not about WWE's inability to conclude, but of a decision to present ambiguity propagated by purpose and design that will, by nature of its bravery, forever transcend WWE's revisionist brutality, heavy-handed morality and oft-limited creative output. #1 is the single time WWE trusted you and me more than it ever had done before, or ever has done since. #1 is the single WWE match you most absolutely must see before you die.

III
Stage, Plot and Character

The format and necessitated structure of the Iron Man genre is so much more naturally exhilarating than any other, and feels as close to a legitimate sport that the performance art will ever come. Its proximity to the connotations of genuine competition is as remarkable as the performances in the better half of the genre's history. There's something about a chronologically traceable story being enacted in a professional wrestling ring that can be utterly spell-binding. The combination of narrative, athletic achievement and such uncanny imitation of legitimate sporting contest is a mind-blowing cocktail to drink in.

In this case, the run time is halved from what had been seen previously. Before this, feature Iron Man bouts were exclusively limited to sixty minute contests in WWE. Halving that would seemingly halve creative potential too, as well as the space in which these two world class competitors could create something as edge-of-your-seat as the Iron Man bouts they'd each wrestled before. Such is not the case here. Even if it were, the important factor to take note of is the above point: *as close to legitimate sporting contest as professional wrestling gets.*

The format plays beautifully up to the situation the two combatants found themselves in. They had already wrestled two incredible matches. At WrestleMania 21, Angle took the victory in what was an exhausting game of athletic chess, while at Vengeance the same year Shawn Michaels was able to even the score with a suitably show-stopping effort. They were all tied up, one a piece; what better stipulation to lead to a final victor than one in which the man with the most falls after a certain time period wins? There is little room for excuse in such an outcome and this was a stipulation selected because of its inarguable finality. Even more appropriate is the reality that the pair had already got two instant classics in the record books and had cemented their feud as the in-ring highlight of the year.

The staging was completed by WWE deciding to host this grand finale on a "Homecoming" show. After years on Spike TV, WWE returned with their flagship show to the USA Network, airing a three hour special that carried the tone of a celebratory happening. This was a celebration of the brand that is now indelibly linked to the company; the brand that is their favourite child and their own television champion. WWE is as much Monday Night Raw as Monday Night Raw is WWE, and this was a night designed to celebrate the show at its very best on the network it originated.

This mix of genre, build and staging is undeniably grand, but then there is the most important factor of all: the talents. Who is Shawn Michaels and who is Kurt Angle?

Take Shawn Michaels first. Shawn Michaels is widely acknowledged by WWE and their loyalists as the greatest of all-time. Admittedly, opinions originated by the WWE propaganda machine do have a tendency to become widespread and infiltrate even the schools of thought among those that many would consider American professional wrestling's intelligentsia. It is because of this that one wonders whether or not the status enjoyed by Shawn Michaels would be what it is if WWE had, instead, opted to champion a different individual. However, reality is lent to the idea by virtue of two means: the absence of scientific fact – inevitable in the case of a matter so subjective – and the presence of a majority opinion, or rather a consensus reality.

His accolades need only be pointed out to understand why it is WWE and its loyalists - a number I belong to - label him as the best of all-time. His classic encounters with The Undertaker in recent WrestleMania history have already been heralded in this book and elsewhere to an exhaustive degree. Though he may not have revolutionised the Ladder match in quite the way he is said to have done, that he popularised it as a genre in WWE is clear. He helped nudge the company, and indeed the wider industry, towards the kind of product now labelled as Attitude: an edgy evolution that was perhaps necessary for professional wrestling to survive; the resulting brand, D-Generation X, has proven an immortal one. He was at the heart of one of the most important events in professional wrestling history – the Montreal Screwjob – and he helped break down the taboo of smaller talent being main event players. Alongside Bret Hart and other contemporaries, Shawn Michaels helped sophisticate the in-ring storytelling of WWE throughout the New Generation and, despite the apparent unavoidable result of a career cut in half by a back injury, he proved himself to be a walking miracle by not only wrestling an encore but going on to have a complete career rebirth; a turn of events that enabled him to forge the moniker of Mr WrestleMania. If Shawn Michaels is not the the greatest professional wrestler of all-time, his library of work and his influence on wider industrial evolution - or at the very worst his presence during those times - certainly means he cannot be far off.

Then there is Kurt Angle, who has not received anywhere near the amount of credit he deserves from a company in whose defining era he headlined, but who nevertheless enjoys a similar status in the minds of many.

In terms of talent, Angle can hang with the best of them. The "only Olympic Gold Medalist" hype may now feel like a cliché, but it was promoted so heavily for a reason. This was as talented an athlete as you could ever hope to find in the professional wrestling industry. With a sickening amateur background, a wonderful understanding of how professional wrestling worked as theatre, an ability to convincingly portray good guy or bad guy with both effortless ease and immense range – intensely, comically, athletically – topped off by a surprising amount of natural charisma, Angle was one-of-a-kind. His own product between the ropes, far more explosive in style than Michaels', never failed to impress and his clinics with the likes of Benoit, Guerrero and Lesnar are as much the bar-setters of their style as his brawls with Austin, Rocky and Triple H were the bar-setters of theirs. His own WrestleMania record is nothing for the man to be shy about either – a match of substance at the otherwise heavily stylistic WrestleMania XVI, a striking dance with Benoit at X-Seven, an in-ring highlight against Kane at X8, a purist main event at XIX, a perfect execution with Guerrero at XX, an explosive triple threat at 22 and, of course, his encounter with Michaels at 21 can all, to some degree, be seen as show-stealers. Ultimately, though, Angle is a legitimate world class sporting athlete who could instantly adjust to the theatricality of professional wrestling and blend immediately with any performer in any genre. From Undertaker to Mysterio, from Flair to Orton, Angle excelled no matter where his match was on the card, no matter which card his match was on.

With as much success as Michaels, if not more, Angle may not quite have been as involved in the growth of the industry as Heartbreak was but that's not to say his own career doesn't carry real world relevance as well. Not only did he help support the Smackdown brand as a key player in the early years of the brand split, he also survived multiple serious neck injuries to go on and cement himself as TNA's answer to Shawn Michaels. His character also happens to be a far more fascinating reflection of his times, in comparison to the relatively reactionary one cultivated by Michaels years earlier. Angle may represent WWE's greatest act of self-deprecating political humour, standing as a parody of the very tropes Hulk Hogan promoted to boost WWE into mainstream popular culture. Prayers and vitamins were replaced by intelligence and integrity, the flag-waving with bannered singlets, the endearing "Real American" was replaced by a preaching "Olympic Hero" and pythons were substituted for milk and cookies; all of it in disparaging fashion. That Angle took his lightweight character and established himself as more than the sum of his parts – a deadly surgeon in the ring capable of amputating a wrestler's ability limb by limb – speaks only to his general top flight attributes as an all-round WWE professional wrestler. JBL likes to tout Randy Orton as what would happen if you built the perfect sports entertainer from the ground up. I'd argue it would actually look like Kurt Angle.

The point is this: crowning the hyperbolic staging is a pair of competitors in the mix for the title of greatest of all-time; and two very strong competitors at that. Obviously, this statement may prove contentious to some. For me and others, the argument *is* between these two. So, what led to the selection of #1 is the nature of what this match is from a performance art point of view; #1 is *the* WWE debate: who was the greatest ever?

IV
Iron Men: A Match Review

The first bout wrestled between these two at WrestleMania 21 consisted largely of explosive aggression born out of unfamiliarity and, perhaps to a certain extent, over-confidence. The dynamic between the two participants was clearly one with room to evolve. Their second match, wrestled at Vengeance, proved to be a superior effort with greater psychological depth and an appearance of two performers now more familiar with one another. Explosive aggression was replaced by a creeping caution that hit its height in a perfectly executed conclusion.

So, what of their third and final match together?

The explosiveness of the first match that transformed into the creeping caution of the second here morphs one final time into gripping urgency; they lunge right into it, Michaels doing away with his psychological feints from March and tactical defensive play from June and instead opting to kick things off with a bare knuckle fight, in turn freeing Angle to instinctively divert right into his comfort zone – mat wrestling. Interestingly, it is Michaels that takes the first advantage in lieu of these respective approaches.

Within two minutes, HBK has gotten two near falls to his name and seems to constantly have Angle's number. Here's a man who has come to fully appreciate the danger of his opponent; in opposition, Angle appears in the early stages to not have learnt a great deal, reeling from the in-your-face onslaught of the Heartbreak Kid, who clearly wants to prove beyond doubt that he is the better man. Michaels' early offensive barrage creates a tone of breathlessness that carries through into the content; this is Angle and Michaels wrestling without the frills, and I think never had it been more important for two guys to do just that.

Once the first five minutes have screamed by, the two seem willing to settle into a more rhythmic routine not too far removed from their previous encounters. It seems a sensible decision, sacrificing the feel of expediency in order to allow the audience room to breathe emotionally so the meaning of the action sinks in appropriately. There are riffs on spots from previous matches, but they're sufficiently different to feel fresh; it's continuity without restriction. Even the falls themselves pay tribute to previous moments in the feud. It is this larger cohesive whole that allows you to see the feud as one match separated into three parts, rather than three matches creating one story.

It's an impressive feat for them to maintain the tone of breathless urgency in the face of a steadier progression beyond those opening five minutes, but it's largely accomplished by the perennial uncertainty regarding momentum and control. When on the back-foot, both men still get regular opportunities to tease a comeback. The falls come in as tit-for-tat a fashion as the rest of the content does; they don't follow the story of a substantial lead as other matches in the format have because the whole point of this entire dialogue is to show how evenly matched they are and, ultimately, make the outcome appear muddy for the entire duration. This feels more like a race than any other match I know.

Their focus is largely on scoring decisions. It only makes sense that they'd waste no time, given the nature of the stipulation and the point at which they're wrestling, but it's refreshing to see nonetheless. Michaels counters anything he can into a pinning combination and, likewise, Angle counters anything he can into the Ankle Lock that had proven so deadly and effective at WrestleMania. These strategies create some of the more exciting moments in the action – witnessing Angle counter a moonsault into an Ankle Lock never gets less pulse-pounding no matter how many times you see it.

By the final portion of the action, Angle dials the pace down a notch – again, it makes sense given how difficult it had proven for him, thus far, to gain even the narrowest margins of victory. It is a method exhibiting shadows of Angle's previous Iron Man encounter with Lesnar, who gained a commanding enough lead to play defensively; here, Angle has a narrow lead and understands, having lost beforehand, how important it is to maintain it, no matter the methodology required. Michaels tries to force him into abandoning that strategy with a number of disrespectful slaps, knowing himself the importance of maintaining an even ground after realising the clock was now working against him; his own experience in the Iron Man format had taught him to hang on, no matter the cost, to drive the match home to sudden death, where an explosive deployment of Sweet Chin Music could pay off immensely.

The final three minutes read as both individuals trying to precariously balance offense and defence as a result. The action morphs into a series of desperate counters-for-counters, each man trying to hit big moves to capture the three seconds or single submission needed to score what had to be the deciding fall at such a late stage. The whole match becomes increasingly tactical and the viewer finds themselves confronted by the same situation Michaels withstood in 1996 to earn his first World title as a tie begins to appear inevitable; ironic, given the entire feud was kick-started by Angle's jealousy of his own accomplishment in '96 being over-shadowed by the aforementioned boyhood dream.

Perhaps haunted by that unsure moment, Michaels is finally able to break out of the threatening submission this time and nail Sweet Chin Music in as shocking a fashion as he did in sudden death overtime all those years ago. Unfortunately, the clock isn't giving enough and the entire affair is cut off right before the moment of climax, met grimly with disdain from the fan base present. Michaels tries for sudden death – it had proven kind to him in the past and was the desperate last play of Angle two years previous.

Angle wants none of it.

WWE put on a beautifully worked feud-ending match that night between arguably the two greatest performers in WWE history and left the result *deliberately ambiguous*. The moment that Angle waves off Michaels' challenge in dismissive fashion isn't WWE backing out of deciding a winner, as sports entertainment would tell you; it's the ultimate exhibition of trust in the audience. Any answer the authors involved give to the question posed – which of these two is better and, as a result, the greatest of all-time – would be rejected by many. Thinking like the audience leads to the understanding they can only ask the question and allow the audience to make up their own minds. Through the decision to have Angle walk out, suddenly the audience is allowed to think like the author; "If this match *represents* the debate as to who the greatest of all-time is, my answer would be...." Ambiguity ensures either side of the argument is as prudent as the other. None of this would have been possible if the match itself had imitated WWE's usual black and white world of good and evil, wins and losses.

V
Trust and Ending

WWE, historically, has proven itself to be the kind of storytelling entity to provide answers. Whether or not you consider that somewhat patronising, there is an element of necessity for it to happen in a constantly progressing animal like professional wrestling. If everything ended ambiguously, there would be no real creative movement and any positioning of talent would lose both its cause and effect. For it to be deployed every once in a while, though, on the rare occasion of a grand conversation, would be refreshing. I prefer the story-teller that asks and says nothing rather than the one who asks and provides the answer as well.

In almost every sense, WWE is a spoon-feeder. Increasingly so as the 2000s wore on, WWE removed decision-making power from the hands of its audience.

While democratic professional wrestling is unfeasible, to act so passive-aggressively towards the fan base appears abhorrent, unappreciative and disrespectful. Only through the mobilising age of social media has it facilitated an overt exhibition of outrage from the bottom up.

This is neither condemnation nor praise of either the promotion or its fan base, but is observed to make the point that WWE has frequently had trouble when it comes to trust, both in its performers – the historical treatment of wrestlers such as Bret Hart and, more latterly, CM Punk – and its audience, as explained above. Indeed, WWE's sometimes condescending creative philosophy could be interpreted as outright distrust. It is because of this core value in the promotion that to see a match wherein that trust is given back - when the viewer is asked to complete the narrative in a manner they see most fit - is to witness something must-see by virtue of its convention-shattering uniqueness.

These are the three central ideas at the heart of #1 that you must take away: the contravention of deep-rooted philosophy, the inclusive nature of the match toward you as a fan courtesy of its open-ended conclusion and the deployment of these tools in the company's most symbolically important match ever.

The result is a validation. Especially if you are a fan who feels abused, distrusted and manipulated by WWE, look no further than #1 for justification of your patience. By asking you to answer for yourself who the greatest of all-time is, WWE gave its audience a wink and a nudge and a reminder that, ultimately, the company isn't about Vince McMahon, it isn't about its greatest stars and, ironically enough, it isn't even about who the greatest star ever was; it's about us.

You may or may not agree that Shawn Michaels and / or Kurt Angle are the two greatest stars to ever lace up a pair of boots but, as has been the point with this entire book, it is not about the match; it's about why the match is must-see. Philosophically, the participants performing are ultimately irrelevant. It's the gesture that matters, as well as when it was made and, of course, its interpretive potential. WWE isn't asking you if Kurt Angle or Shawn Michaels is the better man in this instance; they're telling you that the answer to the question at the centre of this story is whoever you want it to be. They refused to give fans a prescriptive answer and instead asked every fan to come up with their own.

Why is this match the most must-see of all-time? It reassures us it is the fans who dictate meaning and the reality of professional wrestling. Never has that sentiment been in more need of reiterating than now, as the divisive controversies and distinct, increasingly crucial challenges of the age of communication, transparency and the Digital Revolution beats on. #1 is a match that confidently and unapologetically sheds itself of any and all WWE imposed shackles across the board. In WWE, the good guy wins and the bad guy loses. That's just how it goes. But in this one instance, good guys and bad guys and wins and losses just didn't matter. What mattered was the trust and, through that trust, the empowerment of audience. Not only is #1 everything analysed above, it's a reminder that professional wrestling is as much us as we are professional wrestling.

VI
Epilogue

What is WWE? What is professional wrestling? These are the questions that forged this book. To me, it is performance art. To some it is and forever will be simulated sport. To others, sports entertainment. We might debate the positives and negatives of these modes of reception, and others not even touched upon among these pages, infinitely. However, what I have tried to evidence in the case of #1 – and, actually, in my reception and analyses of all 101 of these WWE matches you must see before you die – is that professional wrestling can be whatever *you* want it to be, dear reader, whether you are a performer or a promoter, whether you are new to the world of professional wrestling and WWE and have only recently been indoctrinated, or whether you are, like me, just a long-time fan.

As a result, while I do not contend the performance art view I have presented in this thesis to be the only option with which to approach the world's greatest industry, I will maintain – as I passionately believe it to be true – that it is most certainly the mode of reception best suited to encouraging interpretive potential, legitimising professional wrestling's reputation as an industry, combating the unique challenges presented by our new digital society and, above all else, enabling professional wrestling to transcend in to the state it deserves most, once and for all: as art.

Printed in Great Britain
by Amazon